TEACHER'S EDITION
DAYBOOK
OF CRITICAL READING AND WRITING

GRADE 8

THE AUTHORS
* Fran Claggett
* Louann Reid
* Ruth Vinz

Great Source Education Group

A division of Houghton Mifflin Company

Wilmington, Massachusetts

THE AUTHORS

❊ **Fran Claggett**, an educational consultant, writer, and teacher at Sonoma State University, taught high school and college English for more than thirty years. Her books include *Drawing Your Own Conclusions: Graphic Strategies for Reading, Writing, and Thinking* (1992) with Joan Brown, *A Measure of Success* (1996), and *Teaching Writing: Art, Craft, and Genre* (2005) with Joan Brown, Nancy Patterson, and Louann Reid.

❊ **Louann Reid** taught junior and senior high school English for nineteen years and currently teaches courses for future English teachers at Colorado State University. She has edited *English Journal* and is the author or editor of several books and articles, including *Learning the Landscape* and *Recasting the Text* (1996) with Fran Claggett and Ruth Vinz. She is a frequent consultant and workshop presenter nationally and internationally.

❊ **Ruth Vinz**, currently a professor of English education and Morse Chair in Teacher Education at Teachers College, Columbia University, taught in secondary schools for twenty-three years. She is author of numerous books and articles that focus on teaching and learning in the English classroom. Dr. Vinz is a frequent presenter at conferences as well as a consultant and co-teacher in schools throughout the country.

The authors gratefully acknowledge the assistance of the following teachers in developing the student and teacher material for the *Daybook of Critical Reading and Writing:* Tiffany Hunt, Cammie Kim Lin, Katherine McMullen, and Lance Ozier.

DEVELOPMENT: Bonnie Brook Communications (teacher's edition)
Michael Priestley (assessment)
EDITORIAL: Sue Paro, Lisa J. Clark, Bev Jessen
DESIGN AND PRODUCTION: AARTPACK, Inc.

Printed in the United States of America

International Standard Book Number 13: 978-0-669-53489-4

International Standard Book Number 10: 0-669-53489-7

1 2 3 4 5 6 7 8 9 10 – POO – 11 10 09 08 07 06

CONTENTS

What, exactly, is a *Daybook*, and how can it help my students? Teachers often ask these questions upon their initial encounter with the *Daybook of Critical Reading and Writing*. The answers are simple and compelling:

The *Daybook*

The *Daybook* is a keepable, journal-like book that promotes daily reading and writing experiences. The integrated, interactive pages of the *Daybook* provide students with multiple opportunities to read a variety of literature and other texts, to respond to what they read, and to experiment with their own writing. The *Daybook* honors the relationship between the reader and text, conveying the message that good readers take risks, relate their reading and writing to what they know and want to know, and take ownership of the learning process.

The Literature

Many of the selections complement those commonly found in anthologies or present authors and novels known to be popular with teachers and students. The selections also support curricular content and themes for grades 6-8, reflect the diversity of our world, include a blend of traditional and contemporary authors, and present a wide variety of fiction and nonfiction. Excerpts were chosen carefully to feel "complete" and yet to inspire students to seek out and read the larger works.

The Lessons

Each *Daybook* lesson focuses on a specific strategy or strategies for critical reading and writing, providing students with the tools they need to become more proficient, confident readers and writers. The lessons include instruction on how to respond actively to many kinds of writing, as well as opportunities to practice the strategies, information about writer's craft and genre elements, and support for writing activities.

The Framework

The *Daybook* units are structured around the **Five Essential Strategies of Critical Reading and Writing:**

1. Interacting with the Text
2. Making Connections
3. Exploring Multiple Perspectives
4. Focusing on Language and Craft
5. Studying an Author

These research-based, practical strategies are introduced and summarized in the first unit, "Building Your Repertoire." Subsequent units explore each of the Five Essential Strategies in greater depth. Two assessment units also engage students in an examination of their progress as they move through the book.

HOW TO USE THE DAYBOOK

No two classrooms are alike. That's why the *Daybook* was designed to accommodate a wide range of classrooms and instructional scenarios. The *Daybook's* flexibility and versatility offer something for every teacher.

Supplement an Anthology or Core Novel List

The contemporary selections and multicultural authors provide a needed balance with the more traditional canon in older anthologies. Likewise, for teachers using a list of core novels, the *Daybook* offers a way to add daily writing and reading instruction.

Provide Direct Instruction

The lessons in the *Daybook* are ideal for helping all students develop strong literacy skills. You can use these lessons to

* teach **critical reading skills,** such as predicting, making inferences, and finding the main idea;

* teach **literary elements,** such as plot, setting, characters, and theme;

* teach **writer's craft** and literary devices, such as metaphor, imagery, and dialogue;

* teach **writing traits,** such as organization, word choice and conventions;

* prepare students for **state tests** and teach **standards and benchmarks,** such as writing for a variety of purposes and audiences.

Blend Elements

The *Daybook* allows teachers to provide truly integrated instruction by blending

* direct instruction in how to read and respond to literature critically;

* regular and explicit practice in marking up and annotating texts;

* "writing to learn" activities for each day or week;

* great selections from contemporary and multicultural literature.

WHEN TO USE THE *DAYBOOK*

Each 30-to-40 minute lesson can be used

* as the **core instruction** for a literature or language arts class;

* **before other reading or writing instruction**—to introduce a topic, genre, or author or to teach a particular skill or strategy;

* **after other reading or writing instruction**—to provide additional works by a particular author or to provide practice for students needing skill reinforcement.

Teachers who use the *Daybook* only for homework have not reported much success. The *Daybook* is designed to support interaction among teacher and students; students work collaboratively to reflect, question texts, get feedback on writing, and construct knowledge. These opportunities are lost when students use the *Daybook* in isolation.

STUDENT EDITION

Lesson focus

Lesson title

Literature excerpt

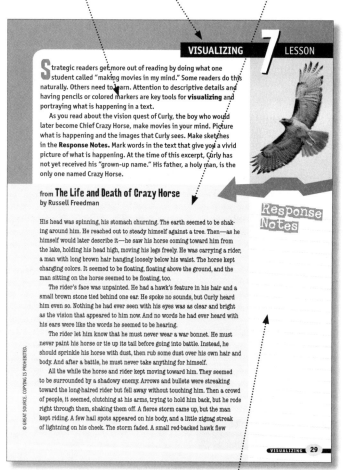

VISUALIZING **7** LESSON

Strategic readers get more out of reading by doing what one student called "making movies in my mind." Some readers do this naturally. Others need to learn. Attention to descriptive details and having pencils or colored markers are key tools for **visualizing** and portraying what is happening in a text.

As you read about the vision quest of Curly, the boy who would later become Chief Crazy Horse, make movies in your mind. Picture what is happening and the images that Curly sees. Make sketches in the **Response Notes.** Mark words in the text that give you a vivid picture of what is happening. At the time of this excerpt, Curly has not yet received his "grown-up name." His father, a holy man, is the only one named Crazy Horse.

from **The Life and Death of Crazy Horse**
by Russell Freedman

His head was spinning, his stomach churning. The earth seemed to be shaking around him. He reached out to steady himself against a tree. Then—as he himself would later describe it—he saw his horse coming toward him from the lake, holding his head high, moving his legs freely. He was carrying a rider, a man with long brown hair hanging loosely below his waist. The horse kept changing colors. It seemed to be floating, floating above the ground, and the man sitting on the horse seemed to be floating, too.

The rider's face was unpainted. He had a hawk's feature in his hair and a small brown stone tied behind one ear. He spoke no sounds, but Curly heard him even so. Nothing he had ever seen with his eyes was as clear and bright as the vision that appeared to him now. And no words he had ever heard with his ears were like the words he seemed to be hearing.

The rider let him know that he must never wear a war bonnet. He must never paint his horse or tie up its tail before going into battle. Instead, he should sprinkle his horse with dust, then rub some dust over his own hair and body. And after a battle, he must never take anything for himself.

All the while the horse and rider kept moving toward him. They seemed to be surrounded by a shadowy enemy. Arrows and bullets were streaking toward the long-haired rider but fell away without touching him. Then a crowd of people, it seemed, clutching at his arms, trying to hold him back, but he rode right through them, shaking them off. A fierce storm came up, but the man kept riding. A few hail spots appeared on his body, and a little zigzag streak of lightning on his cheek. The storm faded. A small red-backed hawk flew

Response Notes

VISUALIZING 29

Response Notes

screaming over the man's head. Still the people grabbed at him, making a great noise, pressing close around him, grabbing, grabbing. But he kept riding.

The vision faded. Curly felt someone kicking him hard. When he looked up, he saw his father. Crazy Horse had ridden out into the prairie to search for the boy. He was angry that Curly had run off alone without saying a word, distracting everyone from the dying Conquering Bear.

When Curly told his father that he had gone out to fast for a vision, Crazy Horse was furious. Seeking a vision without instruction! Without purifying himself! Without any preparation at all! Curly decided not to say anything else, not then. He would tell his father about his vision, but he would wait for the right time. ❖

❃ This vision was very important to Curly later in his life. Because he trusted his sacred vision and followed the instructions in it, Crazy Horse was never injured by enemy bullets and arrows. Use a storyboard to help you see his vision. Don't worry about your artistic ability. Stick figures are fine.

1.	2.
3.	4.

Visualizing the events and details adds to the reader's understanding of nonfiction.

30 **LESSON 7**

Space for students' comments, questions, and annotations

Practice and application of lesson focus

Lesson focus summary statement

TEACHER'S EDITION

Preteaching of difficult or significant selection vocabulary

Prereading activity to build background and/or activate prior knowledge

Suggestion for differentiated instruction for students who need language support

Quickly find out whether students have grasped the main focus of the lesson

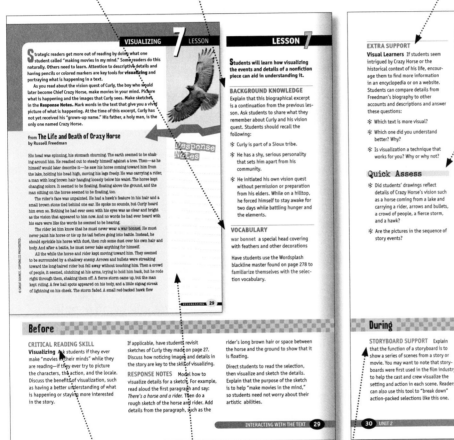

Support for introducing Critical Reading Skill and lesson focus

Reduced facsimiles of student pages eliminate the need for a separate book and include highlighted vocabulary

Support for guiding students through reading the selection and completing response activities

Extension/enrichment activities for further application of the skill or strategy

FREQUENTLY ASKED QUESTIONS

Who is the audience for the Daybook?

The *Daybook* can help all students. The length of selections and the scaffolding built into the lessons support students at all levels, while additional suggestions in the Teacher's Edition offer support for differentiated instruction, collaborative learning, and enrichment.

Are students supposed to write in the book?

Absolutely. The immediacy of responding in the *Daybook* is an integral feature of this program. Interacting with text is one of the Five Essential Strategies of Critical Reading and Writing; only by physically marking the text do students become active readers. Writing in the book provides a natural kinesthetic aid to memory and learning and allows students to refer to and reflect on their thoughts, questions, ideas, and annotations.

How do I know if the readability level is appropriate?

Helping students find materials at their individual reading levels can be a major challenge. Readability levels, which are based on text elements such as word choice, sentence length and complexity, and subject matter, provide a very rough guide. But the readability of a text also depends on the reader's interest and prior knowledge. The engaging, high-interest selections in the *Daybook,* as well as helpful background-building activities in the Teacher's Edition, provide the motivation and prior knowledge students need to access the texts. Additionally, the readability of selections throughout the *Daybook* varies so that students will gain experience reading both easier and more challenging texts.

What do you mean by "texts"?

We could call every work by a professional author *literature,* but some people associate that term only with an aesthetic or artistic approach to writing. While we do often use the term *literature* to refer specifically to "imaginative" works such as poems, short stories, and novels, we also use *literature* and *texts* as broader terms that include all written work. *Texts* also includes what students write and is therefore consistent with the *Daybook* philosophy that students are not only consumers but also creators of the written word.

May I photocopy these lessons?

No, unfortunately not. The selections, instructions, and activities are protected by copyright. To copy them infringes on the rights of the authors of the selections and the book. Writers such as Eric Schlosser, Judith Ortiz Cofer, Linda Sue Park, and Francisco Jiménez have granted permission for the use of their work in the *Daybook;* to photocopy their work violates their copyright. However, a package that includes a CD-ROM of the *Daybook* is available for purchase.

WRITING, VOCABULARY, VISUAL LITERACY, AND ASSESSMENT

Writing in the *Daybook*

The writing activities in the *Daybook* emphasize the idea that reading is a "partnership" between author and reader.

Most of the writing activities in the *Daybook* are not intended to take students all the way through the writing process. Rather they allow students to (1) *explore* texts by questioning, analyzing, connecting with, and reacting to literature; (2) *clarify* their understanding of texts by looking at other perspectives and interpreting or reflecting on their initial impressions; and (3) *apply* what they are learning about structure, genre, and craft by modeling professional writers. The types of writing in the *Daybook* include the following:

❋ **Response Notes** Students keep track of their initial responses to literature by annotating the text as they read. In this way, students develop the habit of recording what they are thinking while they are reading.

❋ **Graphic Organizers** Students collect writing ideas in lists, charts, clusters, diagrams, and so on, while analyzing particular selections or literary elements in the process.

❋ **Short Responses** Students summarize themes and main ideas and write paragraphs of description, explanation, evaluation, interpretation, comparison, and persuasion.

❋ **Personal Narratives** Students write personal stories that connect or relate to what they have read. In some cases, the narratives tell the stories of students' prior reading experiences or how a literary selection relates to their life experiences. Other activities apply and refine students' understanding and use of narrative principles.

❋ **Creative Texts** Students write poems, character sketches, dialogues, vignettes, and descriptions as a way to apply the knowledge about language and craft they are gaining through their reading. They demonstrate and reinforce their understanding of original texts by writing imaginative reconstructions of gaps in the text—adding scenes, rewriting endings, writing from other characters' points of view, and so on.

Vocabulary in the *Daybook*

The connection between reading comprehension and word knowledge has been clear for many years. The units in the *Daybook* give students the opportunity to use words repeatedly within the context of the same theme over time, applied in different ways about different subject matter. At the beginning of most Teacher's Edition lessons, difficult or significant words from the selection are listed, along with their definitions and an activity for preteaching the words.

Visual Literacy in the *Daybook*

Visual literacy—the ability to produce and read graphics—has become an essential skill in today's media-oriented world. Teachers have long known the value of using graphic organizers, photographs, illustrations, and color-coding to present information, represent ideas metaphorically, and help students see connections.

Graphic aids are especially important for students who are just learning English or whose dominant learning mode is visual-spatial. In the *Daybook*, students read and create visuals and graphic organizers such as sequence maps, word webs, Venn diagrams, charts, and illustrations in order to

* organize ideas and information;

* visualize imagery, details, and form;

* perform close observation, personal association, and analysis;

* stimulate long-term memory by integrating both visual and verbal learning.

Several reproducible graphic organizer templates are provided at the back of the Teacher's Edition for use with the activities in the *Daybook*.

Assessment in the *Daybook*

In assessing students' work, it is important to evaluate students' growing facility with reading and writing, not just their finished products. The *Daybook* must be a safe place for students to think things through, change their minds, make mistakes, and start over. Along the way, the *Daybook* provides multiple opportunities for both teachers and students to monitor progress and identify areas of frustration or difficulty:

* **Assessment Units** Two complete units in the *Daybook*, Units 7 and 14, allow students and teachers to take stock of where students are with respect to the Five Essential Strategies of Critical Reading and Writing. Students read and respond to literature, applying all of the strategies they have learned previously, and then reflect on their achievement and identify areas for improvement. A full writing process activity at the end of each unit provides an opportunity for assessment.

* **Quick Assess** In the Teacher's Edition, suggestions are given at the end of each lesson for informal, observational assessment of students' understanding of lesson concepts.

* **Writing Assessment Prompts** At the back of the Teacher's Edition, writing prompts tied to the texts in each unit address commonly tested modes of writing (expository, narrative, persuasive, expressive-descriptive, interpretive) and assess students' ability to interpret, reflect, evaluate, and connect to experience.

* **Reading Strategy Assessments** The assessments, found at the back of this Teacher's Edition, include a Pretest, four Reading Strategy Assessments, and a Posttest. Each assessment includes passages, based on the types of literature found in the *Daybook*, followed by a set of questions. Both multiple-choice and short answer items are included.

* **Self-Assessment** Throughout the *Daybook*, students engage in informal self-assessment as they write short reflections on what they have learned or how well they are doing.

FIVE ESSENTIAL STRATEGIES OF
CRITICAL READING AND WRITING

The *Daybook* is built on a framework of Five Essential Strategies of Critical Reading and Writing.

1. Interacting with the Text

Interacting with text involves physically and mentally engaging with texts. Active readers keep their minds at work throughout reading and writing—they constantly ask questions, make inferences and predictions, and test those inferences and predictions. They write, scratch out, sketch, and rewrite. We use the metaphor of having a "conversation" with a text to describe this process.

2. Making Connections

Making connections means relating the text to oneself, to other texts, and to the rest of the world. Critical readers and writers make relevant connections—a "web of meaning"—between their reading and their experiences, knowledge, memories, and imagination.

3. Exploring Multiple Perspectives

Looking at only one side of an object gives you a limited picture of that object. But when you view it from different angles or points of view, you see the various aspects that make up a whole picture, and you may construct several versions of what the object is or resembles. Likewise, critical readers and writers explore multiple perspectives to generate a more complex understanding of a text.

4. Focusing on Language and Craft

When we take time to focus on how texts work, we analyze how the language and craft of a text—word choice, imagery, style, form, etc.—influence us as readers. This extends our own possibilities as writers. Language has not only meaning but also power, so by understanding how texts work, we gain power to create our own.

5. Studying an Author

Critical readers and writers understand that there is life behind the text and are curious about the author and his or her world. By studying authors—what influences them, where they get their ideas, and how they make decisions about language and craft—students see how they, too, can be authors of works that have personal meaning and relevance.

The Essential Strategies in Action

The essential strategies can be applied to any kind of text—fiction, nonfiction, or poetry. Through the lessons in the *Daybook,* students gradually learn which strategies to use when and why. In so doing, students become independent critical readers and writers.

ESSENTIAL STRATEGIES	STRATEGIES (PURPOSEFUL PLANS)	ACTIVITIES (ACTIONS STUDENTS TAKE)
Interacting with the Text	• underlining key phrases • writing questions/comments in the margin • noting word patterns and repetitions • circling unknown words	• Write down initial impressions. • Reread the text. • Write a summary of the text. • Generate two questions and one "certainty." Then discuss in a small group.
Making Connections	• paying attention to the story being told • connecting the story to one's own experience • speculating on the meaning or significance of incidents	• Create a character map to reveal what you have learned about a person in a story. • Make a 3-column incident chart: Incident, Significance, Related incident in your life.
Exploring Multiple Perspectives	• examining the point of view • changing the point of view • exploring various versions of an event • forming interpretations • comparing texts • asking "what if" questions	• Discuss how you might read a text differently if (1) you think the narrator is female (or male) or (2) you live in a different time or place from the narrator. • Rewrite the text from a different point of view.
Focusing on Language and Craft	• understanding figurative and sensory language • looking at the way the author uses words • modeling the style of other writers • studying various forms of literature	• Use a double-entry log to identify metaphors and the qualities implied by the comparison. • Write to model a type of text.
Studying an Author	• reading what the author says about his/her own writing • reading what others say about the author's writing • making inferences about the connections between an author's life and work • analyzing the author's style • paying attention to repeated themes and topics in the work by one author	• Read about an author's life. Make a chart to record events in the author's life, inferences about how the events affected the author, and how they are manifested in the text. • Read what a critic has said about an author's text. Write a short essay agreeing or disagreeing with the critic.

10 WAYS RESEARCH SUPPORTS THE DAYBOOK

The following research-based principles are key to effective literacy instruction and played a critical role in the development of the *Daybook*. Resources for further reading are listed for each principle.

1. Teach research-based comprehension strategies (i.e. questioning, predicting, connecting, clarifying) and comprehension monitoring strategies (i.e. checking for understanding, reflecting, self-assessing) through direct and explicit instruction. The *Daybook* provides instruction in these strategies and supports strategy development through reading, writing, and assessment activities.

   Guthrie, J. T. and Taboado, A. (2004). "Fostering the Cognitive Strategies of Reading Comprehension." In J. T. Guthrie, A. Wigfield, and K. C. Perencevich, eds. *Motivating Reading Comprehension: Concept-Oriented Reading Instruction,* pp. 87-112. Mahwah, NJ: Erlbaum.

   Melzer, J. (2002). *Adolescent Literacy Resources: Linking Research and Practice.* (ERIC Document Reproduction Service No.ED466788).

2. Integrate reading and writing strategy instruction into a wide variety of texts that build both interest and skill. The *Daybook* provides a wide range of reading and writing activities that help students build habits of mind characteristic of excellent readers.

   Allington, R. L. (2002). You can't learn much from books you can't read. *Educational Leadership, 60*(3): 16-19.

   Alvermann, D. E. (2002, Summer). Effective literacy instruction for adolescents. *Journal of Literacy Research 34(2):* 189-208. (ERIC Document Reproduction Service No. EJ672862).

3. Use modeling, scaffolding, and apprenticing to demonstrate how proficient readers and writers work strategically. The *Daybook* provides explicit step by step processing techniques to help students develop conceptual knowledge of the strategies they use.

   Gere, A. R., Fairbanks, C, & Howes, A. (1992). *Language and Reflection: An Integrated Approach to Teaching English.* Upper Saddle River, NJ: Prentice-Hall, Inc.

   Kingen, S. (2000). *Teaching Language Arts In Middle Schools: Connecting and Communicating.* Mahwah, NJ: Erlbaum.

4. Address the diverse needs of students through targeted instruction with varied reading selections and writing assignments. The *Daybook* provides a wide variety in text difficulty and genre as well as providing the appropriate background knowledge and scaffolding to support student achievement.

   Allington, R. L. (2005, 2nd edition) *What Really Matters for Struggling Readers: Designing Research-Based Programs.* Boston, MA: Allyn and Bacon.

   Kucer, S. B., (2005). *Dimensions of Literacy: A Conceptual Base for Teaching Reading and Writing in School Settings.* Mahwah, NJ: Lawrence Erlbaum.

5. Make reading and writing a daily part of literacy instruction to reinforce the common and shared processes of both sending and receiving information. The *Daybook* provides companion reading and writing activities intended to enhance reading and writing abilities.

   Booth, D. (2001). *Reading and Writing in the Middle Years.* Portland, ME: Stenhouse.

   Fitzgerald, J. (1990). *Reading and writing as "mind meeting." In T. Shanahan (Ed.), Reading and writing together: New perspectives for the classroom*, pp. 81-97. Norwood, MA: Christopher-Gordon.

6. Incorporate visual representations and organizing devices to help students represent and organize ideas and information. The *Daybook* provides multiple and varied opportunities for students to visualize and "picture'"what they are reading, organize text graphically, and engage with visual symbols.

Bustle, L. S. (Ed.). (2003). *Image, Inquiry, and Transformative Practice: Engaging learners in creative and critical inquiry through visual representation.* New York: Peter Lang.

Bustle, L. S. (2004). "The Role of Visual Representation in the Assessment of Learning." *Journal of Adolescent & Adult Literacy.* 47(5): 416-421.

7. Complement strategy-building instruction with opportunities for students to read at their own pace and make their own decisions about what to read.The *Daybook* provides exposure to a wide range of texts and authors that are meant to entice students to read full length works that are introduced to them in excerpts.

Guthrie, J. T. and Humenick, N. M. (2004). "Motivating Students to Read: Evidence for Classroom Practices That Increase Reading Motivation and Achievement." In P. McCardle and V. Chhabra, eds., *The Voice of Evidence in Reading Research,* pp. 329-54. Baltimore, MD: Brookes.

8. Conduct multiple types of assessments and self-assessments to monitor student growth that will inform explicit instruction. The *Daybook* provides students with units for self-assessment and many opportunities for teachers to assess both students' reading and writing skills.

Cohen, J. H. and Wiener, R. B. (2003). *Literacy Portfolios: Improving Assessment, Teaching and Learning.* Upper Saddle River, NJ: Merrill/Prentice Hall.

William, D., and Black, P. (1996). "Meanings and Consequences: A Basis for Distinguishing Formative and Summative Functions of Assessment?" *British Educational Research Journal 22*(5): 537-48.

9. Determine venues for students to share expertise with one another and foster collaborative literacy projects. The *Daybook* provides opportunities for students to share their thinking and writing, and they are encouraged to do that in more depth through various extension activities suggested in the teachers' edition.

Vygotsky, L. S. (1978). *Mind in Society. The development of higher mental psychological processes.* Cambridge, MA: MIT Press.

Wood, K. D., Roser, N. L. and Martinez, M. (2001). "Collaborative Literacy: Lessons Learned from Literature." *The Reading Teacher 55*(2): 102-115.

10. Establish routines that give students ample time to read and write in the classroom, where the teacher can monitor students' progress. The *Daybook* is a resource of multiple and overlapping literacy activities that can support developing and monitoring student understanding.

Gettinger, M. (1984). "Achievement as a Function of Time Spent in Learning and Time Needed for Learning." *American Educational Research Journal 21*(3): 617-28.

Lofty. J. (1992). *Time to Write: The Influence of Time and Culture on Learning To Write.* New York: SUNY.

Contents

4

Focus/Skill		Selection/Author	

7

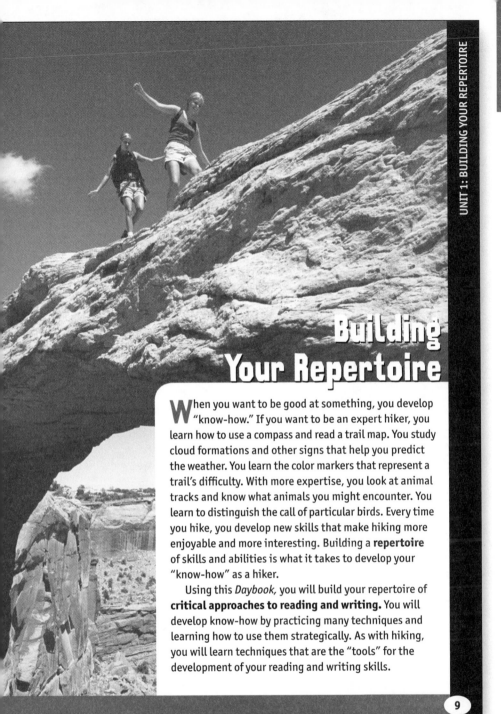

Building Your Repertoire

When you want to be good at something, you develop "know-how." If you want to be an expert hiker, you learn how to use a compass and read a trail map. You study cloud formations and other signs that help you predict the weather. You learn the color markers that represent a trail's difficulty. With more expertise, you look at animal tracks and know what animals you might encounter. You learn to distinguish the call of particular birds. Every time you hike, you develop new skills that make hiking more enjoyable and more interesting. Building a **repertoire** of skills and abilities is what it takes to develop your "know-how" as a hiker.

Using this *Daybook,* you will build your repertoire of **critical approaches to reading and writing.** You will develop know-how by practicing many techniques and learning how to use them strategically. As with hiking, you will learn techniques that are the "tools" for the development of your reading and writing skills.

9

UNIT 1 BUILDING YOUR REPERTOIRE

Lessons 1–5, pages 10–24

UNIT OVERVIEW

In studying six compositions by Langston Hughes, students are introduced to five critical reading and writing strategies that will be used throughout the book.

KEY IDEA

Good readers and writers develop repertoires of skills and strategies to help them read and write effectively.

CRITICAL READING SKILLS
by lesson

1. Interacting with the text
2. Making connections
3. Exploring multiple perspectives
4. Focusing on language and craft
5. Studying an author

WRITING ACTIVITIES
by lesson

1. Write a poem inspired by Hughes's poem.
2. Tell a story that a fellow storyteller might appreciate.
3. Write a few sentences about multiple perspectives.
4. Compose a poem about a person.
5. Write a speech in which you introduce Langston Hughes.

Literature

- **Poems by Langston Hughes**

"Alabama Earth" tells of the enduring message of Booker T. Washington.

"Luck" explores the nature of luck.

"Aunt Sue's Stories" honors Aunt Sue, whose stories about slaves instill pride and a sense of wonder in a young African American boy.

"The Weary Blues" uses the rhythms and flavor of the blues to tell of a weary musician playing and singing his own blues.

- **"The Return of Simple"** by Langston Hughes (article excerpt)

The fictional character, Jesse B. Semple, speaks of the importance of knowing African American history.

- *I Wonder as I Wander* by Langston Hughes (autobiography)

This excerpt discusses the challenges facing a young black writer at the beginning of The Great Depression.

ASSESSMENT See page 231 for a writing prompt based on this unit.

Students will interact with a text by providing initial reactions, questioning it, or "talking back" to the author.

BACKGROUND KNOWLEDGE

The literature in this unit reflects the period known as the Harlem Renaissance, a cultural revolution led by African Americans that took place in the 1920s and 1930s in New York City. The first poem, by Langston Hughes, honors Booker T. Washington, a former slave who became an educator and community leader and helped found Tuskegee Institute in Alabama. The second poem, which explores the nature of luck, is an intriguing expression from a man who clearly depended on drive, perseverance, and goodwill, as well as luck, to achieve his personal goals.

VOCABULARY

unborn not yet born

flung thrown

After discussing each word's meaning, invite students to demonstrate their understanding by replacing each with a synonym as they read the poems.

When you interact with a text, you have a conversation with it. Imagine you are talking to a friend who hums and looks around the room as you try to engage her in a conversation. She probably doesn't hear a word you say. When you're reading, be careful not to do the same thing. You need to hold up your end of the "conversation" by paying close attention to what is going on. Keep your focus and "listen" to what the writer has to say. One way to stay active and focused is to *read with your pen.*

- Circle words you don't know or understand.
- Underline important phrases, repetition, or key images.
- Make notes near confusing parts.
- Ask questions.
- Make comments like: "I wonder..." "What if....." I don't agree...." "I like this." Use phrases that express how you emotionally react.

In the *Daybook,* use the **Response Notes** column to help you carry on a conversation with the text. As you read "Alabama Earth," notice how one reader interacted with the text. Add your responses to the ones already there.

Alabama Earth by Langston Hughes

Response Notes

Do I know him?
I think he was an African American educator.
Find out.
Shows Washington's importance

love this

nonviolent way to make changes

Huh?

(At Booker Washington's grave)
Deep in Alabama earth
His buried body lies—
But higher than the singing pines
And taller than the skies
And out of Alabama earth
To all the world there goes
The truth a simple heart has held
And the strength a strong hand knows,
While over Alabama earth
These words are gently spoken:
Serve—and hate will die unborn.
Love—and chains are broken ✧

Before

CRITICAL READING SKILL

Interacting with the Text Ask students what they do in a conversation. *(talk, ask questions, listen to other people)* Point out that reading is like having a conversation: you consider and react to ideas presented, you ask questions, and you develop new understandings. Model interacting with the text using a think-aloud: *Why did the poet write about Booker*

T. Washington? I'd like to know more about Washington. I can tell the poet admires him because he describes Washington's truth and strength as higher than trees and "taller than the skies." I wonder why the poet used "simple" and "gently spoken" to describe him? Are these qualities the poet admired?

RESPONSE NOTES Point out the sample markings in the *Daybook,* explaining that this is how one student interacted with the text. Encourage students to mark anything they find interesting, important, or puzzling. Point out the on-page model of how to circle the text and make notes. (See *Daybook* page 229 for more about marking text.)

✳ As you read "Luck," another poem by Langston Hughes, read with your pen. Use your **Response Notes** to write questions or emotional reactions you have to the poem. Underline words or phrases that seem important to you.

Luck by Langston Hughes

Sometimes a crumb falls
From the tables of joy,
Sometimes a bone
Is flung.

To some people
Love is given,
To others
Only heaven. ✣

✳ Have a conversation about the poem with a partner or a small group. Compare your **Response Notes.** Discuss what you each think *luck* means to Langston Hughes. What in the poem leads you to think so?

✳ Imagine that you can continue your conversation with the poet. Think about what *luck* means to you and how you would describe the meaning in words. To get started:

■ List a few words or phrases that describe what the word "luck" means to you.

■ List objects, colors, animals, or other concrete details you associate with luck.

■ How does your idea of luck compare to Hughes's idea of luck?

Hughes's description of luck	My description of luck
"tables of joy" luck is like love	

ABOUT THE AUTHOR

Born in 1902 in Joplin, Missouri, Langston Hughes grew up mainly in Kansas, but also lived in Illinois, Ohio, and Mexico. His first book of poetry was published in 1926. Influenced by Walt Whitman, Carl Sandburg, Paul Laurence Dunbar, and Claude McKay. Hughes became a major force of the Harlem Renaissance. His multi-faceted opus, consisting of novels, short stories, plays, essays, articles, and poetry, focuses on themes of racial pride, racism, and artistic indepen- dence. Hughes was the first African American known to support himself entirely by writing and giving lectures. For more information, see http://www .english.uiuc.edu/MAPS/poets/g_l/ hughes/hughes.htm.

TEACHING TIP

Collaboration Have students work in pairs to talk about their reactions. Partners can generate questions and answers together, discuss ideas and reactions, or write additional Response Notes.

During

READING PROCESS Explain to students that good readers keep their minds active when they read. They pre- pare to read by previewing the material and setting a purpose. As they read, they engage with the text and monitor their comprehension. After reading a text, successful readers take time to reflect on what they learned. (See *Daybook* page 226 for more on the Reading Process.)

SHARING RESPONSES Invite volun- teers to share some of their Response Notes with the class. Remind students that there are no right or wrong answers since every person responds to a text in a different way. Compile responses into a chart, sorting them into various ways of interacting with a text, such as, question- ing, circling unfamiliar words, comparing, reacting emotionally, etc.

WRITER'S CRAFT

Word Choice Read aloud the first stanza of "Luck." Discuss how using short words and fragments paint brief but powerful images in the reader's mind. Invite students to share visual images that come to mind as you read the stanza again. Encourage students to review their lists of words and phrases about luck and select those that inspire the most powerful visual images.

EXTRA SUPPORT

Differentiation Before responding to the writing prompt, students who need extra support may benefit from brainstorming with a partner to come up with images and ideas to use in their poems. *You may model a think-aloud, saying: I always think of luck as something that appears suddenly and unexpectedly. For example,*

> *Lightning flashes,*
> *Thunder crashes.*
> *Sometimes luck rolls in*
> *Sprinkling joy.*

Quick Assess

✳ Do students' poems give the reader an impression of luck?

✳ Using your lists as a guide, write a poem to Hughes that portrays what you think *luck* means. You might want to write in the style of Hughes, starting one stanza with *Sometimes* and the other stanza with *To some people.*

> Interact with the text by reacting to, questioning, or talking back to the author.

After

APPLYING THE STRATEGY Provide newspapers, magazines, or other reading materials that students can write on, and have students practice interacting with these texts. Remind students to imagine that they are talking to characters or the author as they write their questions and notes. Then ask: *How does interacting with the text help you understand what you read? Did it help you stay focused on what you were reading? Did it help you make sense of confusing parts? Did it make the text more interesting to you?*

H ave you ever read something that seems like it was written just for you? If so, there is something in the piece that you were able to **connect** to your own experiences and feelings. For example, you might connect what you are reading to something else you read before. You might connect to an event about which you have seen or heard. When you take the time to make these connections, you gain a better understanding of what you are reading by comparing new information to what you know.

As you read "Aunt Sue's Stories," use your **Response Notes** to jot down any connections you make between the people, ideas, or experiences in the story and those from your own life.

Aunt Sue's Stories by Langston Hughes

Aunt Sue has a head full of stories .
Aunt Sue has a whole heart full of stories.
Summer nights on the front porch
Aunt Sue cuddles a brown-faced child to her bosom
And tells him stories.
Black slaves
Working in the hot sun,
And black slaves
Walking in the dewy night,
And black slaves
Singing sorrow songs on the banks of a mighty river
Mingle themselves softly
In the flow of old Aunt Sue's voice,
Mingle themselves softly
In the dark shadows that cross and recross
Aunt Sue's stories.
And the dark-faced child, listening,
Knows that Aunt Sue's stories are real stories.
He knows that Aunt Sue never got her stories
Out of any book at all,
But that they came
Right out of her own life.
The dark-faced child is quiet
Of a summer night
Listening to Aunt Sue's stories. ❖

Response Notes

like my grandfather

Students will learn how to connect their experiences and knowledge to the people and events in a story in order to help them better understand other's lives.

BACKGROUND KNOWLEDGE
Invite students to recall stories that they remember clearly, reflecting on why they remember them so well. Ask: *Did the story remind you of an experience you've had? Did a character remind you of someone? Did the story inspire you to try something challenging?* Explain that making connections between what you read and what you know and feel helps you remember the details of what you read because you already know something about them. Good readers make connections between what they read and what they know and feel about people and the world.

VOCABULARY
dewy covered with dew
mingle to mix or blend together

After discussing each meaning, have students write a sentence using each word, leaving a word out of the sentence. Have students trade papers and complete each other's sentences.

Before

CRITICAL READING SKILL
Making Connections Explain that a word or reference in a poem can remind you of something in your own life or something you've read or heard. This helps you *connect* to the text, relate to what the poet is expressing, and better understand what you're reading. Have students recall storytellers from their own lives or those who tell stories in books, movies, or television shows. Ask students to watch for ways in which Aunt Sue is like or unlike the storytellers they know.

RESPONSE NOTES Remind students that they should mark up the text as they read, noting places in the poem to which they can make connections. Refer to the markings on *Daybook* page 10 as a model. See also *Daybook* page 229.

During

VISUALIZING Explain that one way to connect with the text is to imagine what a scene looks like. Encourage students to close their eyes as you read the poem aloud. Then invite students to share visual images that formed in their minds as they listened to the poem. Ask: *How do these images remind you of a situation in your life or of the way you see the world?*

EXTRA SUPPORT

Differentiation Students who need extra support might benefit from the use of other modalities to complete their charts. One way is for students to draw pictures with captions to explain connections they make with the poem. Another way is to have students prepare collaborative choral readings to present to their classmates.

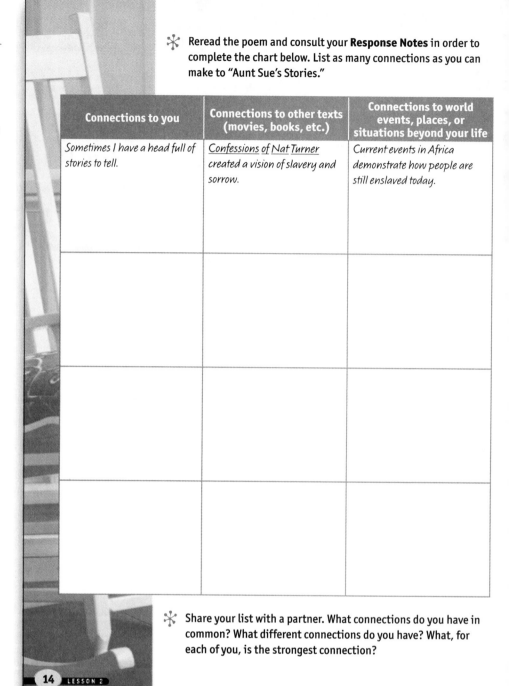

✳ Reread the poem and consult your **Response Notes** in order to complete the chart below. List as many connections as you can make to "Aunt Sue's Stories."

Connections to you	Connections to other texts (movies, books, etc.)	Connections to world events, places, or situations beyond your life
Sometimes I have a head full of stories to tell.	_Confessions of Nat Turner_ created a vision of slavery and sorrow.	Current events in Africa demonstrate how people are still enslaved today.

✳ Share your list with a partner. What connections do you have in common? What different connections do you have? What, for each of you, is the strongest connection?

14 LESSON 2

CONNECTIONS CHART As students complete their charts, help them make connections by asking such questions as: *Does Aunt Sue remind you of someone you know? How would you feel if you were the child in the poem? What does the summer night feel like? What experience of your own does it remind you of? What do you know about slavery that helps you understand how the people in Aunt Sue's stories might feel?*

REFLECTING Have students consider how the connections they made helped them better understand the poem. Could they picture the scenes more clearly? Could they interpret the child's feelings? Did they gain new understanding about others' lives or their life? Encourage students to answer these questions orally or in their Response Notes.

✳ Langston Hughes describes Aunt Sue as having a "head full of stories." You have stories, too. What story of yours do you think Aunt Sue would appreciate hearing? Connect to Aunt Sue, the storyteller, by telling a story of your own back to her.

Connecting your experiences and knowledge to the people and events in the story helps you better understand what you read.

WRITING SUPPORT

Audience Remind students that the audience for their stories is Aunt Sue. Invite students to consider Aunt Sue's personality before they begin writing. Ask: *What does Aunt Sue value? How does she choose the stories she tells? What kind of story would she connect with?* Have partners brainstorm ideas and help each other plan their stories.

TEACHING TIP

Using Graphic Organizers Suggest that students create storyboards or Plot Diagram (see page 276) to plan their stories. The storyboards should include a drawing and brief description of the action in each scene of the story. Encourage partners to give each other feedback on the completeness of their storyboards.

Quick Assess

✳ Were students able to fill in the chart with some connections?

✳ Do students' stories demonstrate an approach appropriate to the audience?

After

WRITING CONNECTION To extend the concept of making connections, suggest that students think about a person who has had an impact on them in a way similar to the way Aunt Sue had an impact on the child. Have students write a short paragraph about this person, explaining the connection they feel and how it affects the way they live their lives.

Students will learn how reading multiple perspectives on a topic can help them understand their own and others' perspectives.

BACKGROUND KNOWLEDGE

In 1942, Langston Hughes began writing a weekly column in the *Chicago Defender*. During the twenty years the column ran, he developed the fictional Harlem character Jesse B. Semple, or Simple, who exchanged commentary about a variety of matters with another customer in a neighborhood bar. Simple became Hughes's most celebrated and beloved fictional creation and the subject of five collections.

VOCABULARY

Mayflower the ship on which the Pilgrims came to America

Jackie Robinson first African American to play major league baseball

Du Bois W.E.B. Du Bois; writer, educator, and civil rights leader

Frederick Douglass African American orator and abolitionist

Harriet Tubman best known for leading slaves to freedom along a route called the Underground Railroad

Divide students into groups and have each group research one word and report its findings.

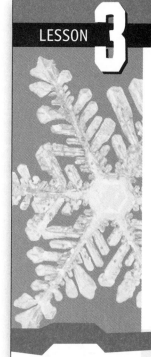

A **perspective** is a way of looking at something. You have certain perspectives because of your experiences. Your perspectives influence how you respond to what you read. Writers often share their perspectives. A writer's perspective is shaped by his or her experiences, education, and feelings. A poet who lives in Canada might have a different perspective on snow, for example, than a poet living in Arizona. The two poets' poems about snow would probably be entirely different—and shaped by their own experience (or inexperience) with winter.

Sometimes authors create characters with definite perspectives. Langston Hughes introduced a fictional character, Jesse B. Semple and a fictional "I" (not given a name) in a newspaper column he wrote for the *Chicago Defender*. This newspaper began in the 1940s and was owned by African Americans. Both Semple (nicknamed "Simple") and "I" have perspectives on the importance of knowing African American history. As you read, use your **Response Notes** to make notes about the differences in Simple's and "I's" perspectives.

Response Notes

from **The Return of Simple** by Langston Hughes

"Next week is Negro History Week," said Simple. "And how much Negro history do you know?"

"Why should I know *Negro* history?" I replied. "I am an American."

"But you are also a black man," said Simple, "and you did not come over on the *Mayflower*—at least, not the same *Mayflower* as the rest."

"What rest?" I asked.

"The rest who make up the most," said Simple, "then write the history books and leave us out, or else put in the books nothing but prize fighters and ballplayers. Some folks think Negro history begins and ends with Jackie Robinson."

"Not quite," I said.

"Not quite is right," said Simple. "Before Jackie there was Du Bois and before him there was Booker T. Washington, and before him was Frederick Douglass and before Douglass the original Freedom Walker, Harriet Tubman, who were a lady. Before her was them great Freedom Fighters who started rebellions in the South long before the Civil War. By name they was Gabriel and Nat Turner and Denmark Vesey."

"When, how, and where did you get all that information at once?" I asked.

Before

CRITICAL READING SKILL
Exploring Multiple Perspectives

Explain that authors choose specific perspectives from which to tell their stories. These choices affect the reader's experience of the story. The perspective determines the style, theme, and other elements of the piece of writing. Explain that, in this selection, Langston Hughes reveals the characters through dialogue alone. The author does not state, explicitly, how the character feels or what the character believes. The reader must infer those aspects of character based on what the character says.

MAKING INFERENCES Explain that discovering character through dialogue alone requires making inferences. Define an inference as "reading between the lines" spoken by a character to determine what a passage means. To model the process, say: *"I" says, "Why should I know* Negro *history? I am an American."* It seems like "I" doesn't see his own history as having any connection to black history. Encourage students to record their inferences in their Response Notes.

"From my wife, Joyce," said Simple. "Joyce is a fiend for history. She belongs to the Association for the Study of Negro Life and History. Also Joyce went to school down South. There colored teachers teach children about *our* history. It is not like up North where almost no teachers teach children anything about themselves and who they is and where they come from out of our great black past which were Africa in the old days."

"The days of Ashanti and Benin and the great trade routes in the Middle Ages, the great cities and great kings."

"Amen!" said Simple. "It might have been long ago, but we had black kings. It is from one of them kings that I am descended."

"You?" I exclaimed. "How so? After five hundred years it hardly seems possible that you can trace your ancestry back to an African king."

"Oh, but I can," said Simple. "It is only just a matter of simple arithmetic. Suppose great old King Ashanti in his middle ages had one son. And that one son had two sons. And them two sons each had three sons—and so on down the line, each bigger set of sons having bigger sets of children themselves. Why, the way them sons of kings and kings' sons multiplied, after five hundred years, every black man in the U.S.A. must be the son of one of them African king's grandsons' sons—including me. A matter of simple arithmetic—I am descended from a king."

"It is a good thing to think, anyhow," I said.

"Furthermore, I am descended from the people who built the pyramids, created the alphabets, first wrote words on stones, and first added up two and two."

"Who said all those wise men were colored?"

"Joyce, my wife—and I never doubts her word. She has been going to the Schomburg Collection all week reading books which she cannot take out and carry home because they is too valuable to the Negro people, so must be read in the library. In some places in Harlem a rat might chaw one of them books which is so old and so valuable nobody could put it back in the library. My wife says the Schomburg in Harlem is one of the greatest places in the world to find out about Negro history. Joyce tried to drag me there one day, but I said I had rather get my history from her after she has got it from what she calls the archives. Friend, what is an archive?"

"A place of recorded records, books, files, the materials in which history is preserved."

"They got a million archives in the Schomburg library," said Simple.

"By no stretch of the imagination could there be that many."

"Yes there is," said Simple. "Every word in there is an archive to the Negro people, and to me. I want to know about my kings, my past, my Africa, my history years that make me proud. I want to go back to the days when I did

During

MARKING THE TEXT   Point out that, in addition to revealing the characters of Simple and "I" through the dialogue, the author also reveals a great deal about Simple's wife, Joyce, so the reader learns about her perspective as well. Suggest that students use a variety of techniques to identify various perspectives in the selection. For example, they might mark comments attributed to different characters (Joyce never speaks for herself) with different colored highlighters. Or they might use different handwriting styles for questions or comments about different characters.

Collaboration Have students form groups to share their inferences about the characters in *The Return of Simple*. Encourage students to explain the thinking that brought them to their inferences about each character. They should identify the author's words and describe their own life experience(s) that led to each inference. Then have groups reach consensus about characters and share their group inferences with the class.

WRITER'S CRAFT

Humor Explain that authors sometimes use humor to write about serious topics. In this selection, Langston Hughes used the discussion about arithmetic to lighten up his very serious discussion of discrimination against African Americans. Have students examine the dialogue for other humorous elements that help reveal the characters' perspectives.

Quick Assess

✳ Did students complete all sections of the Venn diagram?

✳ Did students explain what the conversations between "Simple" and "I" reveal about Hughes's perspective on people's awareness of their own history?

✳ Did students use details from the selection in their writing?

not have to knock and bang and beg at doors for the chance to do things like I do now. I want to go back to the days of my blackness and greatness when I were in my own land and were king and I invented arithmetic."

"The way you can multiply kings and produce yourself as a least common denominator, maybe you did invent arithmetic," I said.

"Maybe I did," said Simple. ❖

✳ On the Venn diagram below, list details that reveal Simple's and "I's" perspectives on African American history. In the center, list any shared perspectives.

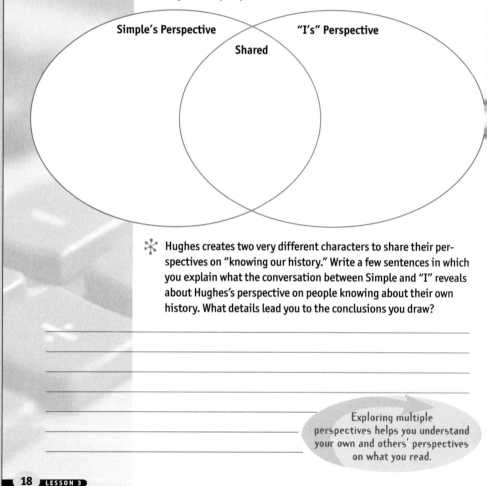

Simple's Perspective   Shared   "I's" Perspective

✳ Hughes creates two very different characters to share their perspectives on "knowing our history." Write a few sentences in which you explain what the conversation between Simple and "I" reveals about Hughes's perspective on people knowing about their own history. What details lead you to the conclusions you draw?

_____

_____

_____

_____

_____

_____

Exploring multiple perspectives helps you understand your own and others' perspectives on what you read.

After

APPLYING THE STRATEGY   Langston Hughes used his column to show various perspectives on the troublesome issues of his time. Many of today's writers do the same thing. Display or read aloud newspaper columns or comic strips that express perspectives on a current issue. Then invite students to find more examples to share with the class. Discuss the multiple perspectives the examples portray.

What are the qualities of writing that make some writers more interesting than others to you? Certainly the subject matter makes a difference. When you have interests in science fiction, adventure, or horror, you naturally gravitate toward those. But the way a writer puts words together also affects a reader's interest. For example, what makes a piece of writing descriptive? Suspenseful? Fast paced? Good writers know how to use words to craft language that captures readers and draws them in. **Language and craft** involve a variety of elements that work together to create certain effects. Here are a few things we will look at in this lesson to focus on Hughes's use of language and craft:

- Choice of words
- Use of sound and rhythm
- Use of repetition

As you read "The Weary Blues," circle or highlight the language that makes the strongest impression on you. In your **Response Notes,** write what comes into your mind because of the language the author uses.

The Weary Blues by Langston Hughes

Droning a drowsy syncopated tune,
Rocking back and forth to a mellow croon,
I heard a Negro play.
Down on Lenox Avenue the other night
By the pale dull pallor of an old gas light
    He did a lazy sway. . . .
    He did a lazy sway. . . .
To the tune o' those Weary Blues.
With his ebony hands on each ivory key
He made that poor piano moan with melody.
    O Blues!
Swaying to and fro on his rickety stool
He played that sad raggy tune like a musical fool.
    Sweet Blues!
Coming from a black man's soul.
    O Blues!
In a deep song voice with a melancholy tone
I heard that Negro sing, that old piano moan—

Response Notes

describes rhythm?

interesting description

repeats, like in a song

Students will learn how focusing on an author's word choice and use of rhythm and/or repetition can help reveal what the author is trying to emphasize.

BACKGROUND KNOWLEDGE

The Weary Blues, from which this poem of the same name is taken, was the first book Langston Hughes published. Flavored by the rhythms of jazz and blues, the poems in this collection, as well as many of Hughes's later works, express the poet's deep devotion to the music that grew out of the African American experience.

VOCABULARY

syncopated a musical device common in jazz consisting of a shift of accent to a normally weak beat

croon to sing with a low, gentle tone

Lenox Avenue a street in Harlem in New York City

pallor a pale or faint color

raggy slang for ragtime, an early form of jazz characterized by uneven rhythms

After discussing the definitions, have students demonstrate understanding by using each word in a spoken sentence.

Before

CRITICAL READING SKILL
Focusing on Language and Craft

In this lesson, students examine the ways an author uses words to develop ideas and create strong images of people, feelings, and situations. Point out that writing is like painting; a good writer paints a picture in your mind.

RESPONSE NOTES   Read the poem aloud and suggest that students draw images that come to mind. For example, the words *Down on Lenox Avenue* or *ebony hands* could elicit an interesting variety of images.

TEACHING TIP

Collaboration Point out that Langston Hughes used words to create visual and auditory images and images of motion. Display a three-column chart with columns labeled accordingly. Arrange students into three groups: one to find words or phrases in the poem that give specific visual details, one to find those that give auditory details, and one to find those that describe motions. Then have groups write their discoveries on the class chart.

> "Ain't got nobody in all this world,
>   Ain't got nobody but ma self.
>   I's gwine to quit ma frownin'
>   And put ma troubles on the shelf."
>
> Thump, thump, thump, went his foot on the floor.
> He played a few chords then he sang some more—
> "I got the Weary Blues
>   And I can't be satisfied.
>   Got the Weary Blues
>   And can't be satisfied—
>   I ain't happy no mo'
>   And I wish that I had died." ❖

✳ What lines of the poem create the strongest impressions? In the Double Entry Chart below, write the line or lines from the poem in the left column. Explain your selections in the right column.

DOUBLE ENTRY CHART

Write the best examples of:	Explain why you think so
Choice of words	
Use of sound and/or rhythm	
Use of repetition	

✳ Share what you listed with a partner or a small group. After listening to what your classmates had to say, what words or phrases would you add to your chart?

During

ELEMENTS OF LANGUAGE Explain that poets use various devices to paint word pictures, including precise word choice, repetition, and rhythm and rhyme Read aloud the first five lines of the poem, emphasizing words such as *syncopated, rocking, croon,* and *pallor.* Point out that these word choices communicate images from the writer to the reader. Then read aloud the next two lines and point out that the repetition may remind the reader of songs that use repeated lines. Finally, read aloud the first four lines on page 20, emphasizing their rhythm and rhyme. Discuss the effects of those sound elements, which are typically found in the blues.

MUSIC CONNECTION To support students in relating to the musical references in the poem, play recordings of famous blues musicians of the time, such as Ma Rainey ("The Mother of the Blues"), Bessie Smith, Alberta Hunter, and Ethel Waters. Explain that blues lyrics often deal with hardship, as does Langston Hughes's poem, and are typically arranged in stanzas that include the repetition of certain lines, images, and phrases. Invite students to discuss their responses to the blues they've heard and how they think the characteristics of blues music are related to the subject of the lyrics.

✳ Hughes wrote about a piano player in "The Weary Blues." Think of a person about whom you would like to write a poem. You might choose to write about a friend, a family member, a famous singer, a movie star, or an athlete.

The subject of my poem is _____ .

Spend some time thinking about this person in the following ways:

1 List several words or phrases that describe the person, both physically and emotionally.

2 Use a combination of sound and rhythm to describe the person.

3 Use repetition that will emphasize some particular good or bad quality about the person.

✳ Use your lists above and any other language that comes to mind to write a poem about the person.

Focusing attention on a writer's word choice and the use of sound, rhythm and repetition will help you understand what the author is trying to emphasize.

FOCUSING ON LANGUAGE AND CRAFT **21**

Prewriting Suggest that students work with partners before beginning their writing plans. Each student should name several people to write about and give reasons for choosing each. After partners select the subjects of their poems, they can help each other think of words, phrases, sounds, rhythms, and repetitions they might use in their poems.

Quick Assess

✳ Do students' charts show strong examples of word choice, use of sound/rhythm, and use of repetition from the poem?

✳ Were students able to compose a poem about a person using their notes?

After

SPEAKING/LISTENING CONNECTION   Invite individuals or groups of students to select portions of "The Weary Blues" or another poem by Langston Hughes to perform for the class. Encourage students to choose blues recordings to use as introductory and/or background music. Have students practice their readings with partners or with their groups, who should make suggestions for improvements. After each performance, invite the class to give feedback regarding its interpretation of the language and craft of the poet and the overall effect. Students should consider rhythm, pace, intonation, word emphasis, and gestures of each performance.

Students will learn that knowing about an author's life can help in understanding his or her writing.

BACKGROUND KNOWLEDGE

The Great Depression was a worldwide economic downturn. In the United States, many people were unemployed and thousands of them could not earn enough to feed their families. Obviously this was not a favorable time for a young man, particularly a black writer, to enter the workforce. Langston Hughes was extremely fortunate to have met a wealthy white widow named Charlotte Mason, who supported him for several years as he pursued his dream of living by his pen.

VOCABULARY

patron person who supports an artist or a cause; sponsor

backwash cultural influence

exotic charming because of unfamiliarity

pulps publications containing mostly sensational subject matter

disheartening discouraging

intuitive inborn

Ask students to work in groups to list a synonymous word or phrase for each vocabulary word.

Knowing about an author's life can help you better understand what you are reading. Not every story, poem, or article that a writer composes is autobiographical, of course, but most writers include aspects of their life experiences and memories in their writing. When you know something about a writer's experiences and concerns, you gain other important insights into the writer's craft.

As you read from Langston Hughes's autobiography, use your **Response Notes** to jot down any connections you make between his life and the poems and article you've read in this unit.

Response Notes

from **I Wonder As I Wander** by Langston Hughes

I came out of college in 1929, the year of the Stock Market crash and the beginning of the Great Depression. I had written my first novel, *Not Without Laughter*, as a student on the campus of Lincoln University. I had had a scholarship to college. After graduation a monthly sum from my patron enabled me to live comfortably in suburban New Jersey, an hour from Manhattan, revising my novel at leisure. Propelled by the backwash of the "Harlem Renaissance" of the early 'twenties, I had been drifting along pleasantly on the delightful rewards of my poems which seemed to please the fancy of kind-hearted New York ladies with money to help young writers. The magazines used very few stories with Negro themes, since Negro themes were considered exotic, in a class with Chinese or East Indian features. Editorial offices then never hired Negro writers to read manuscripts or employed them to work on their staffs. Almost all the young white writers I'd known in New York in the 'twenties had gotten good jobs with publishers or magazines as a result of their creative work. White friends of mine in Manhattan, whose first novels had received reviews nowhere nearly so good as my own, had been called to Hollywood, or were doing scripts for the radio. Poets whose poetry sold hardly at all had been offered jobs on smart New York magazines. But they were white. I was colored. So in Haiti I began to puzzle out how I, a *Negro*, could make a living in America from writing.

There was one other dilemma—how to make a living from *the kind of writing I wanted to do*. I did not want to write for the pulps, or turn out fake "true" stories to sell under anonymous names as Wallace Thurman did. I did not want to bat out slick non-Negro short stories in competition with a thousand other commercial writers trying to make *The Saturday Evening Post*. I wanted to write seriously and as well as I knew how about the Negro people, and make *that* kind of writing earn for me a living.

Before

CRITICAL READING STRATEGY
Studying an Author Explain that, while not everything that Langston Hughes wrote was directly about his life, the facts that he was an African American and lived during such historically significant times as the Great Depression and the Harlem Renaissance certainly influenced his work. Encourage students to conduct Internet or library research into the life of Langston Hughes and the Harlem Renaissance. Then have them share information about the poet that enriches their understanding of the poet's perspective and messages.

RESPONSE NOTES   Suggest that students include in their notes information that their Internet research adds to the autobiographical excerpt.

I thought, with the four hundred dollars my novel had given me, I had better go sit in the sun awhile and think, having just been through a tense and disheartening winter after a series of misunderstandings with the kind lady who had been my patron. She wanted me to be more African than Harlem— primitive in the simple, intuitive and noble sense of the word. I couldn't be, having grown up in Kansas City, Chicago and Cleveland. So that winter had left me ill in my soul. ❖

✳ Create a timeline of Hughes's life. List one key event of his life to the right of each number. In the boxes, explain the connections you find between his life events and his poetry and articles.

Born 1902

1.

2.

3.

4.

5.

Died 1967

Collaboration Students may work in small groups on these timelines and then share them with the class. Discussion should include differences and justifications for the key events. Why do readers interpret key events differently?

During

TIMELINES   Before students create their timelines, suggest that they review the information they gained from the Internet research done for page 22. They can use their Response Notes as well as notes from their research. If students encounter gaps as they construct their timelines, suggest that they consult with other students or conduct further research.

WRITING SUPPORT

Organization Suggest the following components for the introduction:

* a "hook" or interesting fact to begin the introduction

* an event or experience that motivated Langston Hughes to become a writer

* a quotation or two from the author's writings that shed light on his thoughts and perspectives

* character traits that are essential elements of the author's outlook

* an important message that the author seems to want to communicate to his readers

* reasons Langston Hughes should receive the award

After students identify these components, they can determine an order that suits their purpose and then write the introduction.

Quick Assess

* Are students' timelines complete?

* Do timelines show connections between the poet's life and his writing?

* Langston Hughes won numerous awards for his writing. Imagine you are introducing him at an awards ceremony. Tell about Hughes's beginnings as a writer, the obstacles he overcame, and the messages that he conveys in his work. Why is he worthy of the award? Write your introduction on the lines below.

> Studying an author's life and perspectives expands your understanding of the author's writing.

After

WRITING/SPEAKING CONNECTION Have partners role-play the introduction of the poet at an awards ceremony. One partner will play the role of Langston Hughes while the other partner will introduce him. Then have students switch roles and repeat the role-play. Invite students to share their responses to the role-plays. For example:

How did it feel to introduce a great poet? How did it feel to take the role of the poet? What did you learn about the poet from the introduction?

REFLECTION Invite students to think about their own career dreams and compare them to those of Langston Hughes. Ask: *Which of Langston Hughes's messages are important to you? How can you use his experiences to promote your dreams? What would you like someone to say, one day, in an introduction of you?*

Interacting with the Text

Reading may be almost second nature to you. After all, you have probably been reading for many years. But what happens when you read about an unfamiliar subject or you read a new genre or type of writing? Readers strengthen their abilities by stretching their skills with new material. In this unit, you will practice **strategies** to help you read **nonfiction** literature about subjects that may be new to you.

This unit includes a biography, an autobiography, and a newspaper account of important people in United States history: a Native American leader, an American first lady, and teenagers who helped change our segregated society of the 1950s. By setting a purpose for reading and by visualizing what you read, you will make connections that will help you understand the information. You will also practice other strategies: questioning the text, building on background knowledge, and evaluating what you read.

25

UNIT 2 INTERACTING WITH THE TEXT

Lessons 6–10 pages 26–38

UNIT OVERVIEW
Students interact with a variety of texts about remarkable people.

KEY IDEA
Good readers use interactive strategies to better understand and evaluate factual texts.

CRITICAL READING SKILLS
by lesson

6 Setting a purpose

7 Visualizing

8 Questioning the text

9 Using background knowledge

10 Evaluating the text

WRITING ACTIVITIES
by lesson

6 Write about setting purposes for reading.

7 Create a storyboard to visualize events.

8 Write a fictional interview with an author.

9 Summarize background knowledge about a subject.

10 Evaluate the accuracy and believability of an author's claims.

Literature

- *The Life and Death of Crazy Horse* by Russell Freedman (biography excerpt)

The famed Sioux warrior and leader's adolescent years are depicted in narrative nonfiction.

- *The Autobiography of Eleanor Roosevelt* by Eleanor Roosevelt (autobiography excerpt)

This notable first lady and activist explains that a change in attitude wiped away her deepest fears.

- "Kids on the Bus: The Overlooked Role of Teenagers in the Civil-Rights Era" by Jeffrey Zaslow (article)

A newspaper columnist ponders teenage activists who, despite their contributions to the civil rights movement, have not achieved the status of their adult counterparts.

ASSESSMENT To assess student learning in this unit, see pages 232 and 256.

Students will learn how setting a purpose for reading helps to maintain focus.

BACKGROUND KNOWLEDGE

Locate North Dakota. Explain that gold was discovered in the Dakotas in the mid-1800s. This led to encroachment on Native American lands by white gold-seekers. Crazy Horse, the courageous chief of the Sioux, led the resistance to the incursion.

Briefly explain *vision quest:* a rite of initiation for adolescent boys that is practiced by some Native Americans. Each boy prepares for manhood by making a journey on his own, seeking a message from a higher spiritual being. For some tribes, this comes in a *vision*, or a hallucination that reveals a significant message.

VOCABULARY

wiry thin

tipi cone-shaped house made of poles, animal skins, and tree bark

hobbled tied the front legs of a horse together to keep it from wandering

breechcloth a cloth worn over the lower body

Have students draw pictures that depict or convey the vocabulary words and share them with each other.

You should think about *why* you are reading something before you start to read it. Strategic readers know that their purposes for reading vary. How you read should change with your **purpose**. If you are reading for information, you might look for subheads or words in bold print that lead you to the information you are looking for. If you are reading for entertainment, you may want to enjoy every word or just read for the plot.

Before you read two excerpts from the **biography** *The Life and Death of Crazy Horse,* about a young Native American boy on a vision quest, ask yourself questions such as these:

- What do I already know about Crazy Horse?
- What do I know about Native American vision quests?
- What do I think I will get out of reading about Crazy Horse?
- Do I expect to be entertained or informed by my reading?

Use the answers to your questions to write one or two sentences that state your purpose for reading this selection.

_____

_____

_____

When he was young, the boy who became the famous Chief Crazy Horse was called Curly because of his unusually soft, curly hair. The first excerpt is a description of the boy and man who later came to be known as Crazy Horse. As you read, mark up the text. Use stars for surprising information, question marks for puzzling spots, check marks for ideas that confirm what you know.

I would never have predicted this!

from **The Life and Death of Crazy Horse**
by Russell Freedman

His own people knew him as "Our Strange One," and at times, he seemed very strange indeed. He wore no war paint, took no scalps, and refused to boast about his brave deeds. A quiet loner, he would walk through the village lost in thought or ride out on the plains to be by himself. His fellow Sioux loved to dance and sing, but [he] never joined a dance, not even the sun dance, and they say that nobody ever heard him sing.

Before

CRITICAL READING SKILL

Setting a Purpose Brainstorm a list of materials students have read in the past week, such as textbooks, novels, magazines, online news or blogs, e-mail, etc. and ask the purpose for reading each one. Possible answers include finding information for an assignment or test, entertainment, staying in touch with current events, or staying in touch with other people.

Discuss how knowing your purpose affects the way you read. For example, ask: *What do you do when you read for entertainment? Do you take notes, or do you just relax? What do you do when you are reading for research? How are the two ways of reading different?*

STATEMENT OF PURPOSE Read
aloud the opening paragraphs. Then guide students through the bulleted

questions. Model answering the questions and writing a statement of purpose. For example: *I've heard about Crazy Horse, but I want to know why he is considered a great leader.*

Have students complete their statements independently, offering assistance as necessary. Then bring students' attention to the directions for responding to the selection before having them read it.

When he was still a boy, grown-ups often discovered him standing in the shadows, listening to their conversation. When he grew up, he continued to listen. "He never spoke in council and attended very few," said his friend He Dog. "There was no special reason for this, it was just his nature. He was a very quiet man except when there was fighting."

Even his appearance set him apart. He was a small man for a fighter, with a wiry frame, soft brown hair, and pale skin. "Crazy Horse had a very light complexion, much lighter than the other Indians," Short Bull remembered. "His features were not like the rest of us. His face was not broad, and he had a sharp, high nose. He had black eyes that hardly ever looked straight at a man, but they didn't miss much that was going on all the same."

✳ What is your initial impression of Curly? Did you read anything that surprised you? Sketch or write your impressions here.

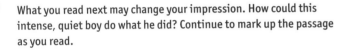

What you read next may change your impression. How could this intense, quiet boy do what he did? Continue to mark up the passage as you read.

One evening, when the Brulés stopped to make camp, Curly caught a glimpse of Conquering Bear as he was being carried into his tipi. Shaken by the sight of the dying chief, who looked so wasted and ghostly, the boy leaped on his pony and rode out on the prairie alone. He hobbled his horse beside a small lake, climbed a hill, stretched out on the ground, and gazed at the night sky.

He was about thirteen now, and he wanted to seek a vision. Sioux boys his age often went by themselves to some lonely place where they could commune with the sacred powers, hoping for a vision that would guide and inspire them

Russell Freedman, born in 1929, grew up in San Francisco and attended the University of California at Berkeley. Working as a journalist cultivated Freedman's passion for research and making facts come alive through compelling nonfiction. This passion has shown itself in his nonfiction titles, which have won countless awards and have been translated into Asian, European, and Middle Eastern languages. In 1994, Freedman's book *Lincoln: A Photobiography* won the Newbery Medal. In 1998, he was the recipient of the Laura Ingalls Wilder Award. See http://www.childrenslit.com/ for more information.

TEACHING TIP

Collaboration Partners can complete the response prompt together. Have each student share at least one impression of Curly. Then, partners can choose an impression to sketch and/or write about in the *Daybook*.

During

PURPOSE After reading each excerpt, have students reread their purpose statements from page 26. Ask: *Did you accomplish your objective?* Explain that revisiting your purpose after reading is a good way of checking whether or not you are getting the most out of reading. Encourage students to return to the excerpt and highlight or underline parts that especially fit their purpose for reading.

WRITING SUPPORT Forming Impressions Explain how readers form impressions. Say: *When you give your impression of someone, you tell what you think of the person.* Briefly discuss what influences personal impressions: what the person says or does; what the person thinks about.

Use a think-aloud to model giving an impression of Curly. For example, *He didn't want to participate in dances, and he was found listening to adults' conversations. It sounds like he was a very serious and thoughtful child.* Remind students that impressions are based on personal opinion; therefore, there are no right or wrong answers. However, impressions should be based on the events of the story.

WRITING SUPPORT

Evaluating Purpose Use think-alouds to model answering the questions in the writing prompt. For example:

❈ *I wanted to know more about Crazy Horse as a leader, but this excerpt just explains what he did as an adolescent.*

❈ *My purpose kept me involved in the text because I kept thinking that I would get to the information I wanted.*

❈ *I'll keep my purpose because I still want to know why Crazy Horse was a good leader. However, I will add "learning about his personality" because the writer seems to think that's important to understanding Crazy Horse.*

Quick Assess

❈ Do students' purpose statements contain specific goals for reading the selection?

❈ Are students' impressions of Curly based on descriptions or events from the story?

❈ Do students' evaluations reflect on whether or not their purpose statement fit the reading and whether it should change?

for the rest of their lives. Usually, a holy man helped a boy prepare for his vision quest. The youngster would fast, purify himself in a sweat lodge, and listen to the holy man's advice and instructions before finally setting out.

Curly had gone out impulsively, without the proper preparation, without telling anyone. Stripped to his breechcloth, he lay on the hilltop, staring at the stars. He had placed sharp stones between his toes and piles of pebbles under his back to keep from falling asleep. He would force himself to stay awake and fast until a vision came. He would try to enter the spirit world, the world that exists behind this one, where there is nothing but the spirits of all things.

For two days he remained on the hilltop without eating, fighting off sleep, his eyes like burning holes in his head, his mouth as dry as the sandhills around him. When he could barely keep his eyes open, he would get up and walk around and sing to himself. He grew weak and faint, but no vision came to him. Finally, on the third day, feeling unworthy of a vision, he started unsteadily down the hill to the lake where he had left his hobbled pony. ❖

❈ Discuss your reading with a partner. How well did you achieve your purpose for reading? How did having a purpose for reading help you stay involved in the text? Write notes from your conversation here and state your purpose for reading the next selection.

SUMMARY OF CONVERSATION WITH YOUR PARTNER

_____

_____

_____

_____

_____

PURPOSE FOR READING THE NEXT SELECTION

_____

_____

_____

_____

_____

> Setting a purpose helps the reader stay focused and gain new knowledge from a text.

■ 28 LESSON 6

After

APPLYING THE STRATEGY Have students keep a weeklong reading journal that records

❈ one reading experience per day;

❈ the purpose for the reading;

❈ a short evaluation of whether or not the experience fulfilled the reader's purpose.

Encourage students to record a variety of reading experiences, including large school assignments, reading for entertainment, and short research tasks such as looking up movie times or homework assignments.

READING/WRITING CONNECTION
Before reading the selection in the next lesson, invite students to speculate on what will happen to Curly after he comes

down the hill. For example: *Will he have a vision? Will his personality change?* Have students write a paragraph that describes what they think will happen. Explain that determining the accuracy of a prediction is an additional purpose for reading in this situation.

Strategic readers get more out of reading by doing what one student called "making movies in my mind." Some readers do this naturally. Others need to learn. Attention to descriptive details and having pencils or colored markers are key tools for **visualizing** and portraying what is happening in a text.

As you read about the vision quest of Curly, the boy who would later become Chief Crazy Horse, make movies in your mind. Picture what is happening and the images that Curly sees. Make sketches in the **Response Notes.** Mark words in the text that give you a vivid picture of what is happening. At the time of this excerpt, Curly has not yet received his "grown-up name." His father, a holy man, is the only one named Crazy Horse.

from The Life and Death of Crazy Horse
by Russell Freedman

Response Notes

His head was spinning, his stomach churning. The earth seemed to be shaking around him. He reached out to steady himself against a tree. Then—as he himself would later describe it—he saw his horse coming toward him from the lake, holding his head high, moving his legs freely. He was carrying a rider, a man with long brown hair hanging loosely below his waist. The horse kept changing colors. It seemed to be floating, floating above the ground, and the man sitting on the horse seemed to be floating, too.

The rider's face was unpainted. He had a hawk's feature in his hair and a small brown stone tied behind one ear. He spoke no sounds, but Curly heard him even so. Nothing he had ever seen with his eyes was as clear and bright as the vision that appeared to him now. And no words he had ever heard with his ears were like the words he seemed to be hearing.

The rider let him know that he must never wear a war bonnet. He must never paint his horse or tie up its tail before going into battle. Instead, he should sprinkle his horse with dust, then rub some dust over his own hair and body. And after a battle, he must never take anything for himself.

All the while the horse and rider kept moving toward him. They seemed to be surrounded by a shadowy enemy. Arrows and bullets were streaking toward the long-haired rider but fell away without touching him. Then a crowd of people, it seemed, clutching at his arms, trying to hold him back, but he rode right through them, shaking them off. A fierce storm came up, but the man kept riding. A few hail spots appeared on his body, and a little zigzag streak of lightning on his cheek. The storm faded. A small red-backed hawk flew

Students will learn how visualizing the events and details of a nonfiction piece can aid in understanding it.

BACKGROUND KNOWLEDGE
Explain that this biographical excerpt is a continuation from the previous lesson. Ask students to share what they remember about Curly and his vision quest. Students should recall the following:

✻ Curly is part of a Sioux tribe.

✻ He has a shy, serious personality that sets him apart from his community.

✻ He initiated his own vision quest without permission or preparation from his elders. While on a hilltop, he forced himself to stay awake for two days while battling hunger and the elements.

VOCABULARY

war bonnet a special head covering with feathers and other decorations

Have students use the Wordsplash blackline master found on page 278 to familiarize themselves with the selection vocabulary.

Before

CRITICAL READING SKILL
Visualizing Ask students if they ever make "movies in their minds" while they are reading—if they ever try to picture the characters, the action, and the locale. Discuss the benefits of visualization, such as having a better understanding of what is happening or staying more interested in the story.

If applicable, have students revisit sketches of Curly they made on page 27. Discuss how noticing images and details in the story are key to the skill of visualizing.

RESPONSE NOTES Model how to visualize details for a sketch. For example, read aloud the first paragraph and say: *There's a horse and a rider.* Then do a rough sketch of the horse and rider. Add details from the paragraph, such as the

rider's long brown hair or space between the horse and the ground to show that it is floating.

Direct students to read the selection, then visualize and sketch the details. Explain that the purpose of the sketch is to help "make movies in the mind," so students need not worry about their artistic abilities.

EXTRA SUPPORT

Visual Learners If students seem intrigued by Crazy Horse or the historical context of his life, encourage them to find more information in an encyclopedia or on a website. Students can compare details from Freedman's biography to other accounts and descriptions and answer these questions:

- Which text is more visual?
- Which one did you understand better? Why?
- Is visualization a technique that works for you? Why or why not?

Quick Assess

- Did students' drawings reflect details of Crazy Horse's vision such as a horse coming from a lake and carrying a rider, arrows and bullets, a crowd of people, a fierce storm, and a hawk?
- Are the pictures in the sequence of story events?

Response Notes

screaming over the man's head. Still the people grabbed at him, making a great noise, pressing close around him, grabbing, grabbing. But he kept riding.

The vision faded. Curly felt someone kicking him hard. When he looked up, he saw his father. Crazy Horse had ridden out into the prairie to search for the boy. He was angry that Curly had run off alone without saying a word, distracting everyone from the dying Conquering Bear.

When Curly told his father that he had gone out to fast for a vision, Crazy Horse was furious. Seeking a vision without instruction! Without purifying himself! Without any preparation at all! Curly decided not to say anything else, not then. He would tell his father about his vision, but he would wait for the right time. ❖

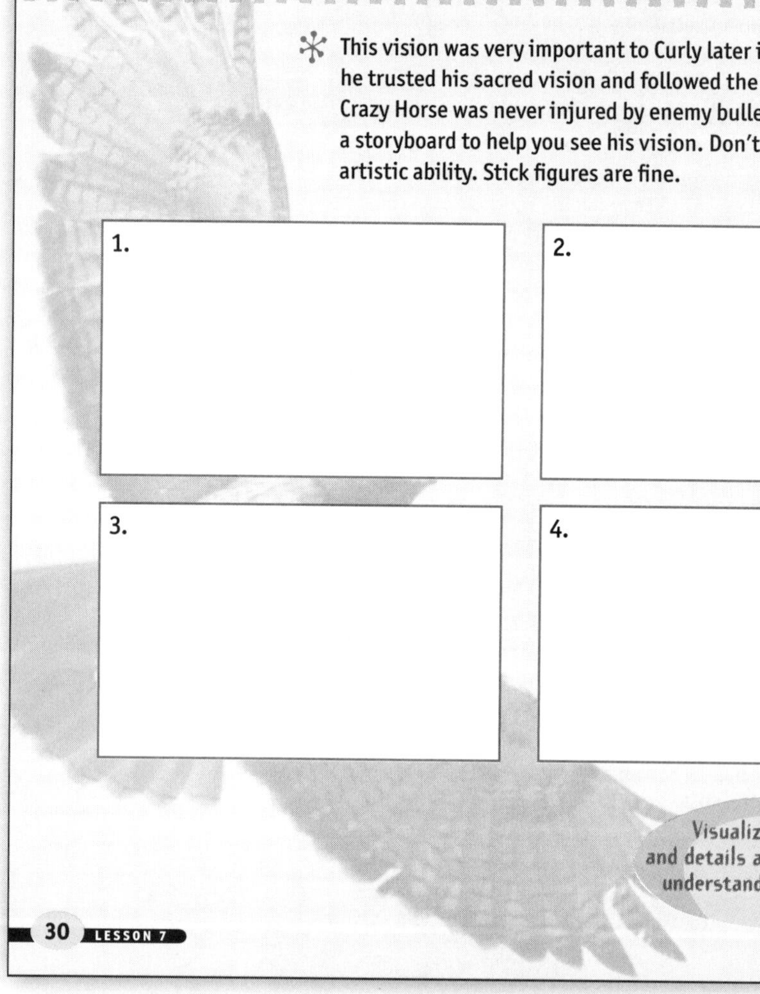

- **This vision was very important to Curly later in his life. Because he trusted his sacred vision and followed the instructions in it, Crazy Horse was never injured by enemy bullets and arrows. Use a storyboard to help you see his vision. Don't worry about your artistic ability. Stick figures are fine.**

1.	2.
3.	4.

Visualizing the events and details adds to the reader's understanding of nonfiction.

During

STORYBOARD SUPPORT Explain that the function of a storyboard is to show a series of scenes from a story or movie. You may want to note that storyboards were first used in the film industry to help the cast and crew visualize the setting and action in each scene. Readers can also use this tool to "break down" action-packed selections like this one.

Since there are four paragraphs with striking images in the selection, suggest using one storyboard box for each. Model choosing a central image from each paragraph, such as a close-up of the rider's head in the second paragraph. Explain that students need not capture fine details; the purpose of the storyboard is to show the movement of events.

After

ART CONNECTION Have groups of students choose a central image from the selections in Lessons 6 and 7. Students can create a detailed poster or mural for presentation and display. Have students incorporate quoted text in the visual to explain the visualization.

from The Autobiography of Eleanor Roosevelt
by Eleanor Roosevelt

In the beginning, because I felt, as only a young girl can feel it, all the pain of being an ugly duckling, I was not only timid, I was afraid. Afraid of almost everything, I think: of mice, of the dark, of imaginary dangers, of my own inadequacy. My chief objective, as a girl, was to do my duty. This had been drilled into me as far back as I could remember. Not my duty as I saw it, but my duty as laid down for me by other people. It never occurred to me to revolt. Anyhow, my one overwhelming need in those days was to be approved, to be loved, and I did whatever was required of me, hoping it would bring me nearer to the approval and love I so much wanted.

As a young woman, my sense of duty remained as strict and rigid as it had been when I was a girl, but it had changed its focus. My husband and my children became the center of my life and their needs were my new duty. I am afraid now that I approached this new obligation much as I had my childhood duties. I was still timid, still afraid of doing something wrong, of making mistakes, of not living up to the standards required by my mother-in-law, of failing to do what was expected of me.

As a result, I was so hidebound by duty that I became too critical, too much of a disciplinarian. I was so concerned with bringing up my children properly that I was not wise enough just to love them. Now, looking back, I think I would rather spoil a child a little and have more fun out of it. It was not until I reached middle age that I had the courage to develop interests of my own,

---

Students will learn how using a standard set of questions can help organize information when reading about an unfamiliar subject.

BACKGROUND KNOWLEDGE
Ask students what they know about Eleanor Roosevelt. Explain that she was the wife of Franklin Roosevelt, U.S. president from 1933 to 1945.

Up to that time, the main role of the first lady was to host guests and foreign visitors. Eleanor was famous for using her position of power, however, to express her views and work for human rights. She has been a role model for many women.

Tell students that they will read an excerpt from Eleanor Roosevelt's autobiography that describes her inner feelings rather than the events of her life.

VOCABULARY
inadequacy lack of ability
obligation something you have to do
hidebound made narrow-minded

Discuss the words using questions such as the following:

✳ *What is one of your* obligations?

✳ *About what are you* hidebound?

Before

CRITICAL READING SKILL
Questioning Post the words *who, what, when, where, why,* and *how.* Explain that using these question words helps readers understand nonfiction.

To illustrate, choose a selection the class has read and ask volunteers to answer questions about it. For example:

✳ Who wrote the piece?

✳ What was it about?

✳ When did the events take place?

✳ Where did they take place?

✳ Why was the subject important?

✳ How did the subject become important?

Then summarize the importance of questioning. For example, say the following: *If you can answer all six of these questions, you have a good understanding of what you've read.*

RESPONSE NOTES Model how to find information that answers the question words. For example, read aloud the first paragraph of the selection and point out the words or phrases that answer questions: *a young girl* answers *who; an overwhelming need to be approved* answers *what; I did whatever was required of me* answers *how;* etc.

ABOUT THE AUTHOR

Eleanor Roosevelt lived from 1884 to 1962. Born in New York City to an upper-class family—President Theodore Roosevelt was her uncle—Eleanor was taught the values of community service from a young age. Both of her parents died when she was a little girl, and she attended boarding school in England. After returning to the U.S., she married Franklin Delano Roosevelt (a distant cousin). Eleanor bore six children and attended to the social duties of being a political wife while bringing attention to issues such as child welfare, humanitarian aid, and civil rights. After Franklin's death in 1945, she was appointed as a U.S. delegate to the United Nations' Commission on Human Rights and continued working for social causes until her death. Though she earned criticism for eschewing the traditionally quiet role of first lady, she has been praised for being most influential in a time when women had little to no political power.

EXTRA SUPPORT

Differentiation Since students will not be familiar with Eleanor Roosevelt or the time period in which she lived, find websites or books that have pictures of her to provide a visual context for the selection.

outside of my duties to my family. In the beginning, it seems to me now, I had no goal beyond the interests themselves, in learning about people and conditions and the world outside our own United States. Almost at once I began to discover that interest leads to interest, knowledge leads to more knowledge, the capacity for understanding grows with the effort to understand.

From that time on, though I have had many problems, though I have known the grief and the loneliness that are the lot of most human beings, though I have had to make and still have to make endless adjustments, I have never been bored, never found the days long enough for the range of activities with which I wanted to fill them. And, having learned to stare down fear, I long ago reached the point where there is no living person whom I fear, and few challenges that I am not willing to face. ❖

❊ What are your first impressions of Eleanor Roosevelt after reading this excerpt? Explain.

During

CHECKING COMPREHENSION

Discuss students' responses to the selection before completing the writing prompt on page 33. Solicit answers to *who, what, when, where, why,* and *how* questions, such as: *What is this excerpt about? When was Eleanor afraid? Why did she change her outlook on life?*

WRITING SUPPORT
Remind students what an impression of a person is: an opinion of the person, based on what the person says, does, thinks about, reacts to, etc. Because impressions are based on personal opinion, there are no right or wrong answers to the prompt. However, the impressions should be based on what the author says in the excerpt.

✳ Imagine that you interviewed Mrs. Roosevelt for a publication for teenagers. Use the 5 Ws and H to write your questions. Follow your questions with what you think Mrs. Roosevelt's answers would be. When you write your interview, use the Question and Answer format, often known as Q and A, to help the reader identify who is speaking, as in this example:

[Q] Mrs. Roosevelt, what was your main objective when you were a child?

[A] To do my duty. This had been drilled into me as far back as I could remember.

_____

_____

_____

_____

_____

_____

_____

_____

_____

_____

_____

_____

_____

_____

_____

_____

_____

_____

> Using a standard set of questions is one way to organize information when reading about an unfamiliar subject.

WRITING SUPPORT

Prewriting Explain that students will be answering their own questions with information in the excerpt. Then have them return to their circled details in the excerpt. Say: *The information in this selection answers* who, what, when, where, why *and* how *questions. Now you will think of and write the actual questions.* Point out the example in the prompt and explain that a main idea from the story—Eleanor's objective was to do her duty—was turned into a question.

TEACHING TIP

Collaboration Students can complete their interviews in pairs. Have each pair exchange at least three questions. Then, using the excerpt, answers to each other's questions. Ask volunteers to perform their interviews for the class, with each partner taking the role of the interviewer or Eleanor.

Quick Assess

✳ Do students' questions reflect their use of the 5Ws and H?

After

LISTENING/SPEAKING CONNECTION

Have groups turn their written interviews into a script for a "talk show" to perform for the class:

✳ Discuss what makes an interview interesting to read or watch. Explain the importance of detailed questions and enthusiastic participants.

✳ For the subject, groups can combine and expand their interviews of Eleanor Roosevelt or write another interview for a different person or character.

✳ Groups should collaboratively write the interviews. For the performance, individuals can play the show host, guest, and viewers who "call-in" with questions.

✳ After each performance, briefly discuss which questions students found most interesting and why.

READING/WRITING CONNECTION

Invite students to interview a community leader about his or her personality and approach to life as a young person. Before the interview, have students formulate thoughtful questions about the issues brought up by Roosevelt: discipline versus fun, fear versus freedom, etc. Students should transcribe their subjects' answers and report what they learned to the class.

Students will learn something new by connecting it to something in their own background knowledge.

BACKGROUND KNOWLEDGE

To understand the article, students should know the following:

✳ Until the 1950s, many southern states had laws to segregate African Americans and whites.

✳ In 1955, Rosa Parks, an African American woman, was arrested for refusing to give up her seat to a white passenger.

✳ Parks's action sparked the Montgomery bus boycott.

VOCABULARY

segregated having separate laws or facilities for separate groups of people

integrated open to all people

unconstitutional not in agreement with the U.S. Constitution

Discuss the words using questions such as these:

✳ *A school that separates children based their race is what?* (segregated)

✳ *A law judged to be inconsistent with the Constitution is what?* (unconstitutional)

Did you know that you can learn something new by **connecting** it to something you already know? In fact, some people would say that that is the *only* way to learn something new. But how do you do that? When you read strategically, you think about what you know about the topic before you read. While you read, you compare what you are reading with what you know. By adding to and modifying what you know, you will build your knowledge.

You have probably learned about the U. S. civil rights movements of the 1950s and 1960s. But, in the newspaper column that follows, you may find some information that you did not know. Before you read, write in the box words and phrases for everything you can think of about the civil rights movements. Include names and places, too. You may create a web or a bulleted list.

✳ Write three sentences using some of your words and phrases. This will help you organize your thoughts before you read.

1 _____

2 _____

3 _____

As you read, put check marks next to new information.

34 LESSON 9

Before

CRITICAL READING SKILL

Using Background Knowledge Define *background knowledge*: things that you already know about a subject before you read about it. Then compile a class list of students' sources of background knowledge about the civil rights era. Possibilities include textbooks, people they know, and the media, including the Internet.

Use a think-aloud to model the process of listing words or phrases about the civil rights movement. For example: *I'll write* Martin Luther King, Jr., *because I know he was a leader of the movement.* Or, *I've heard that people were sometimes attacked during this era just because of their race or political views. So, I'll write* dangerous.

WRITING SUPPORT   Making Connections

After students write their words and phrases in the box, ask volunteers to share some examples. After listing a few, model how to write a sentence that shows how they connect. For example: *Martin Luther King, Jr., was a leader who spoke out for civil rights during a dangerous era.*

from **"Kids on the Bus: The Overlooked Role of Teenagers in the Civil-Rights Era"** by Jeffrey Zaslow

Response Notes

There's a true story we should tell our children about a bus, an African-American citizen and her yearning for equality in the segregated South of the 1950s.

No, Rosa Parks is not part of this story. This story is about Barbara Johns.

In 1951, Barbara was a 16-year-old student at a segregated school in Farmville, Va. About 450 black students were crowded into a school built for 200. Overflow classes were held in leaky, tar-paper shacks and on school buses, with kids shivering in the winter. Books and supplies were in tatters.

One day, Barbara missed the bus to school, and waited by the road, hoping someone would pick her up. A bus, filled with white children heading to their far-superior school, passed by. After it drove off, Barbara bravely decided to organize a walkout of her entire student body. Her leadership would help change America.

Our children are taught about Rosa Parks's refusal to give up her seat on a bus in 1955. They know about the Rev. Martin Luther King Jr. and his "I Have a Dream" speech. But many don't realize that the early civil-rights movement was often led by unsung teens. Some academics and activists now argue that by not sharing this hidden history, parents and teachers are missing crucial opportunities to energize and inspire today's kids, especially African-Americans.

"Rosa Parks, an older woman, is a wonderful symbol, but most black teenagers don't have a sense of the role played by people their own age," says Clayborne Carson, director of the Martin Luther King Jr. Research and Educational Institute at Stanford University. "When we speak about Rosa Parks, let's speak about these other people."

USING BACKGROUND KNOWLEDGE 35

ABOUT THE AUTHOR

Jeffrey Zaslow was born in 1958 in Philadelphia and studied creative writing at Carnegie-Mellon University. As a columnist for *The Wall Street Journal,* Zaslow wrote a recurring feature about the *Chicago Sun-Times'* contest to replace famed advice columnist Ann Landers. Besides getting a good story for the *Journal,* Zaslow wound up beating out 12,000 applicants for the job! He penned a *Sun-Times* column for 14 years, while publishing three books and winning the Will Rogers Humanitarian Award for the fundraising and attention to children's causes that he achieved through his writings. His current column, which centers on life transitions, appears in *The Wall Street Journal.*

During

ACTIVATE PRIOR KNOWLEDGE

Before students read the excerpt, have a brief discussion about perceptions of teenagers. Ask: *How often do you hear of teenagers taking risks to improve the world?* (rarely) *How often do you hear about adults doing so?* (most days) *How would you explain this difference?* (Teenagers don't take risks, or we don't hear about it because people think teenagers are self-centered.)

Introduce the term *unsung hero* and define it: someone who has done something heroic but has not received public praise for it. Invite students to talk about people they consider unsung heroes.

RESPONSE NOTES Have students revisit the background knowledge they noted on page 34. Then ask volunteers to read the first three paragraphs of the selection as you model noting new infor-

mation. For example: *I didn't know that African American students had to study in such poor conditions. I'll put a check mark here.* Direct students to respond to the rest of the selection independently.

WRITING SUPPORT

Summarizing Model how to write a summary sentence by using the sentence frame provided. For example, write: *Although I knew that African American adults took a stand against segregation, I didn't know that students did, too.* Encourage students to use a graphic organizer, such as the outline of a hand, to collect the most important information they learned for inclusion in the summary sentences. Students should write the main idea on the palm of the hand and the details on the fingers.

Main Idea

Detail
Detail
Detail
Detail

Quick Assess

✳ Do students' summary sentences link their old and new knowledge? Are the pieces of information in each sentence related to each other?

Barbara Johns led Moton High School students on a two-week strike. The NAACP offered to help their cause if they agreed to sue for an integrated school, not merely a school equal to the white one. The case was one of five reviewed by the U.S. Supreme Court when it declared segregation unconstitutional in the 1954 Brown v. Board of Education case. That year, Ms. Johns's family home was burned to ashes. She died from cancer in 1991.

"There were thousands of Barbara Johnses," says Doreen Loury, a professor of sociology and African-American studies at Arcadia University in Glenside, Pa. These were kids who made a stand to integrate lunch counters, community centers, sports leagues. As children in Columbus, Ohio, in the 1950s, Dr. Loury and her brother courageously entered a community pool and took a swim, even as white people got out and chanted, "We don't want you in our pool!" ✧

✳ Write two summary sentences that combine your new knowledge and your old knowledge. You could use a pattern such as "Although I knew _____, I didn't realize that _____."

1 _____

2 _____

Use your background knowledge to gain new understandings by connecting what you know to what you don't know.

After

APPLYING THE STRATEGY Have students analyze what they know and what they have learned using a K-W-L chart. Have students choose a topic and

✳ write about their background knowledge of it in the *K* column;

✳ write questions they have about the topic in the *W* column;

✳ read about the topic in an encyclopedia or other student reference;

✳ write answers to the questions and anything else they have learned in the *L* column.

Have volunteers share their charts with the class. Then lead a discussion about the process, asking: *Does your own chart show that you learned a little or a lot about the topic? Explain.*

READING/WRITING CONNECTION
Invite students to do a freewrite on unsung heroes. Post these questions:

✳ Why do you think some heroes are celebrated, while others are not?

✳ Do you have a favorite story about a hero? What was special or different about this hero?

After students have had time to write, ask volunteers to share their responses.

10 LESSON

Strategic readers make judgments about what they read. Anyone can say, "That's boring!" or "That's awesome!" But strategic readers go beyond such easy judgments. When reading nonfiction, they look for main ideas and evidence to support them. They question the authority and reliability of the evidence used. They also ask if there is another side of the story. Looking for information, asking questions about it, and thinking about it are all part of **evaluating** what you read.

Keep these considerations in mind as you continue reading about teenagers and their role in the civil rights movement. Mark places in the text that help you evaluate the key ideas.

from "Kids on the Bus: The Overlooked Role of Teenagers in the Civil-Rights Era" by Jeffrey Zaslow

One reason young activists have faded into history is because, early on, they didn't fit the image that civil-rights leaders wanted to project. Some were deemed too militant, rebellious or immature to be useful rallying symbols.

Claudette Colvin never became a household name. In Montgomery, Ala., nine months before Mrs. Parks took her stand, Ms. Colvin, then 15, refused to give up her seat on a bus and was arrested. Because she soon became pregnant, civil-rights leaders worried that her morals might be attacked, reflecting poorly on the movement if her case were taken to court. They preferred to showcase the 42-year-old Mrs. Parks, an upstanding citizen. Ms. Colvin, now 66, attended Mrs. Parks's funeral last week in Detroit, and was mentioned only briefly during the seven-hour memorial service.

In our sound-bite culture, we often simplify history into tidy stories: Dr. King was the black Moses who led his people to freedom. The saintly Mrs. Parks sat on that bus and became the mother of the civil-rights movement. ...

The lauding of superstars oversimplifies the real history. "The civil rights movement would have happened without Martin Luther King and Rosa Parks," says Dr. Carson, who is editor of Dr. King's papers. Because the movement was often "the story of teenage revolt," he adds, stories of young heroes would resonate with young people today.

As Dr. Loury sees it, learning about these brave young people can give children today "a moral and academic compass" that will guide and fortify them on issues far beyond civil rights.

But the old guard—institutions protecting the legacies of civil-rights icons—can be resistant to sharing glory.

Response Notes

Rosa Parks was not the 1st person to keep her seat on a bus.

Students will learn how to evaluate text by considering the authority and reliability of the sources, as well as inquiring into other sides of the story.

BACKGROUND KNOWLEDGE

Students will read a continuation of the previous lesson's article. Ask volunteers to name the article's topic and the author's point of view. Students should know that the article is about teenage activists in the civil rights era and that the author thinks that the teenagers' contributions have not been given as much credit as the adults' contributions—especially famous adults, such as Rosa Parks.

VOCABULARY

sound-bite culture group of people who only pay attention to small bits of information and do not take the time to understand longer discussions

Moses a Hebrew leader who led his people away from enslavement

saintly completely good or unable to be criticized

lauding praising

icon someone who receives a lot of attention for he or she symbolizes

Use the Word Splash activity on page 278.

Before

CRITICAL READING SKILL

Evaluating Ask this question to start the discussion: *Do you believe everything you read?* Invite students to share times they have questioned something they read. For example, students may have questioned claims in advertisements.

Explain that good readers question, or evaluate, everything they read. Post these questions to help students evaluate the selection:

✽ What evidence does the author give?

✽ What are the sources of the evidence? Are they trustworthy?

✽ Does the author tell both sides of the story?

Direct students to highlight or underline parts of the text that answer these questions.

RESPONSE NOTES Model how to evaluate a piece of the text. For example, ask a volunteer to read the fourth paragraph aloud. Then say: *I'll highlight the fourth paragraph. Since the source of the evidence, Dr. Carson, is the editor of Dr. King's papers, he or she must know a lot about the movement. So he or she is likely to be a trustworthy source.*

WRITING SUPPORT

Evaluating Explain that students should summarize whether or not they think the author has a well-supported, or valid, opinion. Then students should answer the questions in the prompt. You may want to explain *reliability* and *authority*:

✳ Information that comes from a source that is known to give accurate, unbiased information has *reliability*. Give examples of sources that are generally reliable (encyclopedias, museums) versus unreliable (anonymous websites).

✳ Sources that have the most reliable and up-to-date information have *authority*. An encyclopedia may have authority on history, but a teen magazine would have authority on the latest fashion trends.

TEACHING TIP

Collaboration Students can pair up to brainstorm and question each other's evaluations before completing the prompt independently.

Quick Assess

✳ Do students' evaluations explain whether they think the article presents another side of the story and is accurate and believable?

The Rosa and Raymond Parks Institute for Self-Development in Detroit, a nonprofit education group founded by Mrs. Parks, chose not to get involved in a new traveling exhibit by the Smithsonian Institution called "381 Days." The exhibit focuses on the 381-day Montgomery Bus Boycott that followed Mrs. Parks's arrest.

While the exhibit shows that Mrs. Parks sparked the movement, it also recognizes the 50,000 people, young and old, who joined the boycott, walking miles to school and work, says a Smithsonian spokeswoman. At the Parks Institute, president emeritus Lila Cabbil says that the Smithsonian "wanted to feature other unsung heroes. We were concerned that [Mrs. Parks] wasn't featured prominently."

Actually, the Smithsonian is taking a worthy stand. The story of the bus boycott "has been recounted as a lone act of heroism," the exhibit's introduction explains. "But the truth is more powerful." ✦

✳ Write an evaluation of this newspaper article, which was written shortly after Rosa Parks died in 2005. Before writing, look back at the first part in Lesson 9. In your evaluation, (1) tell whether you think that this article presents another side of the story; (2) tell whether you think the story is accurate and believable; and, (3) explain your reasons, referring to the authority and reliability of the evidence and the treatment of all sides of the story.

> Evaluate nonfiction by considering the accuracy and believability of the evidence. Ask if there are other sides of the story that should be presented.

During

SHARING RESPONSES After students have completed reading the selection, ask volunteers to share the evidence they found and their evaluation of it. Ask: *Was the evidence from a trustworthy source? What other side of the story could have been told?* Answers will vary but should be supported by the text on pages 35–38.

After

APPLYING THE STRATEGY Have students apply their new evaluation skills to other opinion pieces. Direct students to find a newspaper editorial or column about an issue that interests them. In groups, have students

✳ choose and read one opinion piece;

✳ summarize the author's viewpoint;

✳ identify the supporting evidence;

✳ evaluate the opinion based on the evidence's reliability and authority.

Debrief on the process, asking: *Are you now more or less concerned about believing everything you read? Why?*

Making Connections

Have you ever experienced one of those "aha" moments when you were reading a story? It's when you think to yourself, "Yes, I've felt that way, too!" Or, "Yes, I understand how this character feels." The "aha" moment usually results from **feeling connected** to the story because of similarities between the story and your own experiences.

Sometimes a story takes you into unfamiliar places. Your response then might be: "I've never thought about that before. This character teaches me something new." Or you might think, "This character makes me see a different world than I have seen before."

Sometimes a story can draw you in so that you feel as if you are living inside the story. When a story keeps you on the edge of your seat, makes you laugh or cry, or helps you to see things differently, it's because you've become emotionally involved. You are **connecting to the story.**

39

UNIT 3 MAKING CONNECTIONS

Lessons 11–15, pages 40–52

UNIT OVERVIEW
In this unit, students practice making connections with texts related to migrant farm workers.

KEY IDEA
Proficient readers make connections within a story, with other stories, and to world events.

CRITICAL READING SKILLS
by lesson

11 Stepping into the story
12 Deciding what's important
13 Inferring meaning through the story
14 Connecting the story to the world
15 Responding to the issues

WRITING ACTIVITIES
by lesson

11 Make statements that demonstrate comprehension and the reader's reactions.
12 Describe what the characters experience.
13 Fill in an inference chart.
14 Identify a problem and offer solutions with support from the text.
15 Write a letter about an issue that needs attention.

Literature

■ **"The Circuit"** by Francisco Jiménez (autobiographical fiction)

Jiménez writes of his childhood in California, alternating between the classroom and migrant farm work, and portrays the life of migrants who move from job to job.

■ **"In the Strawberry Fields"** by Eric Schlosser (nonfiction article)

In this award-winning article, investigative journalist Schlosser reports on workers' rights by exposing the journey of a strawberry from farm to market, while exposing America's reliance on illegal immigrants.

■ **"A Street Name That Hits Home"** by Tara Malone (nonfiction article)

In this article written for Chicago's *Daily Herald,* journalist Malone describes a student-led campaign to rename a local street after activist César Chávez.

ASSESSMENT To assess student learning in this unit, see pages 233 and 259.

Students will step into a story by connecting to the plot and characters.

BACKGROUND KNOWLEDGE

Migrant farm workers play a major role in the agricultural areas of many states, California in particular. Invite students to share anything they may know about these seasonal work-ers who travel from place to place to help bring in crops. Help students understand that the families of these farm workers travel with them, and the women and children often also work with the men in the fields. Invite students to talk about what life must be like for a teenager who moves from place to place and lives in temporary housing.

VOCABULARY

sharecropper a tenant farmer who gives a share of the crops to the land-lord as rent for the land

bracero a Mexican laborer permitted to enter the United States and work for a limited period of time, often in agriculture

Have students use context clues in the first two paragraphs of the selection to determine the meaning of *sharecropper* and *bracero*.

When you go to the movies, you ease yourself into a comfortable seat. You have snacks to enjoy. You wait for the lights to dim. Once the images flicker across the screen, you are in the story world.

Written stories work this way too. Writers hope you will care and understand when you read their stories. They also create a world for you to enter. Here are some ways to **step into a story:**

1 Ask yourself: What's going on? What's interesting about it?

2 Think about: What are my first impressions of the characters? Whom do I like? With whom do I sympathize?

3 Predict: What do I think might happen? What do I hope will happen?

Read the first part of "The Circuit," a short story based loosely on the author's life as the son of migrant farm workers. In your **Response Notes,** make notes about the three ways to step into a story.

Response Notes

The narrator seems friendly — he gets to know other workers.

from "The Circuit" by Francisco Jiménez

It was that time of year again. Ito, the strawberry sharecropper, did not smile. It was natural. The peak of the strawberry season was over and the last few days the workers, most of them braceros, were not picking as many boxes as they had during the months of June and July.

As the last days of August disappeared, so did the number of *braceros.* Sunday, only one—the best picker—came to work. I liked him. Sometimes we talked during our half-hour break. That is how I found out he was from Jalisco, the same state in Mexico my family was from. That Sunday was the last time I saw him.

When the sun had tired and sunk behind the mountains, Ito signaled us that it was time go home. "*Ya esora,*" he yelled in his broken Spanish. Those were the words I waited for twelve hours a day, every day, seven days a week, week after week. And the thought of not hearing them again saddened me.

As we drove home Papá did not say a word. With both hands on the wheel, he stared at the dirt road. My older brother, Roberto, was also silent. He leaned his head back and closed his eyes. Once in a while he cleared from his throat the dust that blew in from outside.

Yes, it was that time of year. When I opened the front door to the shack, I stopped. Everything we owned was neatly packed in cardboard boxes. Suddenly I felt even more the weight of hours, days, weeks, and months of work.

Before

CRITICAL READING SKILL

Stepping into the Story In this lesson, students learn strategies for making con-nections with a story by thinking about what draws them into it. They are also asked to keep track of their thinking and level of engagement as they read. Read the first paragraph or two with students, stopping a couple times to ask them to retell what is going on, what they already know about the characters, and what they speculate this story will reveal.

SETTING A PURPOSE Remind stu-dents that successful readers read for a purpose. In this case, they will be reading to see how they can connect with, or "step into" the story.

In their Response Notes, students should keep track of their responses to the three ways of "stepping into a story" on page 40. They should mark references to the following:

1. plot (what's going on)

2. characters

3. predictions

I sat down on a box. The thought of having to move to Fresno and knowing what was in store for me there brought tears to my eyes.

That night I could not sleep. I lay in bed thinking about how much I hated this move.

A little before five o'clock in the morning, Papá woke everyone up. A few minutes later, the yelling and screaming of my little brothers and sisters, for whom the move was a great adventure, broke the silence of dawn. Shortly, the barking of the dogs accompanied them. ❖

✳ Complete the following chart to record how you are stepping into the story world. Use your Response Notes. Then share your finished chart with a partner.

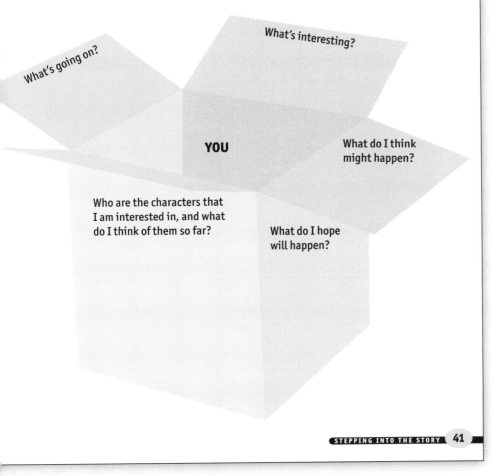

What's going on?

What's interesting?

YOU

What do I think might happen?

Who are the characters that I am interested in, and what do I think of them so far?

What do I hope will happen?

ABOUT THE AUTHOR

Francisco Jiménez came from a family of migrant workers in California. Although Jiménez was born in Mexico (1943), most of his childhood was spent following the crop harvests around California. He was one of many children of migrant farmers who grew up without access to permanent housing. Because of these constant moves, Jiménez did not have the benefit of attending the same school for long. Despite the odds, he finished school and went on to college. He graduated from Santa Clara University in California and holds Master's and doctoral degrees from Columbia University in New York. Jiménez's first story for young people is the award-winning short story, "The Circuit," which is based on his childhood.

EXTRA SUPPORT

Differentiation If any students have trouble stepping into the story—as evidenced by their Response Notes and marks on the text—confer with them about the reading. Consider reading a paragraph or two aloud with the student, pausing to ask the questions posed in the beginning of the lesson. Point out the annotation on page 40 as a starting point.

During

MAKING CONNECTIONS Model how to make connections with the text by reading aloud from the beginning of this story and using think-alouds.

✳ *What's going on? What's interesting to me?*

✳ *What do I think of these characters? Who do I like? With whom do I sympathize?*

✳ *What do I think might happen next? What do I hope will happen?*

SPANISH WORDS AND PHRASES

Invite Spanish speakers to read aloud and translate the Spanish words and phrases in the story for the rest of the class. If no one speaks Spanish, invite students to look up words and phrases in a Spanish-English dictionary (printed or online).

SHARING RESPONSES After students fill in the chart on page 41 and draw their pictures on page 42, have them share with a partner and then with the class.

Using a Graphic Organizer: Story Frame Using a Story Frame helps students think about what they've read by forming pictures in their minds of scenes from a story. Before students begin to fill out the Story Frame, have them stop to think about scenes from the selection that have stayed in their minds. Then ask students to sketch those scenes on the Story Frame. Allow them to go back over the text on pages 40–41 to refresh their memories of what they've read.

Quick Assess

✳ Do students' charts demonstrate they can retell what is going on, comment on the characters, and state their own reactions?

✳ Do students' Story Frames reflect an ability to visualize the story world?

✳ Another way to step into the story world is to envision what is going on by creating pictures in your mind. In the following Story Frame, sketch two key scenes that you can visualize from the story so far. Give as much attention to detail as you can. Use colored pencils or markers if you wish.

Step into the story by imagining what is going on and visualizing the story world in your mind.

42 LESSON 11

After

SOCIAL STUDIES CONNECTION
Have students research the use of migrant labor in the United States. Students can research the topic by using encyclopedias, the Internet, magazine articles, and nonfiction books. Encourage students to note the point of view of the source, comparing an account from an objective source such as an encyclopedia with a first-person account from someone who has experienced the migrant life.

Just as at the movies, once you step into the story you start to "feel" it through your senses and your heart. If you do more than sit back and watch, you start to care about what happens. It's like that with a written story, too. As you get into the story, you start to care about the characters and what happens to them. You start to explore their situation and problems and "feel" for them. When you start reading a story in these ways, you **decide what matters.**

Continue reading "The Circuit." In your **Response Notes,** keep track of your emotional reactions. Record your responses and what you are feeling for the narrator and his family. Write down what matters to you.

from "**The Circuit**" by Francisco Jiménez

As we drove away, I felt a lump in my throat. I turned around and looked at our little shack for the last time.

At sunset we drove into a labor camp near Fresno. Since Papá did not speak English, Mamá asked the camp foreman if he needed any more workers. "We don't need no more," said the foreman, scratching his head. "Check with Sullivan down the road. Can't miss him. He lives in a big white house with a fence around it."

When we got there, Mamá walked up to the house. She went through a white gate, past a row of rose bushes, up the stairs to the front door. She rang the doorbell. The porch light went on and a tall husky man came out. They exchanged a few words. After the man went in, Mamá clasped her hands and hurried back to the car. "We have work! Mr. Sullivan said we can stay there the whole season," she said, gasping and pointing to an old garage near the stables.

The garage was worn out by the years. It had no windows. The walls, eaten by termites, strained to support the roof full of holes. The dirt floor, populated by earth worms, looked like a gray road map.

That night, by the light of a kerosene lamp, we unpacked and cleaned our new home. Roberto swept away the loose dirt, leaving the hard ground. Papá plugged the holes in the walls with old newspapers and tin can tops. Mamá fed my little brothers and sisters. Papá and Roberto then brought in the mattress and placed it on the far corner of the garage. "Mamá, you and the little ones sleep on the mattress. Robert, Panchito, and I will sleep outside under the trees," Papá said.

Early next morning Mr. Sullivan showed us where his crop was, and after breakfast, Papá, Roberto, and I headed for the vineyard to pick.

Response Notes

Students will connect to a story by deciding which aspects of the characters' lives are important to them.

BACKGROUND KNOWLEDGE
Continue the discussion begun in Lesson 11 about the life of migrant farm workers by sharing the following information: migrant farm workers have long been the source of cheap, seasonal labor on farms, orchards, vineyards, and groves throughout the United States. The history of migrant farm laborers demonstrates the difficulty of following the crops. Migrant families live in a constant state of uncertainty. Will there be a job in the next town? What will the housing conditions be like? What if the crop fails? Invite students to predict what awaits the narrator and his family when they get to Fresno.

VOCABULARY
foreman a person who serves as the leader of a work crew

Break the word apart into its prefix and base word: *fore, man*. The prefix *fore* means "in front of," so a foreman is a person in front of, or in charge of, a work crew.

Before

CRITICAL READING SKILL
Deciding What's Important Strategic readers are able to connect with a story, deciding what is significant about it and what that means to them. The more a reader cares about and becomes involved with a text, the more a reader gets out of the text. In this lesson, students record their reactions to and feelings for the characters. They connect to the story by identifying what matters most about what they are reading.

RESPONSE NOTES Encourage students to take the time to record their thoughts and reactions to what's happening to the characters in the stories. Invite them to imagine what it would be like to be the narrator. Prompt students' thinking with questions such as these: *How would you feel? What would be important in your day-to-day life? What would your fears be? For what would you wish?*

WRITER'S CRAFT

Show, Don't Tell Talk with students about how good writers demonstrate "show, don't tell" by letting the characters' actions and words speak for themselves. Ask students to find examples that demonstrate "show, don't tell." Point out how masterfully Jiménez does this. For example, in the third paragraph on page 44, Jiménez doesn't tell us how Papá feels. Instead, he describes Papá's actions: the writing and crossing out of numbers and the murmured "Quince" (fifteen). The fact that Papá is concerned about how much money they made that day comes across in his actions. Challenge students to find several examples of this use of details to convey the characters' feelings in the story.

Response Notes

Around nine o'clock the temperature had risen to almost one hundred degrees. I was completely soaked in sweat and my mouth felt as if I had been chewing on a handkerchief. I walked over to the end of the row, picked up the jug of water we had brought, and began drinking. "Don't drink too much; you'll get sick," Roberto shouted. No sooner had he said that than I felt sick to my stomach. I dropped to my knees and let the jug roll off my hands. I remained motionless with my eyes glued to the hot sandy ground. All I could hear was the drone of insects. Slowly I began to recover. I poured water over my face and neck and watched the dirty water run down my arms to the ground.

I still felt a little dizzy when we took a break to eat lunch. It was past two o'clock and we sat underneath a large walnut tree that was on the side of the road. While we ate, Papá jotted down the number of boxes we had picked. Roberto drew designs on the ground with a stick. Suddenly I noticed Papá's face turn pale as he looked down the road. "Here comes the school bus," he whispered loudly in alarm. Instinctively, Roberto and I ran and hid in the vineyards. We did not want to get in trouble for not going to school. The neatly dressed boys about my age got off. They carried books under their arms. After they crossed the street, the bus drove away. Roberto and I came out from hiding and joined Papá. *"Tienen que tener cuidado,"* he warned us.

After lunch we went back to work. The sun kept beating down. The buzzing insects, the wet sweat, and the hot dry dust made the afternoon seem to last forever. Finally mountains around the valley reached out and swallowed the sun. Within an hour it was too dark to continue picking. The vines blanketed the grapes, making it difficult to see the bunches. *"Vámonos,"* said Papá, signaling to us that it was time to quit work. Papá then took out a pencil and began to figure out how much we had earned our first day. He wrote down numbers, crossed some out, wrote down some more. *"Quince,"* he murmured.

When we arrived home, we took a cold shower underneath a waterhose. We then sat down to eat dinner around some wooden crates that served as a table. Mamá had cooked a special meal for us. We had rice and tortillas with *carne con chile,* my favorite dish.

The next morning I could hardly move. My body ached all over. I felt little control over my arms and legs. This feeling went on every morning for days until my muscles finally got used to the work.

It was Monday, the first week of November. The grape season was over and I could now go to school. I woke up early that morning and lay in bed, looking at the stars and savoring the thought of not going to work and of starting sixth grade for the first time that year. Since I could not sleep, I decided to get up and join Papá and Roberto at breakfast. I sat at the table across from Roberto, but I kept my head down. I did not want to look up and face him. I knew he was sad. He was not going to school today. He was not going tomorrow, or next week, or next month. He would not go until the cotton season

During

CONNECTING WITH THE CHARACTERS Review with students what they have read in Lesson 11. Then read the first four paragraphs on page 43 with them, modeling how to keep track of their feelings in the Response Notes. Use a think-aloud: *I just can't imagine how it would feel to move so suddenly. Just as you get to know one place and feel comfortable there, you are asked to move. In my Response Notes I'll write that it makes me sad to think what they have to go through, but I think they are a really strong family.*

was over, and that was sometime in February. I rubbed my hands together and watched the dry, acid stained skin fall to the floor in little rolls.

When Papá and Roberto left for work, I felt relief. I walked to the top of a small grade next to the shack and watched the *Carcanchita* disappear in the distance in a cloud of dust.

Two hours later, around eight o'clock, I stood by the side of the road waiting for school bus number twenty. When it arrived I climbed in. Everyone was busy either talking or yelling. I sat in an empty seat in the back. ❖

❊ Stories talk to us. What are the four most important things this part of the story says to you? List them in order of importance, starting with the most important.

1 _____

2 _____

3 _____

4 _____

❊ Describe your feelings about the family and their situation. What aspects of their situation matter to you? When you finish writing, share what you wrote with a partner or a small group.

_____

_____

_____

_____

_____

_____

Connect to the story by deciding what's important to you as you learn what the characters are feeling and experiencing.

EXTRA SUPPORT

Differentiation Some students may be unfamiliar with the idiom *a lump in my throat*. Explain that there are phrases in English that carry a meaning different from the meanings of the individual words. In this case, the narrator does not have a physical lump in his throat; rather, he is expressing his sadness for moving.

Collaboration Students can use a Think-Pair-Share approach to the activity at the bottom of page 45.

1. **Think** Students review their own Response Notes to determine what they want to say to partners about their feelings toward the family and their situation.
2. **Pair** Ask students to discuss their reactions and feelings with a partner.
3. **Share** Ask pairs to share with the class or with another pair.

Quick Assess

❊ Did students identify the four most important things to them in the story?

❊ Are students able to express their feelings about the family and their situation and provide details to support the way they feel?

After

READING/WRITING CONNECTION

To extend the activity at the bottom of page 45, ask students to write a personal letter to a character from the story, sharing personal feelings and thoughts about the family's situation. (It need not be to the narrator, Panchito.) Remind students to use the form of a friendly letter, including the date, the greeting, the body, the closing, and the signature.

Students will learn to make inferences about the meaning of a story in order to better understand what it says about human experience.

BACKGROUND KNOWLEDGE

Activate prior knowledge by inviting students to talk about their experiences starting at a new school. When was the last time they started at a new school? How did they feel at first? Have students think about what they've read so far in "The Circuit"—especially about how the family moves around from place to place and how the narrator is starting school in November. Ask students to talk about how he must be feeling and about some of the challenges he is facing. As students read, have them reflect on how the narrator's telling of the story gives us clues as to what his feelings are and what type of person he is.

VOCABULARY

corridos Mexican ballads or folk songs

Have students use the context in the second and third paragraphs on page 47 to determine the meaning of *corridos*.

A story sometimes has meaning beyond the literal meaning of the words and the action of the story. The story may imply, or suggest, other interpretations of the words or actions. Ask yourself: What ideas and meaning does this story explore? What does this story teach you about migrant farm workers and the life they live?

Read the last part of "The Circuit." In your **Response Notes**, keep track of what you are learning from the story and your thoughts and feelings about it.

from "**The Circuit**" by Francisco Jiménez

Response Notes

I wonder how many schools the author went to.

When the bus stopped in front of the school, I felt very nervous. I looked out the bus window and saw boys and girls carrying books under their arms. I put my hands in my pants pocket and walked to the principal's office. When I entered I heard a woman's voice say: "May I help you?" I was startled. I had not heard English for months. For a few seconds I remained speechless. I looked at the lady who waited for an answer. My first instinct was to answer her in Spanish, but I held back. Finally, after struggling for English words, I managed to tell her that I wanted to enroll in the sixth grade. After answering many questions, I was led to the classroom.

Mr. Lema, the sixth grade teacher, greeted me and assigned me a desk. He then introduced me to the class. I was so nervous and scared at that moment when everyone's eyes were on me that I wished I were with Papá and Roberto picking cotton. After taking roll, Mr. Lema gave the class the assignment for the first hour. "The first thing we have to do this morning is finish reading the story we began yesterday," he said enthusiastically. He walked up to me, handed me an English book, and asked me to read. "We are on page 125," he said politely. When I heard this, I felt my blood rush to my head; I felt dizzy. "Would you like to read?" he asked hesitantly. I opened the book to page 125. My mouth was dry. My eyes began to water. I could not begin, "You can read later," Mr. Lema said understandingly.

For the rest of the reading period I kept getting angrier and angrier with myself. I should have read, I thought to myself.

During recess I went into the restroom and opened my English book to page 125. I began to read in a low voice, pretending I was in class. There were many words I did not know. I closed the book and headed back to the classroom.

Mr. Lema was sitting at his desk correcting papers. When I entered he looked up at me and smiled. I felt better. I walked up to him and asked if he could help me with the new words. "Gladly," he said.

Before

CRITICAL READING SKILL
Inferring Meaning Through the Story
Proficient readers make inferences as they read, based on what they know and on what is said in the text. Making inferences is "reading between the lines." Good readers ask, "What important thing is this story or scene telling me?

How do I know?" Remind students of the discussion you had in Lesson 12 about Jiménez's ability to "show, not tell" about the characters in a story. Help students understand that by grasping what a character is like through his or her actions, they are making inferences.

RESPONSE NOTES Tell students to note the inferences they make about the characters and action in the story. Point out the annotation on *Daybook* page 46 as a model.

The rest of the month I spent my lunch hours working on English with Mr. Lema, my best friend at school.

One Friday during lunch hour Mr. Lema asked me to take a walk with him to the music room. "Do you like music?" he asked me as we entered the building.

"Yes, I like *corridos*," I answered. He then picked up a trumpet, blew on it and handed it to me. The sound gave me goose bumps. I knew that sound. I had heard it in many *corridos*. "How would you like to learn how to play it?" he asked. He must have read my face because before I could answer, he added: "I'll teach you how to play it during our lunch hours."

That day I could hardly wait to get home to tell Papá and Mamá the great news. As I got off the bus, my little brothers and sisters ran up to meet me. They were yelling and screaming. I thought they were happy to see me, but when I opened the door to our shack, I saw that everything we owned was neatly packed in cardboard boxes. ❖

✳ Review what you've written in your **Response Notes.** Do a quick write to explore what you think are the big issues and ideas behind the story.

_____

_____

_____

_____

_____

_____

✳ Turn to a partner and share what each of you has written. Compare your impressions of the ideas and messages behind the story.

When you look at the meaning *behind* the story, you figure out what particular words, actions, or gestures mean. For example, if you turned to a classmate right now and said: "I wouldn't want to live on the circuit," that person would probably understand your reference to the title of the story you just read. Your classmate **infers** meaning beyond the word *circuit*. **Inferences** are the small understandings that you make while you read. Inferences become the meaning behind the story.

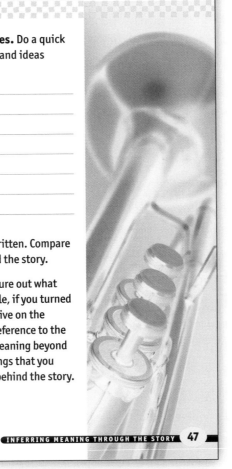

Collaboration After students have completed their quick writes, ask them to compare and discuss them with a partner. Remind students that they should think about what in the story leads them to identify the major issues that they've written down. After partners have had a chance to talk about their analyses, have them report on their discussions. Chart the big issues and ideas they identified and discuss them as a group.

During

MAKING INFERENCES   Ask students to think about what kind of person Mr. Lema seems to be. Help them make their own inferences about him by modeling with a think-aloud: *At first Mr. Lema asks the narrator to read aloud to the class on his first day. I know the boy doesn't feel comfortable doing that, so I wonder if Mr. Lema is being mean. But it says he asks "hesitantly." Then he says, "You can read later," and it says he says it "understandingly," so I infer that he sees how uncomfortable the boy is and doesn't want to put him on the spot. I think Mr. Lema is a very nice teacher who wants to help the boy.*

Using a Graphic Organizer:
Inference Chart Have students go back over the text and review their Response Notes to help them fill in the Inference Chart. You may want to do the first one with them. Ask: *Why does he feel a lump in his throat at this particular moment? What makes you think that?*

Quick Assess

✳ Do students' quick writes examine the major issues and ideas behind the story, using evidence from the text to support their impressions?

✳ Do students' Inference Charts indicate an understanding of the story's main ideas?

✳ In the following chart, write your best understanding of what the following story elements mean and why you think so.

INFERENCE CHART

From the story	What it means	Why I think so
"As we drove away, I felt a lump in my throat." (p. 43)		
"Here comes the school bus," he whispered loudly in alarm. (p. 44)		
Neatly packed cardboard boxes (p. 47)		
The narrator isn't named.		
Title "The Circuit"		
Choose a sentence or an idea.		
Choose a sentence or an idea.		

Make inferences about the meaning behind the story in order to better understand what it has to say about life and human experiences.

After

READING/WRITING CONNECTION
Have students step into the shoes of the narrator and write a journal entry about how he felt the moment he got home and saw the boxes packed. Encourage them to think about how they related to what the character might be feeling and to use details that show the character's emotion.

Some students may prefer to begin the activity with a sketch of what they visualize and then do their writing.

from "In the Strawberry Fields" by Eric Schlosser

The San Andreas labor camp is a small slum set amid rolling hills and strawberry fields not far from Watsonville. For most of the year this bleak collection of gray wooden barracks has about 350 residents, mainly strawberry workers and their families, but at the peak of the harvest hundreds more cram into its forty apartments. Last summer there was a major outbreak of tuberculosis at the camp, fueled by crowded living quarters and poor building design. The bedrooms occupy a central corridor of the barracks; none has a window. A superior-court judge recently held the landlord responsible for maintaining "a public nuisance" and for violating local fire, health, safety, building, and zoning codes. Nevertheless, the tenants continue to pay 500 a month for their two-bedroom apartments and feel lucky to have a roof over their heads. As I walked around the camp, there were children everywhere, running and playing in the dirt courtyards, oblivious of the squalor.

It was mid-April, and heavy rains the previous month had flooded hundreds of acres, scattering bright-blue plastic barrels from the nearby Smuckers plant across local strawberry fields and embedding them in the mud. Many fields that had not been flooded had still been damaged by the rains. The sky was overcast, more bad weather was coming, and a year's income for these workers would be determined in the next few months. Half a dozen strawberry pickers, leaning against parked cars, told me that at this point in the season they usually worked in the fields eight or ten hours a day. Only one of them was employed at the moment. Each morning the others visited the strawberry farm on a nearby hillside, inquired about work, and were turned away. The foreman, who had hired them for years, said to try again next week.

Harvest work in the strawberry fields, like most seasonal farm work in California, is considered "at will." There is no contract, no seniority, no obligation beyond the day-to-day. A grower hires and fires workers as necessary, without need for explanation. It makes no difference whether the migrant has been an employee for six days or six years. The terms of employment are laid

Response Notes

CONNECTING THE STORY TO THE WORLD **14** LESSON

Another way a reader can **connect** to a story is by researching information about the issues raised. For example, in "The Circuit" the family lives in difficult conditions. They find it necessary to move frequently. What are the conditions that make this necessary? Read the following excerpt from a newspaper article that examines migrant farm workers' issues. In your **Response Notes,** record connections you make to the story and your reactions to the information provided.

LESSON **14**

Students will learn to connect what they read to larger issues by researching the issues and sharing their understanding of them.

BACKGROUND KNOWLEDGE

Eric Schlosser has spent his career investigating topics of social importance, including the effects of fast food on American society (*Fast Food Nation*). His investigative reporting on the lives of migrant farm laborers involved many visits to labor camps, as well as interviews with the workers, growers, and community members. Schlosser has said that this research led him to realize what a difficult life these farm workers have.

VOCABULARY

barracks a large, plain building used for temporary occupancy

tuberculosis a contagious lung disease with symptoms that include fever, weight loss, chest pain, and coughing up sputum

squalor dirty and in bad condition due to poverty and neglect

Use the Word Splash activity on page 278 to preview the vocabulary.

Before

CRITICAL READING SKILL
Connecting the Story to the World
Strategic readers make connections between the things they read. They also make connections between what they read and world events. The selection in this lesson sets up a clear connection to the story "The Circuit" in Lessons 11–13.

SETTING A PURPOSE Ask students to make connections between this informational article and the fictional short story "The Circuit." They should highlight (underline or circle) places in "In the Strawberry Fields" that connect or relate to "The Circuit." For example, the second sentence mentions strawberry workers and their families, which describes Francisco Jimenez and his family.

During

Read the first paragraph with students, if necessary, to help them make a connection with the story. After reading the paragraph, ask: *"What in this paragraph sounds similar to what the Jiménez family experienced?* They may note that the narrator of the story mentions poor housing conditions several times *(paper and lids were used to fill holes; the family brings its own mattress)* and housing conditions are also very poor at the ▶▶▶

Visual Learners This selection contains many strong images of the conditions in the strawberry fields and in a nearby labor camp in California. Check students' comprehension by asking individuals what they picture as they read. Ask: *How were the pictures in your head similar to and different from those you had of the life of migrant farm workers described in "The Circuit"?*

To engage and encourage students' visual abilities, have them sketch a picture of what they're picturing as they read the article. You may also want to ask them to make a companion sketch for "The Circuit."

TEACHING TIP

Using a Graphic Organizer: Problem Chart As a class, brainstorm some of the key problems faced by the migrant workers in both the story and the article. Make a list. Then ask students to complete the graphic organizer independently or with a partner.

Quick Assess

✳ Are students able to identify three key problems and supporting details from the story and article?

✳ Are students able to explain why an issue is an important problem and suggest possible solutions?

Response Notes

down on a daily basis. If the grower wants slow and careful work, wages are paid by the hour. If the grower wants berries quickly removed from the field, the wages are piece-rate, providing an incentive to move fast. A migrant often does not know how long the workday will last or what the wage rate will be until he or she arrives at the field that morning. There might be two weeks of ten-hour days followed by a week of no work at all, depending on the weather and the market. ✧

✳ Both the story and the article you just read give you information about the difficult circumstances that migrant farm workers face. Lack of adequate housing, for example, is a problem. Select three key problems and record them on the chart. Use details from both the story and the article.

Problem:
Details:
Problem:
Details:
Problem:
Details:

✳ Select one of the migrant worker problems. Explain why it is an important problem and how the problem might be solved.

1 The issue: _____

2 Why it is an important problem: _____

3 Possible solutions: _____

Connect what you read to the larger issues in the world by researching the issues and sharing your understanding of them with others.

After

San Andreas labor camp. This will give students a good start at making connections between the two texts.

ADDITIONAL READING For students looking for more stories about migrant-child labor:

✳ *The Circuit: Stories from the Life of a Migrant Child,* by Francisco Jiménez; anthology includes the story "The Circuit"; available in English and Spanish

✳ *Breaking Through,* by Francisco Jiménez; the sequel to "The Circuit"; available in English and Spanish

✳ *Esperanza Rising,* by Pam Muñoz Ryan; available in English and Spanish

Here's an example of a high school student's response to learning about the migrant farm workers' situation. Gloria Verastegui read about Cesar Chavez (photo right), a man who took action to organize the grape pickers in California so they would have better wages and working conditions. While his efforts were not entirely successful, he did help bring attention to the issues.

from "**A Street Name That Hits Home**" by Tara Malone

His was a name relegated to history books, where she read of his efforts to shield migrant workers from awful work conditions and miserly pay. But it wasn't until the Elgin High School junior recently launched a campaign to give Maroon Drive outside her school the honorary name of Cesar Chavez Drive that Verastegui learned how many Elgin residents Chavez affected with his grape boycotts, hunger fasts and community organizing.

Her dad included. A former potato picker, Verastegui's father ditched school for the fields, where he worked all day and much of the night to help his family in Mexico. Also among them was James Logan, the Elgin High dean's assistant who gave up grapes and wine in the early 1970s when Chavez called for a boycott demanding farm workers' right to organize and bargain collectively.

Chavez founded and led for 31 years the United Farm Workers of America. He died in 1993.

"His legacy is still going on," Verastegui said Monday. "There's a lot of people around Elgin who worked with him or who felt his work in their lives." To celebrate Chavez's efforts, which warranted the 1994 Presidential Medal of Freedom, Verastegui and four other Elgin High students hatched a plan to give a second, honorary name to the road in front of their school. They will unveil the proposal to Elgin High administrators, Elgin City Council members and Lt. Gov. Pat Quinn in the coming weeks. They also will go door to door along Maroon Drive collecting petition signatures.

"Everyone thinks education is about getting a good job, getting a good car," Verastegui said. "But it's really about improving your community. . . . We want people when they drive by Maroon Drive, we want them to think they can make a difference because he [Chavez] did." ❖

Response Notes

Students will learn to connect to a text by using the information in it as support for action on an issue.

BACKGROUND KNOWLEDGE
Ask students to share what they know about César Chávez and unions. Share the following biographical information. César Estrada Chávez (March 31, 1927–April 23, 1993) founded the National Farm Workers Association, which became the United Farm Workers Union, a labor union that fights for the rights of migrant farm workers. He is known for his commitment to using nonviolent means to fight for workers' rights, including organizing boycotts, work stoppages, and hunger strikes.

VOCABULARY

relegate assign to an unimportant place

miserly small and insufficient

boycott to avoid purchasing or using a product to make a statement

Have students see if they can figure out the meanings from context. Then compare their guesses with the definitions listed above.

Before

CRITICAL READING SKILL
Responding to the Issues In this lesson, students connect the selections in this unit with ways to make a difference in the world. Students read a newspaper article about a high school junior who campaigned to have the street in front of her school renamed César Chávez Drive. Students are then asked to consider an action they could take to effect positive change.

During

RESPONDING TO THE TEXT Read aloud the introductory paragraph at the top of page 51. Begin a discussion about the ability of young people to effect change. Ask students if they can think of any young people who have done things to improve their communities or the world. Are there things in their own neighborhood or school that have been improved because of students' willingness to take action? Then have students read the selection independently. When they finish reading, have them write their reactions on page 52.

WRITING SUPPORT

Supporting Arguments Once students have determined topics for their letters, help them identify the audiences, such as the mayor, a congressperson, peers, the school principal, or parents. Remind students that they will need to use strong examples and details to support their arguments. You may want to have students use the drafts they wrote on page 52 and take them through the writing process, choosing to mail, as a class, the most convincing letters.

Quick Assess

✳ Did students express their reactions to Gloria Verastegui's campaign on behalf of César Chávez? Did they make connections with what they read?

✳ Were students able to write a persuasive letter identifying a problem, supporting their argument, and offering possible solutions?

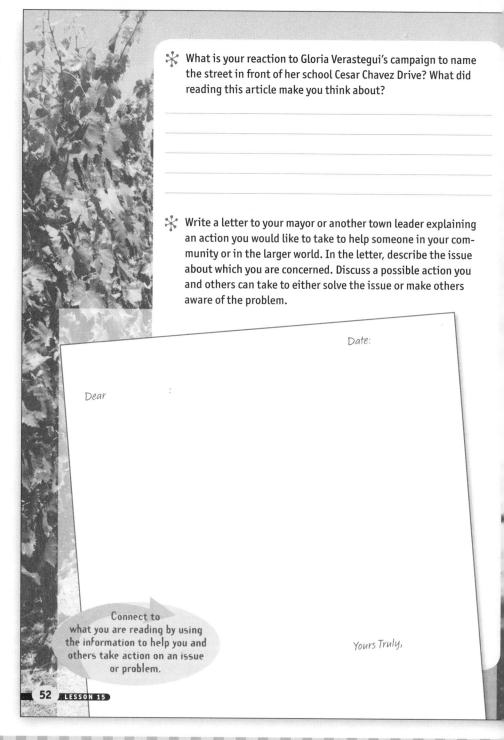

✳ What is your reaction to Gloria Verastegui's campaign to name the street in front of her school Cesar Chavez Drive? What did reading this article make you think about?

✳ Write a letter to your mayor or another town leader explaining an action you would like to take to help someone in your community or in the larger world. In the letter, describe the issue about which you are concerned. Discuss a possible action you and others can take to either solve the issue or make others aware of the problem.

Date:

Dear   :

Connect to what you are reading by using the information to help you and others take action on an issue or problem.

Yours Truly,

52 LESSON 15

After

WRITING A LETTER Remind students of standard business letter format: heading (inside address, date), greeting (*Dear —:*), body (the message), closing (*Yours truly,*), and signature. Discuss the purpose and audience of the letter, both of which will influence the voice or tone of the letter (probably formal and persuasive).

COMMUNITY INVOLVEMENT
Have students develop their own social action projects. Working in groups of four or five, students can select an issue and design a specific action plan. Be sure to help students choose something that is feasible and design the project to ensure follow-through. Students can engage a variety of literacy, language arts, and social studies skills—reading, researching, writing letters, speaking publicly, conducting surveys, and so on, as they work on their projects.

Examining Multiple Perspectives

You know from your own life experiences that there are many sides to every story. Did one friend ever tell you a one version of an event, only to have another friend report a different version? Different versions depend on the perspective of the person describing the event. This does not mean that one version of the story is more correct than another. A reader can learn more about a subject by **examining multiple viewpoints**.

In this unit, you will read several different perspectives about the atomic bomb that dropped on Hiroshima, Japan, in 1945. You will examine multiple viewpoints and consider how each portrays the bombing in a different light. You can compile these multiple points of view to develop your understanding of what happened on that day and its significance to humanity.

53

UNIT 4
EXAMINING MULTIPLE PERSPECTIVES

Lessons 16–20 pages 54–68

UNIT OVERVIEW
Students read multiple accounts of the 1945 bombing of Hiroshima in order to analyze, compare, and evaluate different perspectives.

KEY IDEA
Good readers consider multiple perspectives in order to understand an event.

CRITICAL READING SKILLS
by lesson

16 Analyzing perspective and slant
17 Focusing on details and perspective
18 Focusing on the eyewitness perspective
19 Comparing perspectives
20 Evaluating perspectives

WRITING ACTIVITIES
by lesson

16 Write a paragraph to compare information in two texts.
17 Write a paragraph that speculates on an author's purpose.
18 Write a newspaper article based on an eyewitness account.
19 Compose a dialogue between two characters.
20 Write a newspaper article.

Literature

- *Hiroshima* by John Hersey (nonfiction excerpt)

A war correspondent pieces together a narrative describing the morning activities of Hiroshima's victims.

- from **The Avalon Project** at Yale Law School (government report excerpt)

Data and statistics about the city of Hiroshima are part of this U.S. Army-compiled report.

- "Summer Flower" by Tamiki Hara (nonfiction excerpt)

This eyewitness account relays the fear and confusion at one residence during and after the bombing.

- *Shockwave* by Stephen Walker (nonfiction excerpt)

Historical documents form the basis of this description of the scene inside the airplane that bombed Hiroshima.

- *Hiroshima* by Laurence Yep (novella excerpt)

This story tells about a little girl who survives the bombing but must live with the disturbing and harmful after effects.

ASSESSMENT To assess student learning in this unit, see pages 234 and 262.

Students will identify an author's perspective and determine how it reveals the author's purpose.

BACKGROUND KNOWLEDGE

Ask students what they know about Hiroshima, a town on the southeast coast of Japan's mainland. Explain that the world's first atomic bomb was exploded over this city in 1945. U.S. President Harry S. Truman authorized the bombing in order to put an end to World War II.

Over 100,000 Japanese people were killed on impact, and thousands more died as a result of injuries, radiation illnesses, or environmental damage. Explain that, in this unit, students will read several descriptions of the day that Hiroshima was bombed.

VOCABULARY

B-29 a military plane that carried heavy bombs

Chugoku Hiroshima's newspaper

hullabaloo a loud noise

prefectural relating to government officials

localize to keep from spreading

ration food given by the government during war or other emergencies

Use the Word Splash activity on page 278 to preview the vocabulary.

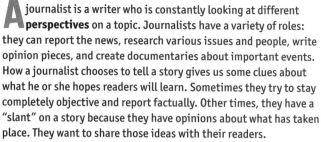

A journalist is a writer who is constantly looking at different **perspectives** on a topic. Journalists have a variety of roles: they can report the news, research various issues and people, write opinion pieces, and create documentaries about important events. How a journalist chooses to tell a story gives us some clues about what he or she hopes readers will learn. Sometimes they try to stay completely objective and report factually. Other times, they have a "slant" on a story because they have opinions about what has taken place. They want to share those ideas with their readers.

John Hersey was a war correspondent during World War II. As you read an excerpt from Hersey's book on the bombing of Hiroshima, record reactions and questions in your **Response Notes**.

from **Hiroshima** by John Hersey

Response Notes

Did the people have any idea about what might happen?

At nearly midnight, the night before the bomb was dropped, an announcer on the city's radio station said that about two hundred B-29's were approaching southern Honshu and advised the population of Hiroshima to evacuate to their designated "safe areas." Mrs. Hatsuyo Nakamura, the tailor's widow, who lived in the section called Nobori-cho and who had long had a habit of doing as she was told, got her three children—a ten year-old boy, Toshio, an eight-year-old girl, Yaeko, and a five-year-old girl, Myeko—out of bed and dressed them and walked with them to the military area known as the East Parade Ground, on the northeast edge of the city. There she unrolled some mats and the children lay down on them. They slept until about two, when they were awakened by the roar of the planes going over Hiroshima.

As soon as the planes had passed, Mrs. Nakamura started back with her children. They reached home a little after two-thirty and she immediately turned on the radio, which, to her distress, was just then broadcasting a fresh warning. When she looked at the children and saw how tired they were, and when she thought of the number of trips they had made in past weeks, all to no purpose, to the East Parade Ground, she decided that in spite of the instructions on the radio, she simply could not face starting out all over again. She put the children in their bedrolls on the floor, lay down herself at three o'clock, and fell asleep at once, so soundly that when planes passed over later, she did not waken to their sound.

The siren jarred her awake at about seven. She arose, dressed quickly, and hurried to the house of Mr. Nakamoto, the head of her Neighborhood Association, and asked him what she should do. He said that she should

---

Before

CRITICAL READING SKILL
Analyzing Perspective and Slant
Before students read the selections, you may want them to do a quick-write to answer these questions:

❊ Is it acceptable to cause mass destruction if it will end a war?

❊ Was the United States right to have bombed Hiroshima and Nagasaki?

Review or define the term *perspective* as "the point of view from which a writer sees something based on his or her location, opinions, and experience." Then read aloud or ask a volunteer to read aloud the introduction. Explain that, in this lesson, students will read two different perspectives of the bombing. Say: *While you're reading, think about whether the author thinks that the bombing was right or wrong or has no opinion of it.*

RESPONSE NOTES Read aloud or ask a volunteer to read aloud the first paragraph of the excerpt. Then model a response to the above question. For example: *The author is describing only what happened to Mrs. Nakamura. So he's not telling us his opinion. But he does make us feel sympathy for her, so maybe he thinks the bombing was wrong.*

remain at home unless an urgent warning—a series of intermittent blasts of the siren—was sounded. She returned home, lit the stove in the kitchen, set some rice to cook, and sat down to read that morning's Hiroshima *Chugoku*. To her relief, the all-clear sounded at eight o'clock. She heard the children stirring, so she went and gave each of them a handful of peanuts and told them to stay on their bedrolls, because they were tired from the night's walk. She had hoped that they would go back to sleep, but the man in the house directly to the south began to make a terrible hullabaloo of hammering, wedging, ripping, and splitting. The prefectural government, convinced, as everyone in Hiroshima was, that that the city would be attacked soon, had begun to press with threats and warnings for the completion of wide fire lanes, which, it was hoped, might act in conjunction with the rivers to localize any fires started by an incendiary raid; and the neighbor was reluctantly sacrificing his home to the city's safety. Just the day before, the prefecture had ordered all able-bodied girls from the secondary schools to spend a few days helping to clear these lanes, and they started work soon after the all-clear sounded. ❖

❋ In the excerpt above, Hersey describes the hours leading up to the bombing through the thoughts and actions of Mrs. Nakamura. Write a paragraph that describes what you learned from her perspective about the city of Hiroshima.

_____

_____

_____

_____

_____

_____

_____

_____

_____

_____

_____

On page 56 is a factual account about Hiroshima at the time of the bombing. In your **Response Notes,** record questions and reactions.

ABOUT THE AUTHORS

John Hersey was born in 1914 in Tientsin, China. His parents were American missionaries, and his family returned to the United States when John was ten years old. He attended Yale University, and as a summer job he worked for novelist Sinclair Lewis. He soon got a job for *Time* magazine, writing from their Chungking, China, bureau. During World War II, Hersey covered both the Italian and Asian fronts. His first book, *A Bell for Adano,* won the Pulitzer Prize for Novels in 1945. Hersey followed up with *Hiroshima* and many other acclaimed works, publishing until his death in 1993.

The Avalon Project is a compendium of legal, historical, and diplomatic documents held by Yale Law School in New Haven, Connecticut. Among its findings is *The Atomic Bombings of Hiroshima and Nagasaki,* a report compiled by the U.S. Army. A searchable database of the Avalon Project's holdings is available at: www.yale.edu/lawweb/avalon/avalon.

TEACHING TIP

Collaboration Use the Think-Pair-Share method to have students discuss and share their paragraphs.

❋ Have students share their completed paragraphs with a partner.

❋ Have each pair share one thing they learned with the class.

During

CHECKING COMPREHENSION

Before students complete the writing prompt, briefly discuss the main events of the passage. Ask:

❋ *Who is Mrs. Nakamura?* (a widow and mother of three)

❋ *What had she done earlier that morning?* (She had already evacuated with her children and returned home.)

❋ *What had life been like for people in Hiroshima?* (Evacuations were common, people were ordered to dismantle their homes for fire-safety purposes, and children were taken from school to aid in war preparations)

WRITER'S CRAFT

Choosing Details Explain a writer includes or omits details to support his or her slant. Guide students to interpret the broader meaning of the details in The Avalon Project excerpt by asking the following questions:

✻ *Given the materials from which most of Hiroshima's buildings were built, was it logical for the Japanese to expect an incendiary attack, or fire-bombing, as noted in Mrs. Nakamura's story?*

✻ *The population of Hiroshima is compared to that of Providence or Dallas. Does this mean that it was a fairly big city?*

WRITING SUPPORT

Before students complete the writing prompt, briefly discuss the two passages.

✻ *If people knew only* The Avalon Project *data, how would they feel about Hiroshima?*

✻ *What perspective does Hersey provide that cannot be found in* The Avalon Project?

Quick Assess

✻ Are students able to describe major differences between the two accounts (e.g., one is more personal and one is more objective)?

---

from **The Avalon Project** at Yale Law School

The center of the city contained a number of reinforced concrete buildings as well as lighter structures. Outside the center, the area was congested by a dense collection of small wooden workshops set among Japanese houses; a few larger industrial plants lay near the outskirts of the city. The houses were of wooden construction with tile roofs. Many of the industrial buildings also were of wood frame construction. The city as a whole was highly susceptible to fire damage.

Some of the reinforced concrete buildings were of a far stronger construction than is required by normal standards in America, because of the earthquake danger in Japan. This exceptionally strong construction undoubtedly accounted for the fact that the framework of some of the buildings, which were fairly close to the center of damage in the city, did not collapse.

The population of Hiroshima had reached a peak of over 380,000 earlier in the war but prior to the atomic bombing the population had steadily decreased because of a systematic evacuation ordered by the Japanese government. At the time of the attack the population was approximately 255,000. This figure is based on the registered population, used by the Japanese in computing ration quantities, and the estimates of additional workers and troops who were brought into the city may not be highly accurate. Hiroshima thus had approximately the same number of people as the city of Providence, R.I., or Dallas, Texas. ✣

✳ Discuss with a partner what you learned in this account.

✳ Describe the major differences in what you learned from each account.

Consider why authors choose a particular perspective to write about a subject and what that might reveal about their purpose or "slant."

After

READING/WRITING CONNECTION

Explain that for decades after World War II the fear of atomic bombings was prevalent. Invite students to interview someone who remembers the bombing of Hiroshima, the Cuban Missile Crisis of 1962, or bomb shelters or air raid drills in their schools or communities.

Have students prepare questions that focus on how their interviewees felt about the events and what their daily lives were like at the time. Students can turn the answers into a narrative told from the perspective of the interviewees.

FURTHER RESEARCH Have groups research related topics, such as the Japanese bombing of Pearl Harbor, the development of the atomic bomb, or President Truman's decision to use the atomic bomb.

✻ Each group should use both print and online sources for their research.

✻ Have each group give a brief presentation on their findings.

✻ Discuss how the additional perspectives provided by these topics make for a fuller understanding of the bombing of Hiroshima.

A moment in time is experienced differently by each person. Imagine that you were alive in 1945, right before the bombing of Hiroshima. If you were Mrs. Nakamura, you were at home with your children and thinking about their safety. If you were on your way to work, you might have heard loud engines and looked up at the sky to see a plane. If you were one hundred miles from Hiroshima, you might have seen the mushroom cloud before anything else. Each of these stories would have different **details** because each person's perspective on the subject is different.

In the section below, Hersey retells Mrs. Nakamura's experience as the bomb's impact is felt. In your **Response Notes,** record your reactions.

from Hiroshima by John Hersey

As Mrs. Nakamura stood watching her neighbor, everything flashed whiter than any white she had ever seen. She did not notice what happened to the man next door; the reflex of a mother set her in motion toward her children. She had taken a single step (the house was 1,350 yards, or three-quarters of a mile, from the center of the explosion) when something picked her up and she seemed to fly into the next room over the raised sleeping platform, pursued by parts of her house.

Timbers fell around her as she landed, and a shower of tiles pummeled her; everything became dark, for she was buried. The debris did not cover her deeply. She rose up and freed herself. She heard a child cry, "Mother, help me!," and saw her youngest—Myeko, the five-year-old—buried up to her breast and unable to move. As Mrs. Nakamura started frantically to claw her way toward the baby, she could see or hear nothing of her other children.

Response Notes

✳ Reread the excerpt and circle the three details that are most meaningful to you.

EXAMINING THE DETAILS **57**

Students will learn to examine the descriptive details of a text in order to better understand the perspective of a writer and his or her message.

BACKGROUND KNOWLEDGE
Ask students to review what they learned about the bombing of Hiroshima in 1945 from the previous lesson. Review the character of Mrs. Nakamura from the *Hiroshima* excerpt. Then explain that students will read a continuation of her story, along with the story of another woman who was in Hiroshima at the time of the bombing.

VOCABULARY

mushroom cloud the kind of cloud that is caused by a nuclear explosion, usually appearing in the shape of a mushroom

artillery large, heavy weapons operated by more than one person

personnel employees of a company

employee discharges people who have been relieved of their war duties

atomic age the period after World War II, when people realized that mass destruction could be caused by nuclear bombs

Have students choose a word or phrase and sketch images they associate with it. Have students share their drawings with the class.

Before

CRITICAL READING SKILL
Focus on Details and Perspective
Ask: *What is John Hersey's perspective on the bombing of Hiroshima?* Briefly discuss students' opinions. Then explain the importance of details: *An author has a purpose for each detail that is included or omitted, so details can reveal the perspective of an author.*

Read aloud or ask volunteers to read aloud the introduction and first paragraph of the excerpt. Then model using details to visualize the action. For example, say: *I can see the bright white and the explosion sending Mrs. Nakamura into the other room.*

Then model an analysis of Hersey's perspective. For example, ask: *Why does Hersey want you to know the effect of the bombing on individual people?* Direct students to read the selection twice, circling details that help them understand the author's perspective.

TEACHING TIP

Collaboration   Form heterogeneous reading groups to read and respond together. Have each student read a portion of the page aloud. After each reading, have the group members

✳ summarize the action;

✳ decide on details that indicate the author's perspective;

✳ write individual Response Notes in the text.

Continue reading Hersey's report from the perspective of another person. Use your **Response Notes** to record reactions and questions.

Miss Toshiko Sasaki, the East Asia Tin works clerk, got up at three o'clock in the morning on the day the bomb fell. There was extra housework to do. Her eleven-month-old brother, Akio, had come down the day before with a serious stomach upset; her mother had taken him to the Tamura Pediatric Hospital and was staying there with him. Miss Sasaki, who was about twenty, had to cook breakfast for her father, a brother, a sister, and herself, and—since the hospital, because of the war, was unable to provide food—to prepare a whole day's meals for her mother and the baby, in time for her father, who worked in a factory making rubber earplugs for artillery crews, to take the food by on his way to the plant. When she had finished and had cleaned and put away the cooking things, it was nearly seven. The family lived in Koi, and she had a forty-five-minute trip to the tin works, in the section of town called Kannonmachi. She was in charge of the personnel records in the factory. She left Koi at seven, and as soon as she reached the plant, she went with some of the other girls from the personnel department to the factory auditorium. A prominent local Navy man, a former employee, had committed suicide the day before by throwing himself under a train—a death considered honorable enough to warrant a memorial service, which was to be held at the tin works at ten o'clock that morning. In the large hall, Miss Sasaki and the others made suitable preparations for the meeting. This work took about twenty minutes.

Miss Sasaki went back to her office and sat down at her desk. She was quite far from the windows, which were off to her left, and behind her were a couple of tall bookcases containing all the books of the factory library, which the personnel department had organized. She settled herself at her desk, put some things in a drawer, and shifted papers. She thought that before she began to make entries in her lists of new employee discharges, and departures for the Army, she would chat for a moment with the girl at her right. Just as she turned her head away from the windows, the room was filled with a blinding light. She was paralyzed by fear, fixed still in her chair for a long moment (the plant was 1,600 yards from the center).

Everything fell, and Miss Sasaki lost consciousness. The ceiling dropped suddenly and the wooden floor above collapsed in splinters and the people up there came down and the roof above them gave way; but principally and first of all, the bookcases right behind her swooped forward and the contents threw her down, with her left leg horribly twisted and breaking underneath her. There, in the tin factory, in the first moment of the atomic age, a human being was crushed by books. ✣

During

SHARING RESPONSES   Solicit students' circled details and/or responses in order to prepare them for completing the chart on page 59. Then model how to complete the chart, using the sample answers. Say:

✳ *Mrs. Nakamura rushed toward her children. Hersey could be showing that she is always thinking about her children. She is like many parents.*

✳ *Miss Sasaki's father worked in a rubber earplug factory. Hersey is showing how the war affected people's lives. It seems as if nearly everyone was doing something related to the war, all of the time.*

Suggest that students complete the left portion of the chart individually. Then, in pairs or groups, they can discuss the significance of the details they listed and complete the right portion of the chart.

✳ Fill in the chart below to help you understand how Hersey uses details to reveal particular perspectives on the bombing.

Details of the incident	What the incident reveals
Mrs. Nakamura's Account ✳ *Rushes toward her children* ✳ ✳ ✳ ✳	✳ *Her children are always on her mind.* ✳ ✳ ✳ ✳
Miss Sasaki's Account ✳ *Father makes rubber earplugs* ✳ ✳ ✳ ✳	✳ *Many jobs were related to the war.* ✳ ✳ ✳ ✳

✳ Explain why you think Hersey chose to tell the story focused on the perspectives of those who experienced the bombing rather than writing a strictly factual account.

_____

_____

_____

_____

✳ Based on the excerpts, write what you think Hersey wants you to understand about the bombing of Hiroshima. List the details in his writing that lead you to this understanding.

_____

_____

_____

_____

Examine the details used to describe events and people in order to better understand the opinions and the perspective of a narrator or writer.

WRITING SUPPORT

Speculating on Motive With students, brainstorm possible motives for Hersey's portrayal of Hiroshima residents. Use a think-aloud to model speculating on a motive. For example: *He wanted to show that Mrs. Nakamura was a good parent. Maybe he wants to show that, even though Japan was our enemy, the average Japanese person's priorities were not that different from the average American's.*

Encourage students to come to their own conclusions for the first writing prompt. Assure them that no answer is wrong, as long as it is based on the details Hersey uses.

Finding the Author's Message For the second writing prompt, ask: *Now that you know Hersey's perspective, and you've speculated on his motive, what is his message? What does he want you to think about or take action on?* Solicit students' opinions.

Quick Assess

✳ Do students find details that help reveal the perspective and indicate what those details reveal?

✳ Can students speculate on reasons for Hersey's inclusion of personal details and support their opinions with details?

After

APPLYING THE STRATEGY Invite students to read additional chapters from John Hersey's *Hiroshima*. For each chapter, have students respond to these questions:

✳ From whose perspective is the chapter written?

✳ What do this perspective and the descriptive details tell you about Hersey's motive?

✳ Do you think Hersey's message is similar to or different from that of the accounts of Mrs. Nakamura and Miss Sasaki?

ART CONNECTION Have groups use the passages to create visual perspectives of Hiroshima.

✳ Assign each group a perspective: Mrs. Nakamura's, Miss Sasaki's, or The Avalon Project's.

✳ Have the group choose an image or scene from their assigned passage.

✳ The group should collaboratively draw the scene or image, using the passage's description as a guide.

✳ Have each group copy the sentences with the descriptions they used and include them with the illustration.

Students will determine how eyewitness accounts are important perspectives on the understanding of an event.

BACKGROUND KNOWLEDGE

Explain that John Hersey wrote stories about people after he interviewed them. The U.S. Army wrote the report in The Avalon Project based on what was seen, heard, and studied by them. Then tell students they will read an account of the bombing of Hiroshima written by one of its survivors.

VOCABULARY

veranda a porch or balcony that has a roof

beheld looked at and studied

tatami a straw mat that is laid on the floor

scullery a room for washing dishes

dumfounded surprised and confused (usually spelled *dumbfounded*)

magnesium a metal that sizzles when burned

Assign a word to each student and have him or her write a sentence that uses the word. Students can also make a quick sketch to illustrate their sentences. Have students share their sentences.

LESSON 18 — IN THEIR OWN WORDS

Sometimes the best way to find out information about an event is to talk to someone who was actually there. **Eyewitnesses** often give dramatic and detailed accounts. They rely on their memory to record the events. In the excerpt below, you will read how a survivor of the Hiroshima bombing felt and what he saw at the moment the bomb exploded. Circle words that reveal Hara's attitude toward the bombing.

from "Summer Flower" by Tamiki Hara in *The Crazy Iris and Other Stories of the Atomic Aftermath* edited by Kenzaburo Oe

Response Notes

My life was saved because I was in the bathroom. On the morning of August 6th, I had gotten up around eight o'clock. The air-raid alarm had sounded twice the night before and nothing had happened, so that before dawn I had taken off my clothes and slept in my night robe, which I had not put on for a long time. Such being the case, I had on only my shorts when I got up. My younger sister, when she saw me, complained of my rising late, but I went into the bathroom without replying.

I do not remember how many seconds passed after that. All of a sudden, a powerful blow struck me and darkness fell before my eyes. Involuntarily I shouted and held my hands over my head. Aside from the sound of something like the crashing of a storm, I could not tell what it was in the complete darkness. I groped for the door, opened it, and found the veranda. Until then, I had been hearing my own voice exclaiming, "Wah!" amid the rushing sounds, agonized at not being able to see. But after I came out to the veranda, the scene of destruction gradually loomed in the dusk before my eyes and I became clearly conscious.

Loathsome is a powerful word of hatred.

It looked like an episode from a (loathsome) dream. At first, when the blow struck my head, and I lost my sight, I knew that I had not been killed. Then I became angry, thinking that things had become very troublesome. And my own shouts sounded almost like the voice of somebody else. But when I could see, vaguely as it was, the things around me, I felt as if I were standing stage center in a tragic play. Certainly I had beheld such a scene in a movie. Beyond the clouds of dust, patches of blue sky began to come into view. Light came in through holes in the walls and from other unexpected directions. As I walked gingerly on the boards where the tatami flooring had been blown off, my sister came rushing toward me. "You weren't hurt? You weren't hurt? Are you all right? Your eyes are bleeding. Go wash right away." She told me that there was still water running in the kitchen scullery.

60 LESSON 18

Before

CRITICAL READING SKILL
Focus on the Eyewitness Perspective

Although eyewitnesses can provide dramatic accounts of an event, one has to remember that eyewitnesses know only what they see and hear. In fact, these accounts can be quite limited because each eyewitness's perspective determines what

information is presented. Discuss what an eyewitness account can add to the description of an event. Emphasize that when learning about an event, it is important to consider multiple perspectives.

SET A PURPOSE Remind students that successful readers read for a specific purpose, perhaps to find out particular information. Direct students to read and respond to the passage, paying special attention to details that have not been revealed in the previous two lessons' readings.

✳ Based on what this eyewitness has said so far, what is different about this perspective and the Hersey accounts?

_____

_____

Continue reading Tamiki Hara's account. Keep track of your reactions in your **Response Notes.**

My brother had been seated at a table in his office when a flash of light raced through the garden. The next instant, he was blown some distance from his seat and for a while found himself squirming around under the wreckage of the house. At last he discovered an opening and succeeded in crawling out. From the direction of the factory he could hear the student workers screaming for help, and he went off to do what he could to rescue them.

My sister had seen the flash of light from the entrance hall and had rushed as fast as she could to hide under the stairs. As a result, she had suffered little injury.

Everyone had at first thought that just his own house had been hit by a bomb. But when they went outside and saw that it was the same everywhere, they were dumfounded. They were also greatly puzzled by the fact that, although the houses and other buildings had all been damaged or destroyed, there didn't seem to be any holes where the bombs had fallen. The air raid warning had been lifted, and shortly after that there had been a big flash of light and a soft hissing sound like magnesium burning. The next they knew everything was turned upside down. It was all like some kind of magical trick, my sister said, trembling with terror. ✧

✳ On the arms of the web, write information that you learned from Tamiki Hara's eyewitness account.

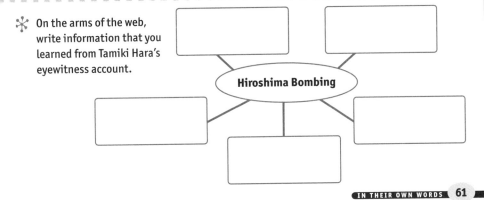

Hiroshima Bombing

IN THEIR OWN WORDS **61**

During

COMPLETING THE WEB After students have read the entire excerpt, have them discuss in groups any new details they learned. Then, have them complete the web together.

✳ Have each group briefly discuss their Response Notes and response to the prompt at the top of the page.

✳ Distribute a large piece of paper to each group.

✳ Have each group copy the empty web from page 61.

✳ Each group member can then write something he or she learned from the excerpt.

✳ When all students are done, have each student with the web pass it to the student on his or her left.

✳ Have that student respond to his or her neighbor's entry. Responses can include a personal connection or a reflection.

After groups have completed the exercise, have a brief discussion about the similarities and differences between Hara's firsthand account and the accounts in the previous two lessons.

WRITER'S CRAFT

Journalistic Writing   Ask students: *What does a reporter do?* Explain that reporters interview people about what they've witnessed or about their views. Then, they write about the interview for a newspaper or other publication.

Instead of including their own views or speculation about what happened, reporters are expected to stay objective and just tell the *who, what, when, where, how,* and *why* of events as told to them in interviews. Explain that students will write an article about the bombing of Hiroshima, using Tamiki Hara's, Mrs. Nakamura's, and Miss Sasaki's experiences. For prewriting, have students create a 5 Ws Organizer.

Hiroshima	
Who	
What	
When	
Where	
How	
Why	

Quick Assess

✳ Do students' webs show information that students learned from the eyewitness account?

✳ Do students include quotations and details from the survivors in their newspaper article?

✳ Imagine that you are a reporter for your school newspaper. You want to give your classmates information about the lessons to be learned from the Hiroshima bombing. There is one person in your community, Tamika Hara, who was an eyewitness to the events. He introduces you to Mrs. Nakamura and Miss Sasaki, who are also survivors. You interview the three of them. Write a short article in which you describe the events. Incorporate quotations and details from the survivors.

WINFORD SCHOOL NEWS

VOL X   OCTOBER 11, 2006

HIROSHIMA REMEMBERED

Determine how eyewitness accounts contribute important perspectives that add to your understanding of an event.

After

APPLYING THE STRATEGY   Invite students to read other eyewitness accounts of war or political upheaval, such as *Anne Frank: The Diary of a Young Girl* by Anne Frank, *Zlata's Diary: A Child's Life in Sarajevo* by Zlata Filipovic, or *Red Scarf Girl: A Memoir of the Cultural Revolution* by Ji-Li Jiang.

✳ Have students research the historical events that are documented in the account.

✳ Have students read an excerpt from the eyewitness account.

✳ Have students compare the eyewitness account to their research findings.

Discuss the power of eyewitness accounts. For example, ask: *Which account did you prefer to read? What did the eyewitness account tell you that your research findings did not?*

R eaders sometimes examine different points of view to gather as many perspectives as they can. As a reader, this might seem like completing a puzzle, since the versions of a story may come from several different sources.

The excerpt below is from the book *Shockwave* by Stephen Walker. The author uses interviews with various participants and survivors of the events to recreate the Hiroshima bombing inside the airplane that carried the atomic bomb. In this particular passage, you will add the pilots' perspective to your other viewpoints. Tom Ferebee and Paul Tibbets were the pilots on the *Enola Gay*, named for Tibbets's mother. As you read from the perspective of those inside the plane, keep track of your questions and reactions.

from Shockwave by Stephen Walker

Now Tibbets took control of the *Enola Gay*, switching off the C-1 autopilot for the last time until the bomb run. Behind him Van Kirk logged the height: they were level at 31,000 feet, their final bombing altitude. Outside the bomber's pressurized hull the temperature was minus twenty-four degrees centigrade, as cold as an Arctic winter, only far more inhospitable. Without oxygen a man would last less than two minutes out there. The sun glared through the windows. They were so high that the skies above them were a deep, burning indigo-blue. Far below, between the gaps in the clouds, the enemy coast slipped by: the flat, unwrinkled ocean suddenly giving way to a strip of land, a muddy carpet of parched browns and greens and hills and the occasional town sparkling in a shaft of sunlight. It looked almost peaceful down there.

Inside *Enola Gay's* waist section, Jake Beser concentrated over his electronic monitoring equipment, intensively searching every enemy frequency for possible interference with the bomb's radars: the result could be catastrophic. So far there was nothing. The air, he said, was "as clean as a hound's tooth." But Beser could also hear a whine through his headphones, and he knew what that meant. The Japanese early warning radar had locked onto the strike force. They were tracking the American bombers across Shikoku.

On the other side of the thirty-foot pressurized tunnel, Deak Parsons stared at the bomb console. All the green lights were still steady. If the enemy attached now, he would have to act very quickly. Typically, he had already worked out exactly what needed to be done. He called it "responding to possible abnormal events." "Possible abnormal events" included such things as being shot down, in which case Parsons would somehow have to climb back

Response Notes

Students will learn how the insights and significance of a perspective add to their understanding of a topic.

BACKGROUND KNOWLEDGE
With students, review the various perspectives of Lessons 16–18: John Hersey's Mrs. Nakamura and Miss Sasaki, The Avalon Project's, and Tamiki Hara's. Then explain that there is one perspective that students have not yet heard: that of the people who dropped the atomic bomb on Hiroshima.

Explain that author Stephen Walker researched historical documents and then wrote a narrative of what he thought happened in the airplane.

VOCABULARY
autopilot an airplane's system for flying itself so a pilot does not have to be at the controls all of the time

Little Boy the code name for the atomic bomb dropped over Hiroshima

Assign one word to a pair or group of students. Have each pair or group research the word and teach it to the class.

Before

CRITICAL READING SKILL
Comparing Perspectives Ask students to imagine what happened in the airplane that dropped the atomic bomb on Hiroshima. Ask: *If you were in the airplane, what might you have seen, heard, felt, or thought?* Have students do a quick-write about the possible perspective of the bombers.

Then read aloud or ask a volunteer to read aloud the introductory paragraphs and the first paragraph of the selection. Review that Tibbetts and Ferebee are the pilots of the plane, and model making a response to the text. For example: *Tibbets describes the "enemy coast" without mentioning the people living on it. He's just thinking about it as a target.*

ABOUT THE AUTHOR

Stephen Walker is a filmmaker. His BBC documentary about Hiroshima, *Days That Shook the World,* won an Emmy award. He has also published *King of Cannes: Madness, Mayhem, and the Movies.* Walker lives in London.

WRITER'S CRAFT

Writing Conventions Point out that, in the excerpt, *Enola Gay, The Great Artiste,* and *Dimples 91* are written in italics. Explain that names of airplanes or ships are italicized, just as titles are.

EXTRA SUPPORT

Differentiation If students seem to have difficulty reading the entire excerpt on their own, you may want to form a guided reading group.

❈ Invite interested students to join you in a group.

❈ Read aloud one paragraph at a time, giving students time to reread it and take response notes.

❈ Briefly discuss each paragraph before moving on to the next one.

Response Notes

into the freezing, unpressurized hell of the bomb bay, dismantle the breech plug with his domestic wrench (another sixteen turns) while the aircraft was screaming or shaking or hurtling to the ground, and disarm the bomb. If he failed, the bomb would almost certainly explode. If they were forced to ditch, it would also very likely explode, since tests in Los Alamos had already demonstrated that seawater leaking into *Little Boy's* casing had an unfortunate tendency to initiate a chain reaction. Parsons had designed as many fail-safes into the bomb as was possible—it could even be dropped if only the pilot and he survived an attack—but in truth there were an infinite number of possible abnormal events, and it was impossible to provide against all of them. In his pocket was a list of coded messages he would shortly use to transmit the result of the drop back to Tinian. There were twenty-eight alternatives on the list. The twenty-fifth was *Returning with unit to indicated place due to damage to aircraft.* If only it were that simple.

Alone in *Enola Gay's* tail, isolated in his capsule from the rest of the crew, Bob Caron stared out at the sky. Despite his sunglasses the glare burned into his eyes. Beneath his windscreen the two .50-caliber machine guns projected into the slipstream. As they approached the enemy coast he had attempted to struggle into his flak suit, but the turret was too cramped. His one protection against anti-aircraft fire lay in a heap on the floor. Now he began scanning every inch of the sky for enemy fighters, mentally tearing it into strips and rigorously examining each strip, up and down, left to right, strip by strip, searching for the dot that could suddenly turn into a fighter and kill you. But that were no dots. The only aircraft out there were American: *The Great Artiste* and *Dimples 91,* hanging off the tail a few hundred feet behind. Otherwise the sky was empty.

Up front, Tibbets also scanned the empty sky. Back in Europe they used to say the antiaircraft fire was so thick you could get out and walk on it. But Shikoku's coastal batteries were silent. No bursts of shrapnel-filled flak greeted them as they crossed the island. The landscape unrolled harmlessly below. Tibbets was convinced that his policy of sending individual or small formations of his bombers to the Empire was paying off. The enemy were simply ignoring

them. The three bombers rode the skies undisturbed, the southerly wind pushing them along at 328 mph—well over five miles a minute—toward their target. Van Kirk passed a new estimate to Tibbets. They would reach their initial point—the start of the bomb run—at exactly 0912. "I was trying to hit it exactly," he said. "By this time it was a game for me." Game or not, he suddenly glanced up, looking past

64 **LESSON 19**

During

CHECKING COMPREHENSION

As students read, you may want to have them pause for brief discussion. Ask for their initial reactions to and comments on the reading, emphasizing how this perspective differs from ones in the previous readings. Ask questions such as the following:

❈ *What kinds of things are the men doing?* (They are focusing on reaching the target and safely releasing the bomb.)

❈ *What could account for the men's very high levels of concentration?* (They are the first people to ever drop this type of bomb on an enemy target.)

❈ *What does Tibbets mean when he says "I was trying to hit it exactly"?* (He wanted to drop the bomb precisely on target.)

the two pilots and through the glass nose. Something glinted on the horizon, a good fifty miles away, beyond Shikoku and across the Inland Sea. He stared in fascination. It was unmistakably a city. ✣

✳ Write a paragraph that describes your reactions to reading the perspectives of people inside the plane. Use quotes from the passage that influence your reactions.

✳ Imagine that some months after the bombing one of the *Enola Gay* pilots meets a Hiroshima survivor. What reactions might they have to each other when they meet? Write a possible dialogue between one of the pilots and one of the survivors.

Decide what insights and significance each perspective adds to your understanding of the subject.

Reacting to the Reading To articulate their reactions to the perspectives of the people inside the plane, students should first look at their Response Notes. If they have insufficient information, they should reread the passage noting where they have any kind of reaction. This will help them identify quotations and details to use in their writing.

Planning a Dialogue Suggest that students collect their thoughts in a two-column chart in which one column is for thoughts about the pilots and one is for the survivors. Prompt students' thinking with questions such as these:

✳ *What were the concerns of the bombers prior to the bombing? How might those concerns have changed after the bombing?*

✳ *What were the concerns of the survivors after the bombing?*

Quick Assess

✳ Were students able to express a reaction to the reading and support it with quotations from the passage?

✳ Do students' dialogues reflect a reasonable reaction based on the readings they have done?

After

FURTHER RESEARCH Students can find out more about the bombing of Hiroshima and its aftermath by visiting these websites:

✳ The Hiroshima Peace Memorial Museum: http://www.pcf.city .hiroshima.jp/index_e2.html.

✳ The Smithsonian Institution's former *Enola Gay* exhibit: http://www.nasm .si.edu/galleries/gal103/gal103_ former.html

Have students summarize what they learn from their research. Then have them compare the information to that in Lessons 16–19, discussing how they corroborate.

ART CONNECTION Have students select one scene from the *Shockwave* excerpt to illustrate. Suggest that they highlight descriptive words and phrases in the text to guide their sketches. Students should also include a description of the scene in their own words.

Students will learn to evaluate the strengths and limitations of a perspective to understand how it adds to their understanding of the subject.

BACKGROUND KNOWLEDGE

With students, review the effects of the bombing of Hiroshima that they have learned about in this unit: there was an explosion accompanied by blinding light; then a shockwave destroyed many buildings, though some were left standing. Introduce the word *radiation* and ask students what they know about it. Explain that a nuclear explosion—the kind that an atomic bomb causes—releases radioactive energy, or energy rays that can harm living things.

Then explain that radiation remained in Hiroshima for some time after the bombing was over. It is known to have caused cancer and other grave illnesses in people who survived the impact of the bomb. Also, hot ash from the explosion rose high into the cold atmosphere, causing caustic, radioactive rain that was black, known as *black rain*. Because these were the world's first atomic bombings, most people near Hiroshima didn't immediately know about the dangers of radiation. Explain that students will read a fictional story of a girl living in the aftermath of the bombing.

LESSON **20** A FICTIONAL ACCOUNT

Historical fiction allows an author to use elements of history to create a believable version of real events. Laurence Yep uses the events of Hiroshima to tell the story of Sachi, a fictional combination of several school children. As you read, make comparisons between this account and the nonfiction passages in earlier lessons. In your **Response Notes,** record reactions and questions.

Response Notes

from **Hiroshima** by Laurence Yep

Sachi wakes a few minutes later when she hears someone screaming. At first, there is so much smoke and dust she feels as if she is staring at a black wall. Then the smoke and dust rise like a curtain. She is stunned when she sees all the damage. One moment there was a city here. Now all the buildings are destroyed. The streets are filled with rubble and ruins. She does not know what could cause such wide destruction.

Shocked, Sachi stumbles through the wasteland until she stops upon a lawn. From the wrecked buildings, people call for help. Before she can help anyone, the buildings go up in flames.

It is so hot around her that the grass catches fire. She crouches down and waits and hopes. The sheet of fire retreats. Flames shoot out of the nearby houses. People continue to scream. Everywhere, there is a sea of fire.

Sachi follows some people as they run into a cemetery. She jumps over tombstones. The pine trees around them catch fire with a great crackling noise.

Ahead she sees a river. People jump into it to get away from the fire. In the panic, some people are crushed. Others drown. Sachi cannot swim. She jumps in anyway. Then she sees a wooden bucket drifting by. She grabs it and holds it desperately.

Soon the water is full of bodies.

The hot ash from all the fires soars high, high into the sky. When the fiery ash mixes with the cold air, it causes rain. It is a horrible kind of rain.

The rain falls in drops as big as marbles. The drops are black and greasy with dust. The drops sting like falling pebbles.

The rain leaves black, oily spots wherever it falls.

The rain is radioactive. It will make people sick, too. They will also die.

After about an hour, the rain puts out the fires. Somebody finds Sachi and brings her to the hospital.

The people living just outside Hiroshima think they are safe. They search through the deadly wasteland for family and friends. They do not know about radiation. Some of these searchers will also fall ill. Many of them will die. ❖

Before

CRITICAL READING SKILL

Evaluating Perspectives By now, students should understand that it is necessary to examine multiple perspectives in order to create a full picture of an event. They should also understand that each perspective has strengths and limitations. The excerpt by Laurence Yep is historical fiction, which blends fictional elements with factual information. Discuss an author's intent in writing historical fiction: why might the author choose historical fiction over a nonfiction account?

RESPONSE NOTES Remind students to keep in mind the excerpts they have already read. As they read and make their Response Notes, have them consider this question:

❖ *What advantage or disadvantage might historical fiction have over a factual or an eyewitness account?*

✳ What new information did you learn from this fictional account?

_____

_____

_____

_____

✳ The excerpts in this unit offer you a variety of perspectives on the bombing of Hiroshima. In the chart below, evaluate each. Indicate the strengths and limitations of each point of view. Focus on what you learned from each account.

Excerpt from	Strengths	Weaknesses
Mrs. Nakamura's account		
The Avalon Project's factual account		
Miss Sasaki's account		
Pilot's account		
Sachi's fictional account		

A FICTIONAL ACCOUNT **67**

ABOUT THE AUTHOR
Laurence Yep was born in San Francisco, California, in 1948. He began publishing fiction, mostly science fiction, in high school. He earned a Bachelor's degree from the University of California at Santa Cruz, and a Ph.D. from the State University of New York at Buffalo. He has taught writing and Asian American studies at the University of California at Santa Barbara and other universities.

Yep published his first novel, *Sweetwater,* in 1973. Since then, he has earned a reputation for thoughtfully conveying complicated emotions in Chinese-American youths. Two of his novels, *Dragonwings* and *Dragon's Gate,* won Newbery Medals. In 2005, Yep won the Laura Ingalls Wilder Medal for his contribution to children's literature.

TEACHING TIP
Collaboration Have groups discuss similarities and differences between Sachi's account and the previous readings in the unit. Each group can make a Venn diagram to record their observations. Each group should share its diagram before students complete the writing prompt independently.

During

SHARING RESPONSES Before completing the writing prompt, invite students to share their responses to the excerpt. Ask: *What did you learn from this passage? What did this new perspective make you think about?*

WRITING SUPPORT
Evaluating Briefly define and discuss strengths and limitations of a perspective. For example, a strength of Tamiki Hara's account is that the author knows firsthand what it was like to witness and survive the bombing of Hiroshima. A limitation of The Avalon Project's account is that it does not tell us the experiences of the people of Hiroshima before, during, or after the bombing. Emphasize that just because a perspective has a limitation, it is not necessarily invalid because all perspectives have strengths and weaknesses.

WRITING SUPPORT

Prewriting Help students brainstorm eventful experiences in their lives. If students have difficulty thinking of an event, ask if they have witnessed any events on live television or through any other media.

After students have chosen an event to write about, suggest that they use timelines to plan their writing. On the timelines, students should note their thoughts and actions before, during, and after the event.

Before students write their articles, remind them of the following:

✳ The article should be written in a journalistic style, giving the *who*, *what*, *where*, *when*, *how*, and *why* information of their experience.

✳ Students should write from the perspective of a reporter who has interviewed them about the event. Therefore, they should refer to themselves in the third person.

Quick Assess

✳ Did students find a strength and a weakness of each perspective?

✳ In their magazine story, do students refer to themselves in the third person?

✳ Do students include a description of their actions before, during, and after the event?

✳ Think of an eventful experience in your life that occurred on what seemed an otherwise normal day. Imagine that a newspaper reporter is trying to capture for a magazine story your perspective of that day and the event. Since a reporter is writing your story, this is not a first-person "I" version. It more closely resembles how Hersey treated Mrs. Nakamura's and Miss Sasaki's accounts. Be sure to include a description of your actions before, during, and after the event.

Evaluate the strengths and limitations of each perspective to understand how it adds to your understanding of the subject.

After

ART CONNECTION Invite groups to create an illustrated timeline of the events of Hiroshima, using the five perspectives in this unit.

✳ Each event should be labeled and illustrated, using description from the excerpt as a guide.

✳ Groups can post their timelines in a history classroom or common area.

FURTHER RESEARCH After completing this unit, students will be in an excellent position to initiate research projects of their own, researching multiple perspectives on an event.

✳ Have students choose another historical event to research.

✳ Help students find one of each type of perspective on the event in print and online sources: a newspaper article, an eyewitness account, a historical fiction piece, and a government document.

✳ Have students write a research report, incorporating facts and description from each perspective. Remind students to properly document each source.

Focusing on Language and Craft

Once you have command of the basic skills of reading and writing, you can attend to the **art of language: style and structure.** You know the differences style in clothes can make; style affects the way you act and how others respond to you. It is the same with language. An **author's style** makes us want to read or not read. Style makes what we read interesting, difficult, funny, or moving. However, style is not the entire issue; the other part is structure. To know how a particular outfit is going to look on you, you have to put it on. A style that looks good on one person may look silly on another.

In this unit, you will learn about some of the features of language that create style and structure. You'll see them in the texts you read, both in poems and in prose. You'll also try to create different structures as you experiment with new ways to develop your own writing style.

UNIT 5 FOCUSING ON LANGUAGE AND CRAFT

Lessons 21–25 pages 70–84

UNIT OVERVIEW
Students learn about style and structure by analyzing related elements in poetry and prose.

KEY IDEA
Paying attention to writers' stylistic and structural choices helps readers improve both their understanding and their writing.

CRITICAL READING SKILLS
by lesson

21 Using opposites
22 Subjective interpretation
23 Focusing on sound and rhythm in poetry
24 Analyzing word choice and structure
25 Analyzing overall style

WRITING ACTIVITIES
by lesson

21 Write a poem that uses similes.
22 Write an interpretation of a poem.
23 Write a poem that uses sound.
24 Write a comparison of authors' word choices.
25 Write a short piece that reflects an author's style and structure.

69

Literature

- **"Simile: Willow and Ginkgo"** by Eve Merriam (poem)

Similes abound in a lighthearted yet profound comparison of two trees.

- **"anyone lived in a pretty how town"** by e. e. cummings (poem)

A popular poet upends the conventions of poetry to paint a beautiful portrait of the cycle of life.

- **"Sledgehammer's Song"** by Mark Turpin (poem)

A poem about demolition provides a study of rhythm and structure.

- *The Pearl* by John Steinbeck (novel excerpt)

The strike of a scorpion is conveyed through artfully chosen words and sensory images.

- **"The Story of My Body"** by Judith Ortiz Cofer (nonfiction excerpt)

A Puerto Rican author retells the pain of adolescent embarrassment in an honest, frank style.

ASSESSMENT To assess student learning in this unit, see pages 235 and 265.

Students will learn that comparing opposites is one way to structure a poem.

BACKGROUND KNOWLEDGE

Students will read a poem that compares a *willow tree* and a *gingko tree*. Ask students if they have ever seen or can describe either kind of tree. You may want to enter *willow tree* and *gingko tree* into an image search engine and display some results. Explain that each tree has different qualities, such as the shape of its branches and leaves. Tell students that the author of this poem will use the differences between the trees to express an opinion about life.

VOCABULARY

willow a species of tree that grows on many continents and has thin, narrow leaves

etching a fine-lined image printed from a cut metal plate

gingko a species of tree that originated in China and has fan-shaped leaves

soprano in music, a voice that can sing the highest notes

nymph an imaginary, fairy-like creature

Review the definitions with students after they read the poem once.

Our language is filled with opposites. Opposition finds its way into stories, television shows, music lyrics, and movies. Almost every story has a balance between opposite poles. Just for fun, see how many pairs of opposites you can come up with in two minutes. We've written a couple of obvious ones to help you get started. How many pairs can you think of? You will use your list later.

hot   cold   *up   down*

                    true   false

Eve Merriam uses opposition to create a series of similes that make a statement in her poem "Simile: Willow and Ginkgo." The use of figurative language like similes is one way writers define their styles. Read the poem, which uses two trees, the willow and the gingko, as the basis of comparison. Underline the similes.

Response Notes

Simile: Willow and Ginkgo by Eve Merriam

The willow is like an etching,
Fine-lined against the sky.
The ginkgo is like a crude sketch,
Hardly worthy to be signed.
The willow's music is like a soprano
Delicate and thin.
The ginkgo's tune is like a chorus
With everyone joining in.
The willow is sleek as a velvet-nosed calf;
The ginkgo is leathery as an old bull.
The willow's branches are like silken thread;
The ginkgo's like stubby rough wool.
The willow is like a nymph with streaming hair;
Wherever it grows, there is green and gold and fair.
The willow dips to the water,
Protected and precious, like the king's favorite daughter.

Before

CRITICAL READING SKILL
Using Opposites Read aloud or ask a volunteer to read the introductory paragraph. Then explain that the word pairs below the paragraph are *opposites,* or words that mean or imply things that *contrast,* or differ greatly, from each other. Give students several minutes to generate their own lists of opposites. Students will return to their lists later in the lesson.

FOCUS ON SIMILE
Review the meaning of *simile:* a comparison that uses the words *like* or *as.* To illustrate, generate one or two similes with the students, such as *The sip of iced tea was like a breeze on a summer day; or, Her lips were as red as a rose.* Then explain that the author uses many similes to compare the two trees in the poem.

RESPONSE NOTES
For the first reading, read the poem aloud so that students can just listen. As students read the poem independently, they should write Response Notes composed of questions, comments, ideas, or connections related to the poem.

The ginkgo forces its way through gray concrete:
Like a city child, it grows up in the street.
Thrust against the metal sky,
Somehow it survives and even thrives.
My eyes feast upon the willow,
But my heart goes to the ginkgo. ❖

❊ Sketch the two trees using words and phrases from the poem to guide your drawing. Try including some of the words as part of your drawings. Choose one shape for the willow and another for the ginkgo.

Name of tree _____   Name of tree _____

❊ Talk with your partner or group about the characteristics of the two trees. It is clear that the narrator of the poem prefers one to the other. Which one do you prefer? Why?

_____

ABOUT THE AUTHOR

Eve Merriam was born in Philadelphia in 1916. She started writing poems at age seven and had her poems published in her high school newspaper. She attended Cornell University and the University of Pennsylvania, but she lived in New York City most of her life. Her poems—for children and adults—both celebrate and lament the realities of urban life. In 1969, she published *The Inner City Mother Goose,* a satiric look at Mother Goose rhymes in the context of inner-city life. Though the book was highly controversial in its time, it was republished in 1996, with illustrations by David Diaz and an introduction by acclaimed poet Nikki Giovanni. Well into her seventh decade, Merriam wrote a book of love poems for teenagers called *If Only I Could Tell You.* Eve Merriam died in 1992.

TEACHING TIP

Collaboration Invite students to complete the sketches in pairs or groups.

❊ Have each student choose one or two images that describe each tree.

❊ Students can then discuss their chosen images with their group or partner.

❊ The group or pair can complete the sketch by incorporating each student's input.

During

CLARIFYING
After students have silently read and responded to the poem, check their comprehension by asking:

❊ *What two things are compared in the poem?* (willow tree and gingko tree)

❊ *Which words describe the willow?* (sleek, silken, fair, etc.)

❊ *Which words describe the gingko?* (crude, leathery, rough, etc.)

WRITING SUPPORT
Drawing Conclusions As students complete the bottom prompt in groups or pairs, pose these questions:

❊ Which tree does the narrator prefer?

❊ How do you know? Which lines in the poem tell you this?

Students should discuss each question. Then allow students to discuss which tree they prefer. Direct students to consider Merriam's descriptions, but encourage them to form an opinion of their own.

WRITER'S CRAFT

Simile Explain that, in this poem, there are two types of comparisons: *two trees are compared to each other, and similes compare each individual tree to something it is unlike in order to describe it.* Then model finding a simile in the poem. For example:

✳ Underline *like* in the first line and say: *I know this comparison is a simile because it uses the word* like.

✳ Draw an arrow from *willow* to etching and say: *The willow is being compared to an etching.*

✳ Ask: *What do the two things have in common?* (They both have fine lines, as explained in the second line.) Encourage students not only to locate the similes but to find the relationship the narrator draws between the two unlike things.

Structure or Form Per the second prompt, direct students to underline each line about the willow. Then discuss the narrator's purpose for using the form. Ask:

✳ *How would the poem be different if the poet had just written one long stanza about the willow and one long stanza about the gingko?*

SIMILES

You have probably written and studied similes many times already, but this is an easy poem that makes the concept clear. A **simile** is a particular kind of **metaphor,** or comparison of two unlike things. The *simile* depends on the use of *like* or *as* for its comparison.

✳ In the **Response Notes,** use arrows or lines to show what two things are being compared. For example, you might draw an arrow from *willow* to *etching.*

STRUCTURE OR FORM

✳ Notice how this poem alternates between the two trees. Underline all lines referring to the willow. Then look at how Merriam shifts back and forth between the willow and the gingko. What lines tell you that the narrator of the poem felt drawn to the gingko?

_____

_____

✳ Look at your list of opposites. Using the list as a starting point, divide your list of pairs into those that refer to *things* and those that are *abstract,* like values. For example, *willow* and *gingko* refer to things, whereas *good* and *bad* refer to abstract qualities.

Pairs referring to things	Pairs referring to abstract ideas
Examples: *willow, gingko* *hill, valley*	*Examples:* *good, bad* *right, wrong*

WRITING SUPPORT

Concrete and Abstract For the third prompt, define *concrete* and *abstract* for students: a concrete word is something we can experience through our senses. An abstract word refers to something that is intangible, such as a quality or a way of acting or being. Use the chart's examples to explain the difference. For example:

✳ *I can touch, see, or hear a willow or gingko tree, so they are concrete.*

✳ *Good* and *bad are qualities. You may be able to sense an object that you judge to be good or bad, but you can never sense the qualities themselves.*

Ask a few volunteers to share their opposite pairs. Model sorting them into things and abstract ideas before having students complete the chart.

EXTRA SUPPORT

Differentiation Students may become confused and argue that they can sense a quality. For example: *I tasted a good pancake.* Explain to the students that they are not really tasting the *good;* they are tasting sugar or other substances that they *judge to be good.* You may want to pair students with on- or above-level partners and have them "talk out" each word pair together.

* Which pairs of words in the poem refer to things? _____

* Which pairs refer to abstract ideas? _____

* What abstract ideas might the willow stand for? _____

* What abstract ideas might the gingko stand for? _____

* Choose one pair of *things* and write your own poem titled
"Simile: _____ and _____ ." Follow Merriam's poem
loosely by first describing one of your "things" and then the other.
Conclude your poem as Merriam did by stating which of the two your
"heart goes to."

Simile: _____ and _____

Comparing opposites
is one way to structure
a poem.

EXTRA SUPPORT

Differentiation If students have difficulty with the questions at the top of page 73, use simple *either/or* questions to elicit answers. For example:

* Direct students to the first four lines of the poem. Ask: *Are the etching and sketch concrete items or abstract ideas?* (things)

* Direct students to the ninth and tenth lines of the poem and ask: *Are* sleek *and* leathery *things you can touch or abstract ideas?* (abstract ideas)

* *Is a willow flexible or stubborn?* (flexible)

* *Is a gingko delicate or forceful?* (forceful)

Quick Assess

* Do students' answers to the questions demonstrate a clear understanding of the difference between things and abstract ideas?

* Are students able to find examples of things and abstract ideas in the poem?

* Do students' poems compare two things?

* Do students' poems use similes to describe the things they are comparing?

After

WRITING SUPPORT

Simile Poem Help students write their poems.

* Have them choose a pair of things from their completed charts on page 72.

* Encourage them to brainstorm ways in which the things are different. Use a think-aloud to model the process. For example: *I want to contrast an apple and an orange. How do they look and feel? An apple is shiny and dry, while an orange is bumpy and juicy.*

* Use the descriptions to form similes. For example: *An apple is as shiny as a mirror.*

* Model concluding the poem as Merriam did. For example: *I think that apples are easier to eat, but I prefer oranges. So, I'll write: My hands stay dry with the apple, but my heart goes to the juicy orange.*

LISTENING/SPEAKING CONNECTION

Students can form groups and have a revising workshop. Encourage them to compare their subjects to interesting objects in order to provide memorable images for their listeners. After revising their poems, have them read their poems to the class. Students may write down at least one simile they heard in the poem.

LESSON 22

Students will learn that if they suspend their expectations of how language is used they may find themselves able to interpret poetry more easily.

BACKGROUND KNOWLEDGE

Ask students to share what they know about the following poetic conventions:

- Rhyme: *What is rhyme? Does all poetry rhyme?* Explain that some poets use internal rhyme, or rhyming words within a line.
- Capitalization: *Does every line of a poem have to start with a capital letter? Why or why not?* Explain that capitalization is up to the poet who may also choose to capitalize letters that wouldn't be capitalized in prose.
- Punctuation: *When you write a paragraph, each sentence should end with punctuation. Are the rules the same in poetry?* Explain that poets may use line breaks and stanzas instead of punctuation to organize their thoughts.
- Parts of Speech: Explain that they will read a poem that also uses verbs in a very different way.

LESSON 22 **BEYOND THE OBVIOUS**

One poet whose **style** is easily recognized is e. e. cummings. One mark of his style is that he never capitalized his name and rarely capitalized words in his poems. Cummings loved to play with the idea of opposites. The opposition in this next poem is not as obvious as it is in Eve Merriam's poem "Simile: Willow and Gingko," but you will find it in almost every line. Note as you read or listen to this poem how cummings "plays" with language in his poetry.

- Use the **Response Notes** column to make observations about the poem.
  - Comment on any ideas you have about the meaning as you read.
  - Note the instances of opposites that occur in the poem.
  - Make notes about what you observe regarding the form of the poem. When you read this poem, suspend your expectations about conventional punctuation, capitalization, and the way words are used. Look particularly at these elements:
    - **rhyme**
    - **capitalization** (Yes, there is one word capitalized twice. Why?)
    - **punctuation** (Did you notice the period? What point does it serve?)
    - **parts of speech** (Notice how words don't fit into their usual parts of speech. Make notes about words that are used in unusual ways. For example, "he sang his *didn't* he danced his *did*.")

anyone lived in a pretty how town by e.e. cummings

Response Notes

anyone lived in a pretty how town
(with up so floating many bells down)
spring summer autumn winter
he sang his didn't he danced his did

Women and men (both little and small)
cared for anyone not at all
they sowed their isn't they reaped their same
sun moon stars rain

Before

CRITICAL READING SKILL

Subjective Interpretation Read the poem aloud, allowing students to hear the rhythm. Then have volunteers take turns reading the poem aloud. Because of the poem's unusual phrases, you may want to have the poem read aloud several times before students write in the Response Notes.

Students' reactions may range from amusement to bewilderment. Solicit their initial impressions, assuring them that there is no one correct way to react. Ask: *What do you think the poet is describing? What is different about this poem?*

Explain that many poems' meanings are not obvious at a first reading. Readers must analyze certain aspects of a poem and then come up with their own interpretation.

children guessed (but only a few
and down they forgot as up they grew
autumn winter spring summer)
that noone loved him more by more

when by now and tree by leaf
she laughed his joy she cried his grief
bird by snow and stir by still
anyone's any was all to her

someones married their everyones
laughed their cryings and did their dance
(sleep wake hope and then) they
said their nevers they slept their dream

stars rain sun moon
(and only the snow can begin to explain
how children are apt to forget to remember
with up so floating many bells down)

one day anyone died i guess
(and noone stooped to kiss his face)
busy folk buried them side by side
little by little and was by was

all by all and deep by deep
and more by more they dream their sleep
noone and anyone earth by april
wish by spirit and if by yes.

Women and men (both dong and ding)
summer autumn winter spring
reaped their sowing and went their came
sun moon stars rain ❖

TEACHING TIP

Collaboration The Response prompt poses a lengthy list of factors to consider in interpreting the poem. Have pairs of students respond to the poem, point by point, using the Think-Pair-Share method.

1. **Think** Have students consider and respond to the first bullet point independently.
2. **Pair** After students discuss their responses to the point in pairs, invite them to share their findings with the class.
3. **Share** Repeat this process for each bullet point in the prompt.

BEYOND THE OBVIOUS 75

During

SHARING RESPONSES Allow pairs or groups to think about the meaning of the poem. Assure students that there is no correct interpretation and that any interpretation is valid, as long as it is supported by aspects of the poem. Encourage students to consider many possibilities, rather than ruling out each other's ideas.

If students seem to struggle with generating any ideas at all, present possibilities for them to ponder. For example: *What do sun, moon, stars, and rain make you think of? What's the difference between* noone *and* anyone?

Though students should be free to interpret the poem, you may want to ground their understandings by sharing themes that have been associated with "anyone lived in a pretty how town." Say: *This is a well-known poem, and many people think it may have to do with life and the changing of seasons, people who live out their entire lives in a small town, or a love story between two people. What do you think it discusses?*

EXTRA SUPPORT

Differentiation

✳ Some students may find it daunting to interpret the entire poem. You may want to have pairs or groups attempt to interpret only one stanza or portion of the poem. Later, they can present their work in sequence.

✳ Prompt analysis with these questions: What is happening in this part of the poem? What are the main images? What could the poet be saying with these images? Encourage students to give several possibilities if they are not comfortable committing to one interpretation.

✳ Some students may insist that they "just don't get" the meaning of the poem. Rather than forcing them to come up with an interpretation, have them write a brief paragraph explaining what confuses them about the poem. Remind them that they must support their opinions with details from the poem.

Quick Assess

✳ Do students use words, phrases, and lines from the poem to support their interpretation?

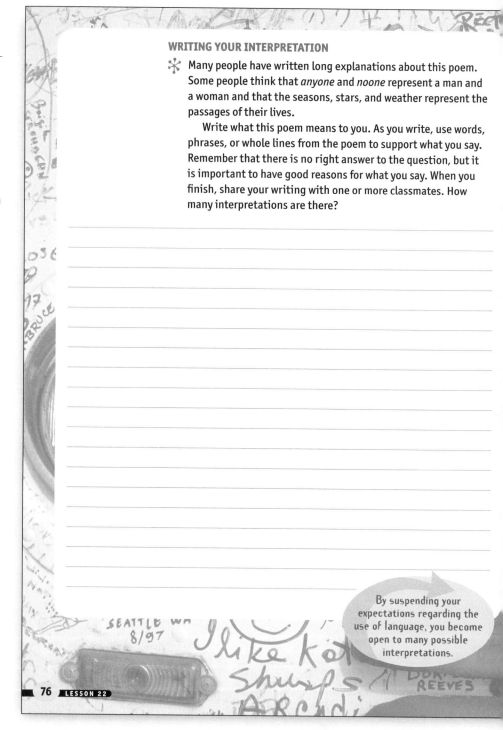

WRITING YOUR INTERPRETATION

✳ Many people have written long explanations about this poem. Some people think that *anyone* and *noone* represent a man and a woman and that the seasons, stars, and weather represent the passages of their lives.

Write what this poem means to you. As you write, use words, phrases, or whole lines from the poem to support what you say. Remember that there is no right answer to the question, but it is important to have good reasons for what you say. When you finish, share your writing with one or more classmates. How many interpretations are there?

> By suspending your expectations regarding the use of language, you become open to many possible interpretations.

76 **LESSON 22**

After

FURTHER READING   Have students read and compare further works by the poet.

✳ Locate more Cummings poems on the Internet or in a poetry anthology.

✳ Invite each group to perform and interpret a Cummings poem for the class.

✳ When each group has read and interpreted their poem, ask the class: *What themes did Cummings write about? What do you think he wanted to tell the world through his poetry?*

READING/WRITING CONNECTION
Invite students to write poetry that "plays with" written conventions.

✳ Have students choose a theme or message they would like to convey.

✳ Encourage students to experiment with only a single convention.

✳ Have them also write a "standard" version of their poems, one that sticks to the rules of prose writing.

✳ Students can read both of their poems to the class. Ask each student: *Which poem was more fun to write? Which one was more creative? Which of these styles would you write in again? Explain why.*

Style is as much about **sound** as it is about imagery. Listen to the rhythm of the sledgehammer in the poem. Turpin combined the worlds of being a construction worker by day and a poet by night. He writes that he likes the attention to detail, to rhythm, both on the construction site and in his poems.

Read the poem. Use the **Response Notes** to write the questions you have about what some words or lines mean. Do any lines catch your interest?

Sledgehammer Song by Mark Turpin

The way you hold the haft,
The way it climbs a curve,
A manswung curve,
The way it undoes what was done.
The way a stake sinks,
Cement splits or a stud
Spins off its nails.

The way shoulders shrug.
The way the breezes waft
And wake and tease a cheek,
The way it undoes what was done.
The way a cabinet cracks
And rakes and bares
The nail-scarred wall beneath.

The way a stance is spread,
The way the steel head pings
And thrums and thuds,
The way it undoes what was done.
The way a bathtub breaks:
Pieces barrowed, porcelain
Left in a bin.

The way sight is stark.
The way the weight wills the arms,
The back and heart,
The way it undoes what was done.
The way the weight is weighed,
Stalling the swing,
The sorrow mid-arc. ❖

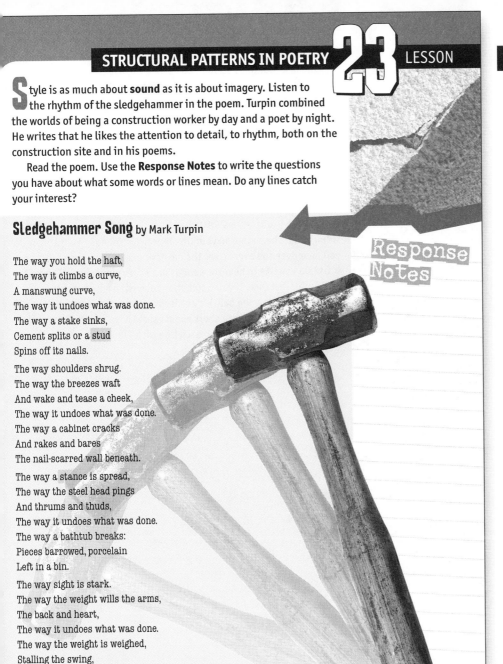

Response Notes

STRUCTURAL PATTERNS IN POETRY **77**

LESSON **23**

Students will learn how sounds and rhythm help make up a poet's style.

BACKGROUND KNOWLEDGE

Ask students what they know about rhythm in poetry. Explain that the rhythm of a poem can be fast or slow, smooth or choppy, but it is often used to make an impression about the subject. For example, a poem about a train may have a fast rhythm. Tell students that they will read a poem that uses rhythm to convey a message.

VOCABULARY

sledgehammer a long, heavy hammer used to break up things

haft the handle of a tool

stud a wooden frame inside a wall

stance the way someone is standing

barrow a cart for moving heavy things

arc a curved path

Note: Students are directed to locate and research unfamiliar words *after* they read the poem (on page 78).

Before

CRITICAL READING SKILL Sound and Rhythm in Poetry Explain or reiterate the idea of poetry as an auditory art form. Explain that poets often read their work aloud in front of an audience, just as musicians perform their songs. Tell students to pay attention to the poem's rhythm as they listen to it.

Then read the poem aloud. When you have finished, ask students: *What is the rhythm of this poem? Is it fast or slow? Is it weak or strong?* Compare the rhythm to the poem's subject: the swing of a sledgehammer. Ask: *When someone swings a sledgehammer, does he or she do it quickly or slowly?*

You may want volunteers to read the poem aloud several more times until students can form a strong sense of the poem's rhythm.

ABOUT THE AUTHOR

Mark Turpin was born in Berkeley, California, in 1953. In high school, he developed a love of writing that followed him through two decades of working as a carpenter. In his thirties, Turpin began taking poetry classes at the University of California at Berkeley. Eventually, he earned a Master's degree from Boston University. Though Turpin's work often centers on images from his construction background, his messages are simple and universal. In 2003, he published *Hammer,* his first book of poetry.

WRITING SUPPORT

Interpretation To help students interpret the ending of the poem, review the last stanza together. Then use questions to spark students' ideas. For example: *How does weight will the arms, back, and heart?* Then use visualization to help students interpret the phrase "the sorrow mid-arc." Ask: *How can sorrow be an arc? What could make sorrow stall?*

Quick Assess

✳ Do students use sound images in their poem?

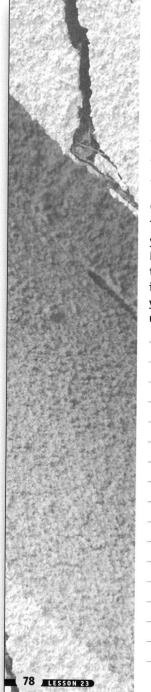

INTERPRETATION

✳ The last four lines seem to go beyond the act of swinging the sledgehammer to something more internal. We have no way of really knowing what the poet means by those lines, but perhaps you can make a good guess. What could he mean by "the sorrow mid-arc"? Try to explain what those lines might mean.

WRITING A POEM USING SOUNDS

Think about the sounds in your life, repetitive sounds. What things do you hear over and over? Does the music you listen to have a repetitive beat? Do you like to hear the sounds of a particular sport? (Think of tennis, for instance. If you watch it on television without the sound, it is hard to follow the ball.) Try to isolate some of the sounds that fill your daily life and write a short poem using those sounds. You might use Turpin's way of beginning each line with "The way . . ."

> Style can be composed of sounds as well as images.

During

RESPONSE NOTES   Direct students to reread the poem silently, noting questions or comments in the Response Notes column. At this point, students should not yet concern themselves with interpretation. Rather, they should circle, underline, or otherwise note specific words or phrases that get their attention or pique their interest.

After students have responded to the poem, have them find the meanings of words they don't know. (Or, distribute the Word Splash blackline master page 272.) If students report many unfamiliar words, you may want to form a class list. In groups, students can research and teach assigned words to the class.

After

APPLYING THE STRATEGY   Invite students to keep a sound journal. Every day, students can notice and write down sounds they hear. Encourage students to observe not only sounds but rhythms while doing daily activities.

After a week, encourage students to share their journal entries. Ask: *Did you notice any sounds or rhythms that were out of the ordinary? Has this changed the way you "hear" the world around you?*

Style is all about choice: what words and sentences to use; whether to use dialogue; how to use description, figurative language, and tone. The **structure** of a piece of writing is the way it is put together. Structure is the arrangement of words into sentences and sentences into paragraphs. In the next two lessons, you will analyze the style and structure of short excerpts by John Steinbeck and Judith Ortiz Cofer.

When you are asked to analyze an author's *style,* you might start by thinking about the author's word choices. Use the **Response Notes** column to comment on these questions:

1 Is the author's language formal or informal?

2 Is the author's vocabulary simple or complex or somewhere in between?

3 Does the author use sensory language—that is, words that can help you see, hear, touch, smell, or taste the thing described?

Read the following selection by John Steinbeck. In this excerpt from *The Pearl,* you will read about a tense moment.

from **The Pearl** by John Steinbeck

The sun was warming the brush house, breaking through its crevices in long streaks. And one of the streaks fell on the hanging box where Coyotito lay, and on the ropes that held it.

It was a tiny movement that drew their eyes to the hanging box. Kino and Juana froze in their positions. Down the rope that hung the baby's box from the roof support a scorpion moved slowly. His stinging tail was straight out behind him, but he could whip it up in a flash of time.

Kino's breath whistled in his nostrils and he opened his mouth to stop it. And then the startled look was gone from him and the rigidity from his body. In his mind a new song had come, the Song of Evil, the music of the enemy, of any foe of the family, a savage, secret, dangerous melody, and underneath, the Song of the Family cried plaintively.

The scorpion moved delicately down the rope toward the box. Under her breath Juana repeated an ancient magic to guard against such evil, and on top of that she muttered a Hail Mary between clenched teeth. But Kino was in motion. His body glided quietly across the room, noiselessly and smoothly. His hands were in front of him, palms down, and his eyes were on the scorpion. Beneath it in the hanging box Coyotito laughed and reached up his hand

Response Notes

Students will learn word choice is an important part of style.

BACKGROUND KNOWLEDGE

Students will first read an excerpt from John Steinbeck's *The Pearl*. Explain that the story takes place in Mexico and involves Kino, his wife, Juana, and their baby, Coyotito. In the excerpt, Kino discovers a scorpion in the baby's hanging box, or crib. The scorpion is dangerous because it can sting and poison the baby. Tell students they will analyze the way the author describes this moment of fear.

VOCABULARY

savage wild, fierce

plaintively sadly

Hail Mary a Roman Catholic prayer to Mary, who was the mother of Jesus

pustules small skin sores

adolescence the period of life between childhood and adulthood

Ask questions to check knowledge of the vocabulary. For example:

✻ *If someone does something* savage, *is it likely to be scary? Why?*

✻ *Who would act* plaintively—*a happy person or a sorrowful person?*

✻ *Which person is in* adolescence—*a baby or a teenager?*

Before

CRITICAL READING SKILL
Analyzing Word Choice and Structure
Use previously studied poems to illustrate the concepts of style and structure.

✻ Have students return to "anyone lived in a pretty how town" on page 74 and summarize Cummings's style. *His word choice was very informal and he mixed up parts of speech. So, one could say his style is playful and imaginative.*

✻ Have students return to "Sledgehammer's Song" on *Daybook* page 77 and summarize Turpin's use of structure. *The same phrase begins lines 1, 2, 4, and 5 of each stanza. So, one could say that Turpin's structure is repetitive.*

RESPONSE NOTES Before students read the excerpt, review Questions 1–3.

1. *Review formal and informal: Formal language follows the rules of English.*

Informal language sounds more like a conversation you'd have with a friend.

2. Define *simple* and *complex* vocabulary: *Simple vocabulary is made up mostly of words you hear every day. Complex vocabulary is made up of more unusual or unfamiliar words.*

3. Have students give examples of sensory language.

ABOUT THE AUTHORS

John Steinbeck (1902-1968) was born in the farming town of Salinas, California. Educated at Stanford University, Steinbeck is known for telling remarkable stories about "ordinary" people who have little power or voice in society. While *The Pearl* concerns a struggling Mexican pearl diver and his family, *The Grapes of Wrath* chronicles the oppression and exploitation of migrant farm workers during the Great Depression. Noted for his impeccable style and his treatment of socially important subjects, John Steinbeck won the Nobel Prize for Literature in 1962.

Judith Ortiz Cofer was born in 1952 in Hormigueros, Puerto Rico. Her father's job brought the family to New Jersey when Cofer was four years old. Though she attended school in New Jersey, Cofer also spent a considerable amount of her childhood in Puerto Rico. The comparison of Puerto Rican and American cultures, along with a child's experience of them, have figured prominently in her work. She has taught creative writing at the University of Georgia in Athens for more than 20 years, while publishing many acclaimed works of poetry, fiction, and essay. Besides winning other prestigious honors, her collection *An Island Like You: Stories of the Barrio* won the Pura Belpré Medal in 1996.

Response Notes

toward it. It sensed danger when Kino was almost within reach of it. It stopped, and its tail rose up over its back in little jerks and the curved thorn on the tail's end glistened.

Kino stood perfectly still. He could hear Juana whispering the old magic again, and he could hear the evil music of the enemy. He could not move until the scorpion moved, and it felt for the source of the death that was coming to it. Kino's hand went forward very slowly, very smoothly. The thorned tail jerked upright. And at that moment the laughing Coyotito shook the rope and the scorpion fell.

Kino's hand leaped to catch it, but it fell past his fingers, fell on the baby's shoulder, landed and struck. Then, snarling, Kino had it, had it in his fingers, rubbing it to a paste in his hands. He threw it down and beat it into the earth floor with his fist, and Coyotito screamed with pain in his box. But Kino beat and stamped the enemy until it was only a fragment and a moist place in the dirt. His teeth were bared and fury flared in his eyes and the Song of the Enemy roared in his ears. ❖

✳ Write a sentence that describes the atmosphere you think Steinbeck creates in this small section from *The Pearl*.

Read the excerpt from an essay by Judith Ortiz Cofer. In the **Response Notes** column, respond to the questions about word choice listed on page 79.

from "**The Story of My Body**" by Judith Ortiz Cofer

I was born a white girl in Puerto Rico but became a brown girl when I came to live in the United States. My Puerto Rican relatives called me tall; at the American school, some of my rougher classmates called me Skinny Bones, and the Shrimp because I was the smallest member of my classes all through grammar school until high school, when the midget Gladys was given the honorary post of front row center for class pictures and scorekeeper, bench warmer, in P. E. I reached my full stature of five feet in sixth grade.

I started out life as a pretty baby and learned to be a pretty girl from a pretty mother. Then at ten years of age I suffered one of the worst cases of chicken pox I have ever heard of. My entire body, including the inside of my

During

DISCUSS *THE PEARL* After reading the excerpt from *The Pearl*, encourage students to attempt the short response prompt before discussing it as a class. For students who have difficulty describing the atmosphere, give possibilities to choose from. For example, ask: *Does the writing make you feel relaxed, sad, or worried?*

After students have had a chance to write their sentences, use Questions 1–3 on page 79 to guide your discussion of *The Pearl*.

INTRODUCE "THE STORY OF MY BODY" Have students locate Puerto Rico on a world map. Explain that, since the Caribbean island is a U.S.

territory, Puerto Ricans are U.S. citizens and can travel freely between the island and the U.S. mainland. Therefore, many Puerto Ricans spend time in both places. Tell students they will read a short excerpt from an essay by an author who moved from Puerto Rico to New Jersey.

ears and in between my toes, was covered with pustules which in a fit of panic at my appearance I scratched off my face, leaving permanent scars. A cruel school nurse told me I would always have them—tiny cuts that looked as if a mad cat had plunged its claws deep into my skin. I grew my hair long and hid behind it for the first years of my adolescence. This was when I learned to be invisible. ❖

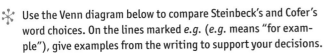

✳ Explain how you think Cofer became "invisible" in this excerpt from "The Story of My Body."

_____

_____

_____

✳ Use the Venn diagram below to compare Steinbeck's and Cofer's word choices. On the lines marked *e.g.* (*e.g.* means "for example"), give examples from the writing to support your decisions.

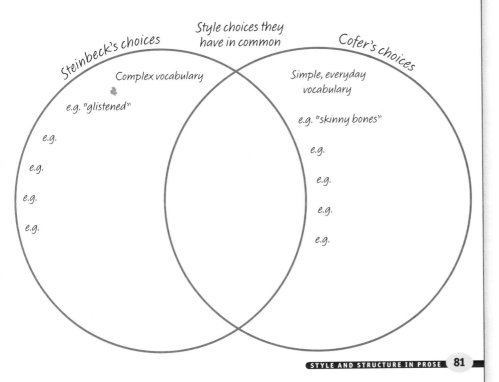

Steinbeck's choices

Style choices they have in common

Cofer's choices

Complex vocabulary

e.g. "glistened"

e.g.

e.g.

e.g.

e.g.

Simple, everyday vocabulary

e.g. "skinny bones"

e.g.

e.g.

e.g.

e.g.

STYLE AND STRUCTURE IN PROSE 81

WRITING SUPPORT

Comparing Style Explain how the Venn diagram is set up: students should write about Steinbeck's style in the left portion, Cofer's style in the right portion, and commonalities between the authors in the middle portion.

The headings establish that Steinbeck uses complex vocabulary, and Cofer uses simple vocabulary. The sample entry for the Steinbeck side is glistened. Explain: *Glistened is a very specific word, more complex than shiny or bright. Find more examples of complex language from the excerpt and write them next to each e.g.*

Direct students to do the same for the Cofer side, finding examples of simple language. For the middle portion of the diagram, direct students to Questions 1–3 on page 79. Students should find aspects of style that are in both excerpts.

TEACHING TIP

Collaboration Have students complete the diagram in pairs using the Think-Pair-Share method. (See page 75.) Each student can look for examples on his or her own diagram and share them with a partner. Have each pair then share an entry from their diagram with the class.

DISCUSS "THE STORY OF MY BODY"

After reading the excerpt from "The Story of My Body," encourage students to attempt the short response prompt before discussing it as a class. For students who have difficulty completing the prompt, ask: *Why would the narrator want to be invisible? What did she do to hide herself?*

After students have had a chance to write their sentences, use Questions 1–3 on page 79 to guide your discussion of "The Story of My Body."

WRITING SUPPORT

Word Choice To prepare students for the prompt, ask: *What is special about each writer's vocabulary? What kind of mood does it create, or how does it make you feel?*

Give students sentence frames to compare points from the Venn diagram. Post:

✳ *While Steinbeck's style is ____, Cofer's style is ____.*

✳ *Steinbeck uses words that ____. Cofer uses words that ____.*

Then use the sample answers in the Venn diagram on page 81 to model forming sentences. For example:

Steinbeck uses words that make a picture, like "glisten." Cofer uses words that make me laugh, like "Skinny Bones."

Quick Assess

✳ Did students fill in the Venn diagram?

✳ Do students support their opinions about the word choices used by Steinbeck and Cofer?

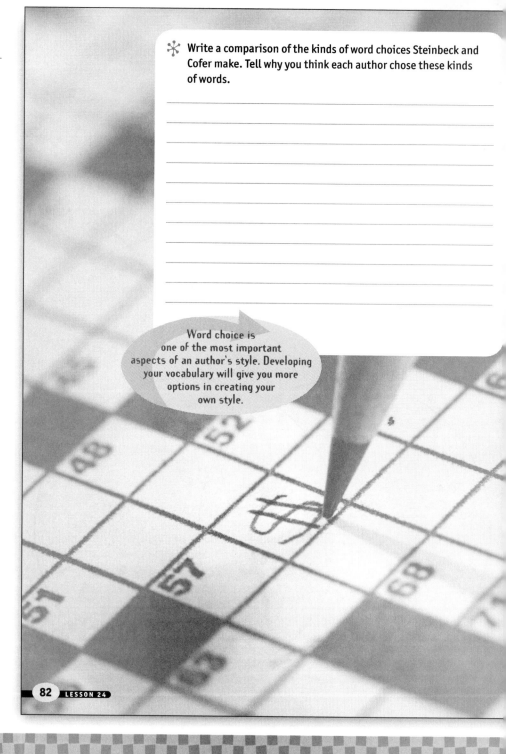

✳ Write a comparison of the kinds of word choices Steinbeck and Cofer make. Tell why you think each author chose these kinds of words.

Word choice is one of the most important aspects of an author's style. Developing your vocabulary will give you more options in creating your own style.

After

APPLYING THE STRATEGY Invite students to compare the word choices of each author in this unit.

✳ Students should note at least three interesting words from each selection.

✳ Have students write a short journal entry answering these questions: *Which is the most interesting author in the unit? What do you like about the author's use of words?*

READING/WRITING CONNECTION Invite students to evaluate a piece of writing from their portfolios and have a short discussion. Ask:

✳ *How would you describe your own style? What kind of words do you use?*

✳ *How does your style reflect you as a person?*

✳ *Would you like to change your own style? If so, in what way?*

If students wish to revise any of their work for word choice, invite them to review those pieces in pairs or groups.

There are many elements, in addition to word choice, that play an important role in an author's style. **Style** involves the way an author uses

- sentence length;
- description;
- figurative language (similes and metaphors, for example);
- tone.

❋ Fill in the Venn diagram with notes about the elements of style listed above.

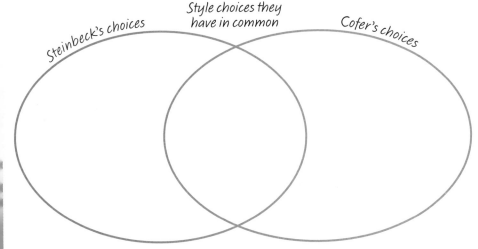

Steinbeck's choices | Style choices they have in common | Cofer's choices

Think about style as evidence of personality; not just the personality of the author, but the personality of the narrator or even the personality of a place. That may sound strange, but if you reread the Steinbeck excerpt, you will see that he has created an atmosphere of the place, which you might think of as its personality. Cofer has created the sense of a young girl whose self-image changes.

Review the lessons in this unit as you think about choices writers make in style and structure. Think about your own writing, the choices you make when you look at your first drafts and want to improve them.

MORE STYLE CHOICES **83**

Students will learn that understanding the style and structure of a piece of writing can help them explore more options for their own writing.

BACKGROUND KNOWLEDGE
Review the elements of author's style by finding examples in the unit's selections.

❋ Sentence Length: Have students return to the fifth paragraph of *The Pearl* on page 80. Ask: *This paragraph starts with a short sentence. How does that fit with the atmosphere of the piece?*

❋ Description: *Which selection has many descriptions of things? Which selections have more descriptions of action or feelings?* Explain that an author's decisions on what to describe play a part in determining his or her style.

❋ Figurative Language: Return to "Simile: Willow and Ginkgo" on page 70. Ask: *Why does an author use a simile or a metaphor?*

❋ Tone: Return to the related prompt on page 80. Ask: *What was the atmosphere, or tone, of* The Pearl?

Before

CRITICAL READING SKILL
Analyzing Overall Style Read aloud the introductory paragraph and bullet points. Then say: *You've already compared John Steinbeck's and Judith Ortiz Cofer's word choice. Now, you will compare their overall style, looking at their use of sentence length, description, figurative language, and tone.*

Direct students to complete the Venn diagram, finding at least one example of each aspect of style from each author's writing.

TEACHING TIP
Collaboration Form groups of mixed-level students to complete a group diagram. Each member can choose an aspect of style and look for examples of it in each selection. After students have had a chance to find these examples, they can discuss their findings and complete the middle portion of the diagram together.

TEACHING TIP

Collaboration Group students according to their favorite writers. Have each group discuss what they like about their writer and find style examples from the text that make the writer interesting to read. After writing their pieces individually, students in each group can exchange *Daybooks* to see how their peers emulate the writer's style.

Quick Assess

✳ Did students complete the Venn diagram?

✳ Did students create a piece of writing in which they showed their own style?

Write a short piece of your own, either a poem or a descriptive piece of prose. You can choose one of the literature pieces you have read in this unit to use as a model for your own poem or prose paragraph. When you finish, exchange your *Daybook* with another student and read each other's writing with an eye for style and structure.

_____

_____

_____

_____

_____

_____

_____

_____

_____

_____

_____

_____

_____

_____

_____

_____

_____

_____

_____

_____

_____

_____

_____

_____

Understanding the style and structure of a poem or prose piece gives you more options in your own writing.

During

WRITING SUPPORT

Brainstorming Explain how a writer's style gives his or her work a certain "personality." For example, John Steinbeck's writing might have a serious and tense personality, while Eve Merriam's writing might be honest and sentimental.

Have students review their completed Venn diagrams on page 83. Ask: *What did your favorite writer do that set him or her*

apart from the rest? What is that writer's "personality"?

Go through the directions at the top of the page, directing students to use their favorite writer's writing as a model for their own. Explain: *In order to model your writing after the writer's, use rhythm, word choice, sentence length, description, figurative language, and tone in the same way that the writer does.*

After

APPLYING THE STRATEGY Have students think of a favorite writer. Have them review a few pages of the writer's work and reflect:

✳ What stylistic choices does the writer make? Consider rhythm, word choice, sentence length, figurative language, description, and tone.

✳ What type of personality does the writing show?

Studying an Author

If I read a book and it makes my whole body so cold no fire can ever warm me, I know *that* is poetry. If I feel physically as if the top of my head were taken off, I know *that* is poetry. These are the only ways I know it. Is there any other way?

Emily Dickinson

In this author study, you will experience some of Emily Dickinson's best-loved poems. Almost unknown as a poet in her lifetime, **Emily Dickinson** is now recognized as one of America's greatest poets and, in the view of some, one of the greatest lyric poets of all time. Emily Dickinson was a passionate poet. She chose to live a secluded life, living within the confines of the family home, the garden, and a small circle of family and friends. Within that seclusion, she felt deeply, wrote with sensitivity, and imagined with intensity. These are the qualities Emily Dickinson shared in her poetry and in her letters.

85

UNIT **6** STUDYING AN AUTHOR

Lessons 26–30, pages 86–100

UNIT OVERVIEW
In this unit, students examine Emily Dickinson's life and poetry.

KEY IDEA
By focusing on approaches to a number of works by one author, students learn ways of reading poetry that they can apply to any poem.

CRITICAL READING SKILLS
by lesson

WRITING ACTIVITIES
by lesson

Literature

■ **Poems by Emily Dickinson**

Poem #288 The first of the Dickinson poems in the unit begins "I'm Nobody! Who are you?" and uses concrete images to express abstract concepts.

Poem #254 "Hope is the thing with feathers" uses a metaphor to make abstract concepts concrete.

Poem #919 "If I can stop one Heart from breaking" is the first line of this well-known poem about living with a purpose.

Poem #435 "Much Madness is divinest Sense" deeply expresses personal feelings and invites readers to connect with their own feelings.

Poem #585 "I like to see it lap the Miles" uses an extended metaphor to relate observations of a rather mundane subject.

Poem #67 The final Dickinson poem in this unit begins "Success is counted sweetest" and is presented in comparison to another poem about winning.

■ **"To an Athlete Dying Young"** by A. E. Housman (poem)

The only non-Dickinson poem in the unit is compared to Poem #67 in content and style.

ASSESSMENT See page 236 for a writing prompt based on this unit.

LESSON 26

Students will learn how poets use concrete images to express abstract ideas.

BACKGROUND KNOWLEDGE

Poem #288 Ask students to think about a time when it seemed like no one was paying attention to them. Ask how it made them feel.

Poem #254 Invite students to think of a time they felt hopeful, and encourage them to describe the circumstances that gave them hope. Then suggest that students reflect on the feelings of hope. In this poem, have students look for clues that reveal the poet's choice of a concrete image with which she represents the abstract concept of hope.

VOCABULARY

dreary dull; boring; gloomy

livelong entire and tedious

bog moist; spongy ground

sore severe

abash to make uncomfortable or ill at ease

extremity a state of extreme need

After discussing the definitions, invite students to write and read aloud sentences that use the words.

Poets choose their words carefully to convey their ideas effectively and economically. Notice how Emily Dickinson uses **concrete images** to express her thoughts about certain **abstract ideas.** Listen to someone read the poem aloud or read it yourself. In the **Response Notes,** capture your initial response by writing or drawing.

Poem #288 by Emily Dickinson

I'm Nobody! Who are you?
Are you—Nobody—Too?
Then there's a pair of us!
Don't tell! they'd advertise—you know!

How dreary—to be—Somebody!
How public—like a Frog—
To tell one's name—the livelong June—
To an admiring Bog! ❖

Response Notes

❋ Write what the poem seems to be about.

❋ Read the poem again. Make some notes about the following elements of the poem. Discuss your ideas with a partner.

■ Dickinson's use of punctuation and capitalization

■ words that are unfamiliar to you

■ words you know but are used in unfamiliar ways

■ connections you made with the meaning of the poem

■ other elements you noticed about the poem

86 LESSON 26

Before

CRITICAL READING SKILL
Making Abstract Ideas Concrete
Define an abstract concept as an idea. Say: *You cannot touch an abstract concept; you cannot take a picture of it. For example,* friendship *is an abstract concept.* Invite students to share other abstract concepts that are important to them.

Define *concrete* as "referring to an object that can be touched or seen." Say: *Something that is concrete can be touched or seen. For example, a clock is concrete.* Invite students to name other things that are concrete. Explain that poems in this lesson use images of concrete things to represent abstract ideas.

Read aloud Poem #288 and ask students to identify touchable "things" in the poem. (frog, bog) Then discuss how these concrete images help readers understand the poet's ideas about the abstract concept of being "nobody."

MAKING AN ABSTRACTION CONCRETE

Poetry uses the poetic device of **metaphor** to make abstract concepts—like *friendship, love, fear,* or *hope*—concrete by relating them to things that we can touch, see, taste, feel, and hear. In this next poem, Dickinson takes a common abstraction—*hope*—and makes it concrete. You may have read the first line of the next poem as it often appears on greeting cards.

Poem #254 by Emily Dickinson

"Hope" is the thing with feathers—
That perches in the soul—
And sings the tune without the words—
And never stops—at all—

And sweetest—in the Gale—is heard—
And sore must be the storm—
That could abash the little Bird
That kept so many warm—

I've heard it in the chillest land—
And on the strangest Sea—
Yet, never, in Extremity,
It asked a crumb—of Me.

Response Notes

✳ Write what you think the poem is about.

✳ As you did before, make some notes about the poem to share with a partner.
  ▪ Does this poem "speak" to you? If so, talk about what it "says."

  ▪ What do you think about Dickinson's metaphor "hope is a thing with feathers"?

Differentiation Students in need of additional support might benefit from an object lesson. Display an object, such as a book or a globe. Share abstract images that come to mind when you look at the object. For example: *This book represents knowledge to me. When I look at it, I think of all the things I can learn from reading.* Then invite students to select other objects and share what the objects represent to them.

During

IDENTIFYING CONCRETE ATTRIBUTES
Remind students that objects have concrete attributes: attributes that can be touched, seen, heard, smelled, and tasted. Suggest that students circle words in the poem that describe concrete attributes of a bird, such as *feathers, perches,* etc. Then invite students to draw a bird, describing its attributes (labeling them when possible) and telling how each attribute relates to the abstract idea of hope.

WRITING SUPPORT

Writing Conventions Remind students that writing conventions include punctuation, capitalization, spelling, grammar, and paragraphing. Explain that these "rules" are really just agreements English speakers and writers keep so that they can understand each other.

Have students identify the conventions Dickinson used. For example, she often used a dash in place of a comma or a period. Invite students to speculate on why the poet used the conventions she does. For example, ask: *How do you think the poet chose which words to capitalize? How do dashes affect the way you read the phrases?* Then discuss the effect of Dickinson's conventions on a reader's understanding of her ideas.

Quick Assess

✳ Are students able to form and express opinions about Dickinson's poetry?

✳ Did students describe an abstract idea in concrete terms?

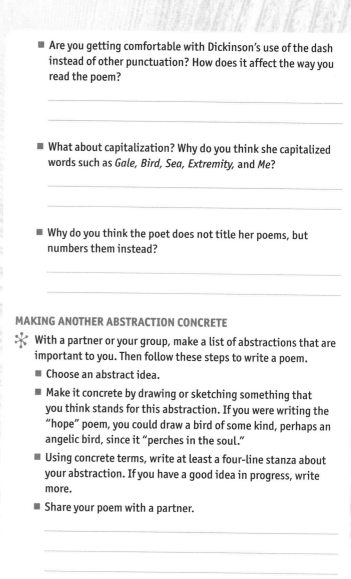

- Are you getting comfortable with Dickinson's use of the dash instead of other punctuation? How does it affect the way you read the poem?

- What about capitalization? Why do you think she capitalized words such as *Gale, Bird, Sea, Extremity,* and *Me*?

- Why do you think the poet does not title her poems, but numbers them instead?

MAKING ANOTHER ABSTRACTION CONCRETE

✳ With a partner or your group, make a list of abstractions that are important to you. Then follow these steps to write a poem.

- Choose an abstract idea.

- Make it concrete by drawing or sketching something that you think stands for this abstraction. If you were writing the "hope" poem, you could draw a bird of some kind, perhaps an angelic bird, since it "perches in the soul."

- Using concrete terms, write at least a four-line stanza about your abstraction. If you have a good idea in progress, write more.

- Share your poem with a partner.

> Concrete images help us understand abstract ideas.

After

LISTENING/SPEAKING CONNECTION Have each student prepare a reading of one of Dickinson's poems.

✳ Remind students to pay special attention to how they interpret the poet's use of writing conventions as they prepare their readings.

✳ Encourage students to practice their readings before a small group of classmates. Then invite volunteers to perform their readings for the class.

✳ Encourage the audience to give positive feedback about each reader's interpretation and to compare and contrast different performances of a single poem.

Good readers always **make connections** when they read. As you read the next two poems, think about your own responses as well as the connections that exist between what you are reading, what you have experienced, and other works you have read. Use the **Response Notes** column to record any connections you make as you read these poems.

Poem #919 by Emily Dickinson

If I can stop one Heart from breaking
I shall not live in vain
If I can ease one Life the Aching
Or cool one Pain

Or help one fainting Robin
Unto his Nest again
I shall not live in Vain. ❖

Poem #435 by Emily Dickinson

Much Madness is divinest Sense—
To a discerning Eye—
Much Sense—the starkest Madness—
'Tis the Majority
In this, as All, prevail—
Assent—and you are sane—
Demur—you're straightway dangerous—
And handled with a Chain— ❖

Response Notes

✳ Discuss these poems with a partner or in a small group. Talk about any difficulties you have in understanding them. Then talk about the connections you made to these two poems.

IMPRESSIONS OF DICKINSON'S POETRY SO FAR

✳ Using your own responses as well as what you learned from your discussions, complete the ten sentences on page 90 with what you know about Dickinson's poetry.

MAKING CONNECTIONS 89

Students will learn that making personal connections to the ideas in a poem can help them understand the meaning of the poem.

BACKGROUND KNOWLEDGE

Explain that the poems in this lesson deal with the purpose of life (#919) and the expectations of society (#435). Invite students to share their ideas of the purpose of life (why we are "here") or of times when they have felt that even though they or someone else was acting against the expectations of their community, it was the right thing to do. In order to facilitate discussion, reassure students that all ideas are welcome.

VOCABULARY

discerning able to see clear differences

starkest most extreme

assent to agree

demur to disagree

straightway immediately

After discussing the definitions, have partners tell about times when they have experienced each word. For example, say: *Tell about a time when you or someone you know* assented *to something or when something had to be done* straightway.

Before

CRITICAL READING SKILL

Making Connections Remind students that successful readers make connections from what they read to their own experiences, to other texts (including movies and television shows), to people they know, and to larger world issues. Readers who make connections when they read gain a deeper understanding of the text.

Read aloud each poem so that students can form a first impression. After reading each poem, Ask students to take a moment to think of connections they can make before turning to a partner and sharing the connections first with the partner and then with the class.

PARAPHRASING Explain that paraphrasing, or expressing something in your own words, can help you to understand

poetry. To model the process, paraphrase the last five lines of "Poem #435" this way: *In this case, the majority wins, as they do in everything. If you agree with the majority, they say you are sane; if you disagree, they call you crazy and lock you up*. Then ask students to make inferences about whether the poet agrees with what most people think or not and explain their inferences.

Quick Assess

✳ Do student's answers reflect familiarity with the poems?

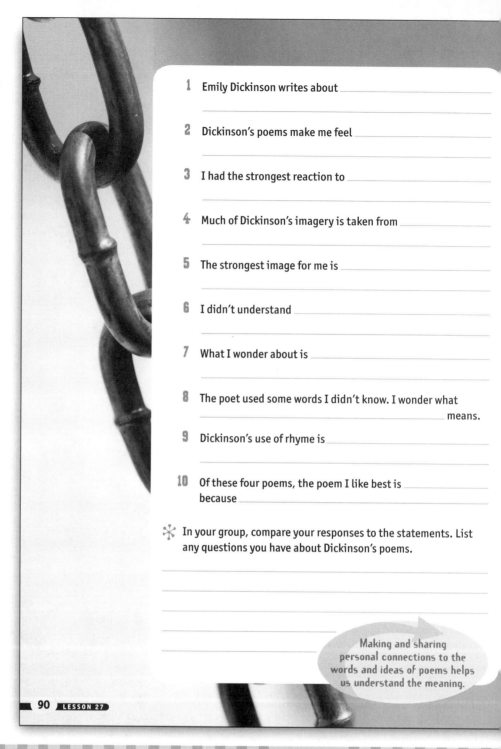

1　Emily Dickinson writes about _____

2　Dickinson's poems make me feel _____

3　I had the strongest reaction to _____

4　Much of Dickinson's imagery is taken from _____

5　The strongest image for me is _____

6　I didn't understand _____

7　What I wonder about is _____

8　The poet used some words I didn't know. I wonder what
_____ means.

9　Dickinson's use of rhyme is _____

10　Of these four poems, the poem I like best is _____
because _____

✳ In your group, compare your responses to the statements. List
any questions you have about Dickinson's poems.

_____

_____

_____

_____

Making and sharing personal connections to the words and ideas of poems helps us understand the meaning.

90　LESSON 27

During

RESPONSE NOTES Suggest that students use two markers of different colors to note the following:

1. lines in the poems that seem particularly powerful and that inspire specific connections

2. lines that reveal the poet's beliefs or thoughts

Then have students record in their Response Notes the connections that they make with the powerful lines and their own beliefs or thoughts in response to the poet's. Students can then use their Response Notes to help them complete the prompts.

After

APPLYING THE STRATEGY Have students select other poetry, including songs, with which they connect profoundly. Have them use the prompts on page 90 to analyze the poetry they chose and share their analyses with their classmates.

Read or listen to poem #585, "I Like to See It Lap the Miles." Do a quick-write or a quick-draw in the **Response Notes** column to solidify your first impression of this poem.

Poem #585 by Emily Dickinson

I like to see it lap the Miles—
And lick the Valleys up—
And stop to feed itself at Tanks—
And then—prodigious step

Around a Pile of Mountains—
And supercilious peer
In Shanties—by the sides of Roads—
And then a Quarry pare

To fit its Ribs
And crawl between
Complaining all the while
In horrid—hooting stanza—
The chase itself down Hill—

And neigh like Boanerges—
Then—punctual as a Star
Stop—docile and omnipotent
At its own stable door—

Response Notes

In "Hope Is the Thing with Feathers" (Poem #254), you dealt with one of Dickinson's metaphors. Sometimes a metaphor deals with two concrete things rather than an abstraction like *hope*. Poem #585 makes use of an extended metaphor, a comparison between *it* in line one, which seems like a horse, and a train.

Chad Walsh, a man who has written extensively about poetry, suggests the exercise on page 92, which will help you explore the metaphor in Poem #585. Rewrite the poem with an *elephant* as the implied comparison, instead of a *horse*.

Students will learn that understanding the metaphors of a poem is essential to understanding the poem's meaning.

BACKGROUND KNOWLEDGE

To help students understand the metaphors in Poem #585, explain that the steam locomotive was developed in 1822, just eight years before Emily Dickinson's birth. Before the development of the steam locomotive, horses were a major source of energy for transporting goods and people on land. Not surprisingly, the locomotive was almost immediately dubbed the "iron horse."

VOCABULARY

lap to be an entire circuit ahead of a competitor on a race around a track; to lick

prodigious enormous; huge

supercilious proud; arrogant

pare to trim away an edge

Boanerges a person who talks very loudly

docile obedient

omnipotent all-powerful

Review the definitions of the words after students read the poem once to form a first impression.

Before

CRITICAL READING SKILL

Analyzing Metaphor and Meaning

Remind students that a metaphor is a comparison that describes one thing as if it *is* the other thing, as distinguished from a simile, which says that one thing is similar to another (and usually uses the word *like*).

Read aloud the poem so that students can form a first impression and listen for a metaphor. (The metaphor describes a train in terms of a horse.)

TEACHING TIP

Use Graphic Organizers Explain that a metaphor may have various elements, particularly when a physical thing is involved. The metaphor in this poem has physical characteristics, personality traits, actions, and sounds. As students read through the poem again, have them record in a chart words that clarify elements of the metaphor:

Actions	Personality traits	
Lick Feed	supercilious	

Discuss how each element applies to both a horse and a train. To model the thinking, say: *A horse stops to eat grass and other plants. A steam locomotive had to stop periodically at storage tanks to fill up with coal. "Stop to feed itself at Tanks" means that, just as a horse stops to fill its belly with grass, a train stops to fill its coal bins with coal.*

❊ In the left column of the chart below write a list of all the words you would have to replace if you were to change the subject.

❊ In the middle column, list the words you would use if the horse were to become an elephant.

❊ In the right column, do the same thing as if the comparison were with a tiger.

Words in the original poem you would have to replace if you changed the subject	Elephant: words that you would substitute for the original "horse" words	Tiger: words that you would substitute for the original "horse" words

❊ On a separate sheet of paper, write the poem twice with your changes: first make the horse an elephant, then a tiger.

❊ Read your versions aloud to a partner, then listen to your partner's versions. Talk about how each of the different animal comparisons changed the poem.

- Did any of the words you removed have a particular sound that made the train image work?
- Has the tone changed?
- Has the feeling changed?
- Does it sound better, worse, or just different?

❊ Go back to the original horse image and note the qualities of the horse that Dickinson chose. (See the left column in the chart.) How does the horse image fit the train image that Dickinson develops in the poem?

CONVENTIONS IN EMILY DICKINSON'S POEMS

As you have probably noticed, Dickinson created her own rules of punctuation and capitalization. She used dashes almost as breathless pauses and capital letters to begin words that she thought were important, regardless of where they fell in a sentence.

During

SHIFTING METAPHORS

Have students read the poem again, marking each term that the poet uses to describe a horse. Then have students complete the chart about how that term will change to fit new animals they will use as they rewrite the poem. To model the thinking, say: *If I'm creating an elephant metaphor, I will change the word* lick, *which describes how a horse* gets water to its mouth. For an elephant, I will use slurp *because that sounds more like the way an elephant gets water to its mouth using its trunk.*

While some of Dickinson's poems use true rhyme, most do not. Rather, Dickinson generally used what is now called *slant rhyme,* which is slightly "off" the complete or true rhyming sound. The critics of her time didn't know what to make of this eccentric woman who violated the traditional rules of poetry. In fact, when her family and a friend first published her poems after her death, they were "corrected" so that the poems had true rhymes and traditional punctuation and capitalization.

The rewritten poems appeared in print for many years after her death. It wasn't until 1955 that they were published the way she wrote them.

❄ Reread Poem #585, "I Like to See It Lap the Miles," then rewrite it with conventional punctuation and capitalization. If you can turn the *slant rhymes* into true rhymes, do that, too, but that is much harder to do. Write your "conventionally correct" version below. The first stanza has been done for you.

I like to see it lap the miles

and lick the valleys up

and stop to feed itself at tanks,

and then, prodigious, step

WRITER'S CRAFT

Rhyme Remind students that poets have many devices to choose from as they write, including rhyme patterns, rhythms, writing conventions, and the shape of the poem. Dickinson's choice of "slant rhyme" confused her contemporaries, but it adds an element of surprise to her poems.

Define *true rhymes* as words that have the same ending sounds, such as *moon/June, love/dove,* etc. Define *slant rhymes* as words whose ending sounds are almost the same. For example, the second and fourth lines of the first stanza of Poem #585 contain the slant rhyme *up/step.* Invite students to identify other slant rhymes in the poem.

WRITING CONVENTIONS

Remind students of the "rules" for writing conventions they discussed in Lesson 26. Suggest that they use a red pen to mark all the unconventional elements of Poem #585 as if they were editing a piece of their own writing. For example, they should mark "Miles" to begin with a lowercase letter and the first dash for deletion. Then they can use their red marks to guide them as the write their "conventionally correct" versions.

Collaboration Form mixed groups, each of which contains some students who prefer the original form of the poem and some who prefer the "corrected" version. Remind students that there may be many "correct" opinions about of a piece of literature. As students state their preferences, encourage them to support their opinions. To model how to support a preference, say: *I prefer the original version. The dashes the poet used give me a feeling of open space and freedom to pause if I want to.*

Quick Assess

* Are students' 3-column charts complete?

* Do students' rewrites contain traditional punctuation and capitalization?

* Compare your version with that of a partner or those of others in your group.

* Write a short paragraph in which you discuss the different effects of the poem as Dickinson wrote it and as you have written it with traditional conventions. Comment on which version you like better and why.

Understanding metaphor is basic to understanding meaning in poetry.

94 **LESSON 28**

After

INTERNET CONNECTION Point out that slant rhyme in poetry has been used by many other poets, including hip-hop musicians and rappers. For more information, see www.flocabulary.com/images/lessonplan.pdf. Encourage students to find other examples of poetry containing slant rhymes and to share them with the class.

OUTWARD ASPECTS OF HER LIFE

The outward facts of Emily Dickinson's life are well known. She was born in 1830 in Amherst, Massachusetts, to a highly respected, prominent family. She was a middle child, devoted to her older brother Austin and her younger sister Lavinia. She was witty, had friends, and went to parties. She went away to college (now Mount Holyoke College), where she was successful but stayed only a year.

INWARD ASPECTS OF HER LIFE

When she returned to her family home in Amherst, she entered into an inward life that deepened into a strong reclusiveness. She loved people, but when they came to visit, she would frequently speak with them from behind a door that was slightly ajar. She also chose to wear only white, and neighborhood children would observe her when she would lower cookies to them on a rope from an upstairs window.

Emily Dickinson was a frequent letter writer. Letters were to Emily Dickinson what email is to people today. She began corresponding with family and friends when she was very young and continued until her death. When she became a recluse, rarely leaving her father's house, she kept up a heavy volume of letters. In her correspondence, she lived a rich life, not unlike the lives of many housebound people today who establish rich and rewarding relationships through the Internet. Her letters were filled with snippets of poetry, but, because her poetry was so strange for its day, readers didn't realize what a treasure it was.

One of the curiosities of Emily's life is that she published only seven of nearly 2,000 poems during her lifetime. The rest she tied in bundles and wrapped in blue ribbon with instructions to burn them after her death. Fortunately, her sister disobeyed her wishes and the poems were saved. Today she is acknowledged as one of the most gifted of all American poets.

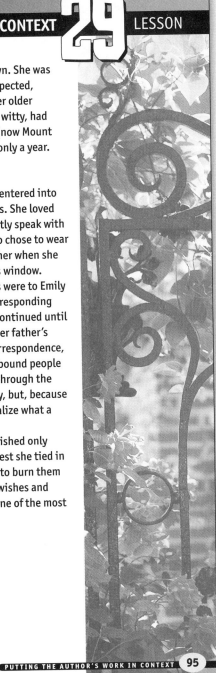

PUTTING THE AUTHOR'S WORK IN CONTEXT **95**

Students will learn that examining an author's life can help them gain a greater understanding of his or her work.

BACKGROUND KNOWLEDGE

Explain that most people have both an outer life and an inner life. Often the person we see on the outside is different from the person who exists in one's private life.

Explain that, while Emily Dickinson displayed many unusual habits in her outer life, such as wearing only white dresses, severely restricting her contacts with the outside world, telling her sister to burn her poetry, and so on, the inner life of Dickinson is also intriguing.

VOCABULARY

recluse a person who stays separate from the rest of the world

Ask students to develop a definition for *recluse* from its context.

Before

CRITICAL READING SKILL

Examining the Context of an Author's Work Explain that almost any kind of writing reflects the experiences and perspectives of the author. Therefore, it is important to know something about the author in order to more deeply understand the author's work.

RESPONDING TO THE ESSAY Invite students to use two different colors of markers to mark salient points in the two parts of the essay.

Use Graphic Organizers Encourage students to create T-charts to record elements of the poet's inner and outer personalities.

Outer Elements	Inner Elements
stayed at home	wrote poetry
spoke from behind a door	loved people
	wrote many letters

TEACHING TIP
Collaboration Encourage students to work together to compare information from a variety of Internet sites before drawing conclusions about the facts of the poet's life. Remind students that not all sites contain reliable information. Suggest that the most reliable sites are those created and maintained by the following types of people:

✳ professional literary organizations

✳ university libraries

✳ English instructors

✳ encyclopedias

✳ publishers of biographies (books)

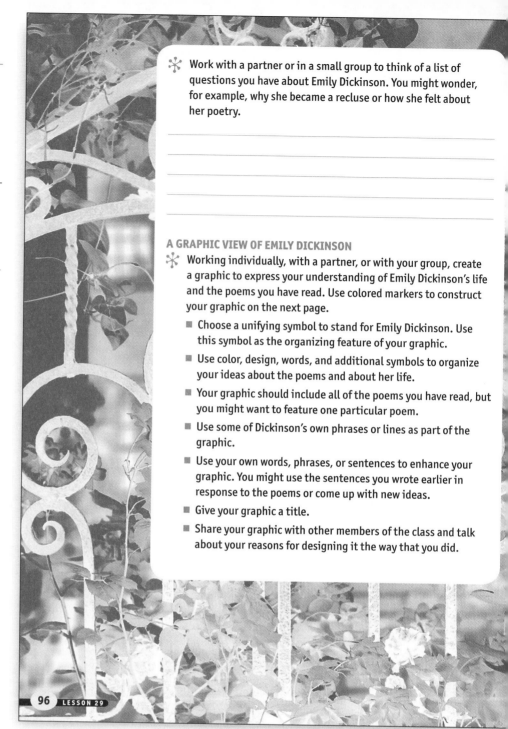

✳ Work with a partner or in a small group to think of a list of questions you have about Emily Dickinson. You might wonder, for example, why she became a recluse or how she felt about her poetry.

_____

_____

_____

_____

A GRAPHIC VIEW OF EMILY DICKINSON

✳ Working individually, with a partner, or with your group, create a graphic to express your understanding of Emily Dickinson's life and the poems you have read. Use colored markers to construct your graphic on the next page.

■ Choose a unifying symbol to stand for Emily Dickinson. Use this symbol as the organizing feature of your graphic.

■ Use color, design, words, and additional symbols to organize your ideas about the poems and about her life.

■ Your graphic should include all of the poems you have read, but you might want to feature one particular poem.

■ Use some of Dickinson's own phrases or lines as part of the graphic.

■ Use your own words, phrases, or sentences to enhance your graphic. You might use the sentences you wrote earlier in response to the poems or come up with new ideas.

■ Give your graphic a title.

■ Share your graphic with other members of the class and talk about your reasons for designing it the way that you did.

During

THINKING METAPHORICALLY
Before students begin drawing their graphics, suggest that they practice thinking metaphorically. After rereading the poems and reviewing the facts of the poet's life, have groups discuss a series of questions about the poet, such as the following:

✳ _If the poem were set to music, what kind of music would it be?_

✳ _If the poet were an animal, what animal would she be?_

✳ _If the poet were a machine, what machine would she be?_

✳ _If the poet were a plant, what plant would she be?_

✳ _If the poem were a building, what kind of structure would it be?_

✳ _If the poet were a sport, what sport would she be?_

Then have students use their answers as inspiration for their graphics.

Symbolism Remind students that symbols are images that represent ideas. Recall the discussion of abstract ideas and concrete images during Lesson 26. Encourage students to examine the attributes of the images they chose for their graphics. For example, ask: *How does the way the object moves remind you of the idea it represents?* To model the thinking, say: *A horse's movements remind me of how swiftly yet smoothly a train moves*. Suggest that students include this type of comment in their analyses of their graphics.

Quick Assess

✳ Do students' graphics represent metaphoric thinking?

✳ Do students' analyses explain the symbolism in their graphics?

✳ Write a short analysis of your graphic. Explain how the symbols, colors, designs, and words work together to portray the meaning or effect of Dickinson's poems.

_____

_____

_____

_____

_____

_____

_____

Glimpses into an author's life can lead to a greater understanding of her or his work.

After

ART CONNECTION Display a variety of works of fine art, including sculpture, paintings, collages, etc. Invite students to interpret what the artists communicate with their images. Ask: *Why did the artist choose this image? What do the attributes of this image remind you of? What message do you think the artist might be trying to communicate with this work?* Suggest that students compare their responses with classmates, noting the similarities and differences in the responses.

Students will learn that comparing and contrasting two poems can lead to a greater understand of both.

BACKGROUND KNOWLEDGE

Explain that the two poems in this lesson approach the topic of success from different and unexpected points of view. Dickinson discusses how success looks to one who has failed in an endeavor. Housman tells the tale of a triumphant athlete who dies young. To prepare students for the comparison of the two poems, invite them to consider such questions as: *Who has a clearer understanding of the value of success—those who succeed or those who fail? Does success have lasting value? Why or why not?*

VOCABULARY

sorest most urgent

host large group of people

chaired lifted up on a chair or on the shoulders of other athletes

betimes quickly

laurel branches of a laurel tree traditionally used to honor athletes

stopped plugged up

rout a retreat or flight from defeat

fleet fast; rapid

lintel top of a door or window

Review the definitions after students have read each poem once.

Sometimes reading two poems by different poets on a similar subject will add to your understanding of both poems. You can think about the subject from two perspectives. In this lesson, you are going to read two poems, the first by Emily Dickinson and the second by A. E. Housman. Use the **Response Notes** to comment on meaning and to capture your questions. Mark lines in the poems with which you make a connection.

Response Notes

Poem #67 by Emily Dickinson

Success is counted sweetest
By those who ne'er succeed.
To comprehend a nectar
Requires sorest need.

Not one of all the purple Host
Who took the Flag today
Can tell the definition
So clear of Victory

As he defeated—dying—
On whose forbidden ear
The distant strains of triumph
Burst agonized and clear!

To an Athlete Dying Young by A.E. Housman

The time you won your town the race
We chaired you through the market-place;
Man and boy stood cheering by,
And home we brought you shoulder-high.

To-day, the road all runners come,
Shoulder-high we bring you home,
And set you at your threshold down,
Townsman of a stiller town.

Smart lad, to slip betimes away
From fields where glory does not stay
And early though the laurel grows
It withers quicker than the rose.

Before

CRITICAL READING SKILL
Comparing and Contrasting Two Poems Remind students that a good comparison includes a discussion of both similarities and differences. To help students keep track of these elements of comparison, have them create a Venn diagram or a T-chart. Read the poems aloud so that students can form a first impression. On their second or third reading of the poems, have students take notes in an organizer about the two poets' topics, messages, points of view, images, and so forth.

Eyes the shady night has shut
Cannot see the record cut,
And silence sounds no worse than cheers
After earth has stopped the ears:

Now you will not swell the rout
Of lads that wore their honours out,
Runners whom renown outran
And the name died before the man.

So set, before its echoes fade,
The fleet foot on the sill of shade,
And hold to the low lintel up
The still-defended challenge-cup.

And round that early-laurelled head
Will flock to gaze the strengthless dead,
And find unwithered on its curls
The garland briefer than a girl's. ❖

❋ Working with your partner or group, talk about both poems. Use
  questions 1-9 to start your discussion.

1 Who is the speaker of the poem? To whom is the poem
  addressed?

2 What is the setting? Is it real or abstract?

3 Is there action in the poem? What is it?

4 What is the form of the poem? Where does the poet depart
  from these patterns and forms? Why?

COMPARING AND CONTRASTING TWO POEMS **99**

ABOUT THE AUTHOR
Alfred Edward Housman was born in
England in 1859 and died in 1936.
During a rather troubled life, the
poet produced a fairly large volume
of work focused primarily on themes
of unrequited love, the oblivion of
death, and idealized military life.
A. E. Housman was trained in classical Greek and Latin literature and
those influences can readily be seen
in his work. For example, meditations
on sporting glory, such as that found
in the poem in this lesson, are found
among the odes of the ancient Greek
poet Pindar. Housman's pessimistic
view of life, however, is more the
product of his own personality.

Although young Housman earned
a scholarship to St. John's College,
Oxford, he failed his final examina-
tions, some believe deliberately, as
a result of a lost love. After another
sad ending to a love affair, Housman
withdrew into monkish seclusion,
not unlike that of Emily Dickinson,
although not so long lived. Housman
finally returned to a career in academia
as Chair of Greek and Latin at University College, London, in 1892, after
which he began to publish the poetry
that ultimately resulted in his current
reputation.

During

INTERPRETING POETRY   Explain
that although the title of "To an Athlete
Dying Young" summarizes the simple
story told in the poem, the poet's beliefs
about the events must be inferred. Have
groups pose questions about especially
powerful lines in the poem and then
examine other parts of the poem to discover the deeper meaning of the line. For
example, for the lines *Smart lad, to slip*
betimes away/From fields where glory does
not stay, groups can pose such questions
as the following: *Does the poet believe*
that athletic glory has no value? What does
the line And the name died before the
man mean?

EXTRA SUPPORT

Differentiation Visual learners might benefit from drawing scenes from the poems to facilitate their interpretations. Students can discuss their drawings, and the interpretations they represent, with their partners or groups.

Quick Assess

✻ Do students' notes from their discussions reflect responses to the questions on pages 99 and 100?

✻ Do students' essays include thoughtful responses to the poetry?

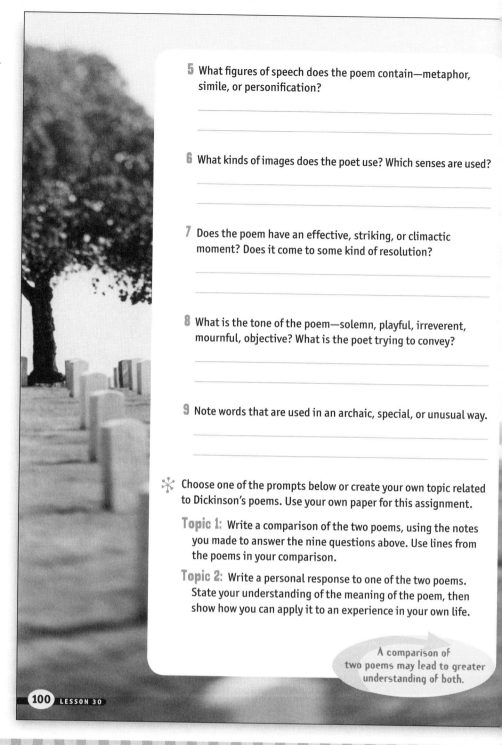

5 What figures of speech does the poem contain—metaphor, simile, or personification?

6 What kinds of images does the poet use? Which senses are used?

7 Does the poem have an effective, striking, or climactic moment? Does it come to some kind of resolution?

8 What is the tone of the poem—solemn, playful, irreverent, mournful, objective? What is the poet trying to convey?

9 Note words that are used in an archaic, special, or unusual way.

✻ Choose one of the prompts below or create your own topic related to Dickinson's poems. Use your own paper for this assignment.

Topic 1: Write a comparison of the two poems, using the notes you made to answer the nine questions above. Use lines from the poems in your comparison.

Topic 2: Write a personal response to one of the two poems. State your understanding of the meaning of the poem, then show how you can apply it to an experience in your own life.

A comparison of two poems may lead to greater understanding of both.

100 LESSON 30

After

POETRY COLLECTIONS Encourage students to read other poems by Emily Dickinson and to collect favorites into personal poetry collections. Suggest that they annotate their collections with drawings or written commentaries of the poems, using the questions on pages 99 and 100 and their previous experience with Dickinson's poetry to guide their responses. Invite students to share their collections with the class.

Assessing Your Strengths

Q What happens when a princess kisses a frog?

A The frog croaks. No, no, that's not right. The frog turns into a prince. And the prince and the princess live happily ever after.

That's one version! In this unit, you'll read not only the "happily ever after" version, but you'll read some of the contemporary versions, too. First, just in case you have forgotten the story, we'll give you the classic Brothers Grimm version. It does have its grim elements, too, as you will see. "The Frog Prince," in several different versions, is the basis for this midway reading and writing opportunity to show your strengths.

101

UNIT 7
ASSESSING YOUR STRENGTHS

Lessons 31-35, pages 102-114

UNIT OVERVIEW
Students will demonstrate how well they can use the reading and writing strategies they have learned so far in the *Daybook*.

KEY IDEA
Students apply what they've learned about reading and writing strategies as they compare different versions of the Frog Prince fairy tale.

CRITICAL READING AND WRITING SKILLS
by lesson

31 Interacting with the text

32 Making connections

33 Exploring multiple perspectives

34 Choosing a topic

35 Revising

WRITING ACTIVITIES
by lesson

31 Write Response Notes.

32 Write a biographical sketch of oneself as an adult author.

33 Compare versions of a fairy tale.

34 Draft an essay.

35 Revise an essay and evaluate progress.

Literature

- **"The Frog Prince"** by the Brothers Grimm (fairy tale)

This fairy tale tells the story of an enchanted frog who turns into a prince.

- *The Frog Prince Continued* by John Scieszka (story)

Scieszka offers a humorous telling of the "happily ever after" part of the Frog Prince tale.

- **"Annunciation"** by Adrianne Marcus (poem)

Told from the princess's point of view, this Frog Prince tale asks the reader "Would you take the chance?"

LESSON 31

Students will interact with the text by responding to this classic version of the Frog Prince fairy tale.

BACKGROUND KNOWLEDGE

Discuss with students the different elements usually found in fairy tales:

- The **beginning** of a fairy tale is often "Once upon a time . . ."
- The **setting** is usually an undefined time and place but recognizable as sometime in the past of the country or region of the tale's origin.
- Fairy tale **characters** are often stereotypical, symbolizing larger issues or values.
- Characters, often royal, usually have a problem to solve.
- Events and people often occur in 3s.
- There is often some kind of transformation, usually physical.
- Fairy tales often teach a lesson.
- The **ending** of a fairy tale is often "they all lived happily ever after."

VOCABULARY

odious hated or disgusting

Ask students to predict how the word *odious* might be used in a tale about an ugly frog and a beautiful princess.

LESSON 31 INTERACTING WITH THE TEXT

Some of you will remember the story of "The Frog Prince," while others in the class may not know it. Before talking about what you remember, jot down as much of the story as you know. Try to include any details that you may remember about it. If you don't remember ever hearing or reading the story, jot down any references with which you are familiar that include the idea of "kissing a frog" or a frog turning into a prince.

INTERACT WITH THE TEXT

This is one of the earliest versions, the most famous of the Grimm brothers' retellings of this tale. In the Response Notes, mark parts of the story that are familiar and parts that are surprising. You may wish to use two different colored pencils.

Response Notes

The Frog Prince as told by Jacob Ludwig Grimm and Wilhelm Carl Grimm

Once upon a time there was a king who had three daughters. In his courtyard there was a well with wonderful clear water. One hot summer day the oldest daughter went down and drew herself a glassful, but when she held it to the sun, she saw that it was cloudy. This seemed strange to her, and she was about to pour it back when a frog appeared in the water, stuck his head into the air, then jumped out onto the well's edge, saying:

> If you will be my sweetheart dear,
> Then I will give you water clear.

Before

CRITICAL READING SKILL

Interacting with the Text Have students write what they know about the Frog Prince before they read the selection. As they read, suggest students circle or underline any surprises they encounter.

RESPONSE NOTES Students are asked to look for parts of the story that are familiar and parts that are surprising. On a second read-through, suggest that students look for such elements of fairy tales as the following:

- the beginning and ending
- setting
- the characters
- stereotypes
- some kind of transformation
- a moral or lesson

"Ugh! Who wants to be the sweetheart of an ugly frog!" exclaimed the princess and ran away. She told her sisters about the amazing frog down at the well who was making the water cloudy. The second one was curious, so she too went down and drew herself a glassful, but it was so cloudy that she could not drink it. Once again the frog appeared at the well's edge and said:

If you will be my sweetheart dear,
Then I will give you water clear.

"Not I!" said the princess, and ran away. Finally the third sister came and drew a glassful, but it was no better than before. The frog also said to her:

If you will be my sweetheart dear,
Then I will give you water clear.

"Why not! I'll be your sweetheart. Just give me some clean water," she said, while thinking, "There's no harm in this. You can promise him anything, for a stupid frog can never be your sweetheart."

The frog sprang back into the water, and when she drew another glassful it was so clear that the sun glistened in it with joy. She drank all she wanted and then took some up to her sisters, saying, "Why were you so stupid as to be afraid of a frog?"

The princess did not think anything more about it until that evening after she had gone to bed. Before she fell asleep she heard something scratching at the door and a voice singing:

Open up! Open up!
Youngest daughter of the king.
Remember that you promised me
While I was sitting in the well,
That you would be my sweetheart dear,
If I would give you water clear.

"Ugh! That's my boyfriend the frog," said the princess. "I promised, so I will have to open the door for him." She got up, opened the door a crack, and went back to bed. The frog hopped after her, then hopped onto her bed where he lay at her feet until the night was over and the morning dawned. Then he jumped down and disappeared out the door.

The next evening, when the princess once more had just gone to bed, he scratched and sang again at the door. The princess let him in, and he again lay at her feet until daylight came. He came again on the third evening, as on the two previous ones. "This is the last time that I'll let you in," said the princess. "It will not happen again in the future."

The king's daughter began to cry, for she was afraid of the cold frog which she did not like to touch, and which was now to sleep in her pretty, clean little bed. When she was in bed he crept to her and said, "I am tired, I want to sleep as well as you, lift me up or I will tell your father." At this she was terribly

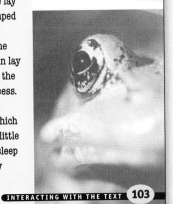

ABOUT THE AUTHORS
The Brothers Grimm are among the most widely read authors of folktales and fairy tales. Born in Germany at the end of the 18th century, these brothers gathered the folktales told by people all over Germany. They published their first volume of folktales in 1812, and their stories have been read all over the world ever since (often in their later, less disturbing versions). The fairy tales recounted by the Grimms capture the good and the bad of human nature, as well as the struggle between human beings and the sometimes menacing world around us. While the tales convey the morals and ideals of the society in which they originated, their universal themes still resonate with people today.

During

VISUALIZATION Instruct students to use their skills of visualization as they read the tale in order to picture and understand its characters. Then lead a discussion of the story, using the questions on page 104.

Explaining Terms Some students may need help with the concepts of *stereotypes* and *transformation story*. Explain that stereotypes are a confining and often prejudiced way of looking at people. Help students understand that fairy tales usually portray men and women in very narrow ways: women are often vain and passive, just waiting for a handsome prince to marry; sisters are often competitive rather than supportive; and men are often on a quest for "the one true love" who will see them for who they are.

Discuss how transformation stories are often tied to that theme of being seen for who you are "on the inside." In this case, the frog is ugly on the outside but a prince on the inside. He is waiting for someone to love him to bring out his true self. Encourage students to discuss other stories they've read or seen in movies that have a similar theme. Invite them to share their own thoughts on the theme of this tale.

Quick Assess

✳ Were students able to identify features of the fairy tale genre in "The Frog Prince"?

✳ Did students contribute to the discussions of their group?

---

angry, and took him up and threw him with all her might against the wall. "Now, will you be quiet, odious frog," said she. But when he fell down he was no frog but a king's son with kind and beautiful eyes.

He told her that he had been an enchanted frog and that she had broken the spell by promising to be his sweetheart. Then they both went to the king who gave them his blessing, and they were married. The two other sisters were angry with themselves that they had not taken the frog for their sweetheart.

✳ Answer the questions below with a few notes. Use the notes to discuss the story with several classmates.

■ What do you think about the violent act of the princess?

_____

_____

■ What stereotypes do you find in the story?

_____

_____

■ If fairy tales were intended to teach children about the values of their society, what might those values be in "The Frog Prince"?

_____

_____

■ "The Frog Prince" is one of many transformation stories. What about the nature of frogs makes the frog a particularly good choice for a "transformation story"?

_____

_____

> Fairy tales embody the values and customs of earlier societies while dealing with issues that remain important to us today.

After

TEACHING TIP

Collaboration You may want to have students write notes responding to the questions on page 104 before they meet in small groups to discuss the Brothers Grimm's version of the Frog Prince tale. When students meet with their groups to discuss those questions, one student can be the moderator, one can be the timekeeper, and one can be the recorder,

writing down the group's collaborative reactions to the questions on page 104. One student from each group can report to the class on the group's discussion.

READING-WRITING CONNECTION

Have students select one of the discussion questions and write a one-page response to it, providing details and examples to support their opinion.

Fairy tales just don't stay the same way. Every writer who reads one seems to want to write his or her own version. "The Frog Prince" has led to an amazing number of spin-offs.

One way writers deal with fairy tales is to give them alternative endings. Read this writer's continuation of "The Frog Prince." As you read, make notes in the **Response Notes** column whenever you find a connection to another fairy tale.

The Frog Prince Continued: A Story
by Jon Scieszka

The Princess kissed the frog. He turned into a prince. And they lived happily ever after... Well let's just say they lived sort of happily for a long time. Okay, so they weren't so happy. In fact, they were miserable.

"Stop sticking your tongue out like that," nagged the Princess. "How come you never want to go down to the pond anymore?" whined the Prince. The Prince and Princess were so unhappy. They didn't know what to do. "I would prefer that you not hop around on the furniture," said the Princess. "And it might be nice if you got out of the castle once in a while to slay a dragon or giant or whatever." The Prince didn't feel like going out and slaying anything. He just felt like running away. But then he reread his book. And it said right there at the end of his story: "They lived happily ever after. The End." So he stayed in the castle and drove the Princess crazy. Then one day, the Princess threw a perfectly awful fit. "First you keep me awake all night with your horrible, croaking snore. Now I find a lily pad in your pocket. I can't believe I actually kissed your slimy frog lips. Sometimes I think we would both be better off if you were still a frog." That's when the idea hit him. The Prince thought, "Still a frog.... Yes! That's it!"

And he ran off into the forest, looking for a witch who could turn him back into a frog. The Prince hadn't gone far when he ran into just the person he was looking for. "Miss Witch, Miss Witch. Excuse me, Miss Witch. I wonder if you could help me?" "Say, you're not looking for a princess to kiss are you?" asked the witch. "Oh, no. I've already been kissed. I'm the Frog Prince. Actually, I was hoping you could turn me back into a frog." "Are you sure you're not looking for a beautiful sleeping princess to kiss and wake up?" "No, no— I'm the Frog Prince." "That's funny. You don't look like a frog. Well, no matter. If you're a prince, you're a prince. And I'll have to cast a nasty spell on you. I can't have any princes waking up Sleeping Beauty before the hundred years are up."

Response Notes

Sleeping Beauty

Students will make connections between the fairy tale they have just read and Jon Scieszka's humorous continuation of the tale.

BACKGROUND KNOWLEDGE
Invite students to speculate on why someone would want to write a continuation of a fairy tale. Help students see that the phrase *and they lived happily ever after* can be an invitation to the curious to imagine what life in the world of "happily ever after" might be like. Invite students to think about what life might be like for other fairy tale characters who lived "happily ever after," such as Cinderella, Sleeping Beauty, and Beauty of "Beauty and the Beast."

Before

CRITICAL READING SKILL
Making Connections Remind students of what they've learned so far in the *Daybook* about constructing meaning for what they read by connecting it with what they already know. Encourage them to use what they read in Lesson 31 plus their knowledge of fairy tales to connect with the text they read in this lesson.

RESPONSE NOTES As students read, they should note any connections they find between Scieszka's story and the Brothers Grimm's tale. Also, encourage them to note any places in the text that refer to other fairy tales.

Jon Scieszka Jon Scieszka was born in Flint, Michigan, in 1954 and has five brothers. He had many different ideas about what he wanted to do with his life, but once he got started writing funny books for children and young adults, he just kept on going. His love of reading and his enjoyment in making people laugh, as well as his experience teaching, have helped inspire him to pursue his career as a writer of fun—and funny—children's books.

Response Notes

The Prince didn't stick around to see which nasty spell the witch had in mind. He ran deeper into the forest until he came to a tiny cottage where he saw another lady who might help him. "Miss Witch, Miss Witch. Excuse me, Miss Witch. I wonder if you could help me. I'm a prince and—" "Eh? What did you say? Prince?" croaked the witch. "No. I mean, yes. I mean, no, I'm not the prince looking for Sleeping Beauty. But, yes, I'm the Frog Prince. And I'm looking for a member of your profession who can turn me back into a frog so I can live happily ever after." "Frog Prince, you say? That's funny. I thought frogs were little green guys with webbed feet. Well, no matter. If you're a prince, you're a prince. And I can't have any princes rescuing Snow White. Here—eat the rest of this apple."

The Prince, who knew his fairy tales (and knew a poisoned apple when he saw one), didn't even stay to say, "No, thank you." He turned and ran deeper into the forest. Soon he came to a strange-looking house with a witch outside. "Ahem. Miss Witch, Miss Witch. Excuse me, Miss Witch. I wonder if you could help me? I'm the Frog—" "If you're a frog, I'm the King of France," said the witch. "No, I'm not a frog. I'm the Frog Prince. But I need a witch to turn me back into a frog so I can live happily ever after can you do it?" said the Prince in one long breath. The witch eyed the Prince and licked her rather plump lips. "Why, of course, dearie. Come right in. Maybe I can fit you in for lunch." The Prince stopped on the slightly gummy steps. Something about this house seemed very familiar. He broke off a corner of the windowsill and tasted it. Gingerbread. "I hope you don't mind my asking, Miss Witch. But do you happen to know any children by the name of Hansel and Gretel?" "Why yes, Prince darling, I do. I'm expecting them for dinner."

The Prince, who, as we said before, knew his fairy tales, ran as fast as he could deeper into the forest. Soon he was completely lost. He saw someone standing next to a tree. The Prince walked up to her, hoping she wasn't a witch, for he'd quite had his fill of witches. "Madam. I am the Frog Prince. Could you help me?" "Gosh, do you need it," said the Fairy Godmother. "You are the worst-looking frog I've ever seen." "I am not a frog. I am the Frog Prince," said the Prince, getting a little annoyed. "And I need someone to turn me back

During

RESPONDING TO THE SELECTION

Read Jon Scieszka's *The Frog Prince Continued* aloud, asking students to use their Response Notes to record their ideas, questions, and connections. (See page 229 for more on marking text.)

Remind students of the various kinds of notes they might make. They can

✻ record their ideas;

✻ ask questions;

✻ make connections;

✻ sketch or draw.

Remind them to note any references to other fairy tales. Use what students write to start a discussion of *literary allusions,* indirect references that writers make to other works of literature. Invite students to find allusions to other fairy tales in the selection. (See the Collaboration on page 107 for a list of the fairy tales to which there are allusions.)

into a frog so I can live happily ever after." "Well, I'm on my way to see a girl in the village about going to a ball, but I suppose I could give it a try. I've never done frogs before, you know."

And with that the Fairy Godmother waved her magic wand, and turned the Prince into a beautiful . . . carriage. The Prince couldn't believe his rotten luck. The sun went down. The forest got spookier. And the Prince became more and more frightened. "Oh, what an idiot I've been. I could be sitting at home with the Princess, living happily ever after. But instead, I'm stuck here in the middle of this stupid forest, turned into a stupid carriage. Now I'll probably just rot and fall apart and live unhappily ever after." The Prince thought these terrible, frightening kinds of thoughts (and a few worse—too awful to tell), until far away in the village, the clock struck midnight.

The Carriage instantly turned back into his former Prince self, and ran by the light of the moon until he was safe inside his own castle. "Where have you been? I've been worried sick. You're seven hours late. Your dinner is cold. Your clothes are a mess."

The Prince looked at the Princess who had believed him when no one else in the world had, the Princess who actually kissed his slimy frog lips. The Princess who loved him. The Prince kissed the Princess. They both turned into frogs. And they hopped off happily ever after. The end. ❖

✳ Use your **Response Notes** to answer these questions.

■ Which other fairy tales are embedded in this story?

_____

_____

■ What do you think of the Prince's solution to his unhappiness?

_____

_____

■ What kind of person would write a story such as this?

_____

_____

WRITER'S CRAFT

Tone Talk with students about how Jon Scieszka is known for his humorous writing. He has a gift for telling a story in a way that makes the reader laugh. His retelling of the story of the three little pigs and the big bad wolf, *The True Story of the Three Little Pigs*, turns that tale on its head by retelling it from the point of view of the wolf, who turns out to be the injured party.

Invite students to talk about how they know the story in this lesson is meant to be funny. Ask: *What is it about this story that tells us it's intended as humorous?* Encourage students to find examples in the story that set the humorous tone, such as the way the princess is always complaining about the Prince's acting like a frog, the silly conversations with the witches, the fact that a character in a fairy tale *knew his fairy tales*, and the fact that prince is mistakenly turned into a carriage by Cinderella's fairy godmother. These all help create the silly, and delightful, tone that Scieszka uses to let his reader know that his fairy tales are "fractured."

COLLABORATION

You may want to have students stay in their groups from the previous lesson to continue their discussion of various versions of the Frog Prince tales. Challenge the groups to come up with a complete list of allusions to other fairy tales ("The Frog Prince," "Sleeping Beauty," "Snow White," "Hansel and Gretel," "Cinderella"). Have them give their opinions on the solution presented in the story and encourage students to develop and express their own opinions, even though others in the group may disagree. Finally, have the groups brainstorm the types of qualities they would expect in someone who would write such a story. Have the recorder in each group write down the qualities, such as *funny, unusual, able to think like a kid,* and *knowledgeable about fairy tales.* Invite each group to report on its discussion.

TEACHING TIP

Connecting the Author with the Work Have students read the excerpt from the interview with Jon Scieszka. Then ask them to write a short response to this question: *How does what Scieszka says about himself fit with the picture you had of the author of* The Frog Prince Continued? Encourage students to be specific and to use details from both the story and the interview to support their point of view. Invite students to share their responses with each other.

FOCUS ON THE WRITER

Here's the answer to the last question on page 107. Read what Jon Scieszka (shown left) says about himself.

Response Notes

I read everything — comic books, newspapers, cereal boxes, poems — anything with writing on it. My favorite things to read are fairy tales, myths, and legends. When I'm not reading, I listen to music, watch cartoons, and sit in my chair and just think about stuff. I've always thought about being an author. One of the first books I read was *Green Eggs and Ham,* by Dr. Seuss. It made me realize that books could be goofy. It's the book that made *The Stinky Cheese Man* possible!

My ideas come from all different things: my kids, kids I've taught, kids I've learned from, watching movies, playing with my cat, talking to my wife, staring out the window, and about a million other places. But what turns the ideas into stories and books is sitting down and writing and re-writing and throwing away writing and writing some more. That's the hard part. I never know exactly how long it takes to write a story. I read a lot of stuff, think about different stories all the time, scribble things down on paper, type them up, change them, scribble again, think some more, add things....

I write books because I love to make kids laugh. I knew Lane Smith (illustrator of *The True Story of the Three Little Pigs!, The Stinky Cheese Man* and *Squids Will Be Squids*) would do a great job because we like a lot of the same cartoons and books and ideas. And we laugh at each other's bad jokes all of the time. Our audience is hardcore silly kids, and there are a lot of 'em out there! My motto in writing is: "Never underestimate the intelligence of your audience." Kids can be silly *and* smart!

Before I became an author, I attended military school, studied pre-med in college, and worked as a lifeguard and house painter. I also taught computers, math, science, and history to kids grades 1-8.

I now live in Brooklyn, N.Y., with my wife Jeri, daughter Casey and my son Jake. I like fruit and a cup of coffee for breakfast, but I usually steal some of Jake's Honey Nut Cheerios or his pancakes. If you'd like to call out my name, it's pronounced "SHEH-ska." It kind of rhymes with Fresca.

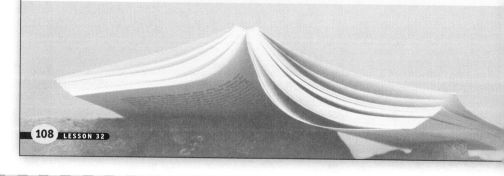

MAKE CONNECTIONS: WRITE YOUR OWN BIOGRAPHY

✳ If you grow up to be a writer, what sort of thing would you write? You might begin by thinking of what you like to read, like Jon Scieszka does in his biography. Imagine that you are grown up and have published something (you decide what). Now write your own biography of how you came to write the kind of thing you do (be specific here). Tell what kind of person you are, using Jon Scieszka's biography as an inspiration. You might even want to illustrate it with a comical self-portrait.

_____

_____

_____

_____

_____

_____

_____

_____

_____

_____

_____

_____

_____

_____

After you have finished, share your writing with your group or the whole class.

Writers are drawn to the possibilities of rewriting or continuing fairy tales, often in a humorous mode.

WRITING SUPPORT

Voice Tell students that *voice* is the author's way of revealing who he or she is. In the interview with Jon Scieszka, it's his voice, or what he says and the tone in which he says it, that gives you a clue to his personality. As students write their autobiographical sketches, encourage them to find the voice of the adult version of themselves. Students should think about the type of person they might grow up to be. Will they be serious? Silly? Dignified? Dedicated to a cause? Fun and friendly? When they write their response to the prompt on page 109, have them use voice to convey the type of person they would be as an adult author. Allow time in class for students to share their "autobiographical" sketches.

Quick Assess

✳ Were they able to make connections between the author and his work?

✳ Were students able to write an "autobiographical" sketch that conveyed an adult version of themselves?

After

WRITING A FRACTURED FAIRY TALE

Ask students to select a fairy tale with which they are familiar and write their own parody, or "fractured fairy tale." Students can work individually or with a partner. You may want to find other examples of humorous versions of well-known fairy tales, such as Scieszka's *The True Story of the Three Little Pigs,* for students to use as models.

Collect students' versions and make a class Fractured Fairy Tales book.

Students will explore another perspective on the Frog Prince tale.

BACKGROUND KNOWLEDGE

Share the information in About the Author on page 111 with students. Remind students that some poems, such as the one in this lesson, have layers of images and themes that require reading and rereading to understand completely. Talk with students about, the use of imagery and themes in other poems they have read in class. Tell students that, as they read, they should think about what the poet is saying in "Annunciation."

VOCABULARY

annunciation an archaic term for the act of announcing; usually refers to the biblical announcement to Mary that she was going to bear Jesus

bulbous rounded, bulb-shaped

Wittgenstein Ludwig Josef Johan Wittgenstein, an Austrian-born British philosopher of the early 20th century

Homer ancient Greek poet credited with writing *The Iliad* and *The Odyssey*

metamorphosizes transforms, changes into a different form

Study the vocabulary with students after they have read the poem once.

Poets, as well as fiction writers, have been intrigued by "The Frog Prince." This is a version of the frog-and-prince story in a poem called "Annunciation" by Adrianne Marcus, who presents another perspective. It closely follows many of the elements of the Grimm brothers' story. It introduces new elements as well, and the last stanza may give you pause as you consider the question it asks.

In the **Response Notes** column, note your comments about elements that are the same as in the classic version and those that are different. It will help to color code the parts of the poem that refer to classic and new.

Response Notes

Wittgenstein is a 20th century philosopher. Homer was a ninth century B.C. Greek writer.

Annunciation by Adrianne Marcus

Disgusting, she thought, as she stroked
that damp green back, noted the fragile
front legs, the muscular thighs. Still, she
had given her word. After all it was her
favorite golden ball, and she had to have
it back He cocked his head, winsomely,
staring at her with bulbous eyes, and his
tongue flicked out, once, then twice.

Revolting, she thought, this stupid bargain
With a talking frog; and talk he did.
Reminded her constantly of promises
made, as he ate off her golden plate,
slept in her bed on the finest Egyptian
linens. By dawn, he was gone, and
she thought that was the end of it.

Unimaginable, she said, when he reappeared
that night, and the next, but by then
she was used to him, and found he could
discuss Wittgenstein, knew a bit of Homer
and offered to help her with her lessons.
By now, his skin felt soft beneath her hand,
his eyes a delicate mixture of hazel and gold,
his forked tongue intriguing.

Before

CRITICAL READING SKILL
Exploring Multiple Perspectives
Briefly review how one's understanding of a story or a situation becomes more complete by considering multiple viewpoints. Have students use what they know about exploring multiple perspectives to compare Adrianne Marcus's views with those of the Brothers Grimm and Jon Scieszka.

RESPONSE NOTES Encourage students to characterize the narrator's opinion toward the frog at the beginning of each stanza.

Fate has a curious way of taking us at
our word, and sometimes the frog
metamorphoses into a handsome
prince and sometimes
he doesn't. Which would you pick?
Remember: the bargain is forever. ❖

Use your **Response Notes** to compare which elements are the same
in both versions and which elements are new in Marcus's poem.

Elements in classic version	New elements

✳ Focus on the last stanza. What do you think Adrianne Marcus
means, especially in the last line? Is the bargain forever,
or isn't it?

Think about the versions of "The Frog Prince" you have read. Make
some notes about these statements:

- Since the frog is an animal that "transforms" itself as it grows
  from a tadpole to a frog, it is a natural for a story about transformation or adopting another persona.
- The idea of transformation underlies a lot of fairy tales and
  myths. In your group, think of some stories or myths you know
  that involve transformations.

Writers get ideas from
looking at familiar stories from
a different perspective.

EXPLORE MULTIPLE PERSPECTIVES **111**

ABOUT THE AUTHOR
Adrianne Marcus is a poet, journalist, food-and-travel writer, and fiction
writer. She wrote her first poem at
age 8 and saw it published in the
Raleigh News and Observer in North
Carolina. Since then, she has published
a number of books of poetry and has
had over 400 poems published in
various magazines and journals. At
home, she lives with her husband, the
futurist and writer Ian Wilson, and her
menagerie, composed of two borzoi
and four silken windhounds. Her latest
chapbook of poems, *Magritte's Stones*,
is dedicated to the memory of her
beloved wolf-hybrid, Lady Macbeth.

Quick Assess

✳ Were students able to distinguish
between the classic and the new
aspects of the Frog Prince tale in
"Annunciation"?

✳ Did students fill out the comparison
chart accurately?

During

COMPARISON CHART   This chart
will provide a comparison of the Brothers Grimm version of the Frog Prince tale
with Adrianne Marcus's "Annunciation."
As students compare the versions, have
them look for elements Marcus kept from
the original, added to the original, and
changed from the original.

You may want students to work with in
groups to complete the chart, since it
demands a detailed comparison of the
selections. Groups can record all their
ideas in their charts.

After

LITERATURE RESPONSE   Ask students to think about how the narrator's
attitude changes. Have them think about
other stories they've read or movies
they've seen in which revulsion turns to
attraction, such as "Beauty and the Beast"
or the Cyrano de Bergerac story. Ask:
*Do you think it's possible for someone to
change from being repulsed by a person to
falling in love with that person? Why?*

Students will show what they have learned by writing to a prompt.

BACKGROUND KNOWLEDGE

The writing assignment in this lesson is a way for you to see what students have internalized about the five essential strategies (Interacting with the Text, Making Connections, Exploring Multiple Perspectives, Focusing on Language and Craft, and Studying an Author) as well as the content of this final unit.

This lesson focuses on selecting a topic, the prewriting stage of the writing process. Students need to understand that they should choose the topic that interests them the most and about which they can write the most. At the end of the lesson students will write their drafts. The following lesson focuses on revision. Suggest that students look ahead to the expectations on page 113 as they plan their writing.

Quick Assess

✳ Do students understand the importance of transformation in the different versions of the Frog Prince story?

✳ Were students able to choose a topic for their writing assessment?

You have now had experience in using all of the essential strategies of reading and writing together in one unit. Using what you have learned in all of the units so far, we want you to demonstrate your best thinking in both reading and writing.

You have three choices for your writing assignment. Choose one. Think about the topic you will write about. What will be your main idea? What are your supporting details? Create a concept web below. Then write a draft of from one to three pages of regular notebook paper.

Choice 1: Think about how people feel free from their own limitations when wearing masks. Consider the positive and negative aspects of adopting another persona. Use examples from your own experience as well as from your reading when you write to this prompt. Refer to "The Frog Prince" in your paper.

Choice 2: Write about the idea of transformation in fairy tales, myths, or stories you have read or watched (television and movies are okay here). Refer to "The Frog Prince" in your paper.

Choice 3: Think about what you have read in this unit, the original classic version of "The Frog Prince" and adaptations. Now write your own adaptation. You may write a continuation, a poem, a story, or even a comic book version.

✳ Write the number of your choice here: _____

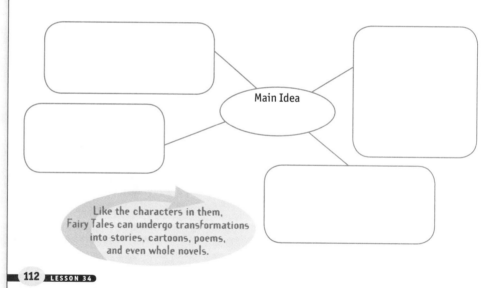

Main Idea

Like the characters in them, Fairy Tales can undergo transformations into stories, cartoons, poems, and even whole novels.

Before

CRITICAL WRITING SKILL

Choosing a Topic Read aloud each choice on page 112 and discuss with students any questions they may have. Tell students to make a few notes or to use a graphic organizer, such as a cluster, to brainstorm what they might say about each one. Students should select the choice about which they have the most to say and/or feel most strongly.

During

WRITING PROCESS As students work on their first drafts, remind them not to get bogged down in the details. Instruct them to make quick notes about parts of the draft they want to go back to and refine later but not to try to resolve all the details now.

After

CONFERENCING Move from desk to desk to conference briefly with students as they continue to work on their drafts in order to check in on their progress, help them move forward when they are stuck, and encourage thoughtful writing.

SHARING YOUR FIRST DRAFT WITH YOUR PARTNER OR GROUP

✻ Meet with a partner or a group to share the first draft of your paper. Before you read each other's papers, we think it is important for you to know what your teacher will look for when he or she reads your story.

An outstanding story will

✻ respond directly to one of the three prompts.

✻ show your understanding of the basic elements of "The Frog Prince."

✻ show how well you are able to
- organize your ideas
- write clear sentences that flow when read aloud
- make good word choices (specific nouns, vivid verbs)
- spell words correctly
- punctuate and capitalize correctly

✻ Read your paper aloud to a partner or members of a small group. When you read your paper, the other members should listen carefully. When each person finishes reading, the other members should tell the writer what they liked about the paper. Then they should use the items in the box to help the reader improve.

✻ As your group talks about your paper, make notes so that when you revise it, you will remember what they suggested.

MAKING A FINAL COPY

✻ Using the suggestions of your group, make the revisions you think will improve your paper. Then make a clean copy of your final draft. Remember to give it a title.

Students will revise their writing and reflect on what they've read and learned in the *Daybook*.

BACKGROUND KNOWLEDGE

It is important to establish the criteria for evaluation before students begin revising their papers. Go over these criteria for an outstanding paper.

✻ Respond directly to the prompt

✻ Show an understanding of the basic elements of the Frog Prince tales

✻ Show how well the student is able to
- organize ideas;
- write sentences that flow when read aloud;
- make effective word choices (specific nouns, vivid verbs);
- punctuate, capitalize, and spell correctly.

Before

CRITICAL WRITING SKILL

Revising Discuss with students how good writers review their drafts to see how they can improve their writing. They often invite feedback from other people to get another viewpoint of how effective their writing is. Tell students that they are now going to improve the drafts they created at the end of Lesson 34 to finalize their papers.

During

REVISING Give students a chance to review their drafts against the criteria on page 113 before they share their work with someone else. Allow students to make notes or to revise their drafts before they invite others to give feedback. Then have students meet with a partner or in a group of no more than four to discuss the paper and invite feedback on ways to make the paper even better.

Once students have revised their papers, they should make a final copy, making sure to give it a title.

Using a Graphic Organizer: Self-Assessment Chart This chart helps students guide their reflections on the reading and writing strategies they have learned so far in the *Daybook*. Help students understand that this is a chance for them to honestly evaluate the progress that they've made in their work this year. It also gives them a chance to set goals for areas in which they would like to improve. Encourage students to focus on the positive, both in their evaluation of their progress as well as in their goals for the future. If students are having trouble with their evaluations, work with them to come up with specific examples of ways in which they've improved and what they'd like to focus on in the future. For example, ask: *Give an example of how you interacted with the text in one of the selections in this unit. What would you like to work on in the future for this strategy?*

REFLECTION

It is important to stop periodically and reflect on what you are learning. Then you can evaluate where you need to go from here. Fill in the chart. Then write about how you have improved as a reader and writer.

Essential Strategies of Reading and Writing	How I rate myself at the beginning of the *Daybook*		How I rate myself now	
	5=High, 1=Low	Comments	5=High, 1=Low	Comments
Example: Interacting with the text	2	*I didn't know how to annotate or ask questions.*	4	*I'm pretty good at it now.*
Interacting with the text				
Making connections				
Exploring multiple perspectives				
Focusing on language and craft				
Studying an author				

Reflecting is an important part of learning how to strengthen your reading and writing skills.

After

RESEARCHING FOLKTALES

Students can read a variety of folktales from various cultures that deal with the issue of how people perceive others, the use of disguises or differing personas to conceal one's true identity, or transformation. Have them report to the class on the examples they've found and how they tie in with the themes found in these different versions of the Frog Prince story.

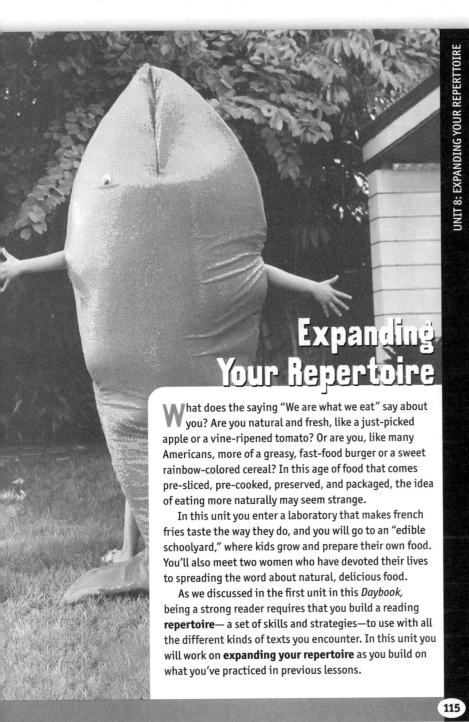

UNIT 8
EXPANDING YOUR REPERTOIRE

UNIT OVERVIEW

By reading texts about food, students will strengthen the basic strategies they have learned.

KEY IDEA

Good readers examine challenging nonfiction texts in multiple ways in order to deepen their understanding of the subject matter.

CRITICAL READING SKILLS

by lesson

36 Interacting with the text

37 Making connections

38 Exploring multiple perspectives

39 Focusing on language and craft

40 Studying an author

WRITING ACTIVITIES

by lesson

36 Write a summary of a nonfiction excerpt.

37 Write a personal essay.

38 Write a paragraph that considers a perspective other than that of the author.

39 Fill in a chart about an author's stylistic techniques.

40 Write a speech.

Expanding Your Repertoire

What does the saying "We are what we eat" say about you? Are you natural and fresh, like a just-picked apple or a vine-ripened tomato? Or are you, like many Americans, more of a greasy, fast-food burger or a sweet rainbow-colored cereal? In this age of food that comes pre-sliced, pre-cooked, preserved, and packaged, the idea of eating more naturally may seem strange.

In this unit you enter a laboratory that makes french fries taste the way they do, and you will go to an "edible schoolyard," where kids grow and prepare their own food. You'll also meet two women who have devoted their lives to spreading the word about natural, delicious food.

As we discussed in the first unit in this *Daybook,* being a strong reader requires that you build a reading **repertoire**— a set of skills and strategies—to use with all the different kinds of texts you encounter. In this unit you will work on **expanding your repertoire** as you build on what you've practiced in previous lessons.

115

Literature

- *Fast Food Nation* by Eric Schlosser (nonfiction excerpt)

In this investigative account of the fast food industry, the author describes the mass production of french fries.

- *"Food Fighter"* by Peggy Orenstein (newspaper article excerpt)

A journalist observes middle school students and a program that teaches them to grow and cook their own food.

- *"Alice Waters"* by Ruth Reichl (nonfiction excerpt)

An expert food writer profiles this restaurateur and activist who wants to change the way that young people eat.

- *"A Taste for Life"* by Jeffrey L. Perlah (interview excerpt)

An interview with Ruth Reichl reveals why food fascinates her and how it has motivated her writing career.

ASSESSMENT See page 237 for a writing prompt based on this unit.

Students will learn about metacognitive awareness and how it can help them interact with and understand challenging texts.

BACKGROUND KNOWLEDGE

Ask students if they are familiar with any controversy about fast food. For example: *What if you ate fast food for every meal, every day?* Explain that, because Americans have come to rely on the convenience of fast food, there is concern about its health effects.

Then post the word *investigate* and ask students to define it. Explain that when a writer investigates a topic, he or she looks for facts in order to figure out the significance of the topic. Tell students that they will read an excerpt from a book that investigates the fast food industry to find out why it is quick, inexpensive, and loved by so many people.

VOCABULARY

blanched parboiled or scalded food before freezing to keep the food from spoiling

centrifugal moving or directed away from the center

Use the Word Splash blackline master on page 278 to preview the selection vocabulary.

When you read, what goes on in your head? If you're really engaged with what you're reading, there is a whole lot going on in there. You are **interacting with the text.** Being aware of what goes on in your head is called *metacognitive awareness. Metacognitive* means "thinking about what's going on in your mind."

Think about the ways you interact with texts that really engage you. Some common ways to interact with texts are these:

- Take notes, highlight, or circle words or phrases.
- Visualize, or picture, what is going on.
- Ask questions or wonder about things you read.
- "Talk back" to the author or characters.
- Pause to think or gather information from a dictionary or another person.

Even if you are a very strong reader, you may find some texts challenging. It could be that you are distracted and have something else on your mind. It could be that the topic is new, complex, or not particularly interesting to you. Or it could be that the writing is challenging, using sophisticated words and complicated sentences. A good way to tackle a challenging text is to practice *metacognitive awareness* and to interact with it as much as possible.

The selection below is an excerpt from a nonfiction book about the author's investigation of the fast food industry. As you read it, practice *metacognitive awareness.* In the **Response Notes** column, record what you are thinking about as you read.

from **Fast Food Nation** by Eric Schlosser

Response Notes

Bud Mandeville, the plant manager, led me up a narrow, wooden staircase inside one of the plant's storage buildings. On the top floor, the staircase led to a catwalk, and beneath my feet I saw a mound of potatoes that was twenty feet deep and a hundred feet wide and almost as long as two football fields. The building was cool and dark, kept year-round at a steady 46 degrees. In the dim light the potatoes looked like grains of sand on a beach. This was one of seven storage buildings on the property.

Outside, tractor-trailers arrived from the fields, carrying potatoes that had just been harvested. The trucks dumped their loads onto spinning rods that brought the larger potatoes into the building and let the small potatoes, dirt, and

---

Before

CRITICAL READING SKILL

Interacting with the Text Read aloud or ask a volunteer to read aloud the first two introductory paragraphs. Then explain *metacognition,* or "thinking about what you're thinking." Then say: *When you're reading and you're thinking about whether or not you understand what you are reading, you are practicing* metacognitive awareness.

Explain that one way to be aware of how you're reading is to interact with the text. Then review the bulleted list of strategies with students. For each strategy, ask volunteers to tell when and how they have used it. For example: *I highlight phrases that I don't understand so I can think about them later, or I make a movie in my mind to visualize what is going on.*

RESPONSE NOTES Read aloud or ask a volunteer to read aloud the first paragraph of the excerpt. Then model a few interactions with the text. For example:

✻ Sketch or use a think-aloud to visualize the french fry factory.

✻ Ask a question, such as: *What is so important about the way french fries are made?*

rocks fall to the ground. The rods led to a rock trap, a tank of water in which the potatoes floated and the rocks sank to the bottom. The plant used water systems to float potatoes gently this way and that way, guiding different sizes out of different holding bays, then flushing them into a three-foot-deep stream that ran beneath the cement floor. The interior of the processing plant was gray, massive, and well-lit, with huge pipes running along the walks, steel catwalks, workers in hardhats, and plenty of loud machinery. If there weren't potatoes bobbing and floating past, you might think the place was an oil refinery.

Conveyer belts took the wet, clean potatoes into a machine that blasted them with steam for twelve seconds, boiled the water under their skins, and exploded their skins off. Then the potatoes were pumped into a preheat tank and shot through a Lamb Water Gun Knife. They emerged as shoestring fries. Four video cameras scrutinized them from different angles, looking for flaws. When a french fry with a blemish was detected, an optical sorting machine time-sequenced a single burst of compressed air that knocked the bad fry off the production line and onto a separate conveyer belt, which carried it to a machine with tiny automated knives that precisely removed the blemish. And then the fry was returned to the main production line.

Sprays of hot water blanched the fries, gusts of hot air dried them, and 25,000 pounds of boiling oil friend them to a slight crisp. Air cooled by compressed ammonia gas quickly froze them, a computerized sorter divided them into six-pound batches, and a device that spun like an out-of-control lazy Susan used centrifugal force to align the french fries so that they all pointed in the same directions. The fries were sealed in brown bags, then the bags were loaded by robots into cardboard boxes, and the boxes were stacked by robots onto wooden pallets. Forklifts driven by human beings took the pallets to a freezer for storage. Inside that freezer I saw 20 million pounds of french fries. . . . ❖

✳ Take a moment to think about what went on in your head as you read, and add comments to your **Response Notes.**

ABOUT THE AUTHOR
Eric Schlosser was born in New York City in 1959. At Princeton University, he studied history while engaging in many writing activities, including playwriting, journalism, and humor. Schlosser turned to journalism full-time and wrote for the *Atlantic Monthly* as well as other publications. After receiving an assignment from *Rolling Stone* to write about the fast food industry, Schlosser took his investigation to deeper levels and penned *Fast Food Nation*. The book was a bestseller for two years and has been translated into twenty languages. Schlosser currently lives in northern California.

EXTRA SUPPORT
Differentiation If a student seems to be having difficulty interacting with the text, consider reading aloud another paragraph, modeling your own interactions. Then, have the student read the next paragraph and note his or her interactions, or you may ask questions to prompt the student's thinking. For example: *What did you picture as you read? Did you already know some of the information? Were you surprised by anything you read?*

During

Ask students to continue making Response Notes. See also page 229 for tips on marking text.

MONITORING UNDERSTANDING
Read aloud the discussion prompt and use questions and statements such as the following to help students monitor their comprehension of the excerpt:

✳ *Tell me what this section was about.*

✳ *Did the text make sense? What can you do if it didn't?*

✳ *Which parts of the excerpt tell about something familiar to you?*

Gauge the responses students are making, offering extra support when necessary.

WRITING SUPPORT

Topic and Main Idea One way to know that you understand what you have read is to be able to summarize it. In order to summarize, students must be able to identify the topic and main ideas. Review that a topic is a subject and the specific point the author makes about it. Review that a main idea is an important point that the author shares about the topic.

1. Sketch the shape of an open hand, Write the topic of the excerpt on the palm.

2. On the fingers, write the main ideas.

3. Use the topic and main ideas from the graphic organizer to write a summary.

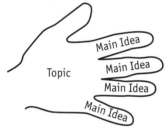

Quick Assess

✳ Were students able to identify a main idea in each paragraph?

✳ Did students use the main ideas to summarize the article?

It is always nice to be able to make sense of everything we read. In reality, though, we better understand some texts and find them more meaningful than others. How hard you work to understand details depends on your purpose for reading. Sometimes, it may be enough to just determine the main point of each paragraph. Other times, every little detail matters.

✳ Imagine that you read the selection above because your friend told you it was interesting. And, you love french fries, so you're curious what it says. In that case, you might decide to read just for the main point of each paragraph. If you missed some details here and there, it would not matter. In the space that follows, explain the main idea of each paragraph.

Paragraph 1: _____

Paragraph 2: _____

Paragraph 3: _____

Paragraph 4: _____

✳ Now imagine that you read the selection because you are writing an article on fast food for your school newspaper. It's important that you get your facts straight. Summarize, in detail and in your own words, what you read.

_____
_____
_____
_____
_____
_____
_____
_____
_____

> Using metacognitive awareness helps you to interact with and understand challenging texts.

After

APPLYING THE STRATEGY Invite students to practice metacognitive awareness when reading more challenging texts.

✳ Ask: *Have you ever seen a book or article that interested you, but you thought it might be too difficult for you to read?* Invite them to choose this kind of book or online article.

✳ Have students attempt to read the text, using the interactive strategies listed on page 116. Encourage them to use self-stick notes to record interactions.

✳ Check in with students after they have read a few pages. Ask: *How challenging was the text? What did you do when you got stuck? Would you feel more comfortable choosing this kind of book or article now?*

FURTHER RESEARCH Explaining that food is the theme of this unit, invite students to create and conduct polls about their peers' eating habits. Poll questions can be written by groups or as a class. Potential questions include: how often they eat french fries, why they like them, and what ingredients they think are in french fries. After students survey their peers, have them compare the results with what they learned from the text.

I n this lesson, you will practice **making connections** with another piece of nonfiction. You might make connections to yourself, to other things you have read, to other things you have learned or know about, or even to the selection in the previous lesson.

In *Fast Food Nation,* Eric Schlosser explains that most processed food is made so that it can be kept and transported easily, such as by picking vegetables or fruits that are not yet ripe or by freezing or dehydrating food. These processes often make the food tasteless. To make up for this, food processing companies such as fast food restaurant chains hire scientists to create flavors that enhance the taste of the food. In the following excerpt, Schlosser visits one of the "flavor labs" in which these flavors are created. A flavorist (a scientist who creates the artificial and "natural" flavors) lets Schlosser smell some of the aromas he has created.

While you read, practice *metacognitive awareness*. Remember to read slowly, pause when you need to, and reread any parts that are unclear. Ask yourself, what do I already know about this topic or these words? What does this remind me of? When you make a connection, write it in the **Response Notes** column.

from Fast Food Nation by Eric Schlosser

…The flavor industry is highly secretive. Its leading companies will not divulge the precise formulas or flavor compounds or the identities of clients. The secrecy is deemed essential for protecting the reputation of beloved brands. The fast food chains, understandably, would like the public to believe that the flavors of their food somehow originate in their restaurant kitchens, not in distant factories run by other firms.

…Grainger [a flavorist] had brought a dozen small glass bottles from the lab. After he opened each bottle, I dipped a fragrance testing filter into it. The filters were long white strips of paper designed to absorb aroma chemicals without producing off-notes. Before placing the strips of paper before my nose, I closed my eyes. Then I inhaled deeply, and one food after another was conjured from the glass bottles. I smelled fresh cherries, black olives, sautéed onions, and shrimp. Grainger's most remarkable creation took me by surprise. After closing my eyes, I suddenly smelled a grilled hamburger. The aroma was uncanny, almost miraculous. It smelled like someone in the room was flipping burgers on a hot grill. But when I opened my eyes, there was just a narrow strip of white paper and a smiling flavorist. ✥

Response Notes

MAKING CONNECTIONS 119

S tudents will learn that making personal connections can help them understand the main idea of a text.

BACKGROUND KNOWLEDGE

Ask students to review the main points from the Lesson 36. Then explain that students will read a continuation of the previous excerpt. This time, the focus will be on manufactured food flavorings. To prepare students for the reading, you may want to have them sample a fresh piece of fruit, along with similarly flavored candy. Ask students: *How does each one taste? Do they taste alike? Which do you like better?*

VOCABULARY

off-notes unintended aromas

conjure to bring about as if by magic

uncanny so amazing as to be almost frightening

Ask questions to check students' understanding. For example:

✲ When food manufacturers use flavorings, what are they trying to *conjure* for you?

✲ Would the smell of skunk be an *off-note* to the scent of an apple?

✲ If something is *uncanny,* does it surprise you?

Before

CRITICAL READING SKILL

Making Connections With students, brainstorm types of texts that are easy or challenging to read. For example, a teen magazine might be easy to read, while an in-depth newspaper editorial about an unfamiliar issue might be challenging.

Then, explain the value of connecting to text. Say: *Often, when we read something that seems really hard, we don't understand it because we can't relate to*

it. Making connections is a way to get the most out of reading something.

Read aloud or have a volunteer read aloud the introductory paragraphs. Then, because the excerpt on page 119 is challenging, you may wish to read it aloud before having students respond. Remind students to be aware of whether they are connecting to the text by asking themselves questions such as these:

✲ How does this relate to the previous lesson?

✲ How do I feel about the information in these excerpts?

✲ How does the information affect me?

Collaboration Have students use the Think-Pair-Share method to compare response notes. Students should compare responses per the prompt at the top of the page. Then, have each pair share a connection one of the students made, and discuss whether or not their connections were similar in front of the class.

WRITING SUPPORT

Making Personal Connections
Explain the third writing prompt. Say: *Now that we've talked about what the author thinks of fast food, it's time for you to say what you think.* Ask questions to help students:

✳ *Does this information matter to you? Why or why not?*

✳ *After reading this, will you eat fast food more often, less often, or as often as you did before?*

Emphasize that students don't have to agree with Schlosser's point of view. Rather, they should form opinions based on the information given and their own background knowledge.

✳ Compare your **Response Notes** with those of a partner. Were your connections similar? Discuss them.

✳ How do your connections help you to understand the text better?

✳ How would you describe the main idea of the excerpts you have read from *Fast Food Nation*? In other words, what do you think is the main point, or the key idea, Eric Schlosser is trying to share with you?

Share your response with your partner. Did you have similar ideas? Discuss why each of you chose the main idea you did.

✳ To make a connection with your own life, consider how what you read could influence your consumption of fast food. Use the space below to list ideas for a personal essay on how you feel about eating fast food. Remember that the beginning of the essay should state your main idea. The middle should expand the idea and present examples and details. The end should restate the focus and make a final statement.

Main idea: _____

Details: _____

_____

_____

Final idea: _____

During

WRITING SUPPORT

Evaluating Explain that, for the first writing prompt, students should write a few sentences to evaluate the process of making connections to the text. Pose these questions to spark students' ideas:

✳ *Did you make connections to the text? If so, how? If not, why not?*

✳ *What connections are most interesting?*

WRITING SUPPORT

Main Idea For the second writing prompt, help students arrive at an overarching connection between the *Fast Food Nation* excerpts. Ask:

✳ *What was the main idea of the previous excerpt?*

✳ *Currently, there is concern over the relationship between heart disease and the*

typical American diet. How is the topic of the production of fast food relevant to this issue?

✳ *By writing about french fry factories and manufactured flavorings, what do you think Schlosser wants you to think about or consider?*

_____

Title

_____
_____
_____
_____
_____
_____
_____
_____
_____
_____
_____
_____
_____
_____
_____
_____
_____
_____
_____
_____
_____
_____
_____
_____
_____
_____
_____

Making personal connections with nonfiction can help you understand the main idea.

WRITING SUPPORT

Organization An important trait of effective writing is organization. The way a writer organizes information determines how well the message will be conveyed to the audience. Review the characteristics of the basic sections of an essay.

✳ A beginning that clearly states their opinion

✳ A middle in which they give reasons for their opinion, including examples that support it. Ask: *What are the reasons for your opinion? What information are you considering?* Also encourage students to use their own experiences to support their opinion

✳ An end that gives implications from the evidence

Quick Assess

Do students' essays

✳ state an opinion about fast food?

✳ contain support for their opinion, such as reasons and examples from the text and their own background knowledge?

✳ have logical organization, with their opinion clearly stated in the beginning and end?

After

READING/WRITING CONNECTION

Invite students to review their personal essays in a writing workshop group. After students revise their essays, you may have them read the essays aloud and/or add artwork to illustrate their point of view. Students can display their finished essays in the school cafeteria or other public place.

FURTHER RESEARCH Introduce the term *muckraking:* a journalistic or literary work that exposes an industry. Explain that, as a result of their writing, muckraking writers have been able to change the way people think. Have students research a famous muckraker, such as Ida Tarbell, Upton Sinclair, or Rachel Carson. Students should find out

✳ what the writer wrote about;

✳ what issues they brought to the public's attention;

✳ what, if any, changes their work brought about (such as laws or regulations).

Have students report their findings to a group or the class.

Students will learn how to examine multiple perspectives in order to better understand all the sides of the argument in a nonfiction text.

BACKGROUND KNOWLEDGE

Ask students: *Has anyone ever urged you to eat more fresh foods instead of "junk food"?* Allow students to relate their experiences.

Explain that in a middle school in Berkeley, a city on the eastern side of the San Francisco Bay, students learn to grow and cook the food they eat.

VOCABULARY

lolling reclining in a relaxed way

foodie's mecca a place where people who love food find many good restaurants and food shops

humanities school subjects of English, history, and social studies

sustainable not permanently removing resources from the environment

restaurateur restaurant owner

impolitic socially unwise

pragmatism practicality

furrowed wrinkled

Have pairs of students each research one word and teach it to the class.

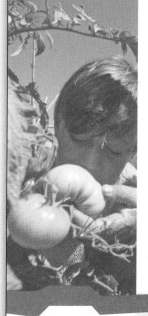

Imagine that you accompany a newspaper reporter on a visit to a middle school in Berkeley, California. The school is famous for its schoolyard, which has been turned into a garden that is cared for by students as part of their schoolwork. A famous restaurant owner, Alice Waters, started the project. You plan to write an article about it for your school newspaper, and the other reporter, Peggy Orenstein, is writing an article for the *New York Times*. Even though you are writing about the same topic, you and Ms. Orenstein will write different articles. This is because no two people have the exact same perspective. You see and feel and respond to things differently.

When you read nonfiction, examine the **perspective** from which it is written. Even though it is factual, the writer's perspective influences what facts are included and how the story gets told. After all, what is important and interesting to one person isn't always the same for another.

The selection you are about to read is an excerpt from a *New York Times* article about the Edible Schoolyard at Martin Luther King Junior Middle School in Berkeley, California. As you read, try to discover the author's perspective. Record your thoughts in the **Response Notes** column. An example is written for you.

from "Food Fighter" by Peggy Orenstein

Response Notes

It sounds like the author thinks the kids eat really badly!

As students from King whirled around, flirting, playing basketball, lolling on the grass, I asked a few of them what they had eaten the previous day. A sixth-grade girl could recall only that she had two doughnuts for breakfast and half a sandwich and candy for lunch. An eighth-grade girl skipped breakfast and lunch altogether and had a soda after school, followed by a sandwich for dinner. The boys ate more consistently, but the nutritional content was not much better. Burgers or pizza for lunch. Lots of chicken for dinner. Vegetables beyond carrots or corn were scarce, unless ketchup counts. The closest thing to fruit for many was a bag of fruit-flavored candy. Only two children had eaten balanced meals within 24 hours. This in a town renowned as a foodie's mecca. Nationally, a third of children eat fast food for at least one meal a day.

... One morning last year, I wandered through the Edible Schoolyard garden reading the student-painted signs for roses, spearmint, grapes, strawberries, fig trees, onions, poppies. The sixth and seventh graders spend 10 weekly 90-minute sessions here as part of their science curriculum and an equal

Before

CRITICAL READING SKILL
Exploring Multiple Perspectives

Define or review *perspective*: the way someone views something. To illustrate the concept, you may want to ask several students to relate their experience of a recently shared event, such as a school assembly. Ask: *What did you see? What did you think of it?* Compare students'

responses, explaining that there are differences because everyone has a unique perspective and interpretation of events.

RESPONSE NOTES Explain that this article is written from the perspective of an adult writer who interviews adolescents about what they eat and observes them in the Edible Schoolyard program. Say: *While you're reading, see if you can*

tell what the author is thinking. Direct students to the sample Response Note as an example of noticing an author's perspective.

Remind students to use the interactive strategies they learned in Lesson 36 to draw information about the author's perspective.

amount of time in the kitchen with their humanities classes. The eighth graders visit each venue about six times a year.

Kelsey Siegel, who works as garden manager, listed the tasks of the day: the students could choose to help build a bench using a sustainable cement mixture of clay and straw. Or they could plant mustard greens or radish seedlings. Or weed the garlic. As a special treat, they also got to make pizza in an outdoor wood-burning stone oven, built by a friend of [restaurateur Alice] Waters's.

Within a few minutes, the students had scattered. By the pizza oven one group rolled out a cornmeal crust, brushed it with a layer of garlic-infused olive oil and sprinkled the top with feta cheese, spring onions, chard, rosemary and mint. "This cheese smells like feet!" announced a compact boy in a red fleece pullover. Then, realizing he'd been impolitic, he added, "I guess it's a good way to eat if you want to be organic and vegetarian."

As I walked back to the kitchen, I bumped into Waters and [Edible Schoolyard program coordinator Marsha] Guerrero. "What did they think of the pizza?" Waters asked expectantly. Before I could reply, Guerrero, the voice of pragmatism, jumped in. "They hated the cheese, didn't they?" Waters furrowed her brow a moment, then brightened. "If the kids think feta is weird, why not have them make their own fresh mozzarella? It's the easiest thing in the world."

…Waters is onto something: teaching about new foods, emphasizing participation and offering choices are all critical to nudging children toward better diets.

ABOUT THE AUTHOR

Peggy Orenstein was born in Minneapolis, Minnesota. She graduated from Oberlin College in Ohio and has written for many national publications, including *The New York Times, The Los Angeles Times,* and the *New Yorker.* In 1995, Orenstein published *Schoolgirls: Young Women, Self Esteem, and the Confidence Gap,* the result of research she did on middle school students. She lives in San Francisco, California.

EXTRA SUPPORT

Differentiation If students seem to have difficulty making inferences about Orenstein's perspective, have them answer these questions:

❉ *How does the author describe the program?*

❉ *Does she use positive or negative words or phrases?*

❉ *Does she present multiple viewpoints—that is, both the positive and negative aspects of the topic?*

❉ How does the author seem to feel about the Edible Schoolyard project?

❉ What evidence from the story suggests that is her perspective?

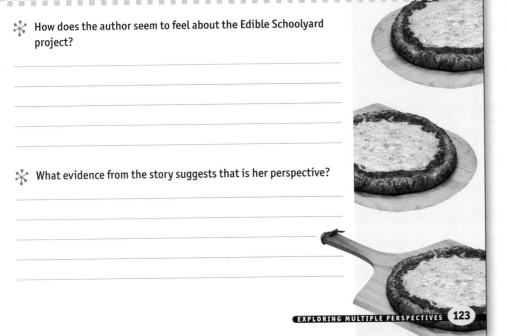

During

MONITORING UNDERSTANDING
Before students complete the writing prompts, discuss Orenstein's perspective. Ask:

❉ *What do you think is the author's opinion of the Edible Schoolyard project?*

❉ *Which parts of the article make you think so?*

Model how to find clues to Orenstein's perspective. For example, in the last paragraph, she states that *Waters is onto something* and that the program could be *nudging children toward better diets.*

WRITER'S CRAFT   Word Choice
Remind students that an author can achieve a stronger impact by showing rather than telling. Including the quotation of the boy who tries the pizza *(This cheese smells like feet!)* is more effective than saying, "The boy didn't like the cheese."

WRITING SUPPORT

Speculating For the first prompt, have students return to the second paragraph on page 123. Then ask:

✳ *What does the boy think of trying these new foods?*

✳ *The author states that the boy's reaction is impolitic, or unwise. But the boy follows his impolitic comment with a different sort of comment. Why?*

Explain that, while students don't have a lot of information about the boy, they can use what he says, along with what they know about teenager's attitudes, to speculate on his perspective.

For the second prompt, have students contemplate how they might feel if they were in the Edible Schoolyard project. Ask:

✳ *What would you like or not like about eating food you have grown?*

✳ *Can you imagine yourself reacting to an unfamiliar food as the boy did?*

Quick Assess

✳ Did students answer all the questions?

✳ Were students able to write from the boy's perspective?

✳ Consider the boy who said, "This cheese smells like feet!" and "I guess it's a good way to eat if you want to be organic and vegetarian." What do these quotes suggest about his perspective?

✳ Now write an article about the Edible Schoolyard from the boy's perspective.

> Examine multiple perspectives to better understand all sides of nonfiction text.

After

ALTERING THE POINT OF VIEW
If students enjoyed writing from a different point of view, have them repeat the exercise with the *Fast Food Nation* excerpts in Lessons 36 and 37.

✳ With students, brainstorm different perspectives, such as that of the french fry factory workers or the flavorist that Schlosser visited.

✳ Ask: How would other people in the excerpt observe things differently than Schlosser did? If you were a factory worker, would you be more or less inclined to eat french fries? If you were the flavorist, how would feel about food flavorings—would you try to avoid them in your food, or would you enjoy trying them?

FURTHER RESEARCH Invite students to find out more about the Edible Schoolyard project by visiting their website (www.edibleschoolyard.org). Have groups discuss the benefits and/or drawbacks of having a similar project at your school.

FOCUSING ON LANGUAGE AND CRAFT

When you imagine studying the **language and craft** of a piece of writing, you probably imagine reading fiction or poetry. The phrase suggests an author *crafting* a great work of literature. Great writing can be found in any genre, however, including nonfiction. Similar to fiction, engaging nonfiction is written with style. All authors have their own style, but they might use similar techniques:

- Ask questions for the reader to think about.
- Choose quotes that are interesting or dramatic.
- Use repetition for emphasis.
- Use words that convey and stir emotions.
- Use descriptive words that help readers develop a mental picture.
- Vary sentence length to keep a reader's interest.
- Write very short sentences to make clear points.
- Use incomplete sentences for impact.

The author of the selection you are about to read is Ruth Reichl (pronounced *RYE-shul*), who became famous for writing about food. The selection is a profile of Alice Waters (at right), the restaurant owner and food activist who started the Edible Schoolyard. Review the techniques listed above. As you read, pay attention to Reichl's writing style. Take notes about language and craft in the **Response Notes** column.

Alice Waters by Ruth Reichl

Alice Waters lies in bed at night worrying about what to feed you. She knows that she can make you happy. She also knows, in her hidden heart, that if she can find the perfect dish to feed each person who comes to her door, she can change the world.

Every great cook secretly believes in the power of food. Alice Waters just believes this more than anybody else. She is certain that we are what we eat, and she has made it her mission in life to make sure that people eat beautifully. Waters is creating a food revolution, even if she has to do it one meal at a time.

Alice didn't set out to change the way America eats. She just wanted to feed her friends. Having been to France, she had seen the way a good bistro could become the heart of a neighborhood, a place where people went for comfort and sustenance. She was not a professional cook, but she enjoyed feeding

Response Notes

Reichl writes smooth and varied sentences.

Students will learn that the writing techniques of nonfiction authors convey their personal styles.

BACKGROUND KNOWLEDGE

Introduce the term *gourmet,* asking students what it means or what they associate it with. Students may volunteer that gourmet food is somehow seen as better than food that people eat every day. Explain that, in the past, gourmet food was served at expensive restaurants and made with unusual, costly ingredients. Now, people may think of gourmet food as being made with natural ingredients and by hand instead of by machines.

Explain that students will read a profile of Alice Waters, a gourmet restaurant owner.

VOCABULARY

bistro a small restaurant

sustenance something that people need to live, such as food

forager someone who "hunts" for food that grows wild

Ask students to give examples of the vocabulary words. For example:

✢ Name a *bistro* in our area.

✢ Name something a *forager* would hunt.

Before

CRITICAL READING SKILL
Focusing on Language and Craft

Ask students what genres of writing they have analyzed an author's language and craft. Students may recall analyzing poetry or fiction. Explain that analyzing the language and craft of an author is also important when reading nonfiction.

Read aloud or ask a volunteer to read aloud the introductory paragraph and bullet points. From previous lessons, students should be familiar with each technique.

RESPONSE NOTES Read aloud the first paragraph and model how to find a style technique: *The first paragraph has two shorter sentences and then a long one. I'll note that the author is varying sentence length.*

Suggest that students work in pairs to find examples of style techniques.

ABOUT THE AUTHOR

Ruth Reichl was born (1948) and raised in New York and attended boarding school in Montreal, Quebec. After earning Bachelor's and Master's degrees in art history from the University of Michigan, Reichl changed her life by moving west to Berkeley, California. There, she became chef and co-owner of a collectively owned restaurant. As her career as a food writer blossomed, Reichl earned the titles of Restaurant Editor and Food Editor at *The Los Angeles Times*. After nine years with the newspaper, she returned to New York and wrote for *The New York Times*. In addition to food journalism, Reichl is known for her recipe-infused memoirs, such as *Tender at the Bone: Growing Up at the Table, which* is the subject of the interview in Lesson 40.

EXTRA SUPPORT

Differentiation Provide additional background information on the importance of food in some people's lives. Students may be more used to quick meals that they can grab in a hurry. Explain that Alice Waters is passionate about food the way some people are passionate about music or sports.

Response Notes

people, and she envisioned a cozy little café, which would be open every day for breakfast, lunch, and dinner, a place where everyone from the dishwashers to the cooks would be well-paid, a sort of endless party where everyone would have fun. Reality soon set in. Faced with financial ruin, Chez Panisse was forced to become a real business. Still, the dream did not die. It just changed.

"I was more obsessed," Alice explains. If she was going to have a restaurant, it was going to be the very best one she could possibly manage. Even if that meant rethinking the whole concept of what a restaurant might be.

She began with the ingredients. Every chef dreams of great produce, but most make do with what is available in the market. Not Alice. Disgusted with the fish that was sold in stores, she bought a truck and sent someone down to the port to find fishermen as they docked their boats. When she could not find the baby lettuces she had loved in France, she tore up her backyard and grew her own. She found foragers to hunt for mushrooms. She persuaded farmers to let their lambs run wild through the hills. She demanded better bread. Before long, she had developed an entire network of people producing food just for her.

✳ Pause for a moment and review your **Response Notes**. Compare notes with a partner and discuss Ruth Reichl's style. Then continue reading and taking notes.

The results were electric. Chez Panisse served only one meal a day, but people reserved months ahead of time and took their chances. You would find them shaking their heads over the menu, wailing, "Chicken? I've come all the way from Maine for chicken?" Then the dish would arrive, and they'd look down with dismay and say, "It's just a piece of chicken," as if they had somehow expected the poor bird to turn into a swan as it cooked. But they'd waited months for the reservation, so they would take a bite of the chicken and a sort of wonder would come over their faces. "It's the best chicken I have ever tasted," they'd whisper reverently. "I never knew that food could taste so good."

And Alice, walking by, would smile her secret little smile. Because once again, she had done it. She had given them food that they would remember, a taste that would linger long beyond that night. And they would know, ever after, how a chicken raised in the open air, fed on corn, and cooked with care, could taste.

She knew that they would carry that flavor away with them, and that every time they ate a chicken, no matter where it might be, they would remember.

And if Alice had her way, they would go looking for that chicken—or that tomato, or that strawberry—until they found it. Because she had given them more than a meal—she had given them a memory.

There is only one Chez Panisse. In this age of multiple restaurants, the restaurant has no clones in London, Las Vegas, or Tokyo. Because Alice Waters

During

MONITORING UNDERSTANDING
Have students pause where the selection breaks. Solicit responses, assessing whether or not students are finding enough examples of Reichl's style techniques.

Some students may have difficulty reading and analyzing the entire selection. Read the selection aloud to them, reviewing the content of each part. Once students understand the excerpt, then have them work on identifying all or a limited number of the techniques listed on page 125.

SHARING RESPONSES Students should share Response Notes with a partner. After students have had a chance to discuss their notes, have each pair share one response with the class. Then have a brief discussion about Reichl's style. For example, ask: *What can you tell about Ruth Reichl's style so far? Does her personality seem cheerful or serious, negative or positive?*

has more than money on her mind. And she has now turned her attention to the next generation. Her latest project? Feeding the children. She wants every school in America to have a garden and every child to have an opportunity to discover the taste of fresh food.

Her fight goes on. Her revolution continues. She knows that all it takes is one taste. It just has to be the right one. ❖

✳ Use your **Response Notes** to fill in the Language and Craft Chart below. An example is done for you.

A stylistic technique Ruth Reichl uses	An example of this technique	The effect of this technique
Uses emotion words	Alice Waters lies in bed at night **worrying** about what to feed you. She knows that she can make you **happy**.	It makes me interested in the writing right away. I feel emotional, too. I feel like I personally know Alice right away, since I can feel what she feels.

Nonfiction authors use writing techniques that convey their own personal styles.

Language and Craft Use the sample entry to explain how to complete the chart.

✳ In the first column, students should note a technique that they spotted while reading the article.

✳ In the second column, students should quote the text that shows this technique.

✳ In the third column, students should describe the effect of the technique on the reader's impression of the article. To explain, ask: *How does the quote in which this technique is used make you feel about the topic? Does it help you connect to it? Does it help you visualize something or give you something to think about?*

Have students consider how they can apply the techniques in the first column to their own writing.

Quick Assess

✳ Did students fill in all the columns of the chart with relevant examples?

✳ Did students explain the effect of the technique convincingly?

After

APPLYING THE STRATEGY Encourage students to look for style techniques in other nonfiction readings. You may want to distribute copies of articles from the food and restaurant sections of newspapers or cooking magazines.

✳ Have students find examples of the style techniques listed on page 125.

✳ Have students share their findings. Then lead a brief discussion about the effects of the techniques that food writers use, e.g. *Which senses do the writers try to appeal to? What do you think their goal is?*

READING/WRITING CONNECTION
Invite students to think of a special meal or eating experience and write a journal entry about it. Before writing, have students contemplate these questions:

✳ What was special about the meal—the ingredients, the person who made it, the people you ate it with, etc.?

✳ How did the food make you feel? What did you taste, touch, smell, or see?

Encourage students to use specific style techniques in their entries.

Students will learn that writers' lives influence the topics and styles of their writing.

BACKGROUND KNOWLEDGE

Ask students to recall who Ruth Reichl is. Students should know that she is a successful writer who writes about food and its importance in people's lives.

Then ask: *What kind of foods do you eat? Do you eat differently when you're alone than when you're with family? How? Do you have certain foods on special occasions?*

Depending on students' experiences, you may want to poll the different kinds of ethnic foods they have tried.

Explain that students will read an interview with Reichl.

VOCABULARY

continental food food of European cultures, such as French or Italian

credible believable or trustworthy

ostracize to exclude someone

Have students give synonyms and/or antonyms for the words, where appropriate. For example:

❋ for *credible:* trustworthy (synonym); unbelievable (antonym)

❋ for *ostracize:* banish (synonym); include (antonym)

LESSON 40 STUDYING AN AUTHOR

Ruth Reichl is one of the most widely respected and influential food writers of our time. Learning about her life and perspective can help us to understand how she became the writer she is today.

The selection that follows is from an interview with Reichl. As you read it, write **Response Notes** as a way to highlight important or interesting facts you learn. After you have read, you will use your notes to write a speech about Reichl.

Response Notes

from "A Taste for Life" by Jeffrey L. Perlah

[While her memoir] *Tender at the Bone* is a celebration of food, Reichl notes that "food has always meant more to me than just eating and recipes. It's about people. And I wanted this book to be about people."

Early on, you discovered that "food could be a way of making sense of the world."

"It's a way of giving yourself something of quality. Just to make yourself a perfect egg in the morning is a way of saying, 'I respect myself.'"

The book points out that sweets are a big part of the beginner's repertoire.

"You learn very early that dessert is sort of a cheap trick. As a beginning cook, you make cookies and brownies, and other sweets, and people love them even if they're not great."

What's challenging about being a restaurant critic in New York City?

"When Craig Claiborne [formerly of the *New York Times*] was doing restaurant criticism, he had to know about French food, continental food, maybe a little bit about Italian food, and that was pretty much it. Today, you have to know about food from all over the world, and, if you don't, you have to learn about it. No credible critic today can talk about Japanese food without really having some knowledge of it. It's more so in New York than in many other places."

Your college friend Mac first made you aware of the way food was bringing people together, and keeping them apart.

"A lot of foods eaten by Europeans are considered disgusting by Americans. If you go to any restaurant in France, you're likely to find kidneys, livers, and brains. And eating a lot of garlic was something that ostracized Jews and Italians from polite society in New York. If you showed up with garlic on your breath, it often classified you as lower class. But one of the great things that has happened today is we eat foods from many different cultures. Food doesn't keep us apart now."

Was your mother's lack of good cooking skills a factor in your approach to food?

Before

CRITICAL READING SKILL

Studying an Author Read aloud or ask a volunteer to read aloud the introductory paragraphs. Then explain the goal of the reading assignment. Say: *You will be writing a speech about the career of Ruth Reichl, so pay special attention to the details she gives in this interview.*

Read aloud the first exchange between the writer and Reichl, using a think-aloud to model how to find interesting details. For example: *Reichl thinks you can respect yourself by eating good food. She must really believe in the power of food!*

Have students read and respond to the interview independently.

"It was not so much her cooking skills as the fact that she was taste blind. She would leave butter uncovered in the refrigerator, put it on the table, and later in the day I would say, 'I can't eat it.' And she would taste it and say, 'there's nothing wrong with it.' I would taste things that she couldn't."

On the other hand, your father was a book designer. Was that an influence on your writing?

"I think so. I was brought up in a world of books. My parents never had a television. Books were really their whole life. And certainly words were. I think I grew up really feeling the importance of telling stories, making a reality out of these little black marks on a paper. I was an only child, and my way of making a world for myself was through reading." ✧

✳ Based on what you read and the **Response Notes** you wrote, what can you infer about Ruth Reichl's personality?

_____

_____

✳ Imagine that you are at an awards dinner for influential writers. You have been asked to introduce Ruth Reichl. Your research has turned up the following details about Ruth Reichl's life:

- Began writing about food in 1972 when she published *Mmmmm: A Feastiary*
- Involved with writing or editing more than 25 books, including three memoirs and numerous cookbooks
- Was chef and co-owner of The Swallow Restaurant in Berkeley, California
- Has been the restaurant critic for *New West* magazine, *California* magazine, the *Los Angeles Times*, and *The New York Times*
- Received the James Beard Award for restaurant criticism and for journalism

On the next page write the speech you would give to introduce Ruth Reichl, using language and craft in a style that is your own. Be sure to include facts about her life and work, as well as comments about her writing.

Collaboration Pair below-level students with those who are on- or above-level for reading the interview aloud. The below-level students can read the interview's questions, and their partners can read the responses. After responding, have partners compare their responses.

WRITING SUPPORT

Making Inferences For the first prompt, remind students that when they infer something, they combine what they've read with what they already know in order to draw a conclusion.

Ask volunteers to share what they have learned about Reichl from the interview. For example, she says that making desserts is an easy way to get people to like your cooking.

Then use a think-aloud to model making an inference about Reichl's personality. For example: *She talks about different ethnic foods and how food can bring people together or keep them apart. She must see food as a tool for building greater understanding among people.* Assure students that there is no "correct" inference about Reichl's personality, though students should base their answers on what is in the interview.

During

WRITER'S CRAFT

Writing for Oral Presentation Briefly discuss how writing an essay differs from writing a speech. For example, a speechwriter would want to write in a lively way that holds the listeners' interest.

Then ask students: *If you were at an awards dinner, what would you want to know about the person who is receiving the award?* Allow students to give input, explaining that listeners would not only

want to know about Reichl's achievements, but little facts and stories that make her interesting and real.

Remind students that their speeches should include the following parts:

✳ An introduction that tells why Reichl is receiving an award

✳ A middle part that gives interesting information about her, such as facts and comments about her writing

✳ A conclusion that gives the listener something to think about

✳ Their own style, using language and craft techniques learned in Lesson 39

Have students practice and deliver their speeches. Suggest that they annotate their speeches by underlining words they want to emphasize and placing slash marks to show where they will pause.

Quick Assess

As students practice their speeches, circulate and check for

✷ an engaging introduction;

✷ accurate facts that illustrate how Reichl stands apart from others and why she deserves an award;

✷ enthusiastic language and style;

✷ clear delivery.

130 LESSON 40

Title

_____

_____

_____

_____

_____

_____

_____

_____

_____

_____

_____

_____

_____

_____

_____

_____

_____

_____

_____

_____

_____

_____

_____

_____

✷ With a partner, practice performing your speech. Compare the differences in your personal styles, as well as different facts and ideas you chose to include.

Writers' lives influence their ideas and styles of writing.

After

LISTENING/SPEAKING CONNECTION   Have students revise their speeches for delivery to a group.

✷ Have students review the bulleted style techniques on page 125.

✷ Remind students to practice good speech delivery, using clear enunciation; strong voice projection; and a confident, fidget-free stance.

READING/WRITING CONNECTION
Invite students to interview a friend or family member about his or her life and work.

✷ Have students brainstorm what they already know about the person.

✷ Have them write questions, using the interview with Reichl as a model. Encourage students to ask questions that address the subject's younger

years and possible motivations for choosing his or her occupation.

✷ Students need to make appointments with their subjects and conduct the interviews.

✷ Have students write profiles of their subjects. Encourage them to use their own language and style as Reichl did in "Alice Waters" (on pages 125–127).

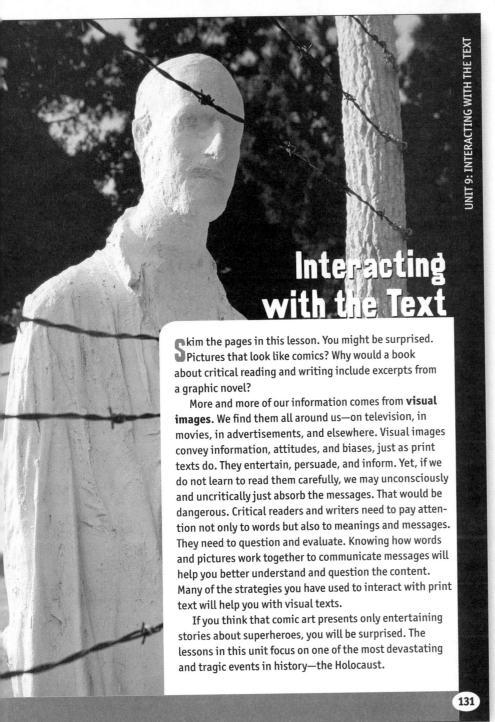

Interacting with the Text

Skim the pages in this lesson. You might be surprised. Pictures that look like comics? Why would a book about critical reading and writing include excerpts from a graphic novel?

More and more of our information comes from **visual images.** We find them all around us—on television, in movies, in advertisements, and elsewhere. Visual images convey information, attitudes, and biases, just as print texts do. They entertain, persuade, and inform. Yet, if we do not learn to read them carefully, we may unconsciously and uncritically just absorb the messages. That would be dangerous. Critical readers and writers need to pay attention not only to words but also to meanings and messages. They need to question and evaluate. Knowing how words and pictures work together to communicate messages will help you better understand and question the content. Many of the strategies you have used to interact with print text will help you with visual texts.

If you think that comic art presents only entertaining stories about superheroes, you will be surprised. The lessons in this unit focus on one of the most devastating and tragic events in history—the Holocaust.

131

UNIT 9 INTERACTING WITH THE TEXT

Lessons 41–45, pages 132–144

UNIT OVERVIEW
In this unit, students will explore the Holocaust through visual and print texts.

KEY IDEA
Comprehending visual texts requires both the adjustment of skills used to comprehend written texts and the development of new skills.

CRITICAL READING SKILLS
by lesson

41 Making inferences
42 Identifying what is important
43 Paying attention to craft
44 Discussing questions
45 Adapting a text

WRITING ACTIVITIES
by lesson

41 Complete an inference chart.
42 Explain how a reader knows what is important.
43 Complete a chart listing elements of craft and explore the significance of images.
44 Summarize how questioning aids understanding.
45 Create visual text for a narrative.

Literature

■ from *Parallel Journeys* by Eleanor Ayer with Helen Waterford and Alfons Heck (memoir excerpt)

In this excerpt, one of the authors offers a brief memory of the Holocaust.

■ from *Maus: A Survivor's Tale* by Art Spiegelman (graphic novel excerpt)

Primarily through visual images, Spiegelman recounts his father's story of living through the Holocaust.

■ from *Memories of Anne Frank* by Alison Gold (memoir excerpt)

This excerpt tells the story of the last encounter that Hannah had with her best friend Anne Frank, the girl whose secret diary later became the world's best-known account of the Holocaust.

ASSESSMENT To assess student learning in this unit, see pages 238 and 256.

Students will learn that making inferences using words, pictures, and background knowledge helps them better understand what they read.

BACKGROUND KNOWLEDGE

The Holocaust took place during the rule of Adolf Hitler and his Nazi party in Germany. To achieve their goal of world domination by a "pure" German race, the dictator and his party attempted to eradicate all Jews and other "non-Aryans" in Germany and countries that came under German rule. Nazi efforts included isolating Jews in ghettos within cities and transporting whole communities of Jews to camps where they were either forced to work to support the German war effort or were killed in gas chambers.

VOCABULARY

protectorate a country or region controlled or protected by another

Reich Germany or the German government during one of the three reichs; in this case, during the Third Reich, 1933–1945

Pole a Polish person

Nazi abbreviated name of the political party headed by Hitler from 1921–1945

Oy gevalt! Yiddish exclamation of surprise or alarm

After discussing the definitions, have partners use each term in a sentence.

Active readers understand what they read by making reasonable guesses, or inferring. When you infer, you combine what you already know with the information provided in the text. Read the following first-person account from a young man who was a teenager during Hitler's rise to power in Germany. What **inference** can you make about his family background?

Response Notes

from **Parallel Journeys** by Eleanor Ayer with Helen Waterford and Alfons Heck

Unlike our elders, we children of the 1930's had never known a Germany without Nazis. From our very first year in the *Volksschule* or elementary school, we received daily doses of Nazisms. These we swallowed as naturally as our morning milk. Never did we question what our teachers said. We simply believed whatever was crammed into us. And never for a moment did we doubt how fortunate we were to live in a country with such a promising future. ❖

❖ Write your inference and the reason for it here. What background knowledge did you combine with clues from the paragraph?

When you read a visual text, you draw inferences from the visual and textual material the author provides. Making inferences about the characters helps you better understand who they are and their relationships to other characters. In *Maus: A Survivor's Tale,* Art Spiegelman tells the story of his father, a Jewish survivor of the Holocaust. Although it is a true story, Spiegelman has chosen to draw all of the characters with animal heads and human bodies. In the excerpt on the following page, Vladek, Spiegelman's father, has been released from a prison camp but ends up in the wrong part of Poland. To return to his town of Sosnowiec requires a dangerous journey. What inferences can you make about the characters' relationships in this excerpt?

132 LESSON 41

Before

CRITICAL READING SKILL

Making Inferences Point out that students make many inferences in their everyday lives. To clarify this concept, play the Found Suitcase game. Bring in a suitcase that contains a variety of objects, such as clothing, personal grooming items, CDs, DVDs, magazines, and books. Invite groups to examine the contents of the suitcase and create a profile of the mystery owner, including gender, age, leisure activities, level of fitness, destination, and purpose of travel.

After groups present their profiles, explain that inferring details such as the fitness level of the owner of the suitcase required putting together new information and background knowledge. Say: *For example, I see used running shoes in the suitcase. When I combine that observation with my background knowledge that running regularly keeps a person physically fit, I can infer that the owner is a fairly fit person.* Explain that students use this process to make inferences as they read.

RESPONSE NOTES Support students in their effort to draw an inference from the paragraph. Ask them to compare their inferences with a partner to see how they used background knowledge and the text to draw a conclusion about the young man's background.

from Maus: A Survivor's Tale by Art Spiegelman

TRAINS WERE STILL GOING FROM PROTECTORATE TO REICH. ONLY, ONE NEEDED LEGAL PAPERS. OF COURSE, THIS I DIDN'T HAVE ...

...BUT ANYWAY I GOT ON THE TRAIN IN THE DIRECTION I WANTED.

I APPROACHED TO THE TRAIN MAN, A POLE...

MAY I TALK TO YOU FOR A MOMENT?

SURE, SOLDIER.

YOU'RE A POLE LIKE ME, SO I CAN TRUST YOU... THE STINKING NAZIS HAD ME IN A WAR PRISON... I JUST ESCAPED.

I STILL HAD ON MY ARMY UNIFORM, AND I DIDN'T LET KNOW I WAS A JEW.

THE POLES WERE VERY BITTER ON THE GERMANS, SO IT WAS GOOD TO SPEAK BAD OF THEM.

I'M TRYING TO GET TO SOSNOWIEC — BACK TO MY FAMILY.

DON'T WORRY... WHEN WE GET TO THE BORDER, HIDE IN HERE.

AND SO THE TRAIN MAN HELPED ME COME BACK TO MY SIDE OF POLAND,

...WHAT I THOUGHT I MIGHT NEVER SEE AGAIN.

OY GEVALT! IT'S VLADEK!

I WALKED FIRST OVER TO MY PARENTS' HOUSE...

ABOUT THE AUTHOR

Art Spiegelman was born in Stockholm, Sweden, in 1948, the child of two survivors of the Holocaust. He began writing, drawing, and printing comics in his teens and was, for a long time, known as an underground artist. In 1986, though, with the publication of the first of the two volumes of *Maus: A Survivor's Tale,* he became known to a wider audience. His recognition increased after he was awarded a Pulitzer Prize Special Award for *Maus* in 1992. From 1991 to 2003, he was a staff artist and writer for the *New Yorker.* Having witnessed the 2001 attacks on New York City from his office near the World Trade Center, he struggled with his emotions and reactions and, not surprisingly, expressed them in the powerful graphic novel *In the Shadow of No Towers* (2004). This was his first graphic novel since the publication of *Maus.*

TEACHING TIP

Collaboration Have students work with partners. Partner A finds details in the pictures that reveal information, while partner B finds information in the written text. Partners then compare their notes to see what information was presented in only one way and what information was confirmed by either the visuals or the text.

During

VISUAL INFERENCES Before students begin reading, remind them that making an inference involves adding what we know from past experience to our reading of a text. The title of the selection, *Maus,* immediately inspires inferences about the main character, who is portrayed as a mouse. Ask: *What characteristics do you think of when you think of a mouse? How do the mouse characters in* Maus *compare to your past impressions of mice?*

Explain that in visual texts, much of the story can be inferred just by studying the pictures. Point out the obvious strings that tie the pig-nose on the main character's face and his hand partially covering his mouth in the third panel. Have students use past experiences of these details to infer the situation. Then invite students to explain how they infer other information from other visual details. Finally, invite students to cite verification from the written text.

WRITING SUPPORT

Prewriting To help students relate animal characteristics to human characteristics, invite groups to draw stick figures of each animal pictured in the graphic novel excerpt. Have groups label various physical characteristics and note human personality traits of which the characteristics reminds them. Then have students check the excerpt to see if those characteristics fit the characters in the graphic literature. To model using a think-aloud, say: *The snout of a pig reminds me of selfish people, who shove other people around. In the excerpt, the pig character is in a position of authority on the train, so he does have the power to push people around.*

Quick Assess

✳ Do students support their inferences with information from the text?

✳ Are students' inference charts complete?

✳ Use the Inference Chart to record your conclusions about the characters. In the third column tell what characteristics and relationships are suggested by the animals Spiegelman uses.

INFERENCE CHART

Animal	Human	Characteristics and Relationships
Pig	Polish train conductor	
Cat	German official	
Mouse	Jew	*Mice are small animals who do not have power over larger animals. They are chased and killed by cats. Vladek disguised himself in Poland by putting on a pig nose so that he would look like a Pole.*

Making inferences from the words, the pictures, and your background knowledge helps you better understand the text.

After

APPLYING THE STRATEGY

Have students look at still photos of animal characters from a fictional television show or movie and make inferences about the characters' personality traits. Then have students view the show. In oral reports to the class, students should describe the personality traits they inferred about the characters and then explain details in the show that verify their inferences.

IDENTIFYING WHAT IS IMPORTANT 42 LESSON

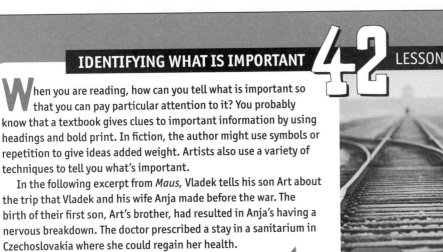

When you are reading, how can you tell what is important so that you can pay particular attention to it? You probably know that a textbook gives clues to important information by using headings and bold print. In fiction, the author might use symbols or repetition to give ideas added weight. Artists also use a variety of techniques to tell you what's important.

In the following excerpt from *Maus*, Vladek tells his son Art about the trip that Vladek and his wife Anja made before the war. The birth of their first son, Art's brother, had resulted in Anja's having a nervous breakdown. The doctor prescribed a stay in a sanitarium in Czechoslovakia where she could regain her health.

from **Maus: A Survivor's Tale** by Art Spiegelman

LESSON 42

Students will learn to use visual and textual clues to more effectively identify what is important in a text.

BACKGROUND KNOWLEDGE

Explain that, since World War II, the swastika has been regarded as the terrifying symbol of Hitler's dictatorship and the brutalities committed by him and his Nazi party. Before Hitler's reign, however, the swastika had been a symbol of largely positive ideas that had been used by many cultures for over 3,000 years. Artifacts such as pottery and coins from ancient Troy show that the swastika was a commonly used symbol as far back as 1000 B.C.E. The word itself comes from the Sanskrit term *svasti* that meant "strength or well-being" and the earliest use of the term *swastika* signified good luck.

VOCABULARY

sanitarium a place for healing; from the root *sanitas,* meaning "good health"

After discussing the definition, encourage students to think of related words from the same root, such as *sanitary, sanitize, sanitation, sanity.*

Before

CRITICAL READING SKILL
Identifying What Is Important

Explain that the written text includes detailed descriptions, explanatory notes, and even grammatical indicators to show what is important in the story. Point out the first panel on page 135 and explain that a narration of the scene could be: *"Oi!" the passenger cried suddenly, gazing out the window with eyes wide*

with terror. A graphic writer, however, must communicate the same information primarily through pictures. Have students identify visual details in the panel that communicate the details given in the verbal narration.

During

TEAM ANALYSIS Invite students to make a game out of identifying details and important ideas. Form two teams. For Round 1, allow ten minutes for teams to list every detail they can identify. Award one point for each detail each team identifies. For Round 2, tell teams to reach consensus on the most important idea in this part of the story and to support their decision with at least three ▶▶▶

Differentiation Auditory learners might benefit from a "narrative walk" through the excerpt. Point to each panel and narrate the details as modeled above for the first panel. Pause occasionally for students to point out the graphic elements that correspond to the details in the verbal narrative.

Quick Assess

✳ Did students list at least five details for this part of the story?

✳ Did students identify and defend what they think is most important in this part of the story?

✳ The visuals for this part of the story contain a lot of information. In the box below, quickly write everything you noticed.

> Use visual and textual clues to identify what is important in a text.

✳ Share what you noticed with a partner. Together, decide what was most important and circle those items. Write an explanation of how you knew one of the items was important.

_____

After

reasons from the text. Award three points to the first team to reach consensus and adequately support their decision. Award another point to each team for every reason they use to support their decisions.

DEBATE LITERARY MERITS Invite students to participate in a debate of the literary merits of graphic and written texts. Assign the question: *Which texts have more literary merit?* Form debate teams. Remind students that *literary merit* is a term that means many things to different people. Encourage them to define what it means to them before they prepare their debate cases. Some of the

usual considerations are aesthetic appeal, effective communication of important ideas, accuracy, and authenticity, but there are others, too. Allow time for teams to prepare their cases. Then conduct the debates according to the standard rules of order.

43 LESSON

W hat makes your favorite writers stand out? You might say it's the way they write the stories they tell. It's how they put words together and the details they include. These are elements of their **style.** Yet, they generally observe the conventions of whatever they are writing. Conventions are the elements that make a science fiction story different from a mystery story. If a story is set in the future, for example, and includes aspects of science such as robots or unusual plants, you expect that it will be science fiction.

Authors of graphic novels work the same way. They observe the conventions of the genre of graphic novels into which they infuse their own individual style. Comic artists use a variety of conventions to show passage of time, to emphasize ideas, and to differentiate between narration and dialogue. Read the following excerpt from *Maus.* This scene is a continuation of the one you read in Lesson 42. Vladek, Anja, and others are on a train on their way to the sanitarium in Czechoslovakia.

from **Maus: A Survivor's Tale** by Art Spiegelman

LESSON **43**

S tudents will learn how the conventions of visual texts show the passage of time, emphasize ideas, and help the reader differentiate between narration and dialogue.

BACKGROUND KNOWLEDGE

Explain that, while many Jews were forced from their homes and massacred, others were persecuted through laws that required Jews to identify themselves as such at all times. Point out the Star of David in the last frame on this page and explain the bitter irony of Nazis appropriating this symbol of religious belief as a means of persecution. Laws also required Jews to wear yellow armbands with the Star of David on them, to label their homes and shops with the word *Jew* (*Jude* in German) in large letters, and to obey curfews that forced them to be inside their homes during specific hours.

VOCABULARY

pogrom organized massacre of a minority group

synagogue a Jewish place of worship

Discuss how these words might relate to a piece of text about the Holocaust.

Before

CRITICAL READING SKILL

Paying Attention to Craft Have students consider how they would describe a visual text to someone who has never seen one. Ask: *What style elements would you mention?* Help students develop a list of style elements used in visual texts:

✳ panels (individual pictures)

✳ captions that reveal details, such as time lapses, locations, characters' feelings

✳ proportion and depth of field to indicate an image's importance

✳ speech balloons to show what characters say

✳ thought balloons to show what characters think

✳ facial expressions and gestures

As an example of how a visual element can uniquely tell a story, point out how the enormous size of the swastika and its hovering presence in the background emphasize the power and ever-present threat of the Nazis. Suggest that students circle examples of these and other visual features and discuss their effects with a group.

WRITER'S CRAFT

Graphic Novels Point out that most people expect to be entertained with a humorous tale when they see a graphic novel. Some scholars, however, feel that the concentrated graphic format stamps the emotions more indelibly on the mind of the reader than words alone can do. Share the following quotation from the author, Art Spiegelman: "The word cartoons implies humorous intent—a desire to amuse and entertain. I'm not necessarily interested in entertainment—in creating diversions." Ask: *Why do you think Mr. Spiegelman chose to tell such a harsh story through this medium?* Facilitate a discussion of the graphic medium as a vehicle for a tale about the Holocaust.

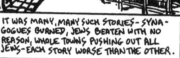

✳ Looking at the excerpts in Lesson 42 and in this lesson, find and label one example of each element of craft. Use the following labels: **T** for time, **E** for emphasis, **N** for narration, and **D** for dialogue. Compare your findings with a partner or a small group. Record your findings in the boxes.

Time	Emphasis
Narration	Dialogue

During

ELEMENTS OF CRAFT Help students understand the elements of craft, abbreviated TEND for Time, Emphasis, Narration, and Dialogue.

T Passage of or a difference in time is conveyed through narration and through illustration (by showing a different scene).

E The relative size of certain items, such as the large swastika in the background of several panels, shows emphasis.

N In *Maus,* author Spiegelman puts the narration in rectangular boxes. Narration fills in background information.

D Dialogue, the spoken words of the characters, is in speech balloons.

* In the frames you just read from *Maus: A Survivor's Tale*, a single image dominates—the Nazi flag. Explain the ways that Spiegelman uses this image and the significance it has in emphasizing certain aspects of the story. Also consider how its presence and absence contributes to the mood of the story. How does it make you feel as a reader?

Visual conventions show the passage of time, emphasize ideas, and help the reader differentiate between narration and dialogue.

After

APPLYING THE STRATEGY

Have students find comic strips or graphic novels and label the elements of craft and style in each. Ask: *What elements of the graphic form did you find that were not used in* Maus? Then have them exchange strips with partners and compare their observations.

LESSON 44

Students will learn how asking questions can help them better understand what they read.

BACKGROUND KNOWLEDGE

Have students recall a literature selection they've recently read in class. Invite volunteers to provide examples of different kinds of questions they might have been asked about the selection; e.g. questions that could be answered directly from information in the text, questions that required students to infer something from the text, or questions that called upon prior knowledge or a reference to another text for further information. Point out that asking questions is one way to clarify our understanding of a selection.

LESSON 44 QUESTIONING

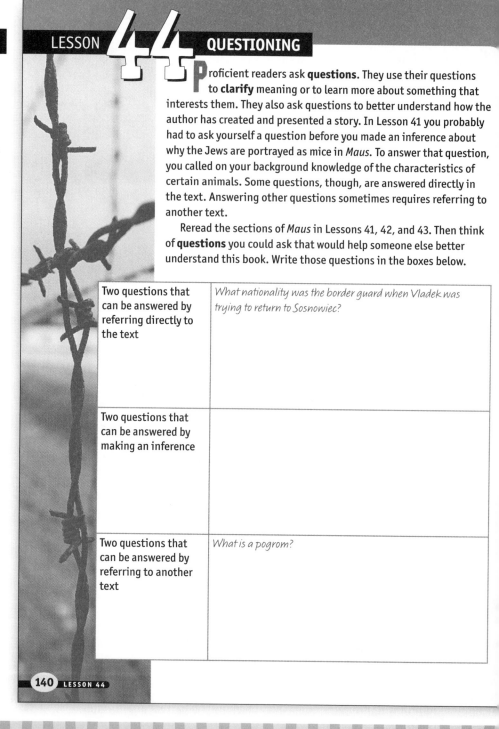

Proficient readers ask **questions**. They use their questions to **clarify** meaning or to learn more about something that interests them. They also ask questions to better understand how the author has created and presented a story. In Lesson 41 you probably had to ask yourself a question before you made an inference about why the Jews are portrayed as mice in *Maus*. To answer that question, you called on your background knowledge of the characteristics of certain animals. Some questions, though, are answered directly in the text. Answering other questions sometimes requires referring to another text.

Reread the sections of *Maus* in Lessons 41, 42, and 43. Then think of **questions** you could ask that would help someone else better understand this book. Write those questions in the boxes below.

Two questions that can be answered by referring directly to the text	*What nationality was the border guard when Vladek was trying to return to Sosnowiec?*
Two questions that can be answered by making an inference	
Two questions that can be answered by referring to another text	*What is a pogrom?*

Before

CRITICAL READING SKILL

Discussing Questions Explain that successful readers keep their minds engaged with the text by asking questions. They ask questions throughout their reading.

- Before: What will this be about? What do I know about the topic?
- During: What does this word mean? What does this remind me of?
- After: What did the author mean by —? How can I use this information in other parts of my life?

Some of the questions can be answered directly by the text, but other questions will be answered by making an inference or referring to another source of information.

Before students complete the chart, have them review the story by retelling the events.

✻ Discuss with a partner or small group two questions that interest you. Write a summary of your discussion below and explain how asking questions helped you understand the story.

_____

_____

_____

_____

_____

_____

_____

_____

_____

_____

_____

_____

_____

_____

_____

_____

_____

_____

_____

_____

_____

_____

_____

Ask questions about what you read if you want to understand it better.

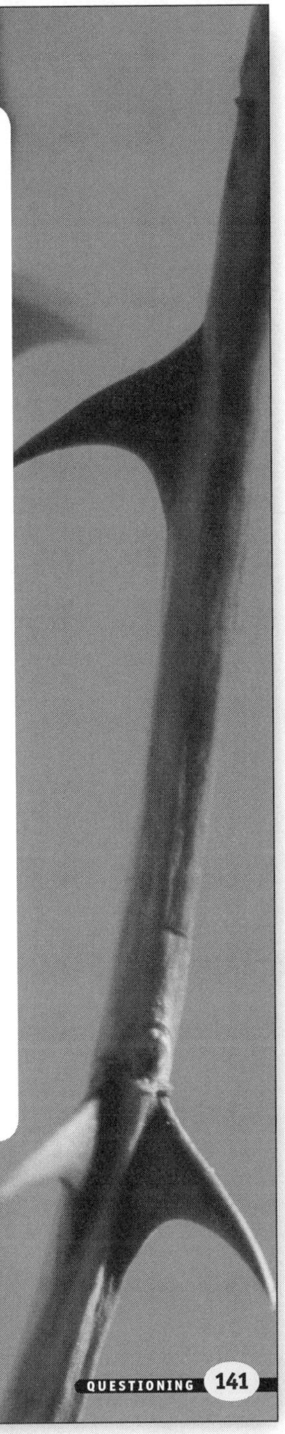

Quick Assess

✻ Do students' charts categorize questions correctly?

✻ Do students' summaries explain how asking two questions helped them understand the story?

During

COLLABORATION Assign students to work in pairs or triads to complete the chart. Listen in as each group discusses the questions and offer support as needed.

After

SPEAKING/LISTENING CONNECTION Have students interview a partner about an important family experience.

First, partners should brainstorm and reach consensus about questions they will ask. Then they should flip a coin to determine who will serve as interviewer first. As the students interview each other, the interviewer should make notes about the partner's answers. After the interviews, students should introduce their partners to the class by reiterating the information they gained during the interview. To debrief the exercise, ask: _How did asking and answering questions affect your understanding of your partner?_

Students will learn that a good way to better understand visual texts is to create one.

BACKGROUND KNOWLEDGE

The excerpt in this lesson comes from Alison Gold's second book about Anne Frank. Her first book, published in 1987, *Anne Frank Remembered,* was co-authored with Miep Gies, a major character in Anne Frank's diary. *Anne Frank Remembered* was made into a TV movie and translated into fifteen languages. To activate prior knowledge, invite students to share what they know about Anne Frank and her diary. To build further background for the students, show one of the many movies made about Anne Frank.

VOCABULARY

barracks temporary housing structures

scrounge to beg or forage

scuffling struggling at close quarters

anguish emotional pain

To preview the words, use the Word Splash activity on page 278.

The best way to learn how visual texts work is to create your own. Art Spiegelman chose the graphic novel as the original form for *Maus.* But graphic novels may also be adapted from short stories or novels. In this lesson, you will create visual panels for a segment of another Holocaust story.

One of the best-known stories of the Holocaust is Anne Frank's diary. The diary tells of the years that Anne (shown left), her family, and others hid in Amsterdam. Anne's story ends when they are discovered and sent to a concentration camp. Her childhood friend, Hannah (who appears as Lies or Hanneli in the published diary), adds to what we know about Anne Frank. She shared her memories with Alison Gold, who wrote *Memories of Anne Frank: Reflections of a Childhood Friend.*

Hannah, who is also in a camp, has learned that Anne Frank is just on the other side of the fence. When the excerpt starts, she has been visiting her father in the hospital. As you read the excerpt, determine what is important and what you might leave out of your graphic text. In the **Response Notes,** jot down some ideas of what to use in a visual presentation of this excerpt.

Response Notes

from **Memories of Anne Frank** by Alison Gold

When Hannah got back to the barracks, there was great excitement. Packages were being distributed. This had never happened before. The packages were from the Red Cross. Hannah was given two packages for her family. One she immediately hid in order to bring it to her father in the hospital.

The packages were small boxes, the shape and size of a book. When she opened hers, she found dry, fried Swedish bread and dried fruit. Quietly she made a package of things for Anne.

Mrs. Abrahams saw Hannah on her way out of the barracks. She warned her that she mustn't go to the fence again. Once she had been lucky but she might not be so lucky again. Hannah explained that she had made contact with her best friend from her childhood. She told Mrs. Abrahams about Anne Frank, what terrible conditions were on the other side of the fence. Immediately Mrs. Abrahams handed Hannah a few scraps of food to put in the package.

The package consisted of a glove, some Swedish bread and dried fruit, and what she had saved from the evening meal. Hannah waited until it was dark and walked across the camp to the barbed-wire fence. Cautiously she whispered, "Anne? Are you there?"

Before

CRITICAL READING SKILL

Adapting a Text Discuss what it means to adapt a text. Point out examples of books, comic strips, and TV shows that have been turned into movies. Ask students to imagine themselves as the person who writes the screenplay. What would they have to consider in making a book work as a movie script?

TEACHING TIP

Use Graphic Organizers Have students review what they learned about the craft of a graphic text in Lesson 43. Suggest that students use a graphic organizer such as the following to plan how they will use each graphic element in their adaptations:

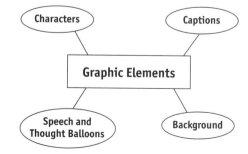

Characters — Captions

Graphic Elements

Speech and Thought Balloons — Background

Immediately the reply came, "Yes, Hanneli, I'm here."

Anne's voice was shaky, and she told Hannah that she had been waiting. Hannah told her she had scrounged up a few things and would throw them over to her.

Hannah felt very weak but summoned her strength and threw the package over the fence.

Immediately there was scuffling noise. Then the sound of someone running and Anne cried out in anguish.

"What happened?"

Anne was crying. "A woman ran over and grabbed it away from me. She won't give it back."

Hannah called, "Anne! I'll try again but I don't know if I'll be able to get away with it."

Anne was crushed.

Hannah begged her not to lose heart, "I'll try. In a few nights. Wait for me."

"I'll wait, Hanneli."

Hannah dashed across the snow, avoiding the searchlight. ❖

The next time Hannah sneaks to the fence, Anne does receive the package. After that, the people in her camp are moved, and Hannah never sees her again.

✳ In the space below, plan your visual text for this excerpt. Decide on the message you want to convey to readers. How will you draw the characters or emphasize what is important?

During

PLANNING THE ADAPTATION

As they read the selection, have students stop and discuss important information that they will communicate in their adaptations. For example, how will they portray the concentration camps? What features of the camps will they include? How many barracks will they show? What do the barracks look like? Where are the guards? How will they show Anne and Hannah evading detection by the guards?

Before students begin creating their adaptations, suggest that they use self-stick notes to create storyboards to serve as rough drafts. To facilitate revision, suggest that students make rough sketches of individual scenes on self-stick notes and arrange them in chronological order. In peer conferences, students can point out gaps and/or out-of-order events that can be easily remedied by adding or rearranging the self-stick notes.

Differentiation Students who are intimidated by the prospect of drawing a story might benefit from teaming up with students who have good drawing skills. Suggest that partners plan the adaptation together. Then the more-artistic student may draw the scenes while the less-artistic student writes the dialogue and the captions.

Quick Assess

✷ Do students create complete plans for their adaptations?

✷ Do students' adaptations communicate the important information and tell the complete story told in this lesson?

✷ Review your plan, and draw as much of the new visual text as you can below. If you do not want to draw, you can use computer graphics or magazine cutouts for the visuals.

A good way to understand how visual texts work is to create your own.

After

READING/SPEAKING CONNECTION Have students prepare speeches to present to the school board or curriculum committee advocating the inclusion of graphic texts in the curriculum. To prepare students for presenting their case, discuss the merits of using graphic texts in school lessons. Ask: *What kinds of learning are best supported through graphic texts? What information cannot be communicated through graphic texts alone?* Then review the elements of persuasion. Allow time for students to prepare their speeches and practice them in front of the class.

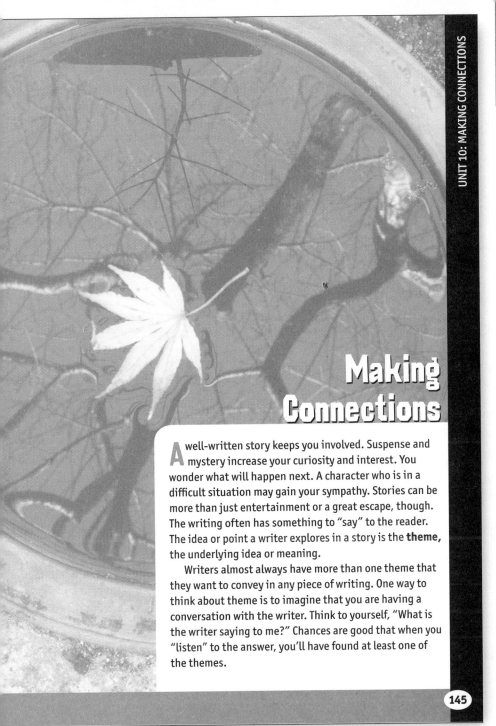

Making Connections

A well-written story keeps you involved. Suspense and mystery increase your curiosity and interest. You wonder what will happen next. A character who is in a difficult situation may gain your sympathy. Stories can be more than just entertainment or a great escape, though. The writing often has something to "say" to the reader. The idea or point a writer explores in a story is the **theme,** the underlying idea or meaning.

Writers almost always have more than one theme that they want to convey in any piece of writing. One way to think about theme is to imagine that you are having a conversation with the writer. Think to yourself, "What is the writer saying to me?" Chances are good that when you "listen" to the answer, you'll have found at least one of the themes.

(145)

UNIT 10 MAKING CONNECTIONS

Lessons 46–50 pages 146–160

UNIT OVERVIEW
Students will track common themes through fiction, poetry, and personal narrative.

KEY IDEA
Skilled readers connect themes to text by studying details, events, images, and symbols.

CRITICAL READING SKILLS
by lesson
46 Connecting details to theme
47 Connecting events to theme
48 Connecting images and symbols to theme
49 Focus on poetry and theme
50 Focus on perspective and theme

WRITING ACTIVITIES
by lesson
46 Write a paragraph describing themes of the text.
47 Write a letter on a theme.
48 Write sentences that relate images and symbols to a theme.
49 Write a poem on a chosen theme.
50 Write a diary entry connecting the themes of three different texts.

Literature

- *When My Name Was Keoko* by Linda Sue Park (novel excerpts)

The Japanese occupation of Korea is described from the perspectives of a fictional Korean girl and boy.

- *Aleutian Sparrow* by Karen Hesse (free-verse novel excerpts)

Told in free verse, an Aleutian girl recounts her people's forced relocation from their island to a desolate encampment in an unfamiliar landscape.

- *Zlata's Diary: A Child's Life in Sarajevo* by Zlata Filipovic (personal diary excerpt)

Personal diary entries give voice to a young Bosnian girl watching her city deteriorate into war.

ASSESSMENT To assess student learning in this unit, see pages 239 and 259.

Students will learn how to identify details that convey themes.

BACKGROUND KNOWLEDGE

Post the word *occupy* and ask: *What if another country occupied ours and made new laws that changed your life? What if you were allowed to speak only the invading country's language and even had to change your name?*

Explain that for hundreds of years, the Korean Peninsula (now known as North Korea and South Korea) has been occupied by other nations. In 1910, Japan claimed control and began a 35-year occupation.

This novel tells the story of a Korean girl, Sun-hee, and boy, Tae-yul, growing up during this time. The novel is titled *When My Name Was Keoko* because Sun-hee is forced to change her name to a Japanese name, Keoko.

VOCABULARY

dregs solid parts left behind in a mostly liquid food or drink

the Emperor the ruler of an empire

Ask questions to check for understanding. For example:

✳ *Would you want to clean the* dregs *out of someone else's soup bowl?*

✳ *Does the United States have an emperor?*

Themes in a piece of writing are the author's underlying statements about life or human nature. Most of the time, the writer does not directly state the **themes.** Instead, you have to read between the lines and figure out what the important ideas are. How can you find the themes? Here are some possibilities:

- Look to see if a theme is stated directly.
- Consider the details the writer emphasizes. If a certain character, for example, acts angry and as a result has no friends, what might the writer be trying to say?
- Read a chunk of the text and then stop and ask: "What is the writer saying to me?" Consider how the details and chunks add up to what is not stated.

When My Name Was Keoko is **historical fiction** that describes the Japanese occupation of Korea. The following excerpt is from the opening chapter which is narrated by a young girl named Sun-hee. Examine **details** as one way to figure out themes. Underline parts of the text that indicate the theme(s). In the **Response Notes,** make notes about what is emphasized.

Response Notes

from **When My Name Was Keoko** by Linda Sue Park

1. Sun-hee (1940)

"It's only a rumor," Abuji said as I cleared the table. "They'll never carry it out."

My father wasn't talking to me, of course. He was talking to Uncle and my brother, Tae-yul, as they sat around the low table after dinner, drinking tea.

I wasn't supposed to listen to men's business, but I couldn't help it. It wasn't really my fault. Ears don't close the way eyes do.

I worked slowly. First I scraped the scraps of food and dregs of soup into an empty serving dish. Then I stacked the brass bowls—quietly, so they wouldn't clang against one another. Finally, I moved around the table and began putting the bowls through the little low window between the sitting room and the kitchen. The kitchen was built three steps down from the central courtyard, and the sitting room three steps up. From the window I could reach a shelf in the kitchen. I put the bowls on the shelf one at a time, arranging them in a very straight line.

The longer I stayed in the room, the more I'd hear.

Uncle shook his head. "I don't know, Hyungnim," he said, disagreeing respectfully. "They're masters of organization—if they want this done, you

Before

CRITICAL READING SKILL

Connecting Details to Theme Define or review *theme:* a comment a writer makes about a specific topic. You may want to illustrate the concept with a work of fiction students read earlier in the *Daybook,* such as Laurence Yep's *Hiroshima* excerpt from Unit 4, page 66. For example, ask: *What was a theme of this story? What was the writer trying to say to you?* (Possible answers: Nuclear

bombs have environmental effects; war is devastating.)

Explain that there are many possible themes for any piece of literature. Good readers think about the theme of what they're reading because it helps them understand what the writer wants to say. Then explain the focus of the lesson. Say: *One way to find the theme of a piece of writing is to pay close attention to the details.*

RESPONSE NOTES Read aloud or ask a volunteer to read aloud the introduction. Stop to explain the bullet points as needed. Then read aloud the first three paragraphs of the excerpt and model a response. For example: *Sun-hee listens to the men and she's not supposed to. One of the themes might be about discrimination against females in that society.*

can be sure they will find a way to do it. And I fear what will happen if they do. Our people will not stand for it. I am afraid there will be terrible trouble—"

Abuji cleared his throat to cut off Uncle's words. He'd noticed me kneeling by the table with the last of the bowls in my hands; I was listening so hard that I'd stopped moving. Hastily, I shoved the bowl through the window and left the room, sliding the paper door closed behind me.

What rumor? What was going to happen? What kind of trouble?

When I asked Tae-yul later, he said it was none of my business. That was his answer a lot of the time. It always made me want to clench my fists and stamp my foot and hit something.

- -

✳ Look at the details the author provides. Circle or underline places that might be clues to the theme or themes.

✳ Write a paragraph that describes possible themes and explain your reasons for what you chose.

_____

_____

_____

_____

_____

Continue reading from the opening chapter.

_They'll never carry it out. . . . They're masters of organization…_I knew who "they" were. The Japanese. Whenever there was talk that I wasn't supposed to hear, it was almost always about the Japanese.

A long time ago, when Abuji was a little boy and Uncle just a baby, the Japanese took over Korea. That was 1910. Korea wasn't its own country anymore.

The Japanese made a lot of new laws. One of the laws was that no Korean could be the boss of anything. Even though Abuji was a great scholar, he was only the vice-principal of my school, not the principal. The person at the top had to be Japanese. The principal was the father of my friend Tomo.

All our lessons were in Japanese. We studied Japanese language, culture, and history. Schools weren't allowed to teach Korean history or language. Hardly any books or newspapers were published in Korean. People weren't even supposed to tell old Korean folktales. But Uncle did sometimes—funny stories about foolish donkeys or brave tigers, or exciting ones about heroes like Tan-gun, the founder of Korea. Tae-yul and I loved it when Uncle told us stories.

ABOUT THE AUTHOR

Linda Sue Park was born in 1960 and raised near Chicago, Illinois. She started writing early in life, and at age 9, one of her poems was published in a children's magazine. Park earned a dollar for the publication of the poem and kept on writing! She continued to publish her poetry throughout middle and high school. She attended Stanford University and earned a Bachelor's degree in English. Her life after college included work in public relations, life in the British Isles, teaching English as a Second Language, and time as a food journalist. At age 37, she wrote her first book, _Seesaw Girl_. Park has since written picture books and young adult novels. In 2002, her novel _A Single Shard_ won the Newbery Medal. Park currently lives in upstate New York.

TEACHING TIP

Collaboration Students may benefit from completing the writing prompt together, using the Think-Pair-Share method.

1. **Think** Have students individually review the first part of the passage for possible clues to the theme.
2. **Pair** In pairs, students can compare ideas and write the paragraph together.
3. **Share** Have each pair share an idea from their paragraph with the class.

During

MONITORING UNDERSTANDING

After students have read the first half of the excerpt, have them stop for discussion. Ask: _Are you finding any possible themes?_ If students seem to be having difficulty, have them return to the reading and circle or underline any interesting details.

Encourage students to think primarily about the details. If they seem to be having trouble correlating the details to

themes, collect the details in a list or in a graphic organizer such as a web so that students can look for patterns and themes in the details.

WRITING SUPPORT

Identifying Possibilities For the writing prompt, explain to students that, having read only one page of the story, they are not encouraged to find a theme but to take notice of points of focus. Ask:

Where do you think the author might be going with this story? What could it really be about?

You might want to explain that _develop_ means "expand" or "make clearer." Remind students to give reasons—details from the text—that support their answers. After students have finished writing, direct them to continue reading the excerpt, continuing to note interesting details.

Identifying Theme Before explaining the chart, you may want to ask students to list themes that they have read in literature.

Then use the list to brainstorm details that would support each theme.

Continue by asking a volunteer to share a noted detail from the story. As a class, decide which theme the detail supports. For example, ask: *Could it be saying something about family? Could it be saying something about freedom?* When students agree on a theme, ask: *What might the author be saying about this?*

Quick-writing Direct students to write without stopping, explaining that writing fast is a way to get a lot of ideas on paper. Use a think-aloud to show how one thought leads to another. For example: *I was thinking how it would feel if I couldn't speak my own language. That makes me think about freedom and how having it taken away would really hurt.*

Quick Assess

✳ Did students connect details to themes in the story?

Response Notes

We still spoke Korean at home, but on the streets we always had to speak Japanese. You never knew who might be listening, and the military guards could punish anyone they heard speaking Korean. They usually didn't bother older people. But my friends and I had to be careful when we were in public.

Every once in a while another new law was announced, like the one when I was little that required us to attend temple on the Emperor's birthday. I decided that this must be the rumor—Abuji and Uncle had heard about a new law. I was right. ✦

✳ What do you think Park is saying about life in Korea during the Japanese occupation? Do a quick-write that answers this question. Explain what details in the story lead you to this understanding.

_____

_____

_____

_____

_____

✳ What details from the story point to the themes you've identified? For each of these details, jot down your ideas about how it supports a potential theme.

Supporting Details	Theme
"I wasn't supposed to listen . . . "	The unequal position of men and women in this family or society

> Examine details that contribute to potential themes and ask yourself, "What is the writer saying to me?"

After

APPLYING THE STRATEGY Invite students to look for thematic clues in the details of a film they like or have watched at school.

✳ Have students watch at least 30 minutes of the film. They should note details that are interesting.

✳ Have students copy the chart on this page, filling it in with details from the film and possible connections to themes.

✳ Have students write a short paragraph about what the filmmakers might be saying in this movie.

When students have completed their analyses, have a brief discussion about connecting details to theme. Ask:

✳ *By looking for details, what did you see in the movie that you hadn't seen before?*

✳ *Now that you've thought about the movie's theme, have you gotten more out of watching it? Explain.*

Often, stories that interest us have memorable events. But how do we as readers learn about themes through these events? Rarely does the writer come out and tell us all we need to know. Instead, writers let the events and actions, as well as the characters' reactions, give us clues about the themes. Think about why a writer includes a particular event in his or her story. It might be to illustrate an aspect of the message he or she is trying to convey.

In *When My Name Was Keoko*, Chapter 2 is narrated by Tae-yul, Sun-hee's brother. He tells how the Japanese have made another law affecting the Koreans. In your **Response Notes**, jot what you think this event reveals about the themes that surface in the novel.

from **When My Name Was Keoko** by Linda Sue Park

2. Tae-yul

Sun-hee is a real pain sometimes. Always asking questions, always wanting to know what's going on. I tell her it's none of her business, which is true. Abuji would tell her if he wanted her to know.

But I don't know what's happening either. Why hasn't he told me? It's not like I'm a little kid anymore—I'm old enough to know stuff.

One day I get home from school and Uncle comes in right after me. He's early, it's way before dinnertime. He's got a newspaper in one hand, and he walks right past me without even saying hello. "Hyungnim!" he calls.

Abuji is in the sitting room. Uncle goes in and closes the door behind him. I listen hard, but I can't hear anything—until Uncle raises his voice. "I won't do it!" he shouts. "They can't do this—they can't take away our names! I am Kim Young-chun, I will never be anyone else!"

Omoni and Sun-hee come out of the kitchen and look at me. I turn away a little, annoyed that I don't know what's going on. Just then Abuji opens the door and waves his hand toward us. So we all go into the room. Uncle is pacing around like crazy.

Abuji reads out loud from the newspaper: "'By order of the Emperor, all Koreans are to be graciously allowed to take Japanese names!'"

"'Graciously allowed...'" Uncle says. His voice is shaking, he's so mad. "How dare they twist the words! Why can't they at least be honest—we are being *forced* to take Japanese names!"

Abuji reads some more to himself, then says, "We must all go to the police station in the next week to register."

Uncle curses and pounds his fist against the wall.

Response Notes

Students will learn to determine how the events of a story can reveal and explain the themes of the story.

BACKGROUND KNOWLEDGE

Students will read another excerpt from *When My Name Was Keoko*. Ask students: *What was the first excerpt about? Who was involved? What was happening?* Students should know the following details:

✤ The story is about a Korean family living in Korea under Japanese occupation.

✤ In the story, a little girl , Sun-hee, is eavesdropping on a conversation between some men as she clears the dinner table. She overhears them discussing a new law imposed by the Japanese.

Explain that this lesson's excerpt will be narrated by Sun-hee's brother, Tae-yul. In this excerpt, the family learns that they have to change their names. Have a brief discussion with students about names and identity. For example, ask: *What is the meaning of your name? Where is it from? How would you feel if you had to change it?*

Before

CRITICAL READING SKILL

Connecting Events to Theme With students, create a web or list of themes discussed in the previous lesson. Then introduce the focus of the lesson. Say: *An author lets themes grow and change through a novel. He or she creates certain events to make their readers think about the themes. Good readers notice each event and how it helps develop a theme.*

Read aloud or ask volunteers to read aloud the introduction and first three paragraphs of the excerpt. Then use a think-aloud to model responding to the events: *Uncle walks right past Tae-yul with the newspaper. He's obviously upset about something he's read. Maybe this has to do with the theme of politics or war.*

Direct students to read and respond to the rest of the excerpt, paying special attention to the events that unfold. To refresh students' memories, you may want to post this cast of characters:

Sun-hee: the daughter
Tae-yul: the son
Abuji: the term for *father*
Omoni: the term for *mother*
Hyungnim: the father's name

Theme Bank Post a list of themes that come up in your class discussions. Add new themes to the list throughout the unit. Draw students' attention to the list each time you begin a new discussion about theme. This will help students keep track of thematic possibilities and make connections between the lessons' selections and their own reading, as well as give them ideas for their writing.

My name, Tae-yul, means "great warmth." My grandfather—Abuji's father—chose it. It's one of our traditions for the grandfather to do the naming. He'd taken it seriously, Omoni once told me; he wanted a name that would bring me good fortune.

For Sun-hee, too—"girl of brightness."

A different name? I can't imagine it. I look at Sun-hee and I can tell she's thinking the same thing.

"Those who do not register will be arrested," Abuji says.

"Let them! Let them arrest me! They will have my body but not my soul—my name is my soul!" Uncle's face is red as a pepper.

Abuji holds up his hand. "Such talk is useless. It must be done. But let me think a while."

We leave him alone. I'm last out of the room, but I don't close the door. I watch him take a few books from the cupboard and turn the pages. Then he gets up again and fetches paper and pencil. Writes something on the paper, looks at it, writes some more. What's he doing?

At last he calls us all back into the room. Sun-hee and I sit on the floor, but Uncle stays standing, his arms crossed. Stubborn. Abuji waits a few moments, until Uncle seems calmer and uncrosses his arms.

"Tae-yul, Sun-hee, you know that the Kim clan is a large and important one," Abuji says. "Long ago, all Kims lived in the same part of Korea, in the mountains. Choosing the word for gold as their name shows what a strong clan they were. Gold was only for kings."

He picks up the sheet of paper from the table and points at it. "I have chosen our Japanese name. It will be Kaneyama. '*Yama*' means 'mountain' in Japanese, and '*ka-ne*' means 'gold.' So the name will honor our family history."

He turns to Uncle. "*They* will not know this. But we will."

Uncle doesn't look so mad now. "Kaneyama," he says quietly, and bows his head. "Hyungnim has chosen well."

"As to our first names," Abuji says, "Sun-hee, fetch your primer."

Sun-hee goes to the cupboard and brings back an old book. I know the book—it was mine first, then hers. The Japanese alphabet is on the first page. Abuji takes the book and opens it.

"We will close our eyes and point. Whatever letter we point to, we will choose a name that begins with this letter. These are not our real names, so we do not care what they are."

Uncle grins. "That's very good, Hyungnim. In fact, I do not care at all—you may choose my letter for me."

Abuji smiles, too. "No, we will each choose for ourselves."

First Abuji, then Uncle. My turn. I close my eyes. Point my finger any old way, and then look.

N. My new initial.

My new name: Kaneyama Nobuo. ❖

During

MONITORING UNDERSTANDING
Circulate and monitor students' reading. As they read, ask questions to check comprehension. For example:

❋ *What are the meanings of Sun-hee's and Tae-yul's names?* (*Sun-hee* means "girl of brightness," and *Tae-yul* means "great warmth.")

❋ *What is the meaning of their family name,* Kim? ("gold")

❋ *Why does Abuji pick the Japanese family name* Kaneyama? (It means "gold mountain"; this way, the family can stay connected to their Korean family name and history.)

CULTURAL NOTE Point out that, at the end of the excerpt, Tae-yul says his new name is Kaneyama Nobuo. Explain that in Korean culture, as in many other cultures, family names come before the individual's name.

* What does this renaming event reveal about the themes in this novel? After you write your thoughts, share them with a partner.

_____

_____

_____

Another way of understanding themes is to put yourself in the position of the characters.

* Imagine that you are forced to change your name. You object and are told that you must write a letter explaining why you don't want to change your name. In your letter you need to answer the following questions: What does your name mean to you? What is the history of how you got your name? If you are still required to change your name, what new name would you take and why?

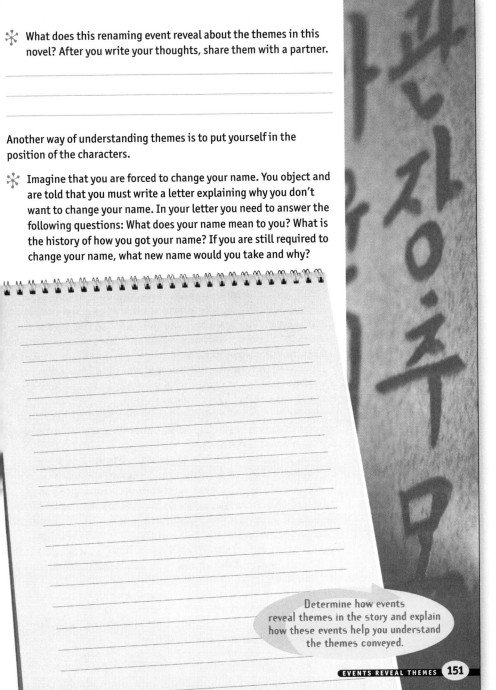

Determine how events reveal themes in the story and explain how these events help you understand the themes conveyed.

EVENTS REVEAL THEMES 151

EXTRA SUPPORT

Differentiation Some students may need to discuss the first writing prompt before completing it. Draw interested students together for a discussion circle or have students form heterogeneous groups. Have the group(s) discuss these questions:

* Why didn't the Kim family want to change their names?

* What was important about being a Kim?

* What is the author saying about identity?

* What is the author saying about Japan's occupation of Korea?

WRITING SUPPORT

Prewriting After reading through the prompt, you may want to suggest that students create a three-row chart to "break down" the prompt. Students can write and list answers to each question in the chart. Though some students may not be opposed to the idea of changing their names, remind them that they should imagine they are Sun-hee or Tae-yul.

Quick Assess

* Do students' letters address the questions listed on page 151?

After

READING/WRITING CONNECTION

Invite students to research their own first, middle, and/or last names.

* Students can interview a family member about the meaning of the name and/or why the family chose that name.

* Students can research the meaning of their first or middle names on the Internet. Have students type the name and the phrase *baby name* into

a protected search engine and browse the results for a definition.

* Students can also find meanings of family names on the Internet. Have students type the family name and the word *surname* into a protected search engine and browse the results.

Have students write a journal entry to reflect on what they found. Use these questions to guide students' responses:

* What have you learned about the meaning or origin of your name?

* Is your name important to you? Does it say something about you as a person?

* Would you change your name if you could? What name would you choose? Why?

LESSON 48   IMAGES AND SYMBOLS SUGGEST THEMES

Students will learn to look for images and symbols that contribute to the themes of a story and to decide what each image or symbol contributes to an understanding of the story.

BACKGROUND KNOWLEDGE

As a class, briefly review the events of the first two excerpts from *When My Name Was Keoko*. Students should know that Sun-hee and Tae-yul's family have been subjected to increasing control by the occupying Japanese.

Ask students if they know what either a cherry tree or a rose of Sharon tree looks like. You may want to display a photograph of each. (Images are easily accessible from the Internet by typing the terms *cherry tree* and *rose of Sharon tree* into an image search engine.) Explain that a cherry tree is common in Japan, whereas a rose of Sharon tree is common in Korea. In the next excerpt, both trees serve as powerful symbols.

VOCABULARY

magenta a bright purplish red

root ball the tangled roots of a plant

trowel a small garden tool with a flat blade for digging

Have students use the Word Splash blackline master found on page 278 to familiarize themselves with the selection vocabulary.

Look for images or symbols that suggest the themes of a story. A written **image** creates a picture in your mind that emphasizes something the writer wants you to notice. A **symbol** shows how one thing can represent something else. As you read another excerpt from *When My Name Was Keoko,* circle or underline images or symbols that you think suggest themes.

Response Notes

from **When My Name Was Keoko** by Linda Sue Park

7. Sun-hee

...Along the back of the vegetable patch was a row of small trees. Really, they were more like large shrubs. In the summer they blossomed—big pink—or white-petaled flowers with magenta throats. They were rose of Sharon trees, the national tree of Korea. Omoni had planted them years before, when she and Abuji had first moved to this house.

One evening in the fall Uncle brought home more news. The government had issued another official order. All families who had cherry trees were to dig up shoots and saplings from around their trees and bring them to police headquarters. The little cherry trees were to be planted all over town, and everyone was supposed to take good care of them.

The government order spoke of wishing to make our land more beautiful, with thousands of cherry trees. But it wasn't just a wish for beauty. The cherry tree was a national symbol of Japan.

And the final part of the order was that all rose of Sharon trees had to be uprooted and burned. The military police would be inspecting gardens to see that the order had been followed.

Omoni stayed inside the house; she couldn't bear to watch as Tae-yal chopped down the rose of Sharon trees one by one and dug out their roots. It was a difficult job; the trees were old and their roots reached deep into the ground. I helped him by dragging the fallen trees to a corner of the yard, where they'd be burned later.

Tae-yul had reached the last tree—a small one that Omoni had planted only a few years before. As he began to dig, Omoni came out of the house and said, "Tae-yul, wait. First go fetch a big pot, or a basin or something."

"What kind of pot?"

"I don't know—it needs to be big. Oh, wait—where you keep the tools, there's an old ceramic pot, with a crack in it. That will do."

I helped Tae-yul carry the pot out to her. It was quite large, as large around as my two arms could make a circle.

Before

CRITICAL READING SKILL

Connecting Images and Symbols to Theme Define or review *image* and *symbol:* An image makes a picture in your mind, and a symbol is something that represents something else. Then ask students to name symbols of their state, nation, or culture, such as a flag, flower, animal, color, etc. Ask: *What would it be like if someone took this symbol away and made*

you replace it with something else? Would it still mean the same thing to you?

Explain that writers commonly use images and symbols of a culture to build a theme pertaining to it. Then review themes that were present in the previous two excerpts. If you created a running list in the previous lessons, return to the list together.

READING FOR A PURPOSE Read aloud or ask a volunteer to read the introduction. Say: *In this excerpt, look for objects or images that could be symbols. The author is using them to build a theme.* Direct students to read and respond to the excerpt.

"Now," Omoni said, pointing to the last little tree. "Dig in a circle, and be careful not to cut any of the roots. I want you to bring the whole root ball out of the ground."

This took a long time. Tae-yul had used an ax to chop up the roots of the other trees and make it easier to dig them out. Now he could only use the shovel. Omoni returned to the house, but she came out from time to time to watch him work.

At last he put down the shovel and wiped his brow. "I think I can get it out now," he said. Although it had been the smallest tree, it was nearly as tall as me. Tae-yul pulled it carefully out of the hole and laid it down on the ground.

"Omoni!" I called.

She came out again and patted Tae-yul's shoulder. "You did a good job," she said. She walked around the little tree. "I think you will need to cut off about this much—" She pointed to a spot about a third of the way down from the top.

While Tae-yul chopped away with the ax, Omoni took up the shovel and began to fill the ceramic pot with dirt from where the tree had been dug up. Now I knew what she was doing. I got a trowel from the tool shelf and helped scoop dirt into the pot.

Omoni and Taw-yul lifted the little tree and settled it into the pot. Then we packed more dirt and mulch around it. Finally I fetched a basin of water and gave the tree a drink.

The three of us stepped back and looked at the tree and then at each other. We were tired and dirty, but we managed to smile. We'd hardly spoken throughout the entire task, yet we'd all known what to do. It felt good to have done this together. ❖

✳ What images stand out in your mind after reading this excerpt? Sketch at least two.

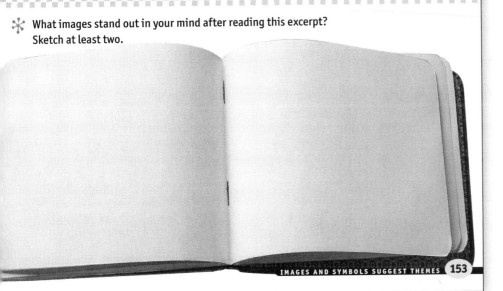

IMAGES AND SYMBOLS SUGGEST THEMES 153

Differentiation Some students may have trouble visualizing what is happening. Encourage students to stop after each paragraph to summarize what is happening. Then, students can complete the sketches together.

During

SHARING RESPONSES   When students have finished reading and responding to the excerpt, invite volunteers to share the images and symbols they noted. Ask: *What did you visualize? What symbols did the author use?* Model making a basic sketch of an image or symbol, such as the image of Sun-hee pouring water into the transplanted tree.

WRITING SUPPORT
Analyzing Theme   With students, go through the questions in the chart. For the left column, ask: *When Omoni decided to save the rose of Sharon tree, what was she saying about the Japanese occupation?* Then review the themes of the novel. Ask students which themes the author is alluding to with Omoni's rebellious act.

For the right column, ask: *Why would a country that is occupying another want to get rid of a cultural symbol, like the rose of Sharon tree?* Discuss what the author might be saying about the methods and intent of the occupying nation.

WRITER'S CRAFT

Symbolism After students finish their sketches, discuss how they contribute to a theme. Ask students: *What does your image or symbol mean? What is the author trying to say with it?*

Specifically, elicit that the rose of Sharon tree is a symbol of Korean culture, and that the family will not allow it to die. Point out the paragraph that starts "Omoni stayed..." on page 152. Repeat the description of the rose of Sharon tree: "the trees were old and their roots reached deep into the ground." Ask students what the roots symbolize. (the strength of the family) This will prepare students for the first writing prompt on page 154.

Quick Assess

✳ Do students identify important images and symbols in the reading?

✳ Do students' sketches accurately reflect the images in the text?

✳ What do the images you sketched tell you about potential themes in the story? When you finish, share your sketches and explanation with a partner.

_____

_____

_____

_____

✳ Reflect on the two questions below. Record your ideas in the space provided.

What does Omoni's resistance to destroying the trees stand for, or symbolize, in the story? How does this reveal one of the themes?	What does the attempt of the Japanese to replace the rose of Sharon with cherry trees suggest about the themes of the story?

Look for images and symbols that contribute to the themes and decide what each contributes to your understanding of the story.

After

APPLYING THE STRATEGY Have students read the remainder of *When My Name Was Keoko.* Then have them track the themes you've discussed in Lessons 46–48. Students can use details, events, images, and symbols to follow the author's themes. Encourage them to use a chart, such as the one on page 148, to connect details to themes.

When students finish reading the final excerpt, have them write a short essay about the theme they consider to be important. Then have a "book club" discussion, allowing each student to share thoughts on what was read.

ART CONNECTION Encourage students to research and write about an important artifact or symbol from their family or culture.

✳ Have students write a short essay about the meaning of the object or symbol.

✳ Students can create a drawing of it to share with the class. The drawings can incorporate words or phrases that convey the symbol's meaning.

✳ Groups of students can create a mural or large visual that conveys several symbols and their meanings.

S tories are not the only types of writing that have themes. Poets convey **themes** in their poetry. And, unlike a story or novel in which the writer has a lot of space to develop themes, a poet has to get to the point much more quickly. As you read a poem, you can use the same strategies for finding themes that you used when reading stories. Look for details, events, symbols, and images that contribute to the themes just as you did in the previous lessons.

At about the same time that the Korean adolescents, Sun-hee and Tae-yul, experienced the Japanese control over their lives, another young person was feeling the effects of war. Vera lived in the Aleutian Islands off the coast of Alaska. For nine thousand years the Aleut people had lived on these islands. Suddenly, the entire population was forced into relocation centers by the U.S. government when the Japanese Navy invaded. Vera's story is told in a series of poems that are written in unrhymed verse. The poems are collected in a book called *Aleutian Sparrow*.

As you read the following poems, jot in the **Response Notes** column your thoughts about possible themes.

And So It Begins: The First Stop on Our Journey by Karen Hesse

In this temporary camp surrounded by trees on the
     grounds of Wrangell Institute
We have little else but the alphabet.
And so we gather together, five villages of Aleuts,
     and start stringing up the lanterns of our lives,
Story by story. ❖

Response Notes

❋ What do you think Vera means by "stringing up the lanterns of our lives"? What is she saying in this poem about the theme of recognizing what is important in life?

Students will learn to explore themes in poems in order to gain insights into a poet's perspective.

BACKGROUND KNOWLEDGE

Ask students what they know about the Aleutian Islands. Help students locate the islands near the southwestern Alaskan coast. Explain that in 1942, during World War II, Japanese and U.S. forces fought over these islands. The Aleutian inhabitants were forced by the U.S. government to relocate into the forests of Alaska. In the 1980s, the U.S. government offered compensation to Aleut families who had to relocate.

Ask students what they know about forced relocations. Students may be familiar with the relocation of Japanese Americans into internment camps during World War II, perhaps through the popular novel *Farewell to Manzanar* by Jeanne and James Houston.

VOCABULARY

Wrangell Institute a large boarding school for Native American children

abandoned cruelly left alone when you need help

suffocation in this context, denseness and airlessness

Ask students to generate their own synonyms and/or antonyms for the first two words.

Before

CRITICAL READING SKILL

Focus on Poetry and Theme Review the meaning of *theme:* a comment a writer makes about a specific topic. Then explain that poets also use themes.

Explain that poetry is more compressed than fiction. That is, poets use fewer words to say more. Whereas novels have themes that develop through the chapters, a poem as short as five lines can also have a theme.

Read aloud or ask a volunteer to read aloud the introduction and first poem. Then ask: *What is happening? What message is the poet trying to convey?* Elicit that the poet might be saying that each family has absolutely nothing except a story to tell about the ways that relocation has affected their lives.

ABOUT THE AUTHOR

Karen Hesse was born in Baltimore, Maryland, in 1952. She had many aspirations in life, but her fifth-grade teacher encouraged her to pursue a career in writing. She earned a Bachelor's degree in English from the University of Maryland and held various jobs while writing books for children and young adults. Hesse has won critical acclaim for her picture books and novels. *Out of the Dust,* about the Great Depression, won the Newbery Medal in 1998.

TEACHING TIP

Collaboration Students will benefit from reading each poem aloud and discussing it together. Have students form pairs or groups. After students have read each poem, have them summarize what is happening and discuss the accompanying writing prompt. Give students time to independently complete each prompt before moving on to the next poem.

Response Notes

Arrival at Ward Lake by Karen Hesse

Not until we are abandoned in the dark suffocation of the
    forest,
Not until we count only two small bunkhouses and two
    cabins for five villages of Aleuts,
Not until the morning, when we wake, on the floor, a
    landscape of bedrolls and blankets,
Do we discover that we cannot, from any corner of the camp,
    catch a glimpse of open water. ❖

✳ **What images does this poem bring to mind? What do you think these images might suggest about the themes of this poem?**

Blanket Houses by Karen Hesse

We have to choose between warmth
And privacy.
We hang blankets to divide the space inside the crowded
    cabins.
I sleep beside my mother, not quite touching. And we shiver. ❖

✳ **What does this poem suggest is important in life? What makes you think so?**

During

WRITING SUPPORT

Analyzing Poetry Circulate and monitor students' progress. As needed, offer explanations of the writing prompts. For the first prompt:

✳ Review the purpose of imagery. Ask: *When you hear the words of the poem, what can you picture in your mind?* Possible answers include people looking lost and confused, people trying to sleep on a crowded floor.

✳ You may also want students to discuss individual images, such as *the dark suffocation of the forest* or *a landscape of bedrolls and blankets.* Ask: *What does the poet want you to know about this situation?*

For the second prompt:

✳ Ask: *What choice did the narrator make?* (giving up the warmth of blankets to keep the family's privacy)

✳ Discuss how the choice shows the narrator's priority. Remind students to quote the poem to support their ideas.

✳ Begin to plan a poem of your own that reveals an important theme. Think of an event from your life that taught you something important. Elaborate about the event and the details of the event in the chart below. Can you think of symbols or images that would represent that theme? In the chart below, plan a poem about the event.

Brief description of the event	Important details that convey themes
Why the event is important and what themes it reveals	Symbols or images that suggest themes

✳ Write your poem in the space below.

Explore the themes in poems to help you gain insights into an author's perspectives.

Prewriting Help students brainstorm subjects for their poems. Post a list of themes you've discussed in the unit. Then ask students: *Which of these themes is important to you? What do you want to say about it?*

Ask students to volunteer themes they would like to write about. Help them decide on events that would convey their thoughts on their themes. For example, ask: *What makes you think this away? What did you do, see, or hear that made you feel this way?*

WRITER'S CRAFT

Composing a Poem Before students write their poems, review some elements of poetry.

✳ Encourage students to use symbols and imagery to convey themes. Ask: *What symbols are you using? What do they represent?*

✳ Point out how Hesse plays with line breaks. Encourage students to experiment with this as well.

Quick Assess

✳ Do students use relevant details, symbols, and imagery to convey theme?

✳ Do students' poems draw on the information in their charts?

After

LISTENING/SPEAKING CONNECTION Have students share and revise their poems.

✳ Divide students into groups.

✳ Ask students to share their poems and offer feedback. For each poem, groups should discuss the questions: *Can we identify the themes of the poem?* Remind students to focus on images and symbols.

✳ Direct students to revise their poems to resolve issues brought up by the groups.

When revisions are complete, have students share their poems with the class. After each poem is read, have a brief discussion about its theme.

APPLYING THE STRATEGY Have students study the theme of a favorite poem or song.

✳ Students should list details, images, or symbols that convey a theme.

✳ Have students write a paragraph identifying the poem's or song's theme. Ask them to support their opinion with quotes from the poem or song lyrics.

✳ Have students read the poem or play the song for the class. Students should also share their opinion about the poem or song.

Students will learn how to explore the themes in an author's personal story in order to gain insights into the writer's perspective.

BACKGROUND KNOWLEDGE

Ask students what they know about the conflict in Yugoslavia in the 1990s. Then, on a world map, help students locate Bosnia and Herzegovina and Yugoslavia in the southern-central portion of Europe. Explain that Yugoslavia used to be a much larger nation that included Slovenia, Croatia, and Bosnia and Herzegovina. In the early 1990s, Slovenia, Croatia, and Bosnia and Herzegovina sought independence from Yugoslavia. Sarajevo, the capital of Bosnia, was bombed by Serbian forces. Thousands of residents were killed or evacuated.

Tell students they will read part of the diary of a 13-year old girl living in Sarajevo at the time of the war. Then ask: *What would it be like if your city were attacked by an enemy? How would your life change? Do you think you'd still be able to spend time with your friends and go about your normal activities?*

A writer's themes provide insights into his or her perspectives. Themes often make a statement about life, the world, or human nature. Themes are more obvious when you are reading **personal narrative,** that is, when the author is talking about his or her own life.

The following excerpt is from a diary written by Zlata, a thirteen-year-old girl who began keeping her diary in September of 1991. In early entries of the diary, Zlata has a very typical preteen life. Then war breaks out in her city of Sarajevo. Life changes. In your **Response Notes,** jot down your thoughts about the possible themes revealed in Zlata's diary entries.

Response Notes

from **Zlata's Diary: A Child's Life in Sarajevo**
by Zlata Filipovic

Sunday, October 6, 1991
I'm watching the American Top 20 on MTV. I don't remember a thing, who's in what place.

I feel great because I've just eaten a "Four Season" PIZZA with ham, cheese, ketchup and mushrooms. It was yummy. Daddy bought it for me at Galija's (the pizzeria around the corner). Maybe that's why I didn't remember who took what place—I was too busy enjoying my pizza.

I've finished studying and tomorrow I can go to school BRAVELY, without being afraid of getting a bad grade. I deserve a good grade because I studied all weekend and I didn't even go out to play with my friends in the park. The weather is nice and we usually play "monkey in the middle," talk and go for walks. Basically, we have fun.

Monday, March 30, 1992
Hey, Diary! You know what I think? Since Anne Frank called her diary Kitty, maybe I could give you a name too. What about:

ASFALTINA	PIDZAMETA
SEFIKA	HIKMETA
SEVALA	MIMMY

Or something else???
    I'm thinking, thinking . . .
    I've decided! I'm going to call you
    MIMMY
    All right, then let's start.

Before

CRITICAL READING SKILL
Focus on Perspective and Theme Ask students: *Do you keep a diary?* Students may volunteer that they keep a diary online or in a notebook or journal. Ask students why they write about their lives in their diaries.

Then explain that because they tell about daily events and feelings, diaries can show a unique perspective on a historical period of time. Briefly review prominent themes in this unit, such as culture, war, and family. Ask students to keep these themes in mind as they read the excerpt.

RESPONSE NOTES Read aloud or ask volunteers to read aloud the introduction and the first entry. Then ask: *What is Zlata's life like? What is she concerned about?* Elicit that Zlata's life is relatively carefree. Then direct students to read and respond to the text, noticing when and how the narrator's life changes.

Dear Mimmy,

It's almost half-term. We're all studying for our tests. Tomorrow we're supposed to go to a classical music concert at the Skendaerija Hall. Our teacher says we shouldn't go because there will be 10,000 people, pardon me, children, there, and somebody might take us as hostages or plant a bomb in the concert hall. Mommy says I shouldn't go. So I won't.

Hey! You know who won the Yugovision Song Contest? EXTRA NENA!!!???

I'm afraid to say this next thing. Melica says she heard at the hairdresser's that on Saturday, April 4, 1992, there's going to be BOOM—BOOM, BANG—BANG, CRASH Sarajevo. Translation: they're going to bomb Sarajevo.
Love, Zlata

Sunday, April 5, 1992
Dear Mimmy,

I'm trying to concentrate so I can do my homework (reading), but I simply can't. Something is going on in town. You can hear gunfire from the hills. Columns of people are spreading out from Dobrinja. They're trying to stop something, but they themselves don't know what. You can simply feel that something is coming, something very bad. On TV I see people in front of the B-H parliament building. The radio keeps playing the same song: "Sarajevo, My Love." That's all very nice, but my stomach is still in knots and I can't concentrate on my homework anymore.

Mimmy, I'm afraid of WAR!!!
Zlata

Monday, June 29, 1992
BOREDOM!!! SHOOTING!!! SHELLING!!! PEOPLE BEING KILLED!!! DESPAIR!!! HUNGER!!! MISERY!!! FEAR!!!

That's my life! The life of an innocent eleven-year-old schoolgirl!! A schoolgirl without a school, without the fun and excitement of school. A child without games, without friends, without the sun, without birds, without nature, without fruit, without chocolate or sweets, with just powdered milk. In short, a child without a childhood. A wartime child. I now realize that I am really living through a war, I am witnessing an ugly, disgusting war. I and thousands of other children in this town that is being destroyed, that is crying, weeping, seeking help, but getting none. God, will this ever stop, will I ever be a schoolgirl again, will I ever enjoy my childhood again? I once heard that childhood is the most wonderful time of your life. And it is. I loved it, and now an ugly war is taking it all away from me. Why? I feel sad. I feel like crying. I am crying.
Your Zlata

ABOUT THE AUTHOR

Zlata Filipovic was born in Sarajevo in 1980. Her diary was like that of many young adults until war broke out in her region in 1992. She kept writing in her diary even as Sarajevo was bombed. At the end of 1993, Zlata's family was rescued from Sarajevo and taken to Paris. Her diary was soon published and translated into more than twenty languages. She has since been an ardent peace activist, working with the United Nations and writing books about teenage writers and the war in the former Yugoslavia. She also earned a Bachelor's degree in Human Sciences from Oxford University and a Master's degree in Peace Studies from Trinity College in Dublin, Ireland. She currently lives in Dublin.

EXTRA SUPPORT

Differentiation If students seem to have difficulty reading the excerpt on their own, you may want to offer support in a small group.

1. Invite interested students to join you in a group.
2. Read aloud one entry at a time, giving students time to reread each and take Response Notes.
3. Briefly discuss each entry before moving on to the next one. Summarize the events of the entry, discussing how they mark the escalation of the war.

During

SHARING RESPONSES   Read separate entries and stop to discuss Zlata's perspective and how it relates to the theme. Ask:

✸ *What did you learn about Zlata's life?*

✸ *What is her perspective? What is she saying about living in a time of war?*

After this discussion, students will be ready to complete the first writing prompt on page 160.

WRITING SUPPORT

Evaluating Perspective For the second writing prompt, discuss how diaries communicate world events. Ask: *If you wanted to know about the war in Yugoslavia, would you rather read an encyclopedia or Zlata's diary? Explain.*

Students may offer that Zlata's description seems more "real," but it does not explain why these events are happening to her. Direct students to complete the prompt with explanations of their own opinions.

Reviewing Themes For the last writing prompt, use questions to stimulate students' thoughts on the unit's themes. For example:

✳ *How has war affected each person I've read about?*

✳ *What do people lose in war?*

✳ *How might I feel or react if I were in the midst of an occupation, relocation, or war?*

Quick Assess

✳ Do students understand how the author's perspective influences what they read?

✳ Do students' diary entries reflect their learning about more than one character in this unit?

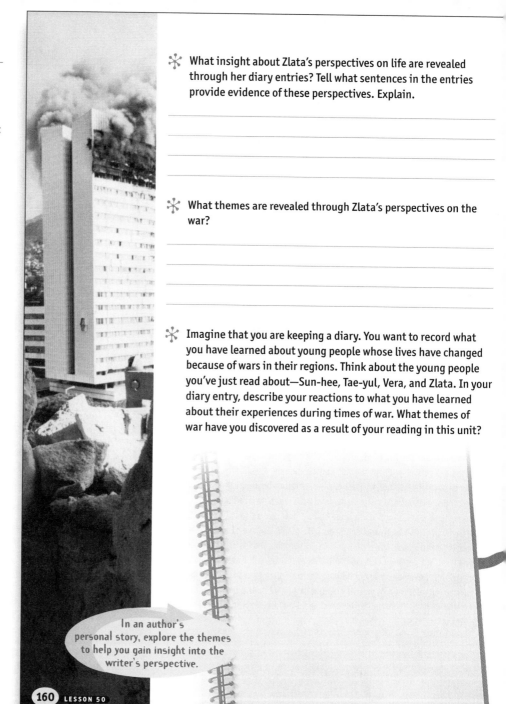

✳ What insight about Zlata's perspectives on life are revealed through her diary entries? Tell what sentences in the entries provide evidence of these perspectives. Explain.

✳ What themes are revealed through Zlata's perspectives on the war?

✳ Imagine that you are keeping a diary. You want to record what you have learned about young people whose lives have changed because of wars in their regions. Think about the young people you've just read about—Sun-hee, Tae-yul, Vera, and Zlata. In your diary entry, describe your reactions to what you have learned about their experiences during times of war. What themes of war have you discovered as a result of your reading in this unit?

In an author's personal story, explore the themes to help you gain insight into the writer's perspective.

After

READING/WRITING CONNECTION

Challenge students to keep a diary for a week or other short period of time. Every day, students can record activities, thoughts, and/or feelings. After students have completed their assignment, have a class discussion about keeping a diary. Ask: *Was it hard to write every day? Are you glad you did? Will you continue to keep a diary? Why or why not?*

READING/ART CONNECTION

In groups, students can create a thematic collage based on the unit's selections.

1. Have each group choose a theme from the unit.
2. Students can choose an image, symbol, detail, or event from each selection that relates to the theme.

3. Students can plan and create an illustration that depicts the chosen images, symbols, details, or events from the selections.
4. Have groups briefly present their collages to the class.

UNIT 11
EXPLORING MULTIPLE PERSPECTIVES

Lessons 51–55, pages 162–176

UNIT OVERVIEW

By reading speeches and essays students will see how writers convey their perspectives on important issues such as racial equality and war.

KEY IDEA

An effective argument makes use of elements such as a thesis statement and supporting evidence, tone, style, and emotional appeal.

CRITICAL READING SKILLS

by lesson

51 Understanding the structure of an argument

52 Analyzing an author's tone

53 Appreciating an author's style

54 Analyzing a persuasive appeal

55 Selecting convincing tools

WRITING ACTIVITIES

by lesson

51 Outline a persuasive letter.

52 Write one paragraph of a persuasive letter previously outlined.

53 Evaluate the effectiveness of a speaker's style.

54 Chart persuasive appeals in three different works.

55 Plan a persuasive speech or letter and write one paragraph of it.

Exploring Multiple Perspectives

When people want to persuade you to think a certain way, they want you to see the issue from a particular **perspective**—theirs! For **powerful persuasion,** writers or speakers use several techniques to convince their audience or move them to action. Historical figures such as Thomas Paine helped convince early American colonists that they should fight the British for their freedom. César Chavez convinced migrant farm workers to join a union, and they convinced grape growers to provide better wages and benefits to their workers. Rosa Parks spoke loudly about segregation through her quiet action of keeping her seat on a Birmingham, Alabama, bus. Powerful persuaders use language and action to convince others.

In this unit, you will learn about tools that persuaders use to structure their **arguments**—thesis statements and supporting evidence, tone, style, and emotional appeals. You will also have a chance to experiment with the power of persuasion.

161

Literature

- **"Memorial and Recommendations of the Grand Council Fire of American Indians"** (letter)

A group of concerned residents appeals to the mayor of Chicago to use his influence to change the curriculum and textbooks used in schools so that all American children will better understand the history and culture of the "First Americans."

- **"Gettysburg Address"** by Abraham Lincoln (speech)

President Lincoln addresses a grieving public at the dedication of a war memorial. He calls them to dedicate themselves to continuing the fight for a nation of freedom and equality for all people.

- **"I Have a Dream"** by Dr. Martin Luther King, Jr. (speech)

This famous speech reviews the major issues of the struggle for civil rights and expresses hope and faith that the dream of equal rights will be a reality.

ASSESSMENT To assess student learning in this unit, see pages 240 and 262.

LESSON **51** STRUCTURING AN ARGUMENT

Students will learn that a writer's perspective is revealed through the thesis of an argument.

BACKGROUND KNOWLEDGE

Tell students the context for this letter. The mayor of Chicago, "Big Bill" Thompson had recently been elected. He had campaigned on a slogan of "America First," advocating that Americans should focus on their country and not on the rest of the world. He had launched an effort to find and remove textbooks that emphasized the part Britain played in American history, calling them "pro-British." The writers of the letter in this lesson refer to Thompson's campaign slogan, "America First," and his claim about textbooks and subtly turn the slogan and claim to suit their purpose: to eliminate the stereotypes of Native Americans that appeared in textbooks and school curricula and present a fuller picture of the First Americans.

VOCABULARY

American Indian Native American

massacre mass murder

treacherous sneaky; likely to betray

medicine man Native American healing priest

Use the Word Splash activity on page 278 to preview the vocabulary.

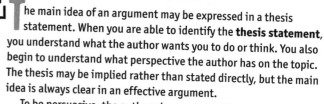

STRUCTURING AN ARGUMENT

The main idea of an argument may be expressed in a thesis statement. When you are able to identify the **thesis statement**, you understand what the author wants you to do or think. You also begin to understand what perspective the author has on the topic. The thesis may be implied rather than stated directly, but the main idea is always clear in an effective argument.

To be persuasive, the author also must provide **reasons** and **evidence.** As a reader or listener, you evaluate the reasons and evidence to see if they are convincing.

Read the letter from the Grand Council Fire of American Indians to the mayor of Chicago. Watch for the main idea and how it is supported. The thesis is directly stated twice. In the **Response Notes**, put a star by the thesis statements and mark any reasons that support the main idea.

Response Notes

"Memorial and Recommendations of the Grand Council Fire of American Indians"

December 1, 1927

To the mayor of Chicago:

You tell all white men "America First." We believe in that.

We are the only ones, truly, that are one hundred percent. We therefore ask you, while you are teaching schoolchildren about America First, teach them truth about the First Americans.

We do not know if school histories are pro-British, but we do know that they are unjust to the life of our people—the American Indian. They call all white victories battles and all Indian victories massacres. The battle with Custer has been taught to schoolchildren as a fearful massacre on our part. We ask that this, as well as other incidents, be told fairly. If the Custer battle was a massacre, what was Wounded Knee?

History books teach that Indians were murderers—is it murder to fight in self-defense? Indians killed white men because white men took their lands, ruined their hunting grounds, burned their forests, destroyed their buffalo. White men penned our people on reservations, then took away the reservations. White men who rise to protect their property are called patriots— Indians who do the same are called murderers.

White men call Indians treacherous—but no mention is made of broken treaties on the part of the white man. White men say that Indians were always fighting. It was only our lack of skill in white man's warfare that led to our

■ 162 **LESSON 51**

Before

CRITICAL READING SKILL

Understanding the Structure of an Argument Explain that the purpose of persuasion is to convince your audience to agree with you or take action on an issue. Remind students that, to accomplish your purpose, you should

✳ state your position about the issue (the thesis);

✳ state the desired outcome (what you want the reader to think or do);

✳ explain reasons for your position;

✳ support your position with strong evidence.

Have students analyze the letter by identifying these elements.

defeat. An Indian mother prayed that her boy be a great medicine man rather than a great warrior. It is true that we had our own small battles, but in the main we were peace loving and home loving.

White men called Indians thieves—and yet we lived in frail skin lodges and needed no locks or iron bars. White men call Indians savages. What is civilization? Its marks are a noble religion and philosophy, original arts, stirring music, rich story and legend. We had these. Then we were not savages, but a civilized race.

We made blankets that were beautiful, that the white man with all his machinery has never been able to duplicate. We made baskets that were beautiful. We wove in beads and colored quills designs that were not just decorative motifs but were the outward expression of our very thoughts. We made pottery—pottery that was useful, and beautiful as well. Why not make schoolchildren acquainted with the beautiful handicrafts in which we were skilled? Put in every school Indian blankets, baskets, pottery.

We sang songs that carried in their melodies all the sounds of nature—the running of waters, the sighing of winds, and the calls of the animals. Teach these to your children that they may come to love nature as we love it.

We had our statesmen—and their oratory has never been equaled. Teach the children some of these speeches of our people, remarkable for their brilliant oratory.

We played games—games that brought good health and sound bodies. Why not put these in your schools? We told stories. Why not teach schoolchildren more of the wholesome proverbs and legends of our people? Tell them how we loved all that was beautiful. That we killed game only for food, not for fun. Indians think white men who kill for fun are murderers.

Tell your children of the friendly acts of Indians to the white people who first settled here. Tell them of our leaders and heroes and their deeds. Tell them of Indians such as Black Partridge, Shabbona, and others who many times saved the people of Chicago at great danger to themselves. Put in your history books the Indian's part in the World War. Tell how the Indian fought for a country of which he was not a citizen, for a flag to which he had no claim, and for a people that have treated him unjustly.

The Indian has long been hurt by these unfair books. We ask only that our story be told in fairness. We do not ask you to overlook what we did, but we do ask you to understand it. A true program of America First will give a generous place to the culture and history of the American Indian.

We ask this, Chief, to keep sacred the memory of our people. ❖

ABOUT THE AUTHORS
Formed in 1923 in Chicago, The Grand Council Fire of American Indians was an activist organization of Native Americans and upper-middle-class whites who were interested in Native American affairs and welfare.

EXTRA SUPPORT

Differentiation Read the first two paragraphs aloud. Then model how a successful reader might stop to think about what he or she has read thus far: *It seems that the letter is asking the mayor to teach the truth about First Americans, which means that the Council believes that First Americans have not been represented fairly in school. I'll continue reading to see if that is true.*

Read aloud the next two paragraphs and stop again. Ask students to write down one belief that the letter writer seems to have. Have them circle words that set up opposites, such as *victories* versus *fearful massacres*. Which words do the letter writers favor?

Then ask questions such as these to help students recognize the thesis:

✳ *What is the main idea that the letter is trying to get across?* (American Indians were treated unfairly in school history books.)

✳ *What is one piece of evidence?* (History books teach that Indians were murders.)

During

RESEARCHING BACKGROUND

Point out references in the letter to events and people many students don't know about. Explain that these references would have been familiar to people of the time. For example, readers of the letter around the time it was written would have detailed knowledge of such events as the Battle of the Little Big Horn (the battle with Custer) and the Wounded Knee Massacre. Suggest that groups of students research Native American history to fill in the context for the letter. Suggested topics for research include the following:

✳ Grand Council Fire

✳ Battle of the Little Big Horn

✳ Wounded Knee Massacre

✳ Potawatomi Chief Black Partridge

✳ Shabbona

✳ Jot down your initial impressions about the letter. Is this letter interesting to you? Is it convincing? From your experience, do you think the same point could be made today?

_____

_____

_____

_____

✳ Good readers carefully evaluate the reasons and evidence that support a thesis. Are the reasons logical? Is there enough evidence to be convincing? Do the facts seem to be accurate? Facts, statistics, examples, observations, quotations, and experts' opinions all can provide **supporting evidence.** Use the following chart to show the reasons and evidence that support the thesis that school history books are "unjust to the life of . . . the American Indian." Label the kind of evidence used.

Reasons	Evidence
Indians are inaccurately portrayed as killers.	Indian victories are called "massacres"; white victories are called "battles."—observation
Indians are inaccurately portrayed as treacherous.	

This argument is/is not persuasive to me because ....

....

....

AUTHOR'S PERSPECTIVE   Remind readers that this letter was written by a group of people. Ask students the following question: *The members of the Grand Council Fire were Native American and white. In what ways might the experiences of the authors have influenced the perspective conveyed in the letter?* (American Indians had been killed by white men, had their land taken away, and had been put on reservations. Therefore, they felt that white men should not be called victorious and patriotic for having mistreated American Indians. Some white men also saw mistreatment and the stereotyping in curricula and schools as serious problems. They agreed with the Native Americans that stereotypical images should be replaced.)

✳ Think of someone whom you feel is portrayed inaccurately. For example, you might think that the media show teenagers as lazy or unruly when that is not true. Briefly outline a letter that you could write to newspaper editors or to another audience to change people's minds. Be sure that your outline includes a thesis (your topic and what you want your audience to think or do about it), reasons, and evidence.

Understanding the structure of an argument helps you evaluate how persuasive it is.

Organizing Ideas Have students create graphic organizers such as the following to outline their letters.

Thesis:		
Desired Outcome:		
Support:	Support:	Support:

To facilitate revision, suggest that students use self-stick notes for each of the boxes. Then they can rearrange them until they achieve the best order.

✳ weaker vs. stronger or vice versa

✳ obvious vs. subtle or vice versa

✳ simple vs. complex or vice versa

Quick Assess

✳ Are students' evaluation charts complete?

✳ Do students' outlines include thesis statements, reasons, and evidence?

After

APPLYING THE STRATEGY

Structuring an Argument Have students read letters to the editors of newspapers and other publications. Then have groups analyze the arguments for their effectiveness. For the letter they deem most effective, have students note the thesis statement and list the reasons and supporting evidence in a chart such as that on page 164.

READING/SPEAKING CONNECTION

Invite students to debate the issue of stereotyping that is at the core of the letter. Assign the question: *Should American Indian names be removed wherever they are used as mascots for sports teams?*

Have groups draw straws for assignments either for or against the change. Provide time for students to plan their arguments; then hold the debates. After the first round, allow students to change sides and argue for the opposite position.

Students will learn that the tone of a piece of writing often reveals the author's opinion or feelings.

BACKGROUND KNOWLEDGE

Invite students to share what they know about the War Between the States and the Gettysburg Address. (Over 48,000 lives were lost in the three days of fighting at Gettysburg, July 1-3, 1863.) The war was still not over when Lincoln was asked to speak at the dedication of a memorial at the battlefield on November 19, 1863.

Myths have grown around the preparation of the speech—that Lincoln wrote it on an envelope on his way to the dedication or that a photographer didn't even have time to take a photo because the speech was so short. What *is* true is that Lincoln's speech was not the main one that day. He had been invited only to make a few "remarks." Yet, his are the words we remember more than one hundred years later.

VOCABULARY

score twenty

consecrate make holy

hallow make holy

After discussing the definitions, invite students to restate the sentence in which each word appears, substituting the definition for the word

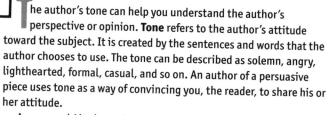

The author's tone can help you understand the author's perspective or opinion. **Tone** refers to the author's attitude toward the subject. It is created by the sentences and words that the author chooses to use. The tone can be described as solemn, angry, lighthearted, formal, casual, and so on. An author of a persuasive piece uses tone as a way of convincing you, the reader, to share his or her attitude.

As you read Abraham Lincoln's Gettysburg Address, think about his opinion and the tone of his speech. The Battle of Gettysburg, which took place in 1863, was one of the bloodiest of the Civil War. Five months after the battle ended, President Lincoln made this speech at a dedication ceremony to honor the thousands of soldiers who had died in that battle. In the audience were grief-stricken mothers, fathers, and children of the men who had died at Gettysburg.

Response Notes

Gettysburg Address by Abraham Lincoln

Four score and seven years ago our fathers brought forth on this continent, a new nation, conceived in Liberty, and dedicated to the proposition that all men are created equal.

Now we are engaged in a great civil war, testing whether that nation, or any nation so conceived and so dedicated, can long endure. We are met on a great battlefield of that war. We have come to dedicate a portion of that field as a final resting place for those who here gave their lives that that nation might live. It is altogether fitting and proper that we should do this.

But, in a larger sense, we cannot dedicate—we cannot consecrate—we cannot hallow—this ground. The brave men, living and dead, who struggled here have consecrated it, far above our poor power to add or detract. The world will little note, nor long remember what we say here, but it can never forget what they did here. It is for us the living, rather, to be dedicated here to the unfinished work which they who fought here have thus far so nobly advanced. It is rather for us to be here dedicated to the great task remaining before us—that from these honored dead we take increased devotion to that cause for which they gave the last full measure of devotion; that we here highly resolve that these dead shall not have died in vain; that this nation, under God, shall have a new birth of freedom; and that government of the people, by the people, for the people, shall not perish from the earth. ❖

Before

CRITICAL READING SKILL

Tone Use the letter in Lesson 51 to discuss tone. Work with students to determine how they would read aloud the fourth paragraph on page 162 (*History books teach that . . .*). Ask students which words should be emphasized and which parts should be read softly or quietly. As you tease out their reasons for how they would read the letter, explain that tone

refers to the author's attitude toward a subject. If the author feels strongly about a serious subject, the words reflect those feelings. In the letter, words such as *unjust, massacre,* and *treacherous* reflect the serious nature of the letter.

RESPONSE NOTES As students read the Gettysburg Address, they should look for words that tell the reader how the author (Lincoln) feels about the subject.

Remind students that, even though the speech was given to dedicate a battlefield that was used in one war, he is really addressing the equality of the whole nation.

✴ What two words would you use to describe Lincoln's tone?

_____

✴ Reread the Gettysburg Address and circle the words that help establish the tone.

✴ Review the outline you developed at the end of Lesson 51. Decide what tone you want to use for the letter you will write and write the first paragraph, selecting words that will help you achieve that tone.

_____

_____

_____

_____

_____

_____

The tone of a piece of writing often reveals the author's opinion or feelings about the subject.

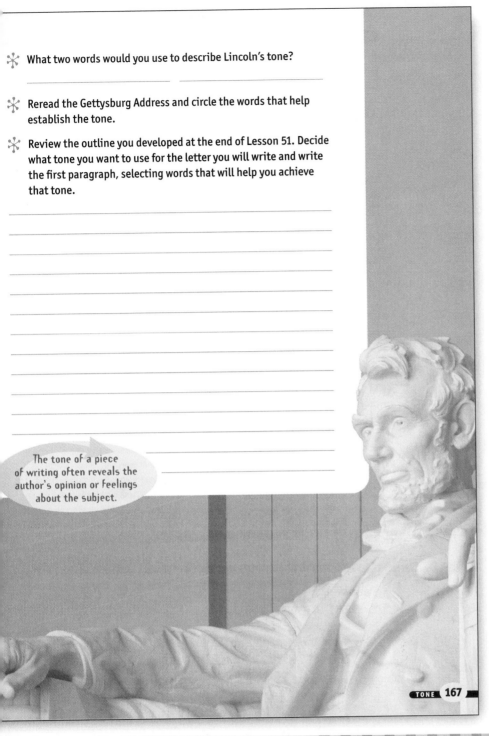

TONE 167

Auditory Learners Auditory learners might benefit from hearing other readings of the famous speech. Present several different treatments by professional actors. Recordings by Jeff Daniels, Sam Waterston, and Johnny Cash are available via the Internet at http://www.learnoutloud.com.

Differentiation The formal language of this speech is challenging for today's students. To help them comprehend, have students listen, *without* following along, as you read the speech aloud with appropriate expression. Then read the speech again as students follow along in their books. Pause at key intervals for students to write "translations" between the lines of the speech or in the Response Notes. For example, above "four score and seven," students can write "87."

TEACHING TIP

Collaboration In groups, have students share their Response Notes and discuss the responses their selected words inspired. Then, have groups brainstorm several labels for the tone of the speech.

Quick Assess

✴ Do students' letters reflect what they have learned about tone ?

During

After

PERSPECTIVE AND TONE Explain that the tone of a piece of writing or a speech reveals the author's perspective. Ask students: *What is Lincoln's purpose in this speech? What does he want the audience to think or do? What is his tone when he addresses them? To describe it, would you use* solemn, sarcastic, sympathetic, *or some other word? Why?*

Have students imagine that they are in the audience that heard the Gettysburg Address for the first time. Suggest that they take on roles, such as mother of a Confederate soldier; survivor of the Battle of Gettysburg; Union politician; etc. As they listen to the speech again, have these students determine what emotional reactions their characters would have

and whether they would be convinced to adopt President Lincoln's perspective. Facilitate a discussion of the characters' various perspectives on the speech.

LESSON 53

Students will learn how an author's style shapes and reinforces the message.

BACKGROUND KNOWLEDGE

On August 28, 1963, Dr. Martin Luther King, Jr. delivered his renowned "I Have a Dream" speech to an unprecedented gathering of 250,000 people at the Lincoln Memorial in Washington, D.C. The event was a rally in support of jobs and equal rights for African Americans, and Dr. King wanted to inspire the crowd to act.

Before students read or hear the speech, have them write down what they know of it.

VOCABULARY

manacles metal shackles for hands or feet, usually attached to chains

promissory note an agreement to pay back a loan

default to fail to pay debts

interposition placing obstacles between people

nullification rejection of federal law, such as racial integration, by a state government

exalted held up in honor

hew carve

Use the Word Splash activity on page 278.

LESSON 53 STYLE

Persuaders know the power of choosing just the right words and arranging them in the most effective way. An author's style is his or her distinctive way of arranging words and constructing sentences. Even without a title or author, you can tell that the writer of the letter from the Grand Council Fire of American Indians is different from the writer of the Gettysburg Address.

In this lesson, you will read a speech that may already be familiar to you. As you read "I Have a Dream," circle words and phrases that seem to make up Martin Luther King, Jr.'s style.

"I Have a Dream" by Martin Luther King, Jr.

Response Notes

Five score years ago, a great American, in whose symbolic shadow we stand, signed the Emancipation Proclamation. This momentous decree came as a great beacon light of hope to millions of Negro slaves who had been seared in the flames of withering injustice. It came as a joyous daybreak to end the long night of captivity.

But one hundred years later, we must face the tragic fact that the Negro is still not free. One hundred years later, the life of the Negro is still sadly crippled by the manacles of segregation and the chains of discrimination. One hundred years later, the Negro lives on a lonely island of poverty in the midst of a vast ocean of material prosperity. One hundred years later, the Negro is still languishing in the corners of American society and finds himself an exile in his own land. So we have come here today to dramatize an appalling condition.

In a sense we have come to our nation's Capitol to cash a check. When the architects of our republic wrote the magnificent words of the Constitution and the Declaration of Independence, they were signing a promissory note to which every American was to fall heir. This note was a promise that all men would be guaranteed the unalienable rights of life, liberty, and the pursuit of happiness.

It is obvious today that America has defaulted on this promissory note insofar as her citizens of color are concerned. Instead of honoring this sacred obligation, America has given the Negro people a bad check; a check which has come back marked "insufficient funds." But we refuse to believe that the bank of justice is bankrupt. We refuse to believe that there are insufficient funds in the great vaults of opportunity of this nation. So we have come to cash this check—a check that will give us upon demand the riches of freedom and the security of justice. We have also come to this hallowed spot to remind America of the fierce urgency of now. This is no time to engage in the luxury of cooling

Before

CRITICAL READING SKILL

Style Have students review the first two selections in this unit to identify elements of style. Point out the following:

- the repetitive use of contrast *White men . . . but . . . ,* etc.
- emotionally charged word choices: *massacre, treacherous, final resting place*, etc.
- references to historical events: Wounded Knee, new nation, Civil War, etc.
- reminders of shared ideals: self-defense, fairness, fitting and proper, etc.

Explain that use of these elements is not accidental. Persuasive writers pay attention to these elements and plan their use very carefully. Invite students to predict which of these elements will appear in the speech by Dr. King.

off or to take the tranquilizing drug of gradualism. Now is the time to make real the promises of Democracy. Now is the time to rise from the dark and desolate valley of segregation to the sunlit path of racial justice. Now is the time to open the doors of opportunity to all of God's children. Now is the time to lift our nation from the quicksands of racial injustice to the solid rock of brotherhood.

It would be fatal for the nation to overlook the urgency of the moment and to underestimate the determination of the Negro. This sweltering summer of the Negro's legitimate discontent will not pass until there is an invigorating autumn of freedom and equality. 1963 is not an end, but a beginning. Those who hope that the Negro needed to blow off steam and will now be content will have a rude awakening if the nation returns to business as usual. There will be neither rest nor tranquility in America until the Negro is granted his citizenship rights. The whirlwinds of revolt will continue to shake the foundations of our nation until the bright day of justice emerges.

But there is something that I must say to my people who stand on the warm threshold which leads into the palace of justice. In the process of gaining our rightful place we must not be guilty of wrongful deeds. Let us not seek to satisfy our thirst for freedom by drinking from the cup of bitterness and hatred. We must forever conduct our struggle on the high plane of dignity and discipline. We must not allow our creative protest to degenerate into physical violence. Again and again we must rise to the majestic heights of meeting physical force with soul force. The marvelous new militancy which has engulfed the Negro community must not lead us to a distrust of all white people, for many of our white brothers, as evidenced by their presence here today, have come to realize that their destiny is tied up with our destiny and their freedom is inextricably bound to our freedom. We cannot walk alone.

And as we walk, we must make the pledge that we shall march ahead. We cannot turn back. There are those who are asking the devotees of civil rights, "When will you be satisfied?" We can never be satisfied as long as the Negro is the victim of the unspeakable horrors of police brutality. We can never be satisfied as long as our bodies, heavy with the fatigue of travel, cannot gain lodging in the motels of the highways and the hotels of the cities. We cannot be satisfied as long as the Negro's basic mobility is from a smaller ghetto to a larger one. We can never be satisfied as long as a Negro in Mississippi cannot vote and a Negro in New York believes he has nothing for which to vote. No, no, we are not satisfied, and we will not be satisfied until justice rolls down like waters and righteousness like a mighty stream.

I am not unmindful that some of you have come here out of great trials and tribulations. Some of you have come fresh from narrow jail cells. Some of you have come from areas where your quest for freedom left you battered by the storms of persecution and staggered by the winds of police brutality. You

STYLE 169

ABOUT THE AUTHOR

Dr. Martin Luther King, Jr. was born on January 15, 1929 in Atlanta, Georgia. His father and grandfather were both ministers, and his mother was a schoolteacher. He went to Morehouse College in Atlanta at age 15. As an adult, he was awarded the Nobel Peace Prize in 1964 for his nonviolent leadership in the American civil rights movement. Later he was the first African American honored by *Time* magazine as "Man of the Year." He died in 1968 from an assassin's bullet.

WRITER'S CRAFT

Metaphor Define *metaphors* as comparisons of two unlike people, objects, or ideas. The writer describes one thing as another thing. For example, *full measure of devotion* (in the Gettysburg Address) implies that devotion can be measured just as we measure a cup of flour or a gallon of water.

Point out Dr. King's metaphor on page 168: *America has given the Negro people a bad check . . . which has come back marked "insufficient funds."* Ask students to identify the comparison. (The promise is like a check sent back to you by your bank because the check writer had too little money to cover it.) Discuss its effectiveness in helping listeners understand and remember the thesis of the speech.

During

LANGUAGE AND STYLE Remind students that a major element of Dr. King's style is the type of language he uses. He often uses figurative language, such as the metaphors mentioned above. Another element of King's style is the rhythm of the language. Point out that, in his introductory comment about the Emancipation Proclamation, King could have said, "Millions of Negro slaves were happy with the announcement." Instead, he crafted the deeply expressive *It came as a joyous daybreak to end the long night of captivity.* Have students include in their Response Notes comments about the rhythm of the language throughout the speech.

PERSPECTIVE Discuss the perspective Dr. King brings to this speech and how it is conveyed. Without his life experiences, would the speech have been as powerful?

WRITER'S CRAFT

Allusion Define *allusion* as a reference to familiar and/or notable historical events, works of literature, myths, or the like. Explain that allusions remind readers of deep meanings and suggest that the present subject should be considered in the same light as the subject of the allusion. For example, Lincoln's use of the phrase "all men are created equal" was intended to remind listeners of the Declaration of Independence, which contains the same phrase, and thus to suggest that the current war was just as important to the nation as the American War of Independence.

Point out Dr. King's allusion *five score years ago* and ask students to discuss why he might have chosen to allude to the Gettysburg Address *(four score and seven years ago)*. Have students reread Dr. King's speech, mark other allusions they find, and explain them in their Response Notes.

have been the veterans of creative suffering. Continue to work with the faith that unearned suffering is redemptive.

Go back to Mississippi, go back to Alabama, go back to South Carolina, go back to Georgia, go back to Louisiana, go back to the slums and ghettos of our northern cities, knowing that somehow this situation can and will be changed. Let us not wallow in the valley of despair.

I say to you today, my friends, that in spite of the difficulties and frustrations of the moment I still have a dream. It is a dream deeply rooted in the American dream.

I have a dream that one day this nation will rise up and live out the true meaning of its creed: "We hold these truths to be self-evident; that all men are created equal."

I have a dream that one day on the red hills of Georgia the sons of former slaves and the sons of former slaveowners will be able to sit down together at the table of brotherhood.

I have a dream that the state of Mississippi, a desert state, sweltering with the heat of injustice and oppression, will be transformed into an oasis of freedom and justice.

I have a dream that my four little children will one day live in a nation where they will not be judged by the color of their skin but by the content of their character.

I have a dream today.

I have a dream that the state of Alabama, whose governor's lips are presently dripping with the words of interposition and nullification, will be transformed into a situation where little black boys and black girls will be able to join hands with little white boys and white girls and walk together as sisters and brothers.

I have a dream today.

I have a dream that one day every valley shall be exalted, every hill and mountain shall be made low, the rough places will be made plain, and the crooked places will be made straight, and the glory of the Lord shall be revealed, and all flesh shall see it together.

This is our hope. This is the faith with which I return to the South. With this faith we will be able to hew out of the mountain of despair a stone of hope. With this faith we will be able to transform the jangling discords of our nation into a beautiful symphony of brotherhood. With this faith we will be able to work together, to pray together, to struggle together, to go to jail together, to stand up for freedom together, knowing that we will be free one day.

This will be the day when all of God's children will be able to sing with new meaning, "My country, 'tis of thee, sweet land of liberty, of thee I sing. Land where my fathers died, land of the pilgrims' pride, from every mountainside, let freedom ring."

WRITER'S CRAFT

Metaphor Each section of this speech is focused on a key metaphor. Point out, for example, that the section that uses the check-cashing metaphor starts with what happened in the past (a promissory note), what the situation is now (insufficient funds), and what needs to be done to remedy the current situation (make real the promises). Have groups of students choose other sections of the speech and analyze them by identifying the overarching metaphor, tracing the supporting statements, and stating the action that Dr. King calls for. Then have groups share their findings with the class.

And if America is to be a great nation this must become true. So let freedom ring from the prodigious hilltops of New Hampshire. Let freedom ring from the mighty mountains of New York. Let freedom ring from the heightening Alleghenies of Pennsylvania!

Let freedom ring from the snowcapped Rockies of Colorado!

Let freedom ring from the curvaceous peaks of California! But not only that; let freedom ring from Stone Mountain of Georgia!

Let freedom ring from Lookout Mountain of Tennessee!

Let freedom ring from every hill and molehill of Mississippi. From every mountainside, let freedom ring.

When we let freedom ring, when we let it ring from every village and every hamlet, from every state and every city, we will be able to speed up that day when all of God's children, black men and white men, Jews and Gentiles, Protestants and Catholics, will be able to join hands and sing in the words of the old Negro spiritual, "Free at last! free at last! thank God Almighty, we are free at last!" ❖

EXTRA SUPPORT

Differentiation Some students may not understand all the references to the various states. Use a United States map to locate the states mentioned and to explain the geographical references (e.g., *the snowcapped Rockies of Colorado*).

✳ What is your initial reaction to this speech? Which words or phrases stayed with you? Which moved you? How do you hear Dr. King's voice delivering this speech?

_____

_____

_____

_____

_____

_____

_____

_____

_____

_____

_____

_____

_____

_____

_____

STYLE 171

WRITER'S CRAFT

Repetition Define *repetition* as "saying the same or very similar words over and over in different contexts to create a pattern of ideas." Point out the *Now is the time . . .* series at the top of page 169 and explain how the device of repetition makes the call for action here seem more urgent than a single statement would. Have groups of students identify other repetitious passages and discuss the effects of the repetitions. Then have each group share their discussion of a passage.

Differentiation Students with strong musical and/or movement skills might enjoy creating and performing presentations that use music, dance, or drama to interpret a segment of the speech.

Quick Assess

✳ Do students express their initial reactions and tell whether the speech persuades them?

✳ Did students identify instances of allusion and repetition accurately?

✳ Did students evaluate the effectiveness of King's speech based on style elements such as metaphor, allusion, repetition, and rhythm?

✳ Dr. King uses **allusion** and **repetition** to make his points and move his listeners to action. Allusions refer to other speeches, songs, and writings that the audience will recognize. Using allusions allows the author to connect his or her message to other ideas that the reader already knows and values. But the author also puts a new twist on the idea. For example, look at the beginning of the Gettysburg Address and the beginning of "I Have a Dream." Why do you think Dr. King started his speech as he did?

Repetition is used to emphasize or connect ideas and to direct attention to the variations. For example, many sentences begin with "I have a dream," but the dreams are all different. Because the sentences begin the same way, they reinforce the idea, but the listener begins to notice the differences, too.

✳ Reread "I Have a Dream" and highlight allusions in one color and repetitions in another.

✳ What is your opinion of the effectiveness of Dr. King's style in this speech?

> An author's style shapes and reinforces the persuasive message of a speech or a piece of writing.

After

LISTENING/SPEAKING CONNECTION
Have each student select a brief segment of the speech to perform before the class. Students should analyze their segments and use highlighters or other markers to plan vocal intonation, pacing, facial expressions, and gestures to enrich their presentations. Encourage students to add to their presentations by adding music or visual aids. Develop a class rubric for evaluating the performances and have students rate each performance using the rubric.

Authors of persuasive arguments may choose to appeal to your feelings as well as to reason. Analyzing those appeals can help you evaluate the argument to determine how convincing it is. Authors sometimes use emotion-laden words to appeal to feelings. An author might want to anger you in order to convince you to act or to think a certain way. In another situation, an author might refer to basic values, such as kindness, justice, responsibility, freedom, or patriotism to persuade you. Both types of appeals can influence a reader's thinking. Critical readers must carefully evaluate the message to be sure they are not persuaded by just their feelings.

Words have two kinds of meanings—**denotation** and **connotation**. The denotation of a word is the dictionary meaning. The connotation is something suggested by a word. For example, the word *freedom* has emotional associations that go beyond the word's literal meaning. A word's connotations can depend on the perspective of the person using it. Look back at Lesson 51 to see how speakers use their point of view to select words with the connotation they think will persuade the listener. If you support the view of the Native Americans, what would you call a fight in which people died? If you do not support their view, what might you call the fight?

Imagine that you want to compliment one person and criticize another one about their body shape and their position on an issue. You can use a connotation ladder to select the right words. In the space below, select words from the word bank and place them on the ladder ranging from most complimentary at the bottom to least complimentary on the top.

Skinny   Firm
Scrawny   Decisive
Slender   Stubborn

VOTES FOR WOMEN ON THE SAME TERMS AS MEN

Students will learn how to evaluate an argument by examining its appeals to reason and emotion.

BACKGROUND KNOWLEDGE

Tell students that they are already experts in persuasion. Have students recall a time when they tried to persuade someone to think about something differently or to do something. For example, they might have tried to get permission from their parents to go somewhere special. Ask: *What kinds of arguments did you use to convince your parents your request was reasonable? Did you appeal to their concern for your happiness? Did you appeal to their desire to be good parents? Did you point out that letting you go to an amusement park with your friends on a school holiday would mean that neither of your parents would need to take time off from work to be home?*

After students share a few examples, point out the types of appeals they used: emotional (use of emotion-laden words such as happiness, or references to basic values such as parental adequacy) or logical (such as saving time and/or money). Explain that these devices are evident in the selections in this unit and that effective persuaders use these devices consciously and plan their use carefully.

Before

CRITICAL READING SKILL

Persuasive Appeals Explain that the authors of arguments choose their words and phrases very carefully in order to have the fullest impact. They consider their purpose and their audience. If their purpose is to incite anger and their audience is capable of using anger to spur action, then the writer will use words and ideas to appeal to the audience's emotions. If a writer's purpose is to objectively and rationally argue a point, then the words and phrases will be very different. The argument will be supported by facts and logical reasons. Appeals to emotion, basic values, and logical reason are all part of an effective persuader's "tool box."

During

KINDS OF EVIDENCE Define an *observation* as "something a person has experienced through his or her senses." For example, in "Memorial and Recommendations of the Grand Council Fire," the authors say, ". . . we do know that [the schools] are unjust to the life of our people." The authors are saying that they have experienced this firsthand. Invite students to identify other examples of observation in each selection.

✳ Do students' charts cite examples of each kind of appeal?

✳ Do students explain clearly which piece is most convincing and how its appeals contribute to its persuasive power?

✳ On the chart below, check the kinds of appeals you find in each piece of writing in this unit. Compare your findings with a partner and label each letter or speech where you find examples of each kind of appeal.

Appeals to Reason	"Memorial and Recommendations..."	"Gettysburg Address"	"I Have a Dream"
Observations			
Examples			
Facts			
Appeals to Emotion			
Emotional language			
Mention of basic values			

✳ Which of the writings in this unit is most convincing to you? How do the appeals that the author uses help persuade you?

_____
_____
_____
_____
_____
_____
_____
_____
_____
_____
_____

Readers can evaluate an argument by examining its appeals to reason and to emotion.

174 LESSON 54

After

Define an *example* as "a specific instance of something happening." For example, the authors of the first selection cite several ways the textbooks teach a biased view of Native American history. Invite students to identify examples in each selection.

Define *facts* as "information that can be checked and either verified or disproven." For example, *History books teach that Indians were murderers* . . . can be checked by reading the history books.

APPLYING THE STRATEGY
Persuasive Appeals Invite students to practice making persuasive appeals by role-playing the letters that they outlined on page 165. Have one student in each pair make an appeal to a partner, and have the partner provide the persuader with feedback about the effectiveness of the appeal.

You have learned many of the persuader's tools:

- Structure an argument with a thesis, reasons, and evidence.
- Select an appropriate tone.
- Use a style that helps you make your point.
- Appeal both to emotion and to reason.

✳ Plan a persuasive speech or letter of your own. You can finish the letter that you began in Lesson 52 or select a new topic.

Possible Topics

Year-round schools
Aid to disaster victims
Required summer reading
Another issue of interest to you

✳ Jot down notes before writing your letter or speech. Decide on the points you want to make.

✳ My topic: _____

✳ My argument: _____

✳ Points I want to make:

- _____
- _____
- _____
- _____

WRITING A SPEECH 175

Students will learn that persuaders carefully select the right tools to help them persuade their audiences.

BACKGROUND KNOWLEDGE

To review each of the persuader's tools, form four groups. Assign a tool to each group and allow time for groups to discuss their notes and products from Lessons 51 through 54. Then have each group share with the class examples of each lesson's tool from the group members' work.

Before

CRITICAL READING SKILL

Writing a Speech Help students plan their speeches by brainstorming additional possible topics as a class. Then model planning a speech by completing the outline on page 175 for one of those topics. Provide a think-aloud, such as: *My topic is that our school should require summer reading for eighth-graders. That is probably not my title, but I'll write it down just to focus my thinking. My main argument is a logical one: I will write that my students need to maintain and improve their reading ability by practicing outside of school.* Continue the think-aloud as you complete the model plan.

* Are students' planning notes complete?

* Do students' paragraphs show a mastery of one of the persuader's tools?

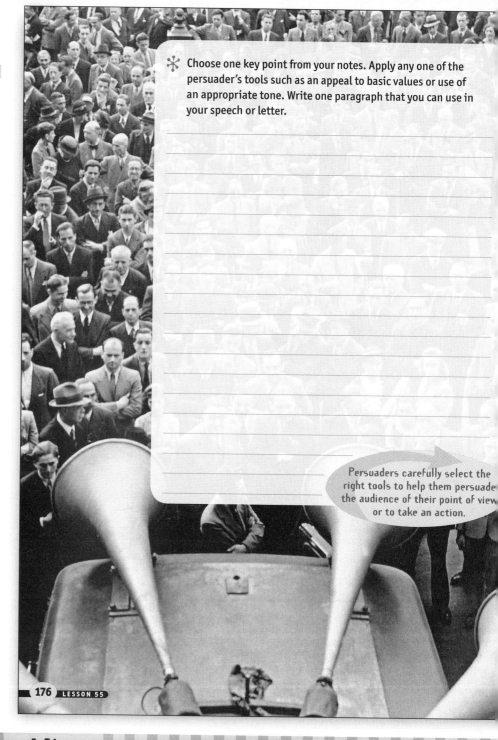

✳ Choose one key point from your notes. Apply any one of the persuader's tools such as an appeal to basic values or use of an appropriate tone. Write one paragraph that you can use in your speech or letter.

Persuaders carefully select the right tools to help them persuade the audience of their point of view or to take an action.

176 LESSON 55

During

USING A GRAPHIC ORGANIZER
Have students use a graphic organizers to plan their speech or letter for this lesson.

Thesis:		
Desired Outcome:		
Support:	Support:	Support:
Appeals to Emotions:		

After

PRESENTING A SPEECH Encourage students to complete their persuasive speeches and present them to the class. Develop a class rubric based on the persuader's tools. Have listeners use the rubric to evaluate the speeches and provide supportive feedback. Then have students use the feedback to decide whether to present their persuasive speeches or letters to those in positions to take action about the issue, such as a school board, a teacher, or a disaster aid agency.

UNIT 12
FOCUSING ON LANGUAGE AND CRAFT

Lessons 56–60, pages 178–192

UNIT OVERVIEW

In this unit, students will explore and create poetry for or by more than one voice.

KEY IDEA

Poetry has its roots in the ancient practices of singing or chanting verses of a story. Hearing and speaking poetry gives readers a better understanding of the genre.

CRITICAL READING SKILLS
by lesson

56 Understanding sound in poetry
57 Creating two voices from one
58 Modeling the poem
59 Studying an author
60 Perceiving a poetic pattern

WRITING ACTIVITIES
by lesson

56 Compose a poem for two voices.
57 Explain how a poem is converted for two voices.
58 Create a poem from a model.
59 Develop a plan for writing a hybrid poem.
60 Write an "I Am" poem.

Focusing on Language and Craft

Poetry is undergoing a big change in cities around the United States these days. Coffee-shops, book stores, libraries—they all have scheduled poetry readings, poetry slams, music and poetry gatherings. Poetry is returning to its roots, where verses were sung or chanted. People are putting the **voice** back into poetry.

Of course, many people still read poetry to themselves and for personal pleasure, but more and more people like to hear it read aloud. They want to hear the poet's voice or the reader's voice. Voice makes poetry come alive.

In this unit, you will "hear" the voice of poetry. You will read it aloud, create poems for two voices, make one poem out of two, and finally write your own poem in your own voice.

177

Literature

- **"Grasshoppers"** and **"Fireflies"** by Paul Fleischman (poems)

The poems in this lesson are among the many for two-voice reading written by a favorite poet of young readers.

- **"On Turning Ten"** by Billy Collins (poem)

Collins recounts memories of the innocence of early childhood.

- **"Life Doesn't Frighten Me"** and **"Alone"** by Maya Angelou (poems)

These two poems on related topics portray two very different views of life.

- **"Ending Poem"** by Rosario Morales and Aurora Levins Morales (poem)

A mother and daughter sing together of the experiences of American immigrants.

ASSESSMENT To assess student learning in this unit, see pages 241 and 265.

Students will learn the importance of sound in poetry.

BACKGROUND KNOWLEDGE

Have students share what they know about grasshoppers and fireflies. Grasshoppers

✳ mature in 40 to 60 days;

✳ jump to escape from enemies;

✳ can leap 20 times their length;

✳ make sounds by rubbing their wings together or rubbing their hind legs across their front wings.

Fireflies

✳ are also called lightning bugs;

✳ female fireflies make short, rhythmic flashes to attract males;

✳ produce light with special cells that are fueled by air tubes.

VOCABULARY

parchment writing surface similar to paper, but made from the skin of a goat or sheep

calligraphers people who create stylized, artistic lettering

After discussing the definitions, ask students to draw a picture showing how fireflies might be *calligraphers* on *parchment*.

Paul Fleischman, the son of the well-known writer Sid Fleischman, grew up surrounded by the sound of language. His father regularly read chapters of his work to the family, and the family gave him suggestions about what should happen next in the story. From this experience, Paul Fleischman says, "We grew up knowing that words felt good in the ears and on the tongue, that they were as much fun to play with as toys." Music was also an important part of the Fleischman household. Fleischman and his mother played the piano, his sisters played the flute, and his father played the guitar. As an adult, Fleischman learned to play the recorder, and he even toured with a recorder group.

Fleischman's love for both music and language has shaped his writing. His books *I Am Phoenix, Joyful Noise,* and *Big Talk* are poems for two or four voices to read aloud, like different voices in a choir or a variety of instruments in an orchestra. Even in his novels and nonfiction books, Fleischman pays careful attention to the rhythm of his sentences and the sounds of the words he puts together. He has received many awards for his books, including the Newbery Medal in 1989 for *Joyful Noise.*

As children, Paul Fleischman and his sisters often biked around the streets and alleys of their hometown, Monterey, California, collecting thrown-out items from other people's trash cans. Fleischman still does this in a way, gathering together forgotten bits of history and quirky facts he learns from old books as he crafts a new piece of writing.

The two poems by Paul Fleischman in this lesson are from *Joyful Noise,* which has poems about the noises of insects. If you have never really listened to the noises of insects, pay close attention to these poems and you will "hear" them in a new way. It will take practice to be able to read this poem effectively because you and your partner have to keep an eye on two columns at one time. When words appear on the same line, they should be spoken together. In some cases, the line that is read together is the same; other times it is different. Think of the poem as music for two instruments or a piano piece for two hands.

Before

CRITICAL READING SKILL
Understanding Sound in Poetry

Remind students that a major attribute of poetry is its musical quality. Explain that much poetry is meant to be read aloud. The poems in this lesson, however, are unique in that they were written specifically to require two readers. Before having students read the poems, read them aloud with a volunteer (who has had an opportunity to practice) and have students listen *without* following along in their books.

Grasshoppers by Paul Fleischman

Sap's rising

    Ground's warming

Grasshoppers are
hatching out
Autumn-laid eggs

    Grasshoppers are
    hatching out

    splitting

Young stepping

    into spring

Grasshoppers
hopping
high

    Grasshoppers
    hopping

Grassjumpers
jumping

    Grassjumpers
    jumping
    far

Vaulting from
leaf to leaf
stem to stem
plant to plant

    leaf to leaf
    stem to stem
    Grass

leapers
Grass-
bounders

    leapers

    bounders
    Grass-

springers
Grass
soarers
Leapfrogging
longjumping
grasshoppers. ❖

    springers

    soarers
    Leapfrogging
    longjumping
    grasshoppers. ❖

Response Notes

❋ Practice reading the poem with a partner. Read the poem several times until you both are reading smoothly.

POEMS FOR TWO VOICES 179

ABOUT THE AUTHOR

Paul Fleischman, born in 1952, has devoted his writing career primarily to the young adult audience, with a particular focus on science and history. In addition to his many books of poetry, several of them for multiple voices, he has also produced a number of novels, historical fiction, and even a play. He seems to always be thinking musically, however. Describing his work, he says: "If I could, I'd write music rather than books. Alas, I don't have that talent— but writing multi-voice poetry at least gives me a taste. Many of my books can be performed as well as read silently. *Bull Run* and *Seedfolks* are collections of monologues suitable for classes. *Mind's Eye* and *Seek* can be performed by high school or adult reader's theater groups. *Zap,* my first play, has just been published."

TEACHING TIP

Collaboration To support students in reading the poems aloud with a partner, suggest that they number each line and highlight the lines each will read in a different color.

During

READING POETRY ALOUD Have students recall the way you and the volunteer(s) read each poem aloud. Point out that reading aloud is more than just saying words. Explain that effective performance requires attention to several aspects of speech:

❋ Intonation: the variations in pitch, loudness, and softness

❋ Rate: saying some lines faster than others

❋ Tone: adjusting seriousness to match mood

Have partners discuss each of these elements and use their Response Notes to plan how to use intonation, rate, and tone to add emphasis, draw attention to specific words, and/or enhance the drama of the work.

WRITER'S CRAFT

Repetition and Alliteration

Remind students that some poems are essentially "sound play" used to express deep emotions and inspire mental pictures in the minds of the audience. Explain that Fleischman's style exhibits particularly colorful uses of two forms of sound play: repetition and alliteration. Define *repetition* as "the appearance of the same or similar words or phrases over and over." Point out the repetitive appearance of such words as *leaf to leaf* and *stem to stem*. Read stanzas that exhibit repetition aloud with emphasis on the repetitions. Then invite students to share the effect of the repetitions on the visual images inspired by the poems.

Define *alliteration* as "the repeated use of the same consonant sound at the beginnings of words." Point out the repeated use of such sounds as the *fl* sound in *flickering, flitting,* and *flashing* in "Fireflies." Read stanzas that exhibit alliteration aloud with emphasis on the repeated consonant sounds. Then discuss the effect of the alliteration on the mental images inspired by the poems.

Response Notes

Here is another of Paul Fleischman's poems. Notice that, again, some lines are read by the first reader, some by the second, and some by both readers together. Practice reading with a partner.

Fireflies by Paul Fleischman

Light	Light
	is the ink we use
Night	Night
is our parchment	
	We're fireflies
fireflies	flickering
flitting	
	flashing
fireflies	
glimmering	fireflies
	gleaming
glowing	
Insect calligraphers	Insect calligraphers
practicing penmanship	
	copying sentences
Six-legged scribblers	Six-legged scribblers
of vanishing messages	
	fleeting graffiti
Fine artists in flight	Fine artists in flight
adding dabs of light	
	bright brush strokes
Signing the June nights	Signing the June nights
as if they were paintings	as if they were paintings
	We're
flickering	fireflies
fireflies	flickering
fireflies. ❖	fireflies. ❖

180 LESSON 56

READING POETRY ALOUD Remind students to think of each voice as a musical instrument. Play recordings of solo instruments, such as oboe, flute, trumpet, trombone, violin, or viola. Have partners discuss the qualities of various musical instruments. For example, ask: *How does an oboe differ from a flute?* Suggest that partners adjust their voices until they reach an effective combination of "instruments" for their readings.

* After you and your partner have perfected your reading, get together with another pair and read to each other.

* Discuss the two poems by Paul Fleischman.
  ■ Select words and phrases that you think are particularly effective.
  ■ Talk about how the poems do or do not describe the grasshopper and the firefly.
    * Are there people in your group who have never seen a firefly? Those who have should explain the firefly's appeal. Has anyone, for instance, ever caught them on a hot summer night and put them in a jar? What happens to them? Did you let them go?
    * What are some other names for the grasshopper and the firefly?
  ■ Talk about how the poems are like music for two voices or instruments.

* Working with a partner or group, compose your own poem for two voices.
  ■ Select a subject.
  ■ Write text for the left and right columns.
  ■ Decide which lines you will say together.
  ■ Copy your poem, then practice reading it before presenting the poem to the class.

> Reading and writing poems for two voices helps you see how important sound is to poetry.

* Do students' readings of the poems demonstrate variations in intonation, rate, and tone?

* Do students' poems follow the form of poems for two voices?

After

LITERATURE/FINE ARTS CONNECTION Encourage students to add other fine arts to performances of their original poems for two voices. They can

* create, download, photocopy, or cut out works of visual arts, such as photographs of insects or animals, Audubon sketches, paintings, and so forth;

* create or record music that suits the rhythms of their poems;

* choreograph original dances to embellish the tone of their works.

Following the performances, have the audience give the performers feedback as to the effectiveness of their fine arts choices in supporting the poetry.

Students will learn that certain poems can convincingly be read with one voice or with two.

BACKGROUND KNOWLEDGE

Ask students to reflect on what they have noticed about growing up. Model the thinking with your own experience. For example, say: *When I was . . . years old, I thought . . . As I grew older, I realized . . .* Then invite volunteers to share similar observations about their growing up process. Note any common themes that emerge from the sharing.

Explain that the poem in this lesson describes stages in one person's process of growing up. Invite students to listen for experiences that are similar to some of their own.

VOCABULARY

psyche human spirit

disfiguring something that leaves a mark on the skin or changes the shape of a feature

chicken pox a disease that leaves crater-like marks on the skin if not treated carefully

solemnly seriously

After discussing the definitions, have partners write one sentence that uses both words so that their meanings are clear.

In Billy Collins's poem "On Turning Ten," we hear the voice of Billy, a ten-year-old. We also hear the voice of the grownup Billy, remembering how he thought when he was a child. First, just read or listen to the poem and try to hear echoes of a ten-year-old in the words.

Response Notes

"On Turning Ten" by Billy Collins

The whole idea of it makes me feel
like I'm coming down with something,
something worse than any stomach ache
or the headaches I get from reading in bad light—
a kind of measles of the spirit,
a mumps of the psyche,
a disfiguring chicken pox of the soul.

You tell me it is too early to be looking back,
but that is because you have forgotten
the perfect simplicity of being one
and the beautiful complexity introduced by two.
But I can lie on my bed and remember every digit.
At four I was an Arabian wizard.
I could make myself invisible
by drinking a glass of milk a certain way.
At seven I was a soldier, at nine a prince.

But now I am mostly at the window
watching the late afternoon light.
Back then it never fell so solemnly
against the side of my tree house,
and my bicycle never leaned against the garage
as it does today,
all the dark blue speed drained out of it.

This is the beginning of sadness, I say to myself,
as I walk through the universe in my sneakers.
It is time to say good-bye to my imaginary friends,
time to turn the first big number.

It seems only yesterday I used to believe
there was nothing under my skin but light.
If you cut me I would shine.
But now when I fall upon the sidewalks of life,
I skin my knees. I bleed. ❖

Before

CRITICAL READING SKILL
Creating Two Voices from One

Remind students of the Fleischman poems for two voices in Lesson 56. Discuss how he used the sound of two voices to give the poem a musical quality. Explain that in the poem they are about to read there is a single narrator but that some people hear the echoes of two people, or, more likely, two parts of the same person.

During

READING POETRY ALOUD Have
partners read the poem aloud together several times, trying out different ways to divide the poem and using a variety of voices. Encourage them to "play" with sounds until they are satisfied with their joint interpretation of the work.

- Re-read the poem, using the **Response Notes** column to indicate where you hear the voice of the ten-year-old and where you hear a grownup remembering. Make notes, too, about any of your own memories of becoming a ten-year-old and your memories of being younger.

- Working with a partner, divide the poem into lines or phrases so that you can read it as a dialogue. Mark the poem so that two people can read it aloud.

- Read the poem to another pair of students, and then listen to them read their version. Talk about the different ways you chose to divide the poem.

- Write a paragraph that explains the way you and your partner chose to divide the poem.

> Reading a poem in two voices helps you focus on the different voices within the poem.

ABOUT THE AUTHOR
Billy Collins, born in 1941, writes poetry that has been described as "reader-friendly, hospitable, congenial, and welcoming." During his tenure as U.S. Poet Laureate, Collins instituted *Poetry 180,* a program designed to make "poetry an active part of the daily experience of American high school students." Although the program focuses on the high school level, many of its ideas are applicable to grades 6–8 as well. For more information, see the Poetry 180 website: www.loc.gov/poetry/180

Quick Assess

- Do partners' readings of the poem make their two-voice interpretations clear?

- Do students' paragraphs explain the partners' decisions about their reading and their feelings about the poem?

After

APPLYING THE STRATEGY
Creating Two Voices from One Have students find other poems that tell stories or otherwise lend themselves to two-voice presentation. Invite students to analyze and perform the poems as they did "On Turning Ten."

LISTENING CONNECTION
Students who prefer to listen to poetry might benefit from listening to professional readings. Readings are available through such organizations as the Academy of American Poets at www.poets.org. Encourage students to listen to each reading several times, while following along with a print version of the work to familiarize themselves with the rhythms and language of the poet. Then invite them to choose another poem by that poet and read it silently. Ask students how hearing poems read aloud affects their understanding and enjoyment of the poems.

Students will learn how the process of modeling a piece of writing can help them attend to its structure as well as its ideas.

BACKGROUND KNOWLEDGE

Have students think about the purposes for modeling in the fashion world. Ask: *Why do stores and fashion designers show clothing on models? How does modeling help consumers?* Explain that authors may also use models in their writing. A good writer sets up a model and then analyzes it, trying out various ways to use it to create new works. Explain that this lesson focuses on using models to help refine sentence structure and to use that structure to communicate meanings effectively.

LESSON 58 MODELING A POEM

Modeling is a strategy that many writers use when they want to focus on the structure of a piece of writing. Writers may model prose or poetry. Modeling prose helps writers get inside the sentences. Modeling poetry can be useful when learning to write different kinds of poems. When you model a poem that has already been written, you are focusing on structure and meaning at the same time.

In this lesson, you will use the structure of Billy Collins's poem to give form to your own memories of being a different age.

* Reread your **Response Notes** about Billy Collins's poem "On Turning Ten" and look at the memories you recorded. Add more memories as they occur to you. Choose an age you want to start with; it might be "On Turning Thirteen" or "On Turning Eleven" or whatever age you choose. Fill in the chart, making up a poem of your own as you go. This is called **modeling.** You owe the structure of your poem to the original poet, but the ideas in your poem are yours.

"On Turning Ten" by Billy Collins	"On Turning _____" by _____
The whole idea of it makes me feel like I'm coming down with something, something worse than any stomach ache or the headaches I get from reading in bad light— a kind of measles of the spirit, a mumps of the psyche, a disfiguring chicken pox of the soul.	The whole idea of it makes me feel *(Write as many lines as you want here)*
You tell me it is too early to be looking back, but that is because you have forgotten the perfect simplicity of being one and the beautiful complexity introduced by two. But I can lie on my bed and remember every digit. At four I was an Arabian wizard. I could make myself invisible by drinking a glass of milk a certain way. At seven I was a soldier, at nine a prince.	You tell me _____, but that is because you have forgotten _____ and _____ But I can lie on my bed and remember every digit. At four I was _____. I could _____. At _____ I was _____, At _____ I was _____

Before

CRITICAL READING SKILL

Modeling the Poem Remind students that modeling can give a poet ideas for both structure and meaning. Point out the structural features of "On Turning Ten" as illustrated by the modeling chart on page 184. For example, the repetitive passage that begins *At four . . .* and ends with *. . . at nine a prince* provides an obvious structure for a new poem. Invite students to identify other structural features in the modeling chart and discuss how they could provide the structure for a new poem. Then have students use a similar process to discuss how the model provides ideas for the meaning of a new poem.

"On Turning Ten" by Billy Collins	"On Turning _____" by _____
But now I am mostly at the window watching the late afternoon light. Back then it never fell so solemnly against the side of my tree house, and my bicycle never leaned against the garage as it does today, all the dark blue speed drained out of it.	But now I _____ _____ . Back then _____ _____ , and my _____ never _____ _____ as it does today, _____ .
This is the beginning of sadness, I say to myself, as I walk through the universe in my sneakers. It is time to say good-bye to my imaginary friends, time to turn the first big number.	This is the beginning of _____ , I say, as I _____ It is time to say good-bye _____ , time to _____ .
It seems only yesterday I used to believe there was nothing under my skin but light. If you cut me I would shine. But now when I fall upon the sidewalks of life, I skin my knees. I bleed. *by Billy Collins*	It seems only yesterday I used to _____ _____ But now when _____ , I _____ . by _____ , *with thanks to Billy Collins*

✷ Share your poem with your group and, perhaps, with the whole class.

Modeling is a strategy that makes you attend to the structure as well as the ideas of the original piece of writing.

MODELING A POEM **185**

Sentence Patterns In addition to focusing on sound, all good poetry exhibits a concentrated use of language. Point out the potency of phrases such as *a disfiguring chicken pox of the soul*. Then invite students to identify other similarly powerful concentrated language choices in "On Turning Ten."

TEACHING TIP

Use Graphic Organizers Provide a stack of small self-stick notes for each student. Have students write words or phrases on the notes and stick them on a larger piece of paper randomly. Once students have written at least 25 notes each, encourage them to begin organizing the notes. They can arrange them in clusters, lists, charts, or other graphic organizer forms that serve their individual organizing purposes.

Quick Assess

✷ Do students' charts utilize the form of the model effectively?

✷ Do students' charts reflect the meanings of the model clearly?

During

FREEWRITING Have each student choose an age for which he or she has vivid memories. Before attempting to follow the model, have students freely brainstorm as many descriptive words and phrases about the time as they can. Discourage the editing of ideas or language at this point. Encourage students to write down any idea, not matter how ridiculous it may seem. They can always discard any unsuitable ideas or words later.

After

CREATING FOUND POETRY Explain that models for poetry literally surround all of us at every moment. Model how to create a "found poem":

✷ Read aloud a short but intriguing news item from a newspaper or magazine.

✷ Point out interesting or emotion-laden words or phrases in the article and have volunteers write them on the board.

✷ Put the words or phrases together in poetic combinations and write them on the board as a poem.

Invite volunteers to read the "found poem" aloud. Discuss how the poetic form of the story differs from the article's account.

Students will learn that creating a hybrid poem helps them focus on the language and meaning of the original poems.

BACKGROUND KNOWLEDGE

Introduce the concept of human interdependency by asking students to recall a time when they were glad to have a friend or confidant to help them through a tough time. Ask: *How did having someone "on your side" help you? After that experience, what conclusion did you reach about "going it alone"?* Explain that this lesson presents two related poems by the same poet, in which she expresses different views of how to handle difficult situations.

VOCABULARY

counterpane an embroidered quilt; a bedspread

banshee a female spirit in Gaelic folklore whose wailing foretold a death

After discussing the definitions, have students reread the lines in which the words appear, replacing the words with synonyms or synonymous phrases.

LESSON **59**   CREATING A HYBRID POEM

You may have read all or part of one of Maya Angelou's best-known books, *I Know Why the Caged Bird Sings*. You may also have found her simple lyrical poems in greeting cards. Maya Angelou is a great inspiration to many people because she was able to survive a tough childhood to become a famous writer, actress, professor, historian, songwriter, playwright, dancer, and civil-rights activist.

Here are a few quotations from Maya Angelou's writing and talks:

- I speak to the black experience, but I am always talking about the human condition—about what we can endure, dream, fail at, and still survive.

- There is nothing so pitiful as a young cynic because he has gone from knowing nothing to believing nothing.

- If you don't like something, change it. If you can't change it, change your attitude. Don't complain.

- We need language to tell us who we are, how we feel, what we're capable of — to explain the pains and glory of our existence.

- If you have only one smile in you, give it to the people you love. Don't be surly at home, then go out in the street and start grinning "good morning" at total strangers.

In this lesson, you will read two of Maya Angelou's poems, then create a new poem from them by selecting words and phrases from each to make a poetic dialogue. You will then read your "hybrid" poem to the class.

Response Notes

Life Doesn't Frighten Me

Shadows on the wall
Noises down the hail
Life doesn't frighten me at all
Bad dogs barking loud
Big ghosts in a cloud
Life doesn't frighten me at all.
Mean old Mother Goose
Lions on the loose
They don't frighten me at all
Dragons breathing flame

Alone   by Maya Angelou

Lying, thinking
Last night
How to find my soul a home
Where water is not thirsty
And bread loaf is not stone
I came up with one thing
And I don't believe I'm wrong
That nobody,
But nobody
Can make it out here alone.

Before

CRITICAL READING SKILL

Studying an Author Have students read the five quotations from Ms. Angelou silently. Then have each student read aloud the quotation that appeals to him or her most and to explain why. After the readings, have volunteers discuss how the meaning of each quotation evolved for them as they heard it repeated and heard others' interpretations of it. Explain that

the quotations express five different components of the poet's outlook on life. Invite students to listen for these different components in "Life Doesn't Frighten Me" and "Alone."

CREATING A HYBRID POEM Put students into pairs; then go over the directions for writing a hybrid poem. Define *hybrid* as something that has two or more different components or origins. Explain that when two purebred dogs of different breeds are mated, you get a crossbreed, or hybrid. A hybrid may have characteristics of both parents or it may resemble one more strongly.

On my counterpane
That doesn't frighten me at all.

I go boo
Make them shoo
I make fun
Way they run
I won't cry
So they fly
I just smile
They go wild
Life doesn't frighten me at all.

Tough guys in a fight
All alone at night
Life doesn't frighten me at all.
Panthers in the park
Strangers in the dark
No, they don't frighten me at all.

That new classroom where
Boys pull all my hair
(Kissy little girls
With their hair in curls)
They don't frighten me at all.

Don't show me frogs and snakes
And listen for my scream,
If I'm afraid at all
It's only in my dreams.

I've got a magic charm
That I keep up my sleeve,
I can walk the ocean floor
And never have to breathe.

Life doesn't frighten me at all
Not at all
Not at all
Life doesn't frighten me at all. ✧

Alone, all alone
Nobody, but nobody
Can make it out here alone.
There are some millionaires
With money they can't use
Their wives run round like banshees
Their children sing the blues
They've got expensive doctors
To cure their hearts of stone.
But nobody
No, nobody
Can make it out here alone.
Alone, all alone
Nobody, but nobody
Can make it out here alone.
Now if you listen closely
I'll tell you what I know
Storm clouds are gathering
The wind is gonna blow
The race of man is suffering
And I can hear the moan,
'Cause nobody,
But nobody
Can make it out here alone.
Alone, all alone
Nobody, but nobody
Can make it out here alone. ✧

CREATING A HYBRID POEM **187**

During

CLOSE READING   Have several students read the poems aloud to the class several times. Have listeners mark in their *Daybooks* points at which the poems seem to intersect. After each reading, have partners discuss similarities and differences in their markings. After all the readings, invite students to share their observations with the class.

RESPONSE NOTES   Have students write in their Response Notes explanations of how the poems intersect. Encourage students to include these explanations in their comparisons with their partners.

WRITER'S CRAFT

Colloquialisms Define *colloquialism* as a nonstandard word or phrase. Cite examples, such as *the wind is gonna blow* and explain that writers use colloquialisms to add authenticity to their work. Point out that the colloquialisms in Ms. Angelou's poems give them an informal, comfortable feeling that invites the reader to share the poet's feelings and experiences. Have students skim through the two poems and identify other examples of colloquialisms. Invite students to imagine the effect of more formal wording and discuss how the poem as a whole would differ.

TEACHING TIP

Differentiation Auditory learners might benefit from hearing two versions of the poems—one as written and one that uses formal language. After the readings, have students discuss how their responses to the two versions varied.

❋ With a partner, take turns reading both of Maya Angelou's poems aloud. Each of you should take major responsibility for one poem, but talk together as you work.

- Talk about what each poem is saying.
  * Who is the speaker?
  * What is she or he saying?
  * How are the two poems related?

- Underline or highlight words, phrases, and lines that stand out for you.

- From these two poems, create a new, "hybrid" poem that conveys the sense of each of the poems, but results in a completely new poem.

- The chart that follows is a sample worksheet on which you can develop your new poem. Copy a blank version onto a piece of paper.
  * Write words, phrases, or complete lines from the two poems in the appropriate column so that when you read them in two voices, they make a new kind of sense.
  * You may use repetition, or you may vary the order in which the words appear, but use only the words of the two poems in your final poem.
  * Write in only one column at a time so you will know when it is your turn to read the lines. See the lines selected for the chart below.
  * Indicate whether the words are to be spoken by one person or by both. If they are to be spoken by both, write them in the center column.

PREWRITING Read aloud the instructions for creating a hybrid poem, stopping after the first two steps for students to follow the directions. Emphasize that there are no "wrong" ways to mark the poem. Invite partners to share their markings and have the class discuss their differences. Encourage partners to change or continue working with their markings until they are satisfied with them. Remind students of the intersection markings they made earlier and encourage them to use those also as they begin to compose their hybrid poems.

Words and phrases from "Life Doesn't Frighten Me" (Speaker A)	Words and phrases to be read together, by both speakers (these can be from either poem)	Words and phrases from "Alone" (Speaker B)
Shadows on the wall		
		Lying, thinking
		How to find my soul
	Life doesn't frighten me at all.	

* Read the new poem with your partner as a dialogue, each reading the words from one of the poems, both reading the lines in the center column.

* Write a paragraph that tells how your understanding of the two Angelou poems was affected by the process of writing a new poem from them. Did your understanding of them change? If so, how?

Creating a "hybrid" poem from two poems helps focus attention on the language and meaning of the original poems.

WRITER'S CRAFT

Repetition Remind students of the discussion of repetition in Lesson 56 (page 180). Point out how the device adds emphasis and encourage partners to consider which lines in their hybrid poems would benefit from the added emphasis.

Quick Assess

✳ Do students' charts clearly indicate the form and content of their hybrid poems?

✳ Do students' paragraphs tell how their understanding of the two poems was affected by writing a hybrid poem?

After

APPLYING THE STRATEGY

Creating a Hybrid Poem Have students read other Angelou poems or works by other poets and identify two candidates for hybridization. Encourage students to work with a partner or small group. Have students create another chart similar to the one on page 189 and create another hybrid poem. Hold a poetry reading so that students can share their hybrid poems with the class or before another audience.

Students will learn that the power of poetry lies in language and structure.

BACKGROUND KNOWLEDGE

Explain that the poem in this lesson is written by two people of mixed heritage. The poem is written in alternating lines that represent the voices of the mother and the daughter.

VOCABULARY

mestiza Spanish term for a girl or woman of mixed blood; usually referring to those of both European and Native American ancestry

diaspora the scattering of a people

jíbara Spanish term for female peasant

shtetl a small Jewish town formerly found in Eastern Europe

mija Spanish term of endearment; literally, "my daughter"

caribeña Spanish term for a girl or woman from the Caribbean

Boricua ancient term for Puerto Rico; now, a person who is Puerto Rican in blood and soul

Taína female member of an ancient Caribbean people

Say each word aloud, define it, and then ask the class to say it aloud. Repeat several times until the pronunciations are smooth.

Getting Home Alive is a book of poems by Aurora Levins Morales and her mother Rosario Morales. In the *Introduction,* Aurora writes, "My mother taught me to read. At some point, interwoven with our book reviews, we began to read each other our writing as well." That early practice led to their collaboration on this book and, later, on the final poem in the book. Aurora and Rosario wrote alternating lines of "Ending Poem."

Divide into groups of 6-10 students each. In your group, have two people read alternating lines for the first stanza. Then have two others read the next stanza. Continue in that pattern through the rest of the poem.

Before you begin, practice saying these words:

mestiza (meh STEE zuh)	*negra* (NEG ruh)
diaspora (die AS por uh)	*ne* (neh)
jíbara (HEE buh ruh)	*caribeña* (car eh BEN ya)
shtetl (SHTET ul)	*Boricua* (bore ee KU uh)
mija (MEE huh)	*Taína* (TYE nuh)

Response Notes

Ending Poem by Rosario Morales and Aurora Levins Morales

I am what I am.
      A child of the Americas.
A light-skinned mestiza of the Caribbean.
      A child of many diaspora, born into this continent at a
      crossroads.
I am Puerto Rican. I am U.S. American.
      I am New York Manhattan and the Bronx.
A mountain-born, country-bred, homegrown jíbara child,
      up from the shtetl, a California Puerto Rican Jew
A product of the New York ghettos I have never known.
      I am an immigrant
and the daughter and granddaughter of many immigrants.
      We didn't know our forbears' names with a certainty.
They aren't written anywhere.
      First names only or mija, negra, ne, honey,
      sugar, dear
I come from the dirt where the cane was grown.
      My people didn't go to dinner parties.
      They weren't invited.
I am caribeña, island grown.

Before

CRITICAL READING SKILL

Understanding Language and Structure Before students read the poem, point out that the poem uses three languages: English, Spanish, and Yiddish. Discuss how this fact symbolizes the theme of the poem: the richness of a mixed heritage. Review the pronunciations of the non-English words before asking students

to read aloud, using the skills of Spanish-speaking volunteers, if possible.

In addition to specific kinds of language, poets also use structure to help convey the message of their poems. Have students make observations about how the poem looks on the page and how the structure and patterns might be an important part of the message.

TEACHING TIP

Differentiation Auditory learners might benefit from hearing the poem before they start to read it for themselves. Invite students to listen *without* following along in their books as you read the poem aloud with appropriate expression. Then invite them to follow along as you read it a second time.

Spanish is in my flesh, ripples from my tongue,
lodges in my hips,
the language of garlic and mangoes.
Boricua. As Boricuas come from the isle of Manhattan.
I am of latinoamerica, rooted in the history of my continent.
I speak from that body.
Just brown and pink and full of drums inside.
I am not African.
Africa waters the roots of my tree, but I cannot return.
I am not Taína.
I am a late leaf of that ancient tree,
and my roots reach into the soil of two Americas.
Taína is in me, but there is no way back.
I am not European, though I have dreamt of those cities.
Each plate is different.
wood, clay, papier mâché, metals basketry, a leaf, a coconut shell.
Europe lives in me but I have no home there.
The table has a cloth woven by one, dyed by another,
embroidered by another still.
I am a child of many mothers.
They have kept it all going.
All the civilizations erected on their backs.
All the dinner parties given with their labor.
We are new.
They gave us life, kept us going,
brought us to where we are.
Born at a crossroads.
Come, lay that dishcloth down. Eat, dear, eat.
History made us.
We will not eat ourselves up inside anymore.
And we are whole. ❖

❋ This poem expresses many facets of the two women. It tells who
they are. Using your Response Notes, comment on the words and
phrases that define the mother and daughter. Look for and label
words that have to do with these aspects of life:

- Geography
- History
- Food
- Names
- Customs
- Language

ABOUT THE AUTHORS

Rosario Morales was born in the Bronx in 1930. A socialist, anti-war activist, and nationalist, she and her husband moved back to Puerto Rico in the 1950s, where they divided their time between university teaching and farming. After the birth of their daughter, Aurora, the couple returned to the U.S., where Ms. Morales continued to teach and write.

Aurora Levins Morales (born 1954) is a poet, essayist, community historian, and activist. She is poet-on-assignment for Pacifica Radio's *Flashpoints* news magazine, where she writes a twice-weekly poetry commentary on current events. Ms. Morales is known for her powerful poetry and prose, in which she uses her ethnically rich heritage to promote the importance of language, reading, words, and writing. *Getting Home Alive,* from which this lesson's work is taken, is a collection of poems, short stories, lyrical prose, essays, and dialogues written with her mother, Rosario Morales. While both composed individual poems for the book, they collaborated on writing "Ending Poem," to show both the mother's and the daughter's senses of identity.

During

RESPONSE NOTES Explain that sometimes the various facets of the women's lives listed on page 191 must be inferred. For example, "mountain-born, country bred" does not name specific geographic locations. It does, however, give the reader images of different areas and lifestyles. Encourage students to write in their Response Notes both the facets words refer to and how the students decided to categorize the words this way.

WRITER'S CRAFT

Metaphor Remind students of the discussion of metaphors in Lesson 53 (page 169). Repeat the definition of *metaphor* as "a comparison that describes one thing as another thing." Explain that "at a crossroads" is a common metaphor for a place in life at which a person or a nation must make a decision about the direction to take for the future. Have students read through the poem to identify other metaphors. Invite volunteers to share their discoveries and explain the meanings of the metaphors.

Quick Assess

✳ Do groups' oral readings demonstrate comprehension of the poem?

✳ Do students' original poems follow the "I Am" poem pattern?

✳ You know something about Rosario and Aurora Morales. What about you? Who are you? Use the following poem format and write a poem describing you. Notice that all the lines involve a particular verb. Verbs are words that show action. In this model, you will use both concrete images, as in "I hear..." or "I touch..." and abstractions, as in "I wonder..." or "I dream..." Notice, too, the importance of nouns, especially place words that are very much a part of "Ending Poem."

✳ Title your poem with a word or phrase that describes some aspect of who you are.

"I Am" Poem Format

I am *(2 special characteristics you have)*
I have lived *(name or list places you have lived)*
I am part of *(name family or group that you feel a part of)*
I treasure *(something you care a lot about)*
I wonder *(something you are curious about)*
I hear *(an imaginary sound)*
I want *(an actual desire)*
I pretend *(something you pretend to do)*
I feel *(a feeling about something imaginary)*
I am *(the first line of the poem repeated)*
I eat *(a few foods that are important to you)*
I touch *(an imaginary touch)*
I worry *(something that really bothers you)*
I cry *(something that makes you sad)*
I understand *(something you know is true)*
I say *(something you believe in)*
I dream *(something you dream about)*
I try *(something you really make an effort to do)*
I hope *(something you hope for)*
I am *(the first line of the poem repeated)*

You may want to make a clean copy of your poem and illustrate it with drawings or a border.

✳ Share your poems with each other in small groups or with the whole class.

> The power of poetry lies in word choice: in nouns that designate place and in verbs that show feeling and movement.

After

APPLYING THE STRATEGY

Pattern Poems Help students locate other literary passages that lend themselves to creating a pattern poem, such as the *I have a dream* passage in Dr. Martin Luther King's speech or the "A House of My Own" passage in Sandra Cisneros' *The House on Mango Street* that begins *Not a flat. Not an apartment in back. Not a man's house. Not a daddy's. A house all my own.*

Have students work in groups to develop a pattern outline similar to the one on page 192 for the work they have chosen. Then they can write poems individually that follow the pattern outline. Invite students to share their pattern poems with the class.

Studying an Author

Look around your classroom. Do you think anyone in your class will become a published author? You never know. When **Walter Dean Myers** was in school, maybe in a class like yours, no one—especially Walter Dean Myers—thought that he would be an author. Now he has published more than thirty novels for young adults, several works of nonfiction for young adults and children, and many picture books for children. The numerous awards for his writing include two Newbery Honor medals, Coretta Scott King Awards, a Michael L. Printz Award, and the Margaret A. Edwards Award for lifetime writing achievement. How could someone who was often in trouble in elementary school and who dropped out of high school become such a famous author? He liked to read and write and, once he knew what he wanted to do, he worked hard at it.

In this unit, you will read some of Walter Dean Myers's writing. By studying the author in depth, you will learn where his stories come from. Throughout the unit, you will have a chance to sharpen your own skills as an author. Who knows where that may lead?

193

Lessons 61–65, pages 194–208

UNIT OVERVIEW

In this unit, students will examine the writing of Walter Dean Myers. They will learn about sources of stories and how an author finds ideas and crafts them into finished pieces.

KEY IDEA

Studying an author in depth leads to greater understanding of the craft of writing.

CRITICAL READING SKILLS
by lesson

61 Finding ideas

62 Developing a theme

63 Building a plot

64 Reading nonfiction

65 Using an author's background to evaluate his or her work

WRITING ACTIVITIES
by lesson

61 Write a story's beginning.

62 Explain how an author uses a character to develop a theme.

63 Plot a story.

64 Outline a short nonfiction piece.

65 Complete a chart that evaluates an author's work.

Literature

- from *Bad Boy: A Memoir* by Walter Dean Myers (memoir)

Myers details some of the trouble he experienced in grade school and the teacher who, perhaps inadvertently, revealed to him the delights of reading.

- from *The Glory Field* by Walter Dean Myers (novel)

Two teenaged runaway slaves seek freedom and dignity in this excerpt from a sweeping family chronicle.

- from *Monster* by Walter Dean Myers (novel)

A fictional journal entry from this novel reveals the main character's confusion and fear about being in jail awaiting trial.

- from "Now Is Your Time!" by Walter Dean Myers (article)

Myers describes a landmark civil rights case, highlighting the contributions of people he considers heroes.

- from "Hope Is an Open Book" by Walter Dean Myers (op-ed piece)

Myers discusses how free libraries became a turning point in his life by providing a desperately needed refuge and a "bridge to self-value."

ASSESSMENT See page 242 for a writing prompt based on this unit.

Students will learn how to find the material for stories in their own lives.

BACKGROUND KNOWLEDGE

Define *memoir* as "a writer's written reflections on his or her life." To distinguish it from an autobiography, say: *A memoir usually tells of a specific experience that has a significant impact on the person's outlook and/or life choices. An autobiography tells a chronology of a person's entire life.* Students should understand that while there are differences, a memoir is often seen as a kind of autobiography since both tell about a real person's life.

VOCABULARY

scenario a setting and brief sequence of events

rouge red coloring for cheeks

Ask several volunteers to briefly tell what happened in a segment of a favorite television show or book. After students have shared, tell them that they have been describing *scenarios* and then ask them how that word might be used in a person's memory entitled *Bad Boy*.

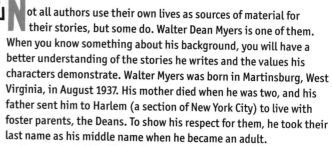

Not all authors use their own lives as sources of material for their stories, but some do. Walter Dean Myers is one of them. When you know something about his background, you will have a better understanding of the stories he writes and the values his characters demonstrate. Walter Myers was born in Martinsburg, West Virginia, in August 1937. His mother died when he was two, and his father sent him to Harlem (a section of New York City) to live with foster parents, the Deans. To show his respect for them, he took their last name as his middle name when he became an adult.

Myers enjoyed his life in Harlem, but he also got into a lot of trouble. In fact, his memoir is titled *Bad Boy* because he was in trouble so much. In fifth grade he went to a new school where he made a poor impression on the teacher on the first day. His relationship with Mrs. Conway did not improve for some time. As you read the excerpt that follows, make check marks or notes in the **Response Notes** for anything Myers says that makes a connection to or reminds you of something in your life.

Response Notes

from **Bad Boy: A Memoir** by Walter Dean Myers

Being good in class was not easy for me. I had a need to fill up all the spaces in my life, with activity, with talking, sometimes with purely imagined scenarios that would dance through my mind, occupying me while some other student was at the blackboard. I did want to get good marks in school, but they were never of major importance to me, except in the sense of "winning" the best grade in a subject. My filling up the spaces, however, kept me in trouble. I would blurt out answers to Mrs. Conway's questions even when I was told to keep quiet, or I might roll a marble across my desk if she was on the other side of the room.

The other thing that got me in trouble was my speech. I couldn't hear that I was speaking badly, and I wasn't sure that the other kids did, but I knew they often laughed when it was my turn to speak. After a while I would tense up anytime Mrs. Conway called on me. I threw my books across that classroom enough times for Mrs. Conway to stop my reading aloud once and for all.

But when the class was given the assignment to write a poem, she did read mine. She said that she liked it very much.

"I don't think he wrote that poem," Sidney Aronofsky volunteered.

I gave Sidney Aronofsky the biggest punch he ever had in the back of his big head and was sent to the closet. After the incident with Sidney,

Before

CRITICAL READING SKILL

Finding Ideas Ask students to brainstorm a list of events in their lives as quickly as they can think of them. Then, have them go back to their list and mark any event or events that influenced them in some way. Have them explain the events and their significance to a partner. Invite students to share events in their lives for which memoirs might be appropriate. For example, they might tell about how an adult influenced their outlook or how they faced a personal challenge.

RESPONSE NOTES As students read the excerpt, suggest that they use the events they shared above as springboards for notes about connections they see between Myers's story and their own life experiences.

Mrs. Conway said that I would not be allowed to participate in any class activity until I brought my mother to school. I knew that meant a beating. I thought about telling Mama that the teacher wanted to see her, but I didn't get up the nerve. I didn't get it up the next day, either. In the meantime I had to sit in the back of the room, and no kid was allowed to sit near me. I brought some comic books to school and read them under my desk.

Mrs. Conway was an enormously hippy woman. She moved slowly and always had a scowl on her face. She reminded me of a great white turtle with just a dash of rouge and a touch of eye shadow. It was not a pretty sight. But somehow she made it all the way from the front of the room to the back, where I sat reading a comic, without my hearing her. She snatched the comic from me and tore it up. She dropped all the pieces on my desk, then made me pick them up and take them to the garbage can while the class laughed.

Then she went to her closet, snatched out a book, and put it in front of me.

"You are," she sputtered, "a bad boy. A very bad boy. You cannot join the rest of the class until your mother comes in." She was furious, and I was embarrassed.

"And if you're going to sit back here and read, you might as well read something worthwhile," she snapped.

I didn't touch the book in front of me until she had made her way back to the front of the class and was going on about something in long division. The title of the book was *East o' the Sun and West o' the Moon*. It was a collection of Norwegian fairy tales, and I read the first one. At the end of the day, I asked Mrs. Conway if I could take the book home.

She looked at me a long time and then said no, I couldn't. But I could read it every day in class if I behaved myself. I promised I would. For the rest of the week I read that book. It was the best book I had ever read. . . .

I realized I liked books, and I liked reading. Reading a book was not so much like entering a different world—it was like discovering a different language. It was a language clearer than the one I spoke, and clearer than the one I heard around me. . . . The "me" who read the books, who followed the adventures, seemed more the real me than the "me" who played ball in the streets. ✥

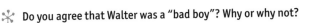

✳ Do you agree that Walter was a "bad boy"? Why or why not?

_____

_____

_____

ABOUT THE AUTHOR

Walter Dean Myers's childhood was influenced by many factors. His life with foster parents Herbert and Florence Dean was a loving one but was not easy. There was little money, and Myers described himself as "a troubled young man." His severe stutter isolated him from his classmates and he turned inward. He filled notebooks with his writing but never thought of himself as a writer. When his fifth-grade teacher encouraged him to read his poems aloud, however, he did not stutter. Although this and other positive experiences ultimately opened a door to his career as a writer, at the time, Myers did not see the value of school for himself. He dropped out of high school twice, joined the Army, and worked at a number of dead-end jobs, all while writing for various periodicals during the evenings. A turning point in Myers's writing career came when he won a contest in 1969. Since then, he has supported himself, his wife, and four children with his very prolific writing of literature for children and young adults.

EXTRA SUPPORT

Visual Learners Visual learners might benefit from drawing the various events in the excerpt. Have students create storyboards with a frame that illustrates each event.

During

MAKING CONNECTIONS Have students read some of the stories in *East o' the Sun and West o' the Moon* and retell the stories to the class. Then invite students to conjecture about the appeal this book had to the young Walter Dean Myers. For example, ask: *How would the kinds of stories in the book help young Walter "fill up all the spaces" in his life?*

Do you think Mrs. Conway knew this particular book would appeal to the boy? Explain your answer.

WRITER'S CRAFT

Drafting Explain that each author has his or her own method for approaching the task of creating a draft. Some take a very structured approach; others require a more free-flowing rhythm. Some write during certain hours of each day; others simply write whatever they feel like on a given day. Walter Dean Myers writes five days a week, seven pages a day. Each day, when he reaches the end of the seventh page, he quits for that day. This approach means that the author often stops in the middle of a scene or an idea, and then he thinks about it until it is time to write again the next day. He is then eager to start writing again every day. Invite students to discuss the approach that works best for them when they need to draft a piece of writing.

Quick Assess

✳ Do students' story beginnings tell about a personal experience appropriate for a memoir?

✳ Look at the connections you marked in the **Response Notes**. Use the connections to begin a story about yourself at school at any time in your past. Or create the beginning of a story about a new, fictional character who might have had an experience similar to Myers's.

Some authors get material for their stories from experiences in their lives.

After

APPLYING THE STRATEGY

Finding Ideas Encourage students to begin keeping logs of events that might provide the seeds for pieces of writing. Suggest that students make regular notes about their lives, daily or weekly, in a 3-column log such as the following. Explain that these logs can become inspirations or resources for future writing tasks.

Date	Event	Significance

Freedom is necessary for humans to have dignity, Walter Dean Myers seems to say in many of his books. It is a **theme** that Myers often uses. The African American characters in his books struggle for both dignity and freedom. They seek freedom from drugs, gangs, prison, and the abuses of white society's laws and prejudices. In *Harlem's Hellfighters,* Myers tells of African American troops who volunteered and fought bravely in World War I, even though white officers did not treat the black soldiers as equals. The black troops therefore served with the French instead of with Americans.

In *The Glory Field,* Myers tells the story of one family descended from an African slave who bought a piece of land and held onto it through several generations. Looking back on the time of slavery, a father says to his son, "Those shackles didn't rob us of being black, son, they robbed us of being human." As you read about Lizzy, a thirteen-year-old runaway slave girl and her friend Lem, mark examples of the search for freedom and dignity.

from The Glory Field by Walter Dean Myers

Lem and Lizzy stayed low as they moved toward the campfires. There were shadows among the fires, and once in a while they could make out a person. They couldn't see what they looked like.

"Hold it!"

Lizzy jumped and grabbed her arms. Lem started to run, and two men with rifles jumped in front of him. One swung his rifle, and Lizzy watched as Lem reeled backwards and fell heavily in the dark field.

"Contraband!" A voice near Lizzy spoke up.

Two other men went over and looked at Lem and then moved away.

"Get on into the camp if you want," the voice nearest Lizzy said.

Lizzy turned and saw the soldier. She couldn't believe her eyes. He was tall and broad-faced, and the rifle he carried looked almost taller than he was. But that wasn't what amazed Lizzy.

"You're black!" she said.

"Glad you noticed it," the soldier grinned. "I had just about forgot it."

Lizzy helped Lem up. Together they started toward the campfires.

"Are they Yankees?" Lem asked.

"I guess they are," Lizzy whispered. "They carrying guns, too!"

As they neared the fires they heard singing. It was black singing, all right, a low praise hymn being crooned sweet and strong in the night.

Response Notes

A MAJOR THEME **197**

Students will learn how an author brings themes to life through the characters in a story.

BACKGROUND KNOWLEDGE

The Glory Field is the story of the Lewis family, which is descended from an African brought to America to be enslaved. Each section tells the story of one generation, focusing on just a few of the family members. Although geographically dispersed, the family members are all drawn back to a piece of land, the glory field. The excerpt in this lesson comes from March 1864, before the family owned the land. The nation is in the midst of the Civil War.

VOCABULARY

contraband smuggled goods

crooned sung in a gentle, murmuring manner

threescore sixty (score = 20)

After showing students the definitions, ask them to think of an application that will help them remember each word. Some prompts might be useful: *If school officials found* contraband *in your desk or your backpack, what do you think would happen to you? Who is more likely to* croon—*a mother with a new baby or a rapper? State the age of an adult you know as a* score.*"

Before

ANTICIPATION GUIDE Explain that American history books cannot tell everything that is interesting about those who fought in the Civil War. Tell them that this selection from *The Glory Field* gives a picture of the fighters that they might not see in their textbooks. Write the four statements below and ask students to decide individually which statements are likely to be true and which are likely to be false.

1. The only soldiers who fought in the Civil War were white. (F)
2. Black men and women helped out in the Yankee camps. (T)
3. Young black women fought beside black and white soldiers for the Confederacy. (F)
4. Black men fought beside white men in Yankee units. (T)

Record students' answers, encouraging students to explain their reasons. Tell students that they should look for how the statements are shown to be true or false as they read the selection. After they read the selection, have students return to the guide to see whether they would respond to the statements in the same way.

Auditory Learners Auditory learners might benefit from research into
music that could have been heard in
a black unit's Civil War camp. Suggest
that students create a multimedia
presentation of some of the music
and explain its origins and meanings.
Invite the class to discuss how Lizzy
knew, "It was black singing, all right."

Response Notes

The Yankee camp was busy. The camp was filled with soldiers, half of them white, the others black.

Snatches of conversation drifted toward them. The voices weren't like the ones they had heard before, and Lizzy was having trouble understanding them. They seemed relaxed, busy with the work of soldiering. There were a lot of other blacks, too. Some of them were just sitting around; others were cleaning boots or saddles.

"You young folks looking for something to eat you can get it around by that wagon." An old man, his white beard contrasting sharply with his black skin, pointed toward a wagon.

"You got black soldiers here!" Lizzy said.

"There's four and forty thousand of them, seven hundred and threescore, all crying out to the Lord for strength," the old man said. "How can they fail?"

✳ What two words would you use to describe Lizzy at this point?

Lizzy and Lem are fed beans and bread in the camp and fall asleep. Lizzy dreams of her recent past—the hounds chasing the runaway slaves—and another dream that involves the 17-year-old white daughter of Lizzy's "owner."

But it was the other dream that filled her, that moved her body in her sleep. It was a dream of being free, of walking across a wide meadow, not even following a road, just going any which way she wanted to go, not caring when she got there. She had the dream over and over again, each time wearing a different one of Miss Julia's dresses. It was a beautiful dream.

✳ What does this dream add to your picture of Lizzy? Add two more words to describe her.

Now read what happens next, continuing to make notes about freedom and dignity. The soldiers—black and white—move out of camp. Lem has joined them.

During

CRITICAL READING SKILL
Developing a Theme Explain that *theme* is not the same as a moral of a story or a lesson learned. A theme is a larger term that refers to the main topic or message that is explored through the characters and plot of a story. Many themes can be expressed quite simply. For example, "helping others usually involves personal risk" is a statement of theme.

Suggest that students make statements of themes for Myers's work by

✳ finding the general topic in the work. For example, freedom and dignity are topics Myers writes about in this excerpt.

✳ noticing the thoughts, words, and actions of characters that reveal what the author believes about the topic. For example, Lizzy's dream of "just going any which way she wanted to go" that "filled her" reveals a belief that freedom is a deeply moving experience.

✳ stating what the author believes in as few words as possible. A good example is the introduction to these excerpts from *The Glory Field* that describes Myers's typical theme as "Without freedom, humans have no dignity."

"What should I do?" Lizzy looked around as the soldiers and wagons started moving out. "What am I going to do?"

"Girl, you can go on with some folks who gonna try to make it North," a woman said. "Or you can stay with the soldiers and help them do what they want. They always need somebody to cook and mend."

Lizzy looked to where the black soldiers had gone down a road, seeing them turn and disappear around a bend. She couldn't see around the bend, or know what she was going to find when she got around it, but she knew she had to find out.

She ran as fast as she could, her feet slapping against the hard road. When she got around the bend, the men were still in sight, tall and proud.

She followed them, never looking back. ❖

Visual Learners Visual learners might benefit from creating posters that represent the big ideas in various sections of The Glory Field.

Quick Assess

✳ Do students explain clearly how the author uses the character of Lizzy to develop his theme?

✳ **How does Walter Dean Myers use the character of Lizzy to portray his theme of freedom and dignity?**

_____
_____
_____
_____
_____
_____
_____
_____
_____
_____
_____
_____
_____
_____
_____
_____
_____
_____
_____

An author's theme can come to life through the characters in the story.

A MAJOR THEME **199**

After

Invite students to think of a statement of theme for *Bad Boy* and practice expressing themes succinctly.

APPLYING THE STRATEGY

A Common Theme Suggest that students read other portions of *The Glory Field* to discover more ways Myers develops themes around the topics of freedom and dignity. Have students share their observations in groups.

Students will learn how the plot of a story can develop from the way a character reacts to a crisis.

BACKGROUND KNOWLEDGE

In most instances, we bear some responsibility for our circumstances. Our actions have placed us in a situation either directly or indirectly. For example, taking too much time to get ready to go somewhere can make us rush. When we rush, we can cause accidents or forget things. Have students reflect on difficult situations they have experienced. Ask: *What actions of yours helped cause the situation?*

Then have students reflect on a time when they were accused of misdeeds that they did not commit. Ask: *What actions of yours helped cause the situation? What did you feel when you were accused? What decisions did you make about your situation?* Have groups discuss various ways people can handle such situations.

VOCABULARY

grainy not clear; appearing to be made out of small (grain-like) particles

prosecutor lawyer whose job it is to prove the guilt of the accused

After discussing the definitions, have students use each term in a sentence that confirms their understanding.

LESSON 63 PLOTTING CONSEQUENCES

nother theme that is important to Walter Dean Myers is dealing with the consequences of one's actions. He develops this theme by building a **plot** from a set of character traits. Lizzy's freedom dream helped her decide what to do. In *Scorpions,* seventh-grader Jamal accepts a gun from an older teen and everything changes. In *The Beast,* Gabi chooses drugs to help her deal with the problems in her life. Not surprisingly, more problems arise. The barber, Duke, in *Handbook for Boys,* could be speaking for Myers when he points out that life doesn't work, people have to. The people who succeed, according to him, are those who know what they want and are willing to work for it.

Sixteen-year-old Steve Harmon made a bad decision. Now he's on trial for murder. Is he guilty? Is he the monster the prosecutor makes him out to be, or was he just in the wrong place at the wrong time? As you read the opening journal entry in *Monster,* use the **Response Notes** space to make notes about Steve's character.

Response Notes

from **Monster** by Walter Dean Myers

The best time to cry is at night, when the lights are out and someone is being beaten up and screaming for help. That way even if you sniffle a little they won't hear you. If anyone knows that you are crying, they'll start talking about it and soon it'll be your turn to get beat up when the lights go out.

There is a mirror over the steel sink in my cell. It's six inches high, and scratched with the names of some guys who were here before me. When I look into the small rectangle, I see a face looking back at me but I don't recognize it. It doesn't look like me. I couldn't have changed that much in a few months. I wonder if I will look like myself when the trial is over.

. . .

They say you get used to being in jail, but I don't see how. Every morning I wake up and I am surprised to be here. If your life outside was real, then everything in here is just the opposite. We sleep with strangers, wake up with strangers, and go to the bathroom in front of strangers. They're strangers but they still find reasons to hurt each other.

Sometimes I feel like I have walked into the middle of a movie. It is a strange movie with no plot and no beginning. The movie is in black and white, and grainy. Sometimes the camera moves in so close that you can't tell what is going on and you just listen to the sounds and guess. I have seen movies of prisons but never one like this. This is not a movie about bars and locked

Before

CRITICAL READING SKILL

Building Plot In a well-written story, the elements (setting, character, plot, theme) all work tightly together. In this lesson, students are asked to identify character traits and then look to see how those traits influence the plot. Use a story or novel familiar to students to illustrate how character traits and plot are related. Ask them to consider how the plot would change if the character had different traits.

GENRE **Journal** Explain that there are many kinds of journals, such as travel journals, scientific journals, news journals, and personal journals. Define a personal journal as an individual's record of his or her life events and reflections about them. Discuss how a personal journal differs from a short story. For example:

✴ It is not fiction.

✴ It is usually told in the first person.

✴ Its emphasis is on thoughts and feelings, rather than on actions and events.

Invite students to look for details that reveal elements of the narrator's character as they read the excerpt.

doors. It is about being alone when you are not really alone and about being scared all the time.

I think to get used to this I will have to give up what I think is real and take up something else. I wish I could make sense of it.

Maybe I could make my own movie. I could write it out and play it in my head. I could block out the scenes like we did in school. The film will be the story of my life. No, not my life, but of this experience. I'll write it down in the notebook they let me keep. I'll call it what the lady who is the prosecutor called me. Monster. ❖

✳ In this journal entry, Steve does not describe himself directly. You have to infer character traits from the thoughts he shares. Discuss with a partner the traits you wrote in the **Response Notes.** Add to your notes any traits you did not think of the first time you read.

Walter Dean Myers often works with groups of student writers. He helps them plot a story by "starting with a simple personality trait of a character and seeing how that character reacts to some crisis."

For example, if the character lacks self-confidence but wants to appear tough, he might be more likely to carry a gun to school. The crisis in the story could begin when he showed that gun to someone. Depending on who saw it, he or she might take any one of several actions, such as reporting him to authorities. The action would then lead to further consequences, and you would have a story.

Differentiation Students in need of more support might benefit from further discussion of character traits. Point out that a character trait is a learned attitude or point of view, as opposed to physical traits, which are inherited genetically. For example, a person who believes that most people are cruel and selfish learned that point of view from his or her life experiences. Remind students of young Walter's attitude toward school: *I did want to get good marks in school, but they were never of major importance to me, except in the sense of "winning" the best grade in a subject.* Discuss what events may have occurred in Walter's life to teach him this attitude.

Explain that people often use adjectives to label character traits. Define such terms as *greedy, compliant, generous, naïve, obedient, defiant,* and *confused.* Invite students to identify thoughts a character might have or actions that a character might take that would support each label.

During

Character's thoughts or actions	What they tell about the character
"...if you sniffle a little, they won't hear you..."	He doesn't want to let the other prisoners know he is afraid.

Point out that the excerpt in this lesson starts in the middle of the action of the story. The narrator is already in jail awaiting trial. Have groups of students brainstorm events that might have led to the situation. Ask: *What events occurred before this point? What actions did the narrator take before this point? What other actions might he have taken to prevent his arrival at this point?* Students might also enjoy predicting the events that follow.

Ask: *What will be the outcome of the trial? What consequences will result from the trial's outcome? What actions will the narrator take after the trial?* Encourage students to make their predictions consistent with the character traits they have identified.

TEACHING TIP

Collaboration To help students develop their thinking about their stories, have them share their completed charts with a partner. Ask each student to tell about a story that they could write using the elements of the chart. Encourage students to revise their charts as a result of their partner's reactions to the story. Partners might ask *How is that action logical if the character has this trait? Could you tell me more about the crisis? I wonder if the character would act differently, given these character traits.*

Quick Assess

✳ Do students' charts show that a character's reactions to a crisis grow from a character trait?

✳ Try your hand at plotting a story that grows from a character trait. You can use Lizzy in Lesson 62, Steve, or a character you create. Tell the name of your character. In the chart below, list the character trait, briefly describe the crisis, and tell the character's reactions.

Name of Character _____

Character Trait	Crisis	Character's Reactions

The plot of a story can develop from the ways in which the character reacts to a crisis.

After

APPLYING THE STRATEGY Have students use their charts from page 202 to write a short story or a scene about a character who faces a crisis that could be included in one of Myers's books. If the partnership collaboration was productive (see above), allow students to choose to work with a partner to develop their scene or short story.

Walter Dean Myers is probably best known for his fiction about teenagers facing the obstacles of inner-city life. But he also writes **nonfiction,** presenting real men and women who, like his fictional characters, show the positive decisions that people can make in troubled circumstances.

In the following excerpt from *Now Is Your Time!* Walter Dean Myers describes a court case, *Brown vs. Board of Education of Topeka*. This case challenged the ruling that "separate but equal" schools for black and white students were constitutional. Thurgood Marshall was the attorney who spearheaded the case against segregation. (Marshall later served on the Supreme Court.) As you read, circle or highlight the names of the people whom Myers would call heroes.

from **Now Is Your Time!** by Walter Dean Myers

It was Thurgood Marshall and a battery of N.A.A.C.P. attorneys who began to challenge segregation throughout the country. These men and women were warriors in the cause of freedom for African Americans, taking their battles into courtrooms across the country. They understood the process of American justice and the power of the Constitution.

In *Brown vs. Board of Education of Topeka*, Marshall argued that segregation was a violation of the Fourteenth Amendment—that even if the facilities and all other "tangibles" were equal, which was the heart of the case in *Plessy vs. Ferguson*, a violation still existed. There were intangible factors, he argued, that made the education unequal.

Everyone involved understood the significance of the case: that it was much more than whether black children could go to school with white children. If segregation in the schools was declared unconstitutional, then all segregation in public places could be declared unconstitutional.

Southerners who argued against ending school segregation were caught up, as then-Congressman Brooks Hays of Arkansas put it, in "a lifetime of adventures in that gap between law and custom." The law was one thing, but most Southern whites felt just as strongly about their customs as they did the law.

Dr. Kenneth B. Clark, an African-American psychologist, testified for the N.A.A.C.P. He presented clear evidence that the effect of segregation was harmful to African-American children. Describing studies conducted by black and white psychologists over a twenty-year period, he showed that black children felt inferior to white children. In a particularly dramatic study that he had supervised, four dolls, two white and two black, were presented to African-

Response Notes

Students will learn that, like fiction, nonfiction can also show people overcoming obstacles.

BACKGROUND KNOWLEDGE

Before the court case discussed in this lesson's excerpt, there were separate public schools for white and black children in 21 southern states. The argument for this segregation was that schools could be "separate but equal." In fact, the separate schools were far from equal in quality. At the trial for *Brown vs. Board of Education of Topeka* (1954), an African American psychologist, Dr. Kenneth B. Clark, demonstrated that a lifetime of segregation was harmful to black children.

VOCABULARY

N.A.A.C.P. National Association for the Advancement of Colored People; an organization formed in support of civil rights for people of color

tangible something "touchable"

intangible not "touchable"; conceptual, as opposed to physical

deliberating considering carefully

prohibitions orders to stop actions

Ask students to provide examples of *tangible* and *intangible* things.

Before

CRITICAL READING SKILL

Nonfiction Have students explain how nonfiction differs from fiction. Reinforce that nonfiction deals with facts and real people. The excerpt in this lesson relates facts about events and people the author considers heroic. Discuss how a fictional hero might differ from a real-life hero. Invite groups of students to create definitions of a real-life hero and share them with the class. Discuss the differences among the definitions. Encourage students to look for a variety of heroic qualities as they read.

GRAPHIC ORGANIZERS Help the class create a mind map of the qualities of real-life heroes. For example:

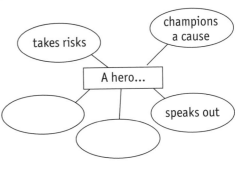

Post the mind map for students to refer to as they read.

WRITER'S CRAFT

Features of Nonfiction Display
other examples of nonfiction, such as
newspaper stories, magazine articles,
history books, science textbooks,
etc. Have each group examine one
example and list the features that
help readers understand the contents.
For example, a textbook usually has
section heads; photographs; captions;
and diagrams, charts, or graphs. Post
a list of features. Then have students
study the Myers article a paragraph at
a time and add features to help clarify
key concepts. Point out that Myers's
article contains facts as well as his
observations and opinions about the
facts. Students might add headlines
or section heads to distinguish one
section from another or they might
create diagrams to distinguish events,
people, and opinions. Then have
students share their additions within
their groups.

American children. From the responses of the children to the dolls, identical
in every way except color, it was clear that the children were rejecting the
black dolls. African-American children did not just feel separated from white
children, they felt that the separation was based on their inferiority.

Dr. Clark understood fully the principles and ideas of those people who
had held Africans in bondage and had tried to make slaves of captives. By
isolating people of African descent, by barring them from certain actions or
places, they could make them feel inferior. The social scientists who testified
at *Brown vs. Board of Education* showed that children who felt inferior also
performed poorly.

The Justice Department argued that racial segregation was objectionable to
the Eisenhower Administration and hurt our relationships with other nations.

On May 17, 1954, after deliberating for nearly a year and a half, the
Supreme Court made its ruling. The Court stated that it could not use the
intentions of 1868, when the Fourteenth Amendment was passed, as a guide
to its ruling, or even those of 1896, when the decision in *Plessy vs. Ferguson*
was handed down. Chief Justice Earl Warren wrote:

We must consider public education in the light of its full development and
its present place in American life throughout the nation. We must look instead
to the effect of segregation itself on public education.

The Court went on to say that "modern authority" supported the idea that
segregation deprived African Americans of equal opportunity. "Modern authority" referred to Dr. Kenneth B. Clark and the weight of evidence that he and
the other social scientists had presented.

The high court's decision in *Brown vs. Board of Education* signaled an
important change in the struggle for civil rights. It signaled clearly that
the legal prohibitions that oppressed African Americans would have to fall.
Equally important was the idea that the nature of the fight for equality would
change. Ibrahima, Cinqué, Nat Turner, and George Latimer had struggled for
freedom by fighting against their captors or fleeing from them. The 54th had
fought for African freedom on the battlefields of the Civil War. Ida B. Wells had
fought for equality with her pen. Lewis H. Latimer and Meta Vaux Warrick had
tried to earn equality with their work. In *Brown vs. Board of Education* Thurgood Marshall, Kenneth B. Clark, and the lawyers and social scientists, both
black and white, who helped them had won for African Americans a victory
that would bring them closer to full equality than they had ever been in North
America. There would still be legal battles to be won, but the major struggle
would be in the hearts and minds of people and "in that gap between law and
custom." ❖

204 LESSON 64

During

EXAMINING DETAILS Form seven
groups. List the names the author cites
in the last paragraph (excluding Marshall
and Clark) and assign one to each group.
Have groups research their assigned personages and report their findings to the
class. Review the discussion of allusions in
Lesson 53. Remind students that the allusions remind readers of historical events
or personages that symbolize specific concepts. Have students discuss why Myers
mentioned each person in his article. Ask
about each person: *Was this person a hero?
Why or why not? With what character trait
would you label this person? Why?*

✳ Return to the excerpt, and in the **Response Notes,** tell why Myers would probably call "heroes" the people whose names you highlighted. Underline the details that he gives in the excerpt.

✳ With a partner, brainstorm a list of other people you would call heroes. They can be from any time period or place. Write their names in the box below. List some qualities that make each one a hero in your opinion.

Name	Qualities

✳ Select one name and outline a short piece you could write about this person. Include in your outline the person's name, the reason you think he or she is heroic, and two or three details you could use.

_____

_____

_____

_____

_____

_____

_____

_____

Nonfiction writing can show real people overcoming obstacles.

Collaboration Define *laws* as "rules enforced by the courts" and *customs* as "rules enforced by peer pressure." Discuss some present-day laws and customs. For example, ask: *What laws apply to cell phone use? What customs apply to cell phone use?* Point out that, as a result of the case of *Brown vs. Board of Education of Topeka,* laws replaced some customs. Invite groups to study the excerpt and record rules of law vs. rules of custom in a T-chart:

Rules of Law	Rules of Custom

Quick Assess

✳ Do students list heroes from various places and periods of history?

✳ Do students' outlines include the hero's name, a reason the person should be considered a hero, and details to support their assertion?

After

SPEAKING/ART CONNECTION Have students prepare oral presentations about heroes. Each presentation should include

✳ a visual aid that either identifies the hero or exemplifies why the person is heroic;

✳ a statement about why the person is a hero;

✳ several details to support the assertion.

Students will learn that reflecting on an author's life can help them to better understand that author's writing and evaluate its quality.

BACKGROUND KNOWLEDGE

Define *op-ed* as "a piece of writing that expresses a point of view." Explain that the genre name derives from the customary placement of such pieces opposite the editorial page of a newspaper. (opposite + editorial = op-ed) Most op-ed pieces take the form of an essay using argumentation to support a point of view. Unlike the opinions on an editorial page, which are endorsed by the newspaper's management, opinions expressed on the op-ed page are those of the writer alone and may be in opposition to the newspaper's position on an issue.

Display several examples of op-ed pieces from newspapers. Form groups and have each group examine an op-ed piece and identify the attributes of the genre, which should include at least the following items:

✳ a thesis statement

✳ opinion statements

✳ several support statements

LESSON **65** REFLECTING ON AN AUTHOR'S LIFE AND WORK

Walter Dean Myers's life and beliefs are evident in his works. He does not just tell the story of his life and the people he knows, though. As an author, he crafts new stories that connect with topics that he knows well—life in Harlem, the army, teenagers, history, and so forth.

In the following excerpt, he reveals his beliefs about the importance of libraries. The 115th Street branch of the New York Public Library in Harlem had been undergoing renovation for more than three years when he wrote this opinion piece for the *New York Times*. As you read, put check marks by the details that connect with any of Myers's other writing that you have read in this unit or elsewhere.

Response Notes

from "**Hope Is an Open Book**" by Walter Dean Myers

As a child growing up in Harlem, I measured my life, and my potential, by what I saw around me. I saw first that I was black and poor. My father was a janitor, and my mother, never very healthy, cleaned apartments when she was well enough to work.

There was no single event that traumatized me, no devastating storm in my life, but slowly the life of the poor began to grind me down. A murdered uncle, an alcoholic parent, the realization that there was no way that I could afford college brought despair to my life. The promising 14-year-old I had been became the 15-year-old chronic truant who had to report to a city agency once a week for supervision.

But amid the chaos, I found a refuge. It was the New York Public Library. Not the research libraries, but the neighborhood branch where I would take out three or four books each week in a brown paper bag to avoid the comments of my friends who thought I was "acting white." When I felt least wanted by the world, the library became my bridge to self-value.

As I stumbled, on the verge of becoming a statistic in the juvenile justice system, increasingly angry at a world that I felt did not belong to me, the George Bruce branch library on West 125th Street was my home away from home. The 115th Street branch is similarly a sanctuary for residents in its neighborhood.

The library was the one place in my world that I could enter and participate in fully despite empty pockets. In the library stacks I could consider a novel by Gide or Balzac or Hemingway, and join a universe that would otherwise be denied me. There was no way I could have afforded to buy the books.

Before

CRITICAL READING SKILL
Putting an Author's Work in Context Authors almost always reflect their beliefs and experiences in their writing. Knowing something about the author helps the reader understand the author's work more deeply.

GENRE **Nonfiction** Have students analyze the excerpt for attributes of an op-ed piece. They should be able to identify, at a minimum, the three attributes listed above.

RESPONSE NOTES Students might benefit from using different colored markers to mark the various attributes. For example, they might mark the thesis statement with one color, opinion statements with another color, and statements that support the opinion with a third color.

In the quiet surroundings of the library, I was safe from the hostility that many inner-city children encounter when they look to extend their lives intellectually. And, if the hostility was there when I was a child, how much more do young people face in an age in which the heroes are gangsta rappers?

I speak with thousands of young people around the country each year: youngsters in middle school, high school students and children in juvenile detention centers. I've learned that they all experience a period of transition, a time when they stop thinking of life as something that will happen to them in the future, and start examining where they are in the moment. It is at this time that their lives are most shaped by the reality of their circumstances and by their ability to escape those circumstances by reaching out for ideas that will eventually define their success in life.

For me, at that moment, the library was crucial—its doors opened onto the American dream. ❖

✳ List two ways that this text connects with other pieces by Walter Dean Myers that you have read in this unit.

1. _____

2. _____

Making connections is one way to start reflecting on the author's work. A second way is to evaluate it. When Myers works with students in schools, he introduces them to his ÉCLAIR formula to criticize material. It looks like this:

E —Emotion

C —Clarity

L —Language that sings

A —Argument

I —Imagination

R —Rhythm

He explains that by *argument* he means "that the writer wants to sway the reader toward a specific point of view. Argument has a utility that, in my view, meaning lacks." He applies this formula to all writing, including poetry.

WRITER'S CRAFT

Explain that drawing on one's life experiences for ideas is not the same as reporting them. Sometimes an author reports aspects of his or her life directly and factually, but even in nonfiction works, such as autobiography or memoir, those reports are colored by the attitude of the author toward those events. In works of fiction, authors may start with aspects of their lives, but may also add incidents, create composite characters, change settings, invent dialogue, and so forth to create an overall effect. In both fiction and nonfiction, although authors may draw on their lives for ideas, they craft their work. The second paragraph of this lesson's excerpt is a good example. Point out that instead of saying something straightforward, like "I had a difficult childhood" or "Life was hard when I was a child" Myers crafts a compelling narrative that draws the reader emotionally into the story. Encourage students to mark other evidence of crafted writing as they read the excerpt.

During

CRITICAL READING SKILL

Reflecting on an Author's Life and Work
Discuss Walter Dean Myers's themes as revealed in the excerpts studied in this unit. Create and post a chart of these observations, such as the following:

Theme	Where revealed
1. Reading is important for all children	1. *Bad Boy: A Memoir* "Hope Is an Open Book"
2.	2.
3.	3.

Point out themes that are explored in more than one work. Ask: *Why do you think these themes show up in Myers's work? What do these common themes show about his purposes for writing?*

WRITING SUPPORT

Evaluating Writing Define *literary criticism* as the evaluation of writing according to certain criteria. The *ÉCLAIR* formula is one set of criteria for such evaluation. To help students use the formula, ask such questions as these:

E – Emotion: *Does the writer use words that express emotions deeply and in ways readers can appreciate?*

C – Clarity: *Does the writer choose words carefully so that meanings are conveyed clearly and accurately?*

L – Language That Sings: *Does the writer make effective word choices and use language that flows smoothly and communicates distinctive personalities?*

A – Argument: *Does the writer state or imply opinions that readers can understand? Does the writer support opinions effectively?*

I – Imagination: *Does the writer paint vivid mental pictures?*

R – Rhythm: *Does the writer use the beat and pacing of language to invite readers into the conversation?*

Quick Assess

✳ Are students able to apply ÉCLAIR to the Myers excerpts?

✳ Use this chart to evaluate the writing you have read in this unit. Do you think Myers follows his own formula? In the top row, write the titles of three excerpts you read. In the other boxes, copy a short sentence or phrase that shows emotion, clarity, or other qualities of the ÉCLAIR formula. Below the chart, write your evaluation of Walter Dean Myers's writing.

Emotion			
Clarity			
Language that sings			
Argument			
Imagination			
Rhythm			

Walter Dean Myers is/is not a good writer because _____

_____

_____

Reflecting on an author's life and work helps you understand the author's writing and evaluate its quality.

After

APPLYING THE STRATEGY

ÉCLAIR Have students apply the ÉCLAIR formula to other works they have read, either in earlier Units of the *Daybook* or independent reading they have done. Hold a Book Share Fair. Suggest that students create charts similar to the one for Myers's writings, complete them for other works, and then share their critiques with the class. Students can then use the ÉCLAIR charts as reading guides as they read books recommended by their peers.

UNIT 14
ASSESSING YOUR STRENGTHS

UNIT OVERVIEW

Using literature on the theme of being an outsider, students will demonstrate how well they can apply the reading and writing strategies they have learned in the *Daybook*.

KEY IDEA

Successful readers and writers use a variety of strategies.

CRITICAL READING AND WRITING SKILLS

by lesson

66 Interacting with the text
67 Analyzing language and craft
68 Making connections
69 Planning and writing a first draft
70 Reflecting

WRITING ACTIVITIES

by lesson

66 Write to show understanding of theme.
67 Write a prose poem.
68 Write to solidify comprehension.
69 Write a response to literature.
70 Write a reflective paper.

Assessing Your Strengths

In this *Daybook,* you have been introduced to a number of ways to become a better reader and writer, building your **repertoire of reading and writing strategies.** You have learned how to interact and connect with the stories and articles you read. You have applied multiple perspectives. You have analyzed language and craft. You have focused on one particular author. Now you are going to use all of those skills and strategies as you read new texts, explore ideas, and demonstrate your proficiency at using the skills and strategies in a piece of writing.

The texts for this unit present three different perspectives on what it means to be an outsider. You will read about ways in which people about your age were transformed by major world events that radically changed their everyday lives. First is a poem written in 1986 by a young Vietnamese refugee shortly after she came to the United States. The next two pieces are set during the era of World War II but depict widely divergent stories of young people during times of great upheaval and displacement.

209

Literature

■ **"You Have to Live in Somebody Else's Country to Understand"** by Noy Chou (poem)

Written in 1984 by a Cambodian-born teenager, this poem captures the vulnerability of a new student in a foreign country.

■ *Aleutian Sparrow* by Karen Hesse (prose poems)

These prose poems are written from the point of view of an adolescent Aleut girl who has been relocated to a camp far from her home during World War II.

■ *The Children of Willesden Lane* by Mona Golabek *(memoir excerpt)*

Concert pianist Mona Golabek tells the story of how music sustained her mother, one of the Jewish children who escaped certain death in Nazi-occupied Austria by being sent to London during the Kindertransport.

Students will interact with and make connections to a poem about how it feels to be a student from another country.

BACKGROUND KNOWLEDGE

Tell students that the poem "You Have to Live in Somebody Else's Country to Understand" was written in 1984 by Noy Chou, a Cambodian-born ninth-grade student attending a high school in a suburb of Boston, Massachusetts. Lead a discussion focused on the following questions:

✻ *In what ways are teenagers thought of or treated as outsiders? (At home? At school? In society?)*

✻ *What books or movies have they read or seen that show teenagers as outsiders? (They may have read* The Outsiders *by S. E. Hinton, for example.)*

✻ *Does the school population encourage the formation of groups, so that some students are always going to be considered outsiders?*

✻ *If there is no such problem in your school, how do the students account for that?*

Read or listen to this poem written by a young woman from Vietnam shortly after she came to the United States. Be aware of your feelings as you read or listen.

Response Notes

You Have to Live in Somebody Else's Country to Understand by Noy Chou

What is it like to be an outsider?
What is it like to sit in the class where everyone has blond hair and
      you have black hair?
What is it like when the teacher says, "Whoever wasn't born here raise
      your hand."
And you are the only one.
Then, when you raise your hand, everybody looks at you and makes fun of you.
You have to live in somebody else's country to understand.
What is it like when the teacher treats you like you've been here all your life?
What is it like when the teacher speaks too fast and you are the only
one who can't understand what
he or she is saying, and you try to tell him or her to slow down.
Then when you do, everybody says, "If you don't understand, go to a
lower class or get lost."
You have to live in somebody else's country to understand.
What is it like when you are an opposite?
When you wear the clothes of your country and they think you are crazy
to wear these clothes and you think they are pretty.
You have to live in somebody else's country to understand.
What is it like when you are always a loser.
What is it like when somebody bothers you when you do nothing to them?
You tell them to stop but they tell you that they didn't do anything to you.
Then, when they keep doing it until you can't stand it any longer, you
go up to the teacher and tell him or her to tell them to stop bothering you.
They say that they didn't do anything to bother you.
Then the teacher asks the person sitting next to you.
He says, "Yes, she didn't do anything to her" and you have no witness to turn to.
So the teacher thinks you are a liar.
You have to live in somebody else's country to understand.
What is it like when you try to talk and you don't pronounce the words right?
They don't understand you.
They laugh at you but you don't know that they are laughing at you, and

Before

CRITICAL READING SKILL
Interacting with the Text and Making Connections Discuss with students about what they have learned in the *Daybook* about how interacting with the text and making connections enhances their reading experience. Remind them that connecting with what they know and have experienced will make what they read more interesting and more meaningful.

RESPONSE NOTES Have students listen quietly as the poem is read aloud, without writing anything in their Response Notes. Then, before discussion, have them read the poem to themselves and write notes in the Response Notes column.

you start to laugh with them.
They say, "Are you crazy, laughing at yourself? Go get lost, girl."
You have to live in somebody else's country without a language to understand.
What is it like when you walk in the street and everybody turns around
to look at you and you don't know that they are looking at you.
Then, when you find out, you want to hide your face but you don't know
where to hide because they are everywhere.
You have to live in somebody else's country to feel it. ✥

INTERACTING WITH THE TEXT AND MAKING CONNECTIONS

✳ Reread the poem, and select phrases, lines, or passages that have meaning for you. Make notes in the **Response Notes** column explaining connections you make to Noy Chou's concerns in the poem. Give examples from your own life experiences.

✳ Write about a time when you felt like an outsider or when someone made a judgment about you based on events or other issues over which you had no control.

_____
_____
_____
_____
_____
_____
_____
_____

✳ Do you think all teenagers experience being "outsiders" in some way? Explain your opinion.

_____
_____
_____
_____
_____
_____

One primary function of literature is to help us understand the feelings and experiences of others and to see how they connect to our own lives.

WRITER'S CRAFT

Voice Tell students that the word *voice* is used to describe how the writer's personality and tone come through in the writing. In this case, the poem has been written by someone who obviously writes from personal experience. The loneliness and sadness of the poem's tone draw us in as readers and help us understand and empathize with the writer. Invite students to find examples in the poem that give clues to what the writer is like and what she's feeling.

Quick Assess

✳ Did students participate thoughtfully in the discussion?

✳ Did students talk knowledgeably about the problem or lack of problem of outsiders in the school?

✳ Were students able to relate to the issue of how an outsider might feel?

During

READING ALOUD After reading the poem aloud, lead a discussion about what it means to be an outsider in a school in America:

✳ *What groups do you think are treated like "outsiders" in American schools today?*

✳ *What are some possible results or consequences in the school when people feel like outsiders?*

✳ *How might feeling like an outsider interfere with a student's ability to learn?*

✳ *What did you learn from this poem that might help you to better understand the feelings of outsiders in your school?*

After

ART CONNECTION Have students create posters to suggest ways in which a school and its students might make the transition easier for new students, especially those coming from other countries. Students can work individually or in small groups to brainstorm ways in which new students can be made to feel welcome. Display the posters in the classroom or throughout the school.

Students will study the language and craft of the author of a series of prose poems.

BACKGROUND KNOWLEDGE

Remind students that they have already encountered the story of Vera, a young Aleut girl, in Unit 10. Review the historical setting for these poems: During World War II, the Japanese bombed and occupied the islands of Kiska and Attu, located at the far western part of North America. The Aleuts were relocated by the U. S. government to a safer but alien inland area for the duration of the war.

Read aloud the first paragraph on page 212 of the *Daybook,* and talk with students about the information in the paragraph. Invite students to talk about what it would be like to be relocated to an environment that is totally different from where they now live. Tell students that they are going to read *prose poems,* poems that read like a narrative, that tell of the Aleuts' experience during relocation and their feelings about the experience.

Aleutian Sparrow by Karen Hesse deals with Vera, a young Aleut girl, during an event in our history that many Americans don't know about. In 1942 the Japanese bombed and occupied the islands of Kiska and Attu, located at the most northwest region of North America. Alaska was not yet a state, but was a territory of the United States. The Japanese campaign to control the North Pacific led the American government to evacuate the majority of Aleut (al-ee-UTE) residents living west of Unimak Island.

The prose poems that make up the novel *Aleutian Sparrow* are best heard read aloud in the oral tradition of the Aleuts. Listen to the first piece, "Who We Were." As you listen, use the **Response Notes** to comment, question, and make your own connections. Some of the images may seem unfamiliar to you, but try to imagine the string of islands that stretch into the Bering Sea from the mainland of Alaska. Remember, too, that an Alaskan summer has almost constant sunlight, while the winter has almost constant darkness.

BACKGROUND NOTES Recall that you read about Vera in Unit 10 of the *Daybook.* Alfred is a close childhood friend of Vera's. Vera spent much of her time in Alfred's house, with his parents and grandparents. Alfred's grandfather is describing their home on the island before they were relocated. The Aleuts refer to the mainland as "outside."

Response Notes

Who We Were from *Aleutian Sparrow* by Karen Hesse

Alfred's grandfather says, "Aleuts have been poets and artists.
We have made music.
We have guided the church and charted the sea.
Now we are trapped like the foot of a bird in the snare of war."

We were not so different, dressed in our Western clothes
    brought by the supply boats from Outside, washing
    laundry, cooking on stoves, sitting around the table
    talking.
Except that in every direction the sea surrounded us. Fierce
    winds boxed with us, like prizefighters sprung from
    four corners.
The fog carried us through the treeless hills in her fat arms,
    our faces pressed against her damp skin.
We were not so different. Except that we lived on the margin
    of a continent, content.

Before

CRITICAL READING SKILL

Analyzing Language and Craft Tell students that being a knowledgeable reader includes appreciating and understanding the craft the writer employs in the words chosen, the images used, and the tone conveyed in the writing. As students read the prose poems, invite them to pay attention to the language and images the author uses, as well as the sense of the

writer's voice. Ask them to think about how those elements make the reading experience more meaningful.

RESPONSE NOTES Encourage students to use their Response Notes to interact with and respond to what they are reading.

BACKGROUND Vera, Alfred, and Pari grew up together; they were best friends. As they grew into teenagers, Pari became sicker every day. Vera slowly became aware of her feelings for Alfred.

The Terrible Beauty of Night from *Aleutian Sparrow*
by Karen Hesse

Escaping outside to the cabin steps,
     Dim lights burning up and down the row,
Alfred and I sit back-to-back and I tremble to be so near him,
     forgetting for a moment the forest and its thousand
     unnamed monsters, and Pari.
"Don't be afraid," Alfred says, sounding like an old man. I put
     my hand over my eyes so the light he makes shine
     inside me won't leak out.

BACKGROUND During the time the Aleuts were living far from their homes, Vera's best friend Pari died from tuberculosis. One in every four of the evacuated Aleuts died from an illness to which they were subjected in that foreign climate and diet.

In the following poem, one of the ancient stories of the Aleuts, you learn of the origin of the book's title.

Trees from *Aleutian Sparrow* by Karen Hesse

The elders from Nikolski tell of the time before the white
     men came, when a single tree grew in the Aleutians
     and the Aleutian sparrow sang as it flew around the
     ascending trunk.
The seasoned tree proudly wore its struggle for life, and it
     alone reached up through the fog into the heavens.
The Russians chopped the tree down and built their Aleutian
     homes from its wood, and all those who touched the
     wood of that tree and lived in those homes met an
     early and mysterious death.
Here in our Southeast camp there are a thousand trees, but
     where is the Aleutian sparrow?

ABOUT THE AUTHOR
An award-winning author of children's books and young adult literature, Karen Hesse often writes stories that take place in historical settings. Her novel *Out of the Dust* won the 1998 Newbery Medal, the Scott O'Dell Award, and many other awards and honors. Her other fact-based books include *Witness and A Light in the Storm: The Civil War Diary of Amelia Martin*. Born in Baltimore, Maryland, in 1952, Hesse discovered writing in school, where she received encouragement from her fifth-grade teacher. Hesse has had many jobs, but writing is what she loves most. She lives with her family in southern Vermont.

LANGUAGE AND CRAFT **213**

During

LISTENING TO POETRY You or a student can read aloud each poem, while the other students listen to the text. Point out to students that while the prose poems don't rhyme and don't have the rhythm of some poems, the author has carefully chosen the language, the images, and a rhythm unique to the prose to make it more poetic than typical prose.

After each poem is read, allow students to write in their Response Notes. Talk about what students have noticed and the questions they might have. Discuss the Background Notes that provide the introduction to each poem.

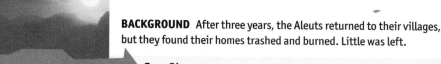

EXTRA SUPPORT

Differentiation Some students may have trouble following the narrative flow of the poems and the information contained in the Background Notes. Review with students the sequence of events:

1. Vera and her family are relocated from their home by the ocean to a place inland.
2. Vera's friend Pari becomes sick, and Vera begins to discover new feelings for her friend Alfred.
3. Pari dies of tuberculosis, and it isn't until the end of the war that Vera and her family are allowed to move back to their home.
4. When they get there, they find most of what they left behind has been destroyed.

BACKGROUND After three years, the Aleuts returned to their villages, but they found their homes trashed and burned. Little was left.

Sea Change from *Aleutian Sparrow* by Karen Hesse

After three years of promises we are back
Where the sun emerges from the galloping clouds,
    Where one moment the rain ices our hair and the next a
        rainbow arches over the volcano.

Where early grass ripples in the wind and violets lead an
        advance of wildflowers across the treeless hills.
It all comes back so quickly, the particular quality of the air
        where the Bering Sea meets the Pacific.
The Aleutian sparrow repeats over and over its welcome of
        fluid notes.
Our resentment folds down into a small package and is
        locked away under the floor of our hearts.
What other chance do we have to survive if we cannot forget?

BACKGROUND This is the last poem in the novel. The people who are still alive return home with the bodies of their friends and relatives, to bury them in their own land. In this poem you feel the spirit of the Aleuts.

Procession from *Aleutian Sparrow* by Karen Hesse

We carried
Pari and her mother home with us
And buried them under the shadow
Of Mount Newhall.

The gulls squeal overhead, and in the harbor
        A murre perches on a half-submerged wreck.
The wind whips our hair across our faces, the sun breaks
        Through to touch the grasses on the mountainside.
And as Aleuts have always done,
We find the will to begin again. ❖

WRITING

Think about your own family's oral traditions. Are there times in your family when you gather together and the "elders" tell stories of how "it used to be"? Do you like to hear stories of when you were little, even though they might be embarrassing?

Many families today are fragmented, with members dispersed geographically. You might not have had the opportunity to hear these stories growing up. If this is the case with your family, you can imagine what stories there might have been. Many "memoirs" are filled with imagined stories.

✳ Choose one of the following two ideas for a short piece of writing. In either case, write it in the form of a prose poem.

1 Write a prose poem in the style of Karen Hesse's poems in *Aleutian Sparrow* about a tradition in your family. You might tell the story in two or three short poems.

2 Write a letter in the form of a prose poem to Vera while she is in a relocation camp. Think about what you could say to her about your own life or what questions you have about hers.

Basing a fictional story on a real historical event gives us insights into how that event affected the people.

Planning Your Writing Once students have chosen the prompt to which they will respond, help them plan and organize the writing of their prose poem. Ask students to think about what their purpose is in writing *(What am I trying to accomplish with this?)*, as well as who the audience is *(Whom am I writing this for?)*. Encourage students to use a graphic organizer, such as a cluster or a sequence chart, to help them plan their writing.

EXTRA SUPPORT

Visual Learners Have students sketch the images that they find in the text Then, after discussing the possible writing prompts, have them choose one to write about. Ask them to draw on their own imagery as they write a prose poem either from their family tradition or as a prose poem letter to Vera.

Quick Assess

✳ Were students able to write a prose poem in the assigned writing

✳ Did students use imagery in their prose poems?

✳ Did their writing show understanding of the situation of the Aleuts?

After

SOCIAL STUDIES CONNECTION

Have students research the relocation of the Aleuts during World War II. Some possible assignments follow:

✳ Map the route of the relocation of the Aleuts.

✳ Write an informational research paper on the invasion of the Japanese in that part of the North American continent.

✳ Give a talk about the Aleut people and their place in Alaskan history.

Students will make connections to the characters and events in this memoir of the Nazi occupation of Vienna.

BACKGROUND KNOWLEDGE

Vienna, Austria, has long been one of the music capitals of the world. Invite students to share what they know about the composers mentioned in the selection: Grieg, Mozart, Beethoven, Schubert, Mahler, Strauss, and Liszt. The Nazis occupied Austria during World War II and tried to dictate the type of music available to the public, going so far as to outlaw the performance of music by Jewish composers, such as Mahler.

VOCABULARY

concerto a musical work that focuses on a soloist or a group of soloists

tympani two or more kettledrums

arpeggio a technique of playing the notes of a chord in a sequence rather than all at once

lyricism a light, bright musical style

legato a smooth tempo

adagio a slow tempo

Give students the list of words and invite them to research their meanings via the Internet or in a musical dictionary or encyclopedia entry.

LESSON 68   RESPONDING TO THE STORY

The following story is in the first chapter of a **memoir** written by world-renowned concert pianist Mona Golabek. In this story Mona tells the true story of her mother's journey during World War II as she was transported from Vienna to England as part of the children's exodus, the Kindertransport. This story shows how a young girl carried with her the music instilled in her by her mother. She was a gifted pianist and became an inspiration to the other children living with her in London after being evacuated from their homes.

In this first chapter of the book, you see young Lisa Jura on a very important day, one of her last in her native city of Vienna. Use the **Response Notes** to record the images, thoughts, questions, or feelings that you have as you read this story. Remember you can cluster, write, or draw. Include notes about connections to your own experience. Put a star by the scenes that are most vivid for you.

Response Notes

from **The Children of Willesden Lane** by Mona Golabek and Lee Cohen

Lisa Jura took her appearance very seriously. She stood in front of the mirror for an eternity, arranging her dark red hair so that it peeked stylishly from under the wool hat she had just bought in the hand-me-down store. The hat needed the perfect tilt . . . just so. She had seen the models do it in the fashion magazines.

She was determined to look more sophisticated than her fourteen years. She was going to her piano lesson and there was nothing more important. Finally turning from the mirror, she smiled at the image of a saucy young girl.

After opening the front door quietly, so as not to disturb her family, she walked down the hallway of the crowded tenement and emerged from the solemn gray building, stepping onto the sidewalk of Franzensbrückestrasse in the heart of the Jewish section of the city.

As she had done every Sunday since her tenth birthday, Lisa boarded the lumbering streetcar and crossed Vienna, heading for Professor Isseles's studio.

She loved the ride.

The images rushed by her window—the glorious Ferris wheel of the Prater amusement park and the blue and serene Danube—eerily accompanied by the distant rhythm of an oompah band. To go across the city was to enter another century—the era of grand palaces and stately ballrooms. Street upon street of marble and granite, of pillar and pediment. The spire of St. Stephen's Cathedral danced by. Her father called it *"Der Alte Steffe"*—"Old Stevie." Lisa

---

Before

CRITICAL READING SKILL

Making Connections Tell students that they are going to read a memoir about a young Viennese girl's experience during World War II. Help them see that the tradition of music is what ties the girl in the story with her mother and her daughter, and it is the daughter of the central character, also a musician, who offers us her perspective of her mother's experience.

Remind students that successful readers make connections while they read. Doing so helps them understand and remember the text.

RESPONSE NOTES   See the instructions following the introduction on *Daybook* page 216. Students can read the story and then go back to make notes about their reactions to the memoir.

thought it a silly name; it was much more grand than that, rising to the heavens like a castle in a fairy tale.

As the streetcar descended the broad avenue and passed Symphony Hall, Lisa closed her eyes, just as she had many times before, and imagined herself sitting perfectly still in front of the grand piano on the stage of the great auditorium. A hush fell over the audience. The keys shimmered in front of her, ebony against ivory. She could hear the opening of Grieg's heroic piano concerto: the soft roll of the tympani building until the moment of her entrance. She straightened her back into the elegant posture her mother had taught her, and when the tension was almost unbearable she took a breath and began to play.

She could sense the excitement of the audience and feel their hearts beat in time with hers. The exhilaration of hearing the music inside her was so extreme that the bumps of the ride and the noise of the street no longer disturbed her.

When she finally opened her eyes, the car was passing the Ringstrasse, the majestic tree-lined boulevard where the Grand Court Opera House stood. She looked out the window in awe and waited for the driver to call her stop.

This was the Vienna of Mozart, Beethoven, Schubert, Mahler, and Strauss, the greatest composers of all time. Lisa's mother had filled her head with their stories, and she had made a secret vow to live up to their legacy. She could hear their music in the marble of the buildings and the stones of the streets. They were here. They were listening.

In a booming voice, the driver called out her stop. But today his words were strange and different. In place of the familiar "Mahler-Strasse" she was expecting, he called another name: "Meistersinger-Strasse." Lisa's heart stopped momentarily.

She climbed down into the great plaza. All the street signs had been changed; the Nazis did not approve of such a grand avenue being named after a Jew. She felt her fury grow but tried to contain herself. Getting upset would only interfere

ABOUT THE AUTHOR

Mona Golabek is an internationally known concert pianist and is the daughter of Lisa, the girl in this memoir.

Golabek is the creator of the Romantic Hours radio program, recordings, and website. She has performed with major orchestras all over the world. Golabek attributes her love of music to a tradition handed down from her mother and her mother's mother. *The Children of Willesden Lane* is Mona Golabek's tribute to her mother's talent and courage.

EXTRA SUPPORT

Differentiation If there are a number of students who will find it difficult to read the entire selection independently, work with them in a small group, reading aloud from the selection, pausing to allow the students to summarize what has happened, and then reading the next part of the selection.

During

MONITORING UNDERSTANDING

While students are reading the selection, stop by individuals to confer quietly. Guide them to monitor their understanding of the text with prompts such as the following:

❋ *Tell me about what you are reading.*

❋ *Is there something you don't understand? What can you do to fix that?*

❋ *Is there a word you don't know? How can you figure it out?*

❋ *What connections have you made thus far?*

WRITER'S CRAFT

Characterization The author creates a strong picture of her mother as a young girl. Discuss with students how Mona Golabek helps the reader see what type of person her mother was as a young girl. For example, Lisa gets angry about the changing of Mahler-Strasse to Meistersinger-Strasse, but she is determined not to let her anger interfere with her music. This dedication and determination carry her through her encounter with the Nazi guard at her music teacher's door. Have students find other examples of Lisa's character, interests, and dreams for the future. After students have finished reading the selection, talk about the characterization of Professor Isseles in the story: *What kind of man is he? How do we know that? Is he a sympathetic character? Why or why not?*

with her music. She forced herself to think about the lesson ahead, knowing that once she was at the piano, the world outside would disappear.

Although it was early, the café-lined streets bustled with energy. The gentle sounds of the "Blue Danube" waltz, mixing with raucous Dixieland jazz, returned the smile to Lisa's face. The aroma of warm, fresh *apfelstrudel*, thick with sliced apples and cinnamon, made her long for a taste of her mother's recipe—surely the best in all of Vienna.

Inside the cafés, well-dressed young men and women sipped their coffee, deep in animated conversation. Lisa imagined them all to be composers, artists, and poets passionately defending their latest works. She yearned to join them, to wear fine clothes and speak of Beethoven and Mozart—to be a part of that intoxicating café society. One day, when she made her musical debut, these streets, these cafés, would be hers.

When Lisa reached her destination, she stopped short. A German soldier, tall and emotionless, stood in the doorway of the old stone building that housed Professor Isseles's music studio. The sun glinted harshly off the black rifle he held against his gray uniform.

She had been coming to the professor's studio for nearly four years, but this was the first time anyone had been standing guard. She shouldn't have been surprised, though; Nazi guards were becoming an increasingly menacing sight on the streets of Vienna.

He asked coldly, "What business do you have here?"

"I have a piano lesson," she replied, trying not to be frightened by the soldier's commanding presence or by the firearm on his shoulder.

"The professor will be waiting," she continued in a loud, clear voice, the force of her words belying her true state of mind. The soldier looked up to the second-floor window. A figure stared down, then motioned that it was all right for the girl to come up. Lowering his weapon, the soldier moved away from the door and grudgingly allowed Lisa to pass.

"Come in, Miss Jura," Professor Isseles said, greeting Lisa with his customary warm handshake. The stoop-shouldered, white-haired gentleman ushered her in past a chipped bust of Beethoven and a sideboard covered with stacks of yellow sheet music. She breathed in the aroma of the professor's pipe tobacco. These sights and scents had become a friendly greeting—a signal that for the next hour, she could turn away from all else and be a part of the music she loved.

The professor's stately Blüthner piano stood in the middle of the studio. It was richly polished, with ornately carved legs and a scroll-patterned music stand. On the wall hung her teacher's prized possession—a photograph of Franz Liszt as an old man, surrounded by several students, including the professor's teacher. He boasted that his teachings were a direct line from the master himself, and there was a worn mark on the photograph where he had so often placed his finger.

FURTHER RESOURCES Online lessons are available for teaching *The Children of Willesden Lane.* Enter key words such as *Mona Golabek, teaching,* and *lessons* into your favorite search engine.

As usual, there was little small talk. Lisa put the score of Beethoven's Piano Concerto no. 1 in C on the music stand and sat on the worn piano bench. She adjusted its height to fit her small stature.

"So, Miss Jura, was it difficult?" asked the professor.

"It was much too easy," she teased.

"Then I expect nothing less than perfection," he responded, smiling.

Lisa began to play the tender C-major opening theme. The professor sat forward in his chair and followed her progress with his copy of the score. When the simple theme erupted into cascades of descending arpeggios, she peered out of the corner of her eye to judge his reaction.

She hoped to catch him smiling. After all, she had learned the complicated first movement in only a week and had often heard him say that she was his best student.

But the professor continued listening with a stern concentration. When he had this expression, she imagined it was his sadness at not being able to play the piano anymore. Arthritis had stiffened his fingers, making it impossible to demonstrate the correct way of playing. What a cruel trick of fate to deny a pianist the ability to perform, she thought. She could not imagine a day when she would not be able to play.

To illustrate his lessons, Professor Isseles would play recordings for her on his gramophone. He was in awe of Horowitz's playing of Rachmaninoff, but it was the lyricism of Myra Hess performing Beethoven that he most appreciated.

"Listen to the tone of her legato," the professor would say with a sigh.

Lisa listened and listened and listened.

For most of the hour Lisa played uninterrupted, as the old man sat in silence, occasionally bringing his hand down to emphasize an accent in the music. Finally, he put down his music and just listened. She looked over and saw a distressed expression on his face. Was she playing that badly?

At the end of the piece, the professor made no comment. Lisa went on to her customary scales and waited anxiously for her assignment. The professor focused on scraping the bowl of his pipe into the ashtray.

"May I do the adagio for next week?" she asked nervously. She loved the second movement and yearned to show him her improving legato.

He looked at her for a long moment, then finally spoke, looking uncomfortable and ashamed: "I am sorry, Miss Jura. But I am required to tell you that I cannot continue to teach you."

Lisa was stunned and unable to move. The professor walked to his window and opened the curtain. He stared at the people in the street. "There is a new ordinance," he said slowly. "It is now a crime to teach a Jewish child." He continued mumbling under his breath, then added in despair, "Can you imagine!"

Lisa felt tears rising.

"I am not a brave man," he said softly. "I am so sorry."

Differentiation The language in this memoir excerpt is rich and lyrical, but because of the German and musical terms in this story, some readers may have difficulty following what's happening. After students have read through the story once, you may want to ask students to summarize the main events. Reread with them the parts that have given them trouble and talk about what is happening. Encourage students not to get stuck on an unfamiliar word but to focus on the important events and their meaning. Students can mark unfamiliar words and look up their meaning after they've read the story to help understand the details and appreciate the author's choice of words.

Collaboration Allow students time to write initial responses to the questions on page 220 before they meet in small groups to discuss them. Remind students that answers to these questions rely on their own reactions to the story and the inferences they make. They don't need to have all the answers before they discuss them with the group, but they should bring their initial responses and update them as the group's discussion inspires them to think about the story more. Have each group assign someone to record the main points of the discussion and someone to act as moderator. A reporter from each group can share with the rest of the class a summary of key points of the discussion.

Quick Assess

✳ Did students' response notes reflect connections they made while reading the story?

✳ Did their participation in the discussion show an understanding of the characters and action in the story?

Response Notes

He came over to the piano, lifted up her slender young hands, and held them in his grip. "You have a remarkable gift, Lisa, never forget that."

Through her tears, she watched the professor pick up a thin gold chain that lay on top of the piano. It held a tiny charm in the shape of a piano.

"It is not much, but perhaps it will help you to remember the music we shared here," he said softly, fastening the gold chain around her neck with trembling fingers.

She stared through her tears at the stacks of music, the picture of Liszt on the wall, and tried to memorize every detail. She was afraid she might never see them again. Gathering her composure, she thanked the professor and collected her things, then turned and fled. ❖

RESPONDING TO THE STORY

✳ Answer these questions.

■ What kind of person is Lisa Jura and how do you know?

■ What do you think of Professor Isseles? What gives you that impression?

■ What are some of the clues that the Nazis are beginning to take over the city?

■ What are some of the things that are as important to you as music is to Lisa Jura?

A memoir is a story based on real people and their lives. The reader gets to know well the subject of a memoir.

After

RESPONDING TO THE STORY

Even though Lisa Jura's story is one of escape, survival, and ultimate triumph, some students might feel disturbed by the prospect of Lisa's separation from her family and their potential mistreatment by the Nazis. Give students an opportunity to talk about their fears and allow them to ask questions. Make sure that students understand that there isn't a right or wrong answer to the questions on page 220. Encourage them to include reasons for why they feel the way they do.

SOCIAL STUDIES CONNECTION

Have students research the Kindertransport during World War II. They may want to focus on specific aspects of the Kindertransport, such as the conditions in Germany and Austria that led to it, how it came about, or the eventual relocation of the children involved. Invite students to present the results of their research.

The three texts in this unit each deal with a young displaced person. In the poem, "You Have to Live in Somebody Else's Country to Understand," the young refugee has not yet found a way to deal with the feelings of being an outsider. In *Aleutian Sparrow*, Vera copes with the displacement, carrying both the sadness and the hope of the Aleuts as she returns home. The young musician in *The Children of Willesden Lane* carries with her the power of music instilled by her mother.

WRITING PROMPTS

✳ Choose one of the following prompts and write two to three pages in response. Use the next page to plan your writing, but use your own paper for the rest of this assignment.

1 Narrative Write a narrative about a time when you had to leave your school or community and felt like an outsider in the new place. Be sure to use specific, sensory details as well as figurative language to allow the reader to see, hear, and feel the actions and emotions of the characters in your narrative. Use quotations in your paper from one or more of the texts you read in this unit.

2 Prose Poems Write a series of prose poems about a time when you felt like an outsider in a new place. Be sure to use specific, sensory details as well as figurative language to allow the reader to see, hear, and feel the actions and emotions of the characters in your narrative. Refer in your paper to one or more of the texts you read in this unit.

3 Reflection Write about the teenager as an outsider in our society. What are the things that make so many teenagers feel like outsiders? What can the school or community do about this situation? Use specific examples in your paper. Refer in your paper to one or more of the texts you read in this unit.

SELECT A TOPIC

✳ After you select a prompt, make a list of possible ideas on which to focus. Then, circle the idea that you will use.

Students will draw on what they have read in this unit to respond to a writing prompt on the theme of being an outsider.

BACKGROUND KNOWLEDGE

Review with students the three writing format choices.

A narrative

✳ Tells a story

✳ Develops the plot through characterization as well as setting and conflict

✳ Has an effective beginning, middle, and end

Prose poetry

✳ Has many elements of traditional poetry

✳ Uses metaphor and imagery

✳ Looks more like prose because it doesn't use traditional line demarcations of poems

A reflective essay

✳ Presents ideas through thoughtful and perceptive personal commentary

✳ May use narrative and descriptive strategies

✳ Focuses on idea rather than story

Before

CRITICAL WRITING SKILL
Planning and Writing a Draft In this lesson, students will think about what they have read in this unit and choose a writing form in which to express their thoughts on the theme of being an outsider.

RESPONSE NOTES Students may want to review their Response Notes from previous lessons in this unit before they begin writing. As they think about what they've read, encourage them to look at the similarities and differences among the different authors' approaches.

WRITING SUPPORT

Using a Graphic Organizer Review with students the types of graphic organizers they've used in past *Daybook* lessons to plan their writing. For the formats listed on page 221, students might want to use one of the following organizers:

✻ *cluster/word web* good for brainstorming words and ideas to use in a prose poem

✻ *sequence chart* good for plotting the order of events in a narrative

✻ *double-entry journal* good for writing reflections and making connections

Quick Assess

✻ Were students able to select a prompt for their writing?

✻ Were they able to narrow their topic and brainstorm details to use in their drafts?

✻ Did students create a draft based on the prompt that they chose?

GATHER DETAILS

✻ Now that you have a topic, you need to decide what to write. Make a list or create a graphic organizer (a web or a chart) in which to collect your details. Include information from your own life to support the prompt. For example, if you're writing about an event, include details about where and when it took place, who was there, what you were thinking, and so forth. Also make a note of details and quotations in the selections that support your writing.

✻ Once you have settled on your topic and gathered supporting details, you can begin to draft your writing on a separate piece of paper.

> Using references to your reading in your writing shows that you understand the important ideas.

During

CHOOSING A PROMPT If students need help trying to decide which writing form to use, help them by asking questions: *Which format feels the most comfortable to you? Which one will allow you to say what you want to say? Would any of the selections you've read be good models to use as you write your first draft?*

After

REVIEWING THE DRAFT Have students reread their drafts to see if they're ready to share it in a peer conference. Allow students time to make changes to the draft without taking the time for a full revision. Students should be able to tinker with a draft, focusing on content and overall organization, before they present something for peer feedback. Once students are ready to move to the revising stage, have them go on to Lesson 70.

SHARING YOUR FIRST DRAFT

As with any craft, an important part of writing is looking to see how it can be improved. In writing, this is called **revision** because you *see* (vision) it *again* (re). Use the list below to evaluate your writing. You might want to meet with a partner and review each other's papers, as well.

- Does my paper respond directly to one of the three prompts?
- Are my ideas about the concept of an outsider clear?
- Are my ideas organized in an appropriate way?
- Does the beginning grab the reader's attention so that he or she wants to read more? If not, how could it be improved?
- Is the end of the paper satisfying? Does it sound "finished"? If not, what could I do to make a better ending?
- Have I chosen my words carefully—specific nouns and vivid verbs?
- Does the language in my paper "show" the reader what is happening, as opposed to just "telling"? In other words, have I used concrete details and sensory language?
- Do my sentences flow so that the paper can be read aloud easily?
- Are the beginnings and lengths of my sentences varied?
- Have I checked for spelling, punctuation, and capitalization errors?

✳ Read your paper aloud to a partner or members of a small group. When each person finishes reading, the other members should tell the reader what they liked about the paper. As you listen, refer to the items in the list to help the reader strengthen the paper. As your group talks about your paper, make notes so that when you revise it, you will remember what they suggested.

MAKING A FINAL COPY

✳ Using the suggestions of your group, make all the revisions you think will improve your paper. Then make a clean copy of your final draft. Remember to give it a title.

Students will finalize the writing they drafted in Lesson 69 and reflect on their progress and future goals.

BACKGROUND KNOWLEDGE

Tap into students' experience with the writing process and revising in particular. Encourage students to talk about what has worked for them in the past and ways in which peer writing conferences should be conducted. Discuss writing-conference etiquette and ways in which to give constructive feedback. Create a list of Rules for Effective Writing Conferences and post it where it can be seen by everyone.

Before

CRITICAL WRITING SKILL

Reflecting Talk with students about how good writers practice the arts of reflection and self-evaluation. They draw on what they've read, what they've learned through their writing experiences, the feedback they get from other readers and writers, and their own best judgment about what works.

EXTRA SUPPORT

Differentiation Some students may need extra support as they try to assess what they have learned and the progress they have made over the year. Help them focus on the positive aspects of what they can do now versus where they were at the beginning of the year. You may want to help them do a comparison and contrast with the beginning of the year, or they could make a progress chart showing something new they learned or mastered each month. Remind students to focus on their progress this year as they set goals they hope to achieve next year.

Quick Assess

✳ Were students able to revise their drafts effectively, based on the feedback they received?

✳ Did students write a paragraph reflecting on their improvement, while setting goals for how they can continue to improve as readers and writers?

A FINAL REFLECTION

As you worked through this *Daybook,* you have had many opportunities to learn and practice skills and strategies to become a better reader and writer.

✳ In this final reflection, consider how much you have improved as a reader and writer during your work with the *Daybook.* Write a few paragraphs reflecting on how you have improved and what you can do to become an even stronger reader and writer than you are now.

_____

_____

_____

_____

_____

_____

_____

_____

_____

_____

_____

_____

_____

_____

_____

_____

_____

_____

Reflection is an important part of learning how to identify and improve on your strengths as a reader and writer.

During

REVISING AND WRITING THE FINAL DRAFT Students should work with partners to review and revise their first drafts. Go over the criteria for evaluation in the student lesson before students begin their reviews. Give them time to read their papers to their partners, then to look at them criterion by criterion to see how they might be improved. Students should then make final copies of their papers.

After

SETTING GOALS **Reading and Writing for the Future** Encourage students to be specific in their goals for building on the progress they have made. Ask them to create a reading list for the summer. They may want to list books that have been excerpted in the *Daybook* or books on topics that have been discussed during the year. Invite students to also create a list of genres that they are interested in exploring, such a prose poems, personal narratives, short stories, nonfiction articles, or persuasive essays. Encourage students to keep a Readers/ Writers Journal in which they track their progress and write about their experiences.

Becoming An Active Reader

Reading can entertain, inform, and reward. Reading also requires some hard work on the part of the reader. The sections that follow will help you get the most out of your reading.

The **reading process** section will guide you through reading a text. It will help you think about how to prepare to read (before reading), what to think about as you read (during reading), and how to get the most out of your reading by reflecting on it (after reading).

The **reading actively** section will show you how to interact with a text in order to get the most meaning out of it. It will show you how to engage with a text by using your brain and your pen—both at the same time!

225

THE READING PROCESS

The Reading Process has three parts: **Before Reading, During Reading,** and **After Reading.**

1. BEFORE READING

Preview the Material
Look over the selection before you read. Does the selection look like a short story or other work of fiction? If so, look at the title, introduction, and illustrations. Does the selection look like nonfiction? If so, look for headings, boldfaced words, photos, and captions. Also, ask yourself how the information is organized. Is the author comparing or contrasting information about the topic? Is the information presented in a sequence using signal words like first, second, third, and finally? Understanding how an author has organized information will help you to recognize key points as you read.

Make Predictions
When you make predictions, you actively connect with the words on the page. Think about what you already know about the subject or the images. Then, think of yourself as a text detective, putting together what you know with new details in the text. Predict what you think will happen, why an event caused something to happen, or what might come next in a series of events.

Set a Purpose
Begin by reviewing what you already know about the topic or situation in the text. Then, think about what you want to find out.

QUESTIONS TO ASK YOURSELF BEFORE READING
- Before I read this material, what do I think it is going to be about?
- After looking over the selection, what do I already know about this subject?
- What should I be thinking about as I read?

---

2. DURING READING

Engage with the Text
As your eyes look at the words, your brain should be working to make connections between the words and what you already know. Have you had an experience similar to that of one of the characters in a story you are reading? Do you know someone like the character? Have you read another book about the topic? You will also want to connect what you read to the predictions you made before reading. *Confirm, revise, predict again* is a cycle that continues until you finish reading the material. All of these questions will go on inside your head. Sometimes, though, it helps to think out loud or write.

Monitor Your Understanding
As you read, stop from time to time and ask yourself, "Do I understand what I just read?" If the text doesn't make sense, there are several steps that you can take.
- Go back and reread the text carefully.
- Read on to see if more information helps you understand.
- Pull together the author's ideas in a summary.
- Retell, or say in your own words, the events that have happened.
- Picture in your mind what the author described.
- Look for context clues or word-structure clues to help you figure out hard words.

This takes some practice. Remember, to be a successful reader, you must be an active reader. Make an effort to check your understanding every so often when you read a new selection.

QUESTIONS TO ASK YOURSELF WHILE YOU ARE READING
- What important details am I finding?
- Which of these ideas seem to be the most important?
- Does this information fit with anything I already know?
- What do I see in my mind as I read this material?
- Do I understand the information in the charts or tables? Does it help me to understand what I am reading?

3. AFTER READING

❋ **Summarize**
Reread to locate the most important ideas in the story or essay.

❋ **Respond and Reflect**
Talk with a partner about what you have read. What did you learn from the text? Were your predictions confirmed? What questions do you still have? Talking about reading helps you to better understand what you have read.

❋ **Ask Questions**
Try asking yourself questions that begin like this:

Can I compare or contrast . . . evaluate . . . connect . . .
examine . . . analyze . . . relate . . .

❋ **Engage with the Text**
Good readers engage with a text all the time, even when they have finished reading. When you tie events in your life or something else you have read to what you are currently reading or have read, you become more involved with your reading. In the process, you are learning more about your values, relationships in your family, and issues in the world around you.

QUESTIONS TO ASK YOURSELF AFTER READING
■ What was this article about?
■ What was the author trying to tell me?
■ Have I learned something that made me change the way I think about this topic?
■ Are there parts of this material that I really want to remember?

© GREAT SOURCE. COPYING IS PROHIBITED.

Make the effort to stay involved with your reading by reading actively. Your mind should be busy reading the text, making connections, making predictions, and asking questions. Your hand should be busy, too. Keep track of what you are thinking by "reading with your pen." **Write** your reactions to the text or connections that you can make. **Circle** words you don't understand. **Draw** a sketch of a scene. **Underline** or **highlight** an important idea. You may have your own way of reading actively. You may develop a style that works better for you, but here are six common ways of reading actively.

MARK OR HIGHLIGHT The most common way of noting important parts of a text is to write on a sticky note and put it on the page. Or, if you can, mark important parts of a text by highlighting them with a marker, pen, or pencil. You can also use highlighting tape. The highlighted parts should provide a good review of the text.

ASK QUESTIONS Asking questions is a way of engaging the author in conversation. Readers who ask a lot of questions think about the text more and understand it better. "Why is the writer talking about this?" "Is this really true?" "What does that mean?"

REACT AND CONNECT When you read, listen to the author and to yourself. Think about what you are reading and relate it to your own life. Compare and contrast what the text says to what you know.

PREDICT Readers who are involved with the text constantly wonder how things will turn out. They think about what might happen. They check their thoughts against the text and make adjustments. Sometimes the author surprises them! Making predictions helps you stay interested in what you are reading.

VISUALIZE Making pictures in your mind can help you "see" what you are thinking and help you remember. A chart, a sketch, a diagram—any of these can help you "see." Sometimes your picture doesn't match what you think the author is telling you. This is a signal to reread to check your understanding of the text.

CLARIFY As you read, you need to be sure that you understand what is going on in the text. Take time to pull together what you have learned. Try writing notes to clarify your understanding. Another way of checking to see that you understand is to tell someone about what you have read.

---

abandoned left alone

abash to make uncomfortable or ill at ease

adagio a slow tempo

adolescence the period of life between childhood and adulthood

allusion an indirect reference

American Indian Native American

anguish emotional pain

annunciation usually refers to the biblical announcement to Mary that she was going to bear Jesus

arc a curved path

argument persuasive language consisting of a main idea supported by details and reasons

arpeggio a technique of playing the notes of a chord one after another

artillery large, heavy weapons operated by more than one person

art of language style and structure

assent to agree

atomic age the period after World War II, when people realized that mass destruction could be caused by nuclear bombs

autopilot an airplane's system for flying itself so a pilot does not have to be at the controls all of the time

B-29 a military plane that carried bombs

backwash cultural influence

banshee a female spirit in Gaelic folklore whose wailing foretold a death

barracks a large, plain building used for temporary housing

barrage an attack coming from many different directions at once

barrow a cart for moving heavy things

Beard, James (1903–1985) an influential cooking teacher

bedroll a mat that is placed on the floor and used for sleeping

beheld looked at and studied

betimes quickly

bistro a small restaurant

Boanerges a person who talks very loudly

bog moist; spongy ground

Boricua a person who is Puerto Rican in blood and soul

boycott to avoid purchasing or using a product because you object to conditions under which it is grown or made

bracero a Mexican laborer permitted to enter the United States and work for a limited period of time

breechcloth a cloth worn over the lower body

bulbous rounded, bulb-shaped

calligraphers people who create stylized, artistic lettering

caribeña Spanish term for a girl or woman from the Caribbean

chaired lifted up on a chair or on the shoulders of other athletes

chicken pox a disease that leaves crater-like marks on the skin if not treated carefully

Chugoku name of Hiroshima's newspaper

collective bargaining negotiation between organized workers and their employer to determine wages, hours, and working conditions

commune with get messages from

conceived envisioned; thought of

concerto a musical work that focuses on a soloist or a group of soloists

conjure to bring about as if by magic

connecting to the story being emotionally involved with the story

© GREAT SOURCE. COPYING IS PROHIBITED.

---

consecrate make holy

continental food food of European cultures, such as French, German, or Italian

contraband smuggled goods

crooned sung in a soft, gentle manner

corridos Mexican ballads or folk songs

counterpane an embroidered quilt; a bedspread

credible believable or trustworthy

croon to sing with a low, gentle tone

cuddles holds someone close

default to fail to pay debts

deliberating considering carefully

demur to disagree

detract reduce in size or impact

dewy covered with dew

diaspora the scattering of a people

Dickinson, Emily reclusive, prolific American poet of the mid-1800s

discerning able to see clear differences

disciplinarian someone who corrects others' behavior with rules and punishments

disfiguring something that leaves a mark on the skin or changes the shape of a feature

disheartening discouraging

docile obedient

Douglass, Frederick African American orator and abolitionist

dreary dull; boring; gloomy

dregs solid parts left behind in a mostly liquid food or drink

Du Bois W.E.B. Du Bois; writer, educator, and civil rights leader in the first half of the 20th century

dumfounded surprised and confused (usually spelled dumbfounded)

Emperor the ruler of an empire; in this case, the Japanese empire

employee discharges people who have been relieved of their war duties

etching a fine-lined image printed from a cut metal plate

evaluating deciding on the value of something

evidence facts that support an argument

exalted held up in honor

examining multiple viewpoints reading different points of view of a story in order to look at a moment or event from more than one angle

exotic charming because of unfamiliarity

extremity a state of extreme need

eyewitness a person who sees an event first-hand

fleet fast; rapid

flung thrown

foodie's mecca a place where food lovers find many restaurants and food shops

forager someone who "hunts" for food that grows wild

foreman a person who serves as the leader of a work crew

furrowed wrinkled

gingko a species of tree that originated in China and that has fan-shaped leaves

grainy not clear; appearing to be made out of small (grain-like) particles

haft the handle of a tool

Hail Mary a Roman Catholic prayer to Mary, who was the mother of Jesus

hallow make holy

hew carve

hidebound made narrow-minded

historical fiction fiction set in the past, in a time of important historical events

© GREAT SOURCE. COPYING IS PROHIBITED.

DATBOOK (?) © GREAT SOURCE. COPYING IS PROHIBITED.

hobbled tied the front legs of a horse together to keep it from wandering

Homer ancient Greek poet credited with the creating of *The Iliad* and *The Odyssey*

host large group of people

hullabaloo a loud noise

humanities school subjects of English, history, and social studies

icon someone who receives a lot of attention for what they symbolize

image mental picture created by a reader as he or she reads

impolitic socially unwise

impulsively without thinking

in vain for no purpose

inadequacy lack of ability

infer to make an inference

inferences reasonable guesses you make by putting together something you have read with something you already know

infused flavored with something, such as garlic (usually said of a liquid)

innocuous harmless

intangible not "touchable"; conceptual, as opposed to physical

integrated open to all people

interacting with the text "carrying on a conversation" with a text; a strategy for effective reading that involves circling, underlining, and writing notes

interposition placing obstacles between people

intuitive inborn

jibara Spanish term for a female peasant

lap to be an entire circuit ahead of a competitor on a race around a track; to lick

lauding praising

laurel branches of a laurel tree traditionally used to honor athletes

legato a smooth tempo

Lenox Avenue a street in Harlem in New York City

lintel top of a door or window

Little Boy the code name for the atomic bomb dropped over Hiroshima

livelong entire and tedious

living inside the story feeling so connected to a story that you are completely drawn in

loathsome much-hated

localize to keep from spreading

lolling reclining in a relaxed way

lyricism a light, bright musical style

magenta a bright purplish red

magnesium a metal that sizzles when burned

making connections a reading strategy that involves comparing what you are reading to something you already know

manacles metal shackles for hands or feet, usually attached to chains

massacre mass murder

Mayflower the ship on which the pilgrims came to America

medicine man Native American healing priest

memoir a writer's written reflections on his or her earlier life

mestiza Spanish term for a girl or woman of mixed blood; usually referring to those of both European and Native American ancestry

metacognitive awareness the process of thinking about what's going on in your mind as you do something

metamorphosizes transforms, changes into a different form

metaphor a technique of figurative language in which one thing is described in terms of something else

mija Spanish term of endearment; literally, "my daughter"

mingle to mix or blend together

miserly extremely small and insufficient

modeling a poem using the structure of a poem as a foundation for a new poem

Moses a Hebrew leader who led his people away from enslavement

mushroom cloud the kind of cloud that is caused by a nuclear explosion, usually appearing the shape of a mushroom

N.A.A.C.P. National Association for the Advancement of Colored People; an organization formed in support of civil rights for people of color

Nazi abbreviated name of the political party headed by Adolf Hitler

nonfiction factual writing

nullification rejection of federal law by a state government

nymph an imaginary, fairy-like creature

obligation something you have to do

odious hated or disgusting

off-notes unintended aromas that arise when a flavor or scent reacts with something

omnipotent all-powerful

organic grown without chemicals

ostracize to exclude someone

Oy gevalt! Yiddish exclamation of surprise or alarm

pallor a pale or faint color

parchment writing surface similar to paper, but made from goat or sheep skin

pare to trim away an edge

patron person who supports an artist or a cause; sponsor

personal narrative a short prose piece in which a writer expresses personal thoughts and makes connections

personnel employees of a company

persuasion an attempt to convince others to feel the same way you do

pigeon-holed strictly categorized; from the old-fashioned desk with small compartments called pigeon-holes because they resemble the compartments that homing and racing pigeons sleep in

perspective the point of view or angle from which you see a subject

plaintively sadly

plot how the characters and events in a story are connected

pogrom organized massacre of a minority group

Pole a Polish person

pragmatism practicality

prefecture government officials of the region

prodigious enormous; huge

prohibitions orders to stop actions

promissory note an agreement to pay back a loan

prosecutor lawyer whose job it is to prove the guilt of the accused

protectorate a country or region controlled or protected by another

psyche human spirit

pulp publication containing mostly sensational subject matter

puritanical related to the Puritans; extremely strict in matters of morals

purpose an author's intent in writing

pustules small skin sores

raggy slang for ragtime, an early form of jazz characterized by uneven rhythms

ration food given by the government during war or other emergencies

recluse a person who stays separate from the rest of the world

Reich Germany or the German government during one of the three reichs; in this case, during the Third Reich, 1933–1945

relegate assign to an unimportant place

repertoire of reading and writing strategies a collection of learned abilities needed by an effective reader and writer

repetition the repeating of a word or phrase to emphasize a point

restaurateur restaurant owner

reverently with awe and respect

revision looking at a draft again in order to find ways to improve it

revolution a big change in the way people think or act

Robinson, Jackie first African American to play major league baseball

root ball the tangled roots of a plant

rouge red coloring for cheeks

rout a retreat or flight from defeat

saintly completely good, or unable to be criticized

sanitarium a place for healing; from the root *sanitas*, meaning "good health"

savage wild, fierce

scenario a setting and brief sequence of events

score twenty

scrounge to beg or forage

scuffling struggling at close quarters

scullery a room for washing dishes

segregated having separate laws or facilities for separate groups of people

sharecropper a tenant farmer who gives a share of the crops to the landlord as rent for the land

shtetl a small Jewish town formerly found in Eastern Europe

simile a technique of figurative language in which the characteristics of one thing are described in terms of something else using the word *like* or *as*

sledgehammer a long, heavy hammer used to break up things

solemnly seriously

soprano in music, a voice that can sing the highest notes

sore severe

sorest most urgent

sound-bite culture group of people who only pay attention to small bits of information and do not take the time to understand longer discussions

squalor dirtiness and poor condition due to poverty and neglect

stance the way someone is standing

starkest most extreme

stopped plugged up

straightway immediately

strategy a carefully designed plan of action for reaching a goal

structure the way a piece of writing is put together, as shown by the arrangement of its words, sentences, paragraphs, chapters, and so on

stud a wooden frame inside a wall

style a writer's unique way of writing, as shown by the decisions the writer typically makes as to sentence length, description, figurative language, and tone

subtle barely noticeable

suffocation in this context, denseness and airlessness

supercilious proud; arrogant

supporting evidence facts, statistics, examples, observations, quotations, and experts' opinions that support an argument

sustainable not permanently removing resources from the environment

sustenance something that people need to live, such as food

symbol image or object that represents other things

synagogue a Jewish place of worship

syncopated a musical device common in jazz consisting of a shift of accent to a normally weak beat

Taina female member of an ancient Caribbean people

tallow fat from cows that is used to make candles, soap, and food

tangible something "touchable"; an object

tatami a straw mat that is laid on the floor

theme the main topic or message that is explored through the characters and plot of a story

thesis statement the part of a persuasive piece of writing that expresses the author's main idea

threescore sixty (score = 20)

tipi cone-shaped house made of poles, animal skins, and tree bark

tone the author's attitude toward his or her subject, as shown by word choice and sentence structure

treacherous sneaky; likely to betray

trowel a small garden tool with a flat blade for digging

tuberculosis a contagious lung disease with symptoms that include fever, weight loss, chest pain, and coughing up sputum

Tubman, Harriet African American "Angel of Mercy" in the mid-19th to early 20th centuries; best known for leading slaves to freedom along a route called the Underground Railroad

tympani two or more kettledrums

unborn not yet born

uncanny so amazing as to be almost frightening

unconstitutional not in agreement with the U.S. Constitution

vegetarian someone who eats no meat

venue place

veranda a porch or balcony that has a roof

visualizing a reading strategy in which a reader makes pictures in his or her mind of a text

voice the narration style of an author

war bonnet a special head covering with feathers and other decorations

willow a species of tree that has thin, narrow leaves

wiry thin

Wittgenstein Ludwig Josef Johan Wittgenstein, an Austrian-born British philosopher of the early 20th century

Wrangell Institute a large boarding school for Native American children

ACKNOWLEDGMENTS

10 "Alabama Earth", "Luck" by Langston Hughes. Used by permission of Random House, Inc.

13 "Aunt Sue's Stories" by Langston Hughes. Used by permission of Random House, Inc.

16 From *The Return of Simple* by Langston Hughes. Used by permission of Random House, Inc.

19 "The Weary Blues" by Langston Hughes. Used by permission of Random House, Inc.

22 From *I Wonder as I Wander* by Langston Hughes. Used by permission of Random House, Inc.

26, 29 Copyright © 1996 by Russell Freedman. All rights reserved. Reprinted from *The Life and Death of Crazy Horse* by permission of Holiday House, Inc.

31 Brief text as submitted from *The Autobiography of Eleanor Roosevelt* by Eleanor Roosevelt. Copyright 1937, 1949, © 1958, 1961 by Eleanor Roosevelt. Copyright © 1958 by Curtis Publishing Company. Reprinted by permission of HarperCollins Publishers.

34, 37 Wall Street Journal.

40, 43, 46 "The Circuit", from *The Circuit: Stories from the Life of a Migrant Child* by Francisco Jimenez. Copyright © 1997 by Francisco Jimenez. Reprinted by permission of Houghton Mifflin Company. All rights reserved.

49 Excerpt from "In the Strawberry Fields" by Eric Schlosser, *The Atlantic Monthly*, Vol 276, Iss 5, Nov 1995. Used by permission.

51 From "A Street Name That Hits Home" by Tara Malone. Reprinted by permission of Daily Herald.

54, 57 From *Hiroshima* by John Hersey. Used by permission of Random House, Inc.

60 Excerpt from "Summer Flower" by Tamiki Hara, from "The Crazy Iris". Used by permission of Grove/Atlantic Inc.

63 From *Shockwave: Countdow to Hiroshima* by Steven Walker. Used by permission of HarperCollins Publishers.

66 From *Hiroshima, A Novella* by Laurence Yep. Copyright © 1995 by Laurence Yep. Reprinted by permission of Scholastic, Inc.

70 From *A Sky Full of Poems* by Eve Merriam. Copyright © 1964, 1970, 1973, 1986 by Eve Merriam. Reprinted by permission of Marian Reiner.

74 "anyone lived in a pretty how town". Copyright © 1940, 1968, 1991 by the Trustees for the E.E. Cummings Trust, from *Complete Poems: 1904-1962* by E.E. Cummings, edited by George J. Firnage. Used by permission of Liveright Publishing Corporation.

77 Mark Turpin, "Sledgehammer Song" from *Hammer*. Copyright © 2003 by Mark Turpin. Reprinted with the permission of Sarabande Books, Inc., www.sarabandebooks.org.

79 From *The Pearl* by John Steinbeck, copyright 1945 by John Steinbeck, © renewed 1973 by Elaine Steinbeck, Thom Steinbeck and John Steinbeck IV. Used by permission of Viking Penguin, a division of Penguin Group (USA).

79 "Skin", an excerpt from "The Story of My Body", from *The Latin Deli: Prose and Poetry* by Judith Ortiz Cofer. Copyright © 1993 by Judith Ortiz Cofer. Reprinted by permission of the publisher, The University of Georgia Press.

86, 89, 91, 98 Reprinted by permission of the publishers and the Trustees of Amherst College from *The Poems of Emily Dickinson,* Thomas H. Johnson, ed., Cambridge, Mass.: The Belknap Press of Harvard University Press, Copyright © 1951, 1955, 1979, 1983 by the President and Fellows of Harvard College.

98 "To an Athlete Dying Young" from Authorised Edition of *The Collected Poems of A.E. Housman*. Copyright 1924, 1965 by Henry Holt and Company. Reprinted by permission of Henry Holt and Company, LLC.

105 From *The Frog Prince Continued* by John Scieszka, © 1991 by John Scieszka. Used by permission of Viking Penguin, A Division of Penguin Young Readers Group, A Member of Penguin Group (USA) Inc., 345 Hudson Street, New York, NY 10014. All rights reserved.

110 "Annunciation" used by permission of Adrianne Marcus.

116, 119 Excerpts from "Food Product Design", from *Fast Food Nation* by Eric Schlosser. Copyright © 2001 by Eric Schlosser. Reprinted by permission of Houghton Mifflin Company. All rights reserved.

122 Copyright © 2004 Peggy Orenstein. Reprinted by permission.

125 Reprinted by permission of *Publicaffairs*, a member of Perseus Books.

128 Excerpt from *Ruth Reichl: A Taste for Life*. Used by permission of the American Booksellers Association.

135, 137 From *Maus I: A Survivor's Tale/My Father Bleeds History* by Art Spiegelman, copyright © 1973, 1980, 1981, 1982, 1984, 1985, 1986 by Art

Spiegelman. Used by permission of Pantheon Books, a division of Random House, Inc.

142 From *Memories of Anne Frank: Reflections of A Childhood Friend* by Alison Leslie Gold. Published by Scholastic Press/Scholastic, Inc. Copyright © 1997. Reprinted by permission.

146, 149, 152 Excerpts from *When My Name Was Keoko* by Linda Sue Park. Copyright © 2002 by Linda Sue Park. Reprinted by permission of Clarion Books, an imprint of Houghton Mifflin. All rights reserved.

155 Reprinted with the permission of Margaret K. McElderry Books, an imprint of Simon & Schuster Children's Publishing Division from *Aleutian Sparrow* by Karen Hesse. Text copyright © 2003 Karen Hesse.

158 "Sunday, October 6, 1991", "Monday, March 30, 1992", "Sunday, April 5, 1992", "Monday, June 29, 1992" from *Zlata's Diary* by Zlata Filipovic, copyright © 1994 Editions Robert Laffont/Fixot. Used by permission of Viking Penguin, a division of Penguin Group (USA) Inc.

162 Excerpt is used with the permission of the Special Collections, University of California, Riverside.

168 Reprinted by arrangement with the Estate of Martin Luther King, Jr., c/o Writers House as agent for the proprietor New York, NY. Copyright 1963 Martin Luther King, Jr., copyright renewed 1991 Coretta Scott King.

178 Text copyright © 1988 by Paul Fleischman. Used by permission of HarperCollins Publishers.

182 "On Turning Ten" is from *The Art of Drowning,* by Billy Collins, © 1995. Reprinted by permission of the University of Pittsburgh Press.

186 "Life Doesn't Frighten Me", copyright © 1978 by Maya Angelou, from *And Still I Rise* by Maya Angelou. Used by permission of Random House, Inc.

186 "Alone", copyright © 1975 by Maya Angelou, from *Oh Pray My Wings Are Gonna Fit Me Well* by Maya Angelou. Used by permission of Random House, Inc.

190 "Ending Poem" from "Getting Home Alive" by Rosario Morales and Aurora Levins Morales, © 1986, Firebrand Books, Ann Arbor, MI.

194 From *Bad Boy: A Memoir* by Walter Dean Myers. Used by permission of HarperCollins Childrens Books.

197 From *The Glory Field* by Walter Dean Myers. Copyright © 1994 by Walter Dean Myers. Reprinted by permission of Scholastic, Inc.

200 From *Monster* by Walter Dean Myers. Used by permission of HarperCollins Childrens Books.

203 From *Now Is Your Time* by Walter Dean Myers. Used by permission of HarperCollins Childrens Books.

206 © 2005, The New York Times. Reprinted by permission.

210 Published in 1986 by the Anti-Defamation League for the "A World of Difference" project.

212 Reprinted with the permission of Margaret K. McElderry Books, an imprint of Simon & Schuster Children's Publishing Division from *Aleutian Sparrow* by Karen Hesse. Text copyright © 2003 Karen Hesse.

216 From *The Children of Willesden Lane* by Mona Golabeck and Lee Cohen. Copyright © 2002 by Mona Golabeck and Lee Cohen. By permission of Warner Books, Inc.

ILLUSTRATIONS

137: © Great Source; **142 *m*:** © Laszlo Kubinyi. Reprinted by permission of Houghton Mifflin Company. All rights reserved. All additional art created by AARTPACK, Inc.

PHOTOGRAPHY

Photo Research AARTPACK, Inc.

cover, 1: © Royalty-Free/Corbis; **3-7:** © Brand X Pictures.

Unit 1 9: © Photodisc/Getty; **10:** © Corbis; **11:** © Royalty-Free/Corbis; **12:** © Royalty-Free/Corbis; **13:** © Royalty-Free/Corbis; **14:** © Royalty-Free/Corbis; **15:** © Royalty-Free/Corbis; **16:** © Royalty-Free/Corbis; **18:** © Photodisc Green/Getty; **19:** © Digital Vision/Getty; **20:** © Getty Images; **21:** © Digital Vision/Getty; **22:** © Royalty-Free/Corbis; **23:** © Corbis; **24:** © Royalty-Free/Corbis.

Unit 2 25: © Stone/Getty; **26:** © Royalty-Free/Corbis; **27:** © Royalty-Free/Corbis; **28:** © Comstock Images; **29:** © Photodisc/InMagine; **30:** © Photodisc/InMagine; **31:** © Getty Images; **32:** © Bettmann/Corbis; **33:** © Royalty-Free/Corbis; **34:** © Flip Schulke/Corbis; **35:** © John Arthur Stokes; **36:** © Bettmann/Corbis; **37:** © Royalty-Free/Corbis; **38:** © Royalty-Free/Corbis.

Unit 3 39: © Steve Starr/Corbis; **40:** © Royalty-Free/Corbis; **42:** © Image Source/Getty; **43:** © Photodisc Green/Getty; **44:** © Photodisc Green/Getty; **45:** © Glowimages/Getty; **46:** © Stone/Getty; **47:** © Photodisc Green/Getty; **48:** © Ryan McVay/Getty Images; **49:** © Image Source/Getty; **51t:** © Najlah Feanny/Corbis; **51b:** © PhotoAlto/Getty; **52:** © Glowimages/Getty.

Unit 4 53: © The Image Bank/Getty; **54:** © Ablestock/InMagine; **55:** © Ablestock/InMagine; **56:** © Murat Taner/

zefa/Corbis; **57t:** © John Van Hasselt/Corbis Sygma; **57b:** © Royalty-Free/Corbis; **58:** © Royalty-Free/Corbis; **59:** © Murat Taner/zefa/Corbis; **60:** © Robert Essel NYC/Corbis; **61:** © Corbis; **62:** © Robert Essel NYC/Corbis; **63:** © Nathan Benn/Corbis; **64:** © Bettmann/Corbis; **65:** © John Van Hasselt/Corbis Sygma; **66:** © John Van Hasselt/Corbis Sygma; **67:** © Brand X Pictures; **68:** © Brand X Pictures.

Unit 5 69: © Royalty-Free/Corbis; **70:** © 1997 PhotoDisc, Inc.; **71t:** © Richard Hamilton Smith/Corbis; **71b:** © Takashi Sato/Sebun Photo/Getty; **72:** © 1997 PhotoDisc, Inc.; **73:** © Richard Hamilton Smith/Corbis; **74:** © Image Source/Getty; **75:** © Image Source/Getty; **76:** © Brand X Pictures; **77t:** © Comstock Images; **77br:** © Photodisc Green/Getty; **77bmr:** © Photodisc Green/Getty; **77bml:** © Photodisc Green/Getty; **77bl:** © Photodisc Green/Getty; **78:** © Comstock Images; **79:** © Digital Vision/Getty; **80:** © Digital Vision/Getty; **81:** © Royalty-Free/Corbis; **82:** © Royalty-Free/Corbis; **83:** © MedioImages/Getty; **84:** © MedioImages/Getty.

Unit 6 85: © Bettmann/Corbis; **86t:** © 1993 PhotoDisc, Inc.; **86b:** © 1993 PhotoDisc, Inc.; **87t:** © 1993 PhotoDisc, Inc.; **87b:** © 1993 PhotoDisc, Inc.; **88:** © Comstock Images; **89t:** © 1993 PhotoDisc, Inc.; **89b:** © 1993 PhotoDisc, Inc.; **90:** © Royalty-Free/Corbis; **91t:** © Royalty-Free/Corbis; **91b:** © 1993 PhotoDisc, Inc.; **92:** © Natphotos/Getty Images; **93:** © Photodisc/InMagine; **94:** © Photodisc/InMagine; **95:** © Indexstock/InMagine; **96:** © Indexstock/InMagine; **97:** © Comstock Images; **98:** © Ingram/InMagine; **99:** © Ingram/InMagine; **100:** © Photonica/Getty.

Unit 7 101: © David Aubrey/Corbis; **102:** © Jim Zuckerman/Corbis; **103:** © Photodisc Red/Getty; **104:** © Photonica/Getty; **105:** © Photodisc Red/Getty; **106:** © Photodisc Green/Getty; **107:** © Photodisc Green/Getty; **108t:** © Scott Gries/Getty; **108b:** © Michele Constantini/Getty; **109:** © 1996 PhotoDisc; **110:** © Stone/Getty; **111:** © 1996 PhotoDisc; **112:** © Photonica/Getty; **113r:** © Blend Images/Getty; **113b:** © Royalty-Free/Corbis; **114:** © Blend Images/Getty.

Unit 8 115: © Stone/Getty; **116:** © Matthew Mcvay/Corbis; **117:** © Comstock, Inc.; **118:** © Royalty-Free/Corbis; **119:** © Tetraimages/InMagine; **120:** © Comstock, Inc.; **121:** © Ross Durant/Jupiter Images; **122:** © Photodisc Red/Getty; **123t:** © Comstock, Inc.; **123m:** © Comstock, Inc.; **123b:** © Comstock, Inc.; **124:** © Royalty-Free/Corbis; **125:** © Roger Ressmeyer/Corbis; **127:** © Royalty-Free/Corbis; **128:** © Foodcollection/InMagine; **129:** © Envision/Corbis; **130:** © MedioImages/Getty.

Unit 9 131: © Medioimages/InMagine; **132t:** © 2005 Comstock Images; **132b:** © Gianni Giansanti/Sygma/Corbis; **134:** © Michael St. Maur Sheil/Corbis; **135:** © Michael St. Maur Sheil/Corbis; **137:** © Corbis; **139:** © Bettmann/Corbis; **140:** © Royalty-Free/Corbis; **141:** © 2005 Comstock Images; **142:** © Reuters/Corbis; **143:** © Hulton Archive/Getty; **144:** © Royalty-Free/Corbis.

Unit 10 145: © Art Wolfe/Getty; **146:** © Robert Essel NYC/Corbis; **147:** © Michael S. Yamashita/Corbis; **148:** © Royalty-Free/Corbis; **149:** © Jason Hosking/zefa/Corbis; **151r:** © Jason Hosking/zefa/Corbis; **151b:** © Royalty-Free/Corbis; **152:** © Tongro/InMagine; **153:** © Royalty-Free/Corbis; **154:** © Tongro/InMagine; **155:** © Kevin Schafer/Corbis; **156:** © 1996 PhotoDisc, Inc.; **157:** © 1996 PhotoDisc, Inc.; **158:** © Reuters/Corbis; **160l:** © Reuters/Corbis; **160b:** © BrandXPictures/InMagine.

Unit 11 161: © Paul Edmondson/Corbis; **162:** © Swift/Vanuga Images/Corbis; **164:** © Patricia Canova Tipton/Jupiter Images; **165:** © Patricia Canova Tipton/Jupiter Images; **166:** © Corbis; **167:** © Royalty-Free/Corbis; **168:** © Flip Schulke/Corbis; **169:** © Flip Schulke/Corbis; **170:** © Hulton-Deutsch Collection/Corbis; **171:** © Hulton-Deutsch Collection/Corbis; **172:** © Flip Schulke/Corbis; **173:** © Bettmann/Corbis; **174:** © Digital Vision/Getty; **175r:** © Time & Life Pictures/Getty; **175m:** © Royalty-Free/Corbis; **176:** © Echos/Jupiter Images.

Unit 12 177: © Sven Hagolani/zefa/Corbis; **178:** © 2005 Comstock Images; **179:** © Photodisc Green/Getty; **180t:** © Photonica/Getty; **180b:** © Photodisc Green/Getty; **181:** © Photonica/Getty; **182:** © Stone/Getty; **183:** © Photodisc Green/Getty; **184:** © Stone/Getty; **185:** © Royalty-Free/Corbis; **186:** © Royalty-Free/Corbis; **187:** © Adnan Abidi/Reuters/Corbis; **188:** © Brand X Pictures; **189:** © Brand X Pictures; **190:** © 1999 PhotoDisc, Inc.; **191:** © Stone/Getty; **192:** © James Sparshatt/Corbis.

Unit 13 193: © Royalty-Free/Corbis; **194:** © Royalty-Free/Corbis; **195:** © Getty Images; **196:** © Royalty-Free/Corbis; **197:** © The Image Bank/Getty; **198:** © 1997 PhotoDisc, Inc.; **199:** © 1997 PhotoDisc, Inc.; **200:** © Royalty-Free/Corbis; **201:** © Photodisc Green/Getty; **202:** © Photodisc Green/Getty; **203:** © Bettmann/Corbis; **204:** © Ablestock/InMagine; **205:** © Photographer's Choice/Getty; **206:** © Rudy Sulgan/Corbis; **207:** © Royalty-Free/Corbis; **208:** © Bettmann/Corbis.

Unit 14 209: © Royalty-Free/Corbis; **210:** © Andrew Holbrooke/Corbis; **211:** © Simon Marcus/Corbis; **212:** © Macduff Everton/Corbis; **213:** © Altrendo/Getty; **214t:** © Shaen Adey/Gallo Images/Getty Images; **214b:** © Tim Thompson/Corbis; **215:** © Shaen Adey/Gallo Images/Getty Images; **216:** © Ingolf Pompe/Getty; **217:** © Hulton-Deutsch Collection/Corbis; **219:** © Stone/Getty; **220:** © Christine Schneider/zefa/Corbis; **221:** © Photodisc/InMagine; **222:** © Photodisc/InMagine; **223:** © Royalty-Free/Corbis; **224:** © Time & Life Pictures/Getty.

Becoming an Active Reader 225: © Rayman/Getty; **226-228:** © 1997 PhotoDisc, Inc.; **229:** © Birgid Allig/zefa/Corbis.

TEACHER'S EDITION CREDITS

cover, i: © Royalty-Free/Corbis; **iii-vii, x-2:** © Glowimages/Getty; **229:** © Indexstock/InMagine; **230:** © 1997 PhotoDisc, Inc.; **231-242, 248-273, 275-276:** © 1993 PhotoDisc, Inc.; **243, 245:** © Comstock Images; **247, 246-247:** Comstock Images; **274:** © Photodisc Green/Getty.

WRITING PROMPTS — 230

ASSESSMENTS — 243

REPRODUCIBLE GRAPHIC ORGANIZERS — 274

The following Writing Prompts are designed for use at the end of each unit of the *Daybook*. You can assign the prompt in a single class period, or you may prefer to have students write over a period of two or three days with time for peer conferences, revising, editing, and reflecting.

Since each prompt is based on the literature and strategies from the corresponding unit, assign the prompt when students have finished the unit. Allow students to refer to their *Daybooks* so they can use the selections as they write.

Please note: The Writing Prompts for Unit 7 and Unit 14 are contained within those units.

✳ **Evaluation criteria accompany each prompt.**
Go over the criteria with students before they begin each assessment so they can use the criteria to inform their writing. Tell students to use resources such as dictionaries or computer programs to check spelling and grammar.

LITERATURE CONNECTION

■ "The Weary Blues"

Literary Analysis

One of the poems you read by Langston Hughes in Unit 1 was "The Weary Blues." This poem especially reflects Hughes's interest in jazz and the blues. Review what you learned about how Langston Hughes used musical elements, such as sound, rhythm, and repetition, in his poetry.

Responding Write a short essay that describes the connection between Hughes's "The Weary Blues" and his love of music. Before you begin your writing, review the poem in Unit 1 and make notes of examples that will support this statement: "The Weary Blues" by Langston Hughes is a poem and a song. Then think about how you want to organize your essay. (You may want to use a Venn diagram.) Be sure to revise your draft and make a final copy.

Evaluation Criteria

The writer responds directly to the prompt and

* ✳ develops and supports the main ideas, using examples from the selection

* ✳ organizes the essay logically (beginning, middle, ending)

* ✳ uses a knowledgeable writer's voice

* ✳ makes effective word choices

* ✳ varies sentence length and structure

* ✳ edits and proofreads for accurate copy

WRITING PROMPT

■ *The Autobiography of Eleanor Roosevelt*

Personal Essay

One of the remarkable people you read about in Unit 2 was Eleanor Roosevelt. In addition to influencing people around the world, she also wrote a newspaper column called "My Day" from 1935 until shortly before her death in 1962. The column was 500 words long and appeared six days a week. Wherever she was—at home in the White House, visiting the troops in the South Pacific during World War II, or in Paris at a UN General Assembly meeting—she wrote the column for the many newspapers that carried it.

Responding Here are four quotations taken from Eleanor Roosevelt's columns over the years. Select the one that means something to you and write an essay about your personal connection.

1. "So often people you admire at a distance do not mean so much to you after you meet them."
2. "All wars eventually act as boomerangs, and the victor suffers as much as the vanquished."
3. "One of the best ways of enslaving a people is to keep them from education."
4. "I found that almost everyone had something interesting to contribute to my education."

Write the quotation you have selected at the beginning of your essay. Use the quotation as a starting point to share your own ideas on the subject. Make a specific connection to something in your own life. It might be to something you have experienced, to something you have read, or to something going on in the world today. Be sure to revise your draft and make a final copy.

Evaluation Criteria

The writer responds directly to the prompt and

* develops and supports the main ideas, using relevant examples

* organizes the essay logically (beginning, middle, ending)

* uses an engaging writer's voice

* makes effective word choices

* varies sentence lengths and beginnings

* edits and proofreads for accurate copy

LITERATURE CONNECTION
- "A Street Name That Hits Home"

Literary Analysis

As you read the story and articles in Unit 3, you got involved by connecting to familiar experiences, but you were also challenged to imagine a life beyond your own, and, in doing so, connect to a world beyond the one you know.

A number of schools around the country celebrate Caesar Chavez's birthday, March 31, by involving students in projects that reflect Chavez's core values. They are summarized below:

1. **Celebrating Community:** Respect one another and treat everyone fairly.

2. **Respect for Life and the Environment:** Respect the land, the people, and all other forms of life.

3. **Knowledge:** Respect education for the purposes of overcoming ignorance and learning to solve problems that everyone faces.

4. **Service to Others:** Respect others and oneself by serving others and practicing self-sufficiency.

Responding Write an essay that analyzes how Tara Malone's article "A Street Name That Hits Home" deals with one or more of Chavez's four core values listed above. Draw on your own experience and what you have read to make connections to these core values. Be sure to revise your draft and make a final copy.

Evaluation Criteria

The writer responds directly to the prompt and

- ✳ develops and supports the main points, using quotations from the selection

- ✳ organizes the essay logically (beginning, middle, ending)

- ✳ uses a knowledgeable writer's voice

- ✳ makes effective word choices

- ✳ varies sentence structure and writes fluent sentences

- ✳ edits and proofreads for accurate copy

WRITING PROMPT

LITERATURE CONNECTION

- *Hiroshima* (John Hersey)
- "The Avalon Project"
- "Summer Flower"
- *Shockwave*
- *Hiroshima* (Laurence Yep)

Position Paper

In Unit 4, the various accounts of the bombing of Hiroshima, Japan, gave you a lot of information about that critical event and its place in history.

Create a two-column chart with these two headings:

✳ Facts about Hiroshima

✳ My Personal Response

In the first column, write the facts that you gathered in reading the selections. In the second column, write how you feel about what you have read. For example, what are your thoughts toward the people in Hiroshima or about the airmen in the *Enola Gay,* the plane that carried the bomb?

Responding Based on what you have learned from the articles in this unit, write an essay in which you state your ideas about the development and use of nuclear energy. Take a position on how nuclear energy should be used in the future. Support your position with reasons, facts, and details from the texts in Unit 4. Also address any opposing viewpoints to your position (counterarguments). Your ending should call your readers to action. Be sure to revise your draft and make a final copy.

Evaluation Criteria

The writer responds directly to the prompt and

✳ states a clear position and supports it with evidence from the readings

✳ organizes the essay logically (states a position, supports the position, ends with a call to action)

✳ uses an objective, polite voice to convince the reader

✳ makes effective word choices

✳ varies sentence structure and writes fluent sentences

✳ edits and proofreads for accurate copy

LITERATURE CONNECTION

- **"Simile: Willow and Ginkgo"**
- **"anyone lived in a pretty how town"**
- **"Sledgehammer Song"**
- ***The Pearl***
- **"The Story of My Body"**

Literary Analysis

In Unit 5, you learned about style and structure. They are part of how a writer achieves a particular effect, creates a specific tone, or elicits a certain reaction from the reader. Look back through the *Daybook* to find a story or article that you enjoyed. Read it through again, this time paying particular attention to how effectively the author uses style and structure to make the writing interesting.

Responding Analyze your favorite selection in the *Daybook*. Use what you have learned about style and structure in this unit to write an essay in which you do the following:

- Tell why you chose this selection.
- Comment on how effectively the writer used any **three** of these literary elements:
  - sentences of varying structure and lengths
  - character dialogue
  - vivid or imaginative description
  - figures of speech, such as similes and metaphors
  - rhythm and sound elements
  - argument and counterargument

Be sure to revise your draft and make a final copy. Remember to include a title.

Evaluation Criteria

The writer responds directly to the prompt and

- develops and supports the main points, using specific examples and quotations from the selection
- organizes the essay logically (beginning, middle, ending)
- uses a knowledgeable writer's voice
- avoids wordiness and repetition of words
- varies sentence structure and beginnings
- edits and proofreads for accurate copy

LITERATURE CONNECTION

- "Poem #288"
- "Poem #254"
- "Poem #919"
- "Poem #435"
- "Poem #585"
- "Outward and Inward Aspects of Her Life"
- "Poem #67"

Literary Analysis

In Unit 6, you learned that Emily Dickinson chose to live a secluded life within the confines of the family home and a small circle of family and friends. Within that seclusion, she wrote poetry about her deepest thoughts. Review the Dickinson poems in Unit 6.

Responding Choose one poem from this unit and think about how it shows emotion, deep thought, and imagination. Find words and phrases in the poems that depict these qualities.

Write the first line of the poem you have chosen here:

_____

_____

Now write a short essay explaining why you chose this poem. Explain how it reveals Dickinson's ability to show emotion, deep thought, and imagination. Identify the poem by its first line for clarity. Use words and phrases from the poem to support your main ideas. Be sure to revise your draft and make a final copy.

Evaluation Criteria

The writer responds directly to the prompt and

* develops and supports the main ideas, using examples and lines from the poem

* uses transition words such as *for this reason, because, likewise,* and *in conclusion* to organize and connect ideas

* uses a personal writer's voice that connects with the reader

* makes effective word choices

* varies sentence structure and writes fluent sentences

* edits and proofreads for accurate copy

LITERATURE CONNECTION

- *Fast Food Nation*
- "Food Fighter"
- "Alice Waters"
- "A Taste for Life"

Persuasive Essay

In Unit 8 you read a number of selections about the nation's interest in food—from raising organic foods to cooking and eating. This interest is evident everywhere: on television, in print materials, and on the Internet. People make choices about food based on what they have learned.

Responding Write a persuasive essay on how school lunch programs might improve students' nutritional habits. Suggest ways to educate people about healthier options available to them, such as the following:

- ✻ advertising healthy options in the school cafeteria

- ✻ creating a poster of nutrition guidelines

- ✻ collecting recipes for healthy snacks

- ✻ publishing a brochure that describes the effects of poor nutrition

Include two quotations from the selections in the unit to give your essay more authority. Be sure to revise your draft and make a final copy.

Evaluation Criteria

The writer responds directly to the prompt and

- ✻ develops and supports the main ideas, using examples and quotations from the selections

- ✻ organizes the writing logically

- ✻ uses a positive and authoritative writer's voice

- ✻ uses specific nouns and strong verbs

- ✻ varies sentence structure and writes fluent sentences

- ✻ edits and proofreads for accurate copy

LITERATURE CONNECTION
- *Parallel Journeys*
- *Maus*
- *Memories of Anne Frank*

Persuasive Letter

In the introduction to Unit 9, you read this question: "Why would a book about critical reading and writing include excerpts from a graphic novel?" You can answer this question because you learned how authors use special techniques, such as dialogue, narration, and sound, to create visual text.

Responding Write a letter to your school librarian explaining the importance of purchasing graphic novels for the library. Your goal is to persuade the librarian that visual texts help build critical reading skills. Use several examples from the selections to support this position. Also include an opposing viewpoint, or counterargument. Be sure to revise your draft and make a final copy. If your teacher approves, send your letter. Remember to use the five parts of a letter:

* the heading (today's date)

* the greeting (*Dear Librarian:*)

* the body (what you want to say)

* the closing (*Sincerely,* or *Yours truly,*)

* your signature (sign your name)

Evaluation Criteria

The writer responds directly to the prompt and

* supports the argument with evidence and counters an opposing argument with a counterargument

* organizes the letter logically (introduction, body, conclusion)

* uses a courteous, knowledgeable, and persuasive writer's voice

* uses effective language

* varies sentence structure and beginnings

* edits and proofreads for accurate copy

WRITING PROMPT

LITERATURE CONNECTION

- ***When My Name Was Keoko***
- ***Aleutian Sparrow***
- ***Zlata's Diary***

Literary Analysis

In Unit 10, you learned that the themes in literature make statements about life, the world, or human nature. You found clues in the details, events, images, symbols, and other literary devices to determine the larger meaning and messages in stories and poems.

Think about some of the novels, stories, and poems you have read in the *Daybook* or elsewhere that invite you to explore big ideas, such as being an outsider, feeling different, getting along with other people, having to make a tough choice, or doing the right thing.

Write down two themes you explored and the title of the stories and/or poems.

Theme #1: ______________________________

Title: ______________________________

Theme #2: ______________________________

Title: ______________________________

Responding Write an essay about how the authors used details, events, images, symbols, and other literary devices to make these themes come alive for you. Give examples from the selections to support your point of view. Be sure to revise your draft and make a final copy.

Evaluation Criteria

The writer responds directly to the prompt and

- develops and supports the main ideas, using examples from the selections
- organizes the essay logically (beginning, middle, ending)
- uses a knowledgeable writer's voice
- makes effective word choices
- varies sentence structure and writes fluent sentences
- edits and proofreads for accurate copy

LITERATURE CONNECTION

- "Memorial and Recommendations of the Grand Council Fire of American Indians"
- "Gettysburg Address"
- "I Have a Dream"

Persuasive Speech

In Unit 11, you read some selections that dealt with people's vision of situations that need to be changed and wrongs that need to be righted. Think of a rule, attitude, or practice that you think should be changed. It may be something that you connect with on a personal level at school or at home, or it may be an issue that affects your community or society as a whole.

1. First, list some issues about which you feel strongly.

2. Next, choose one issue and think about who is in charge of the rules concerning this issue. Make a statement to that person about what you would like to have changed.

3. Then list the kinds of appeals you think would have weight. Sort the arguments or points into two categories: Appeals to Reason (observations, examples, facts) and Appeals to Emotions (emotional language, situations, values).

Responding Write a short speech in which you attempt to persuade your audience to change its rules concerning the issue about which you feel strongly. Use specific examples to make your points clear and persuasive. Keep in mind the persuasive techniques you studied in Unit 11. Be sure to revise your draft and make a final copy.

Evaluation Criteria

The writer responds directly to the prompt and

- develops and supports the main ideas, using examples and quotations from the selections

- organizes the speech logically (introduction, body, conclusion)

- uses a persuasive writer's voice

- avoids weak adjectives such as *good, silly,* or *bad*

- writes fluent sentences that flow when read aloud

- edits and proofreads for accurate copy

LITERATURE CONNECTION

- "On Turning Ten"

Personal Essay

Reread Billy Collins' poem "On Turning Ten" on page 188, paying special attention to the last stanza. Think of something you've learned about life since you were ten. Notice that Billy Collins says "I used to believe . . . but now . . ." Use the same format to plan your essay. Then make a few notes about how you changed.

I used to believe _____

But now _____

Notes:

Responding Write an essay in which you describe what changed your belief. Be as precise as you can, using images, events, and even dialogue to describe what changed and why.

Evaluation Criteria

The writer responds directly to the prompt and

* develops and supports the main ideas, using examples from the selections

* organizes the essay logically (beginning, middle, ending)

* uses an engaging writer's voice

* makes effective word choices

* varies sentence structure and writes fluent sentences

* edits and proofreads for accurate copy

WRITING PROMPT

LITERATURE CONNECTION
- *Bad Boy: A Memoir*
- *The Glory Field*
- *Monster*
- "Now Is Your Time"
- "Hope Is an Open Book"

Review

In Unit 13, you read different selections from Walter Dean Myers's body of work. Which was your favorite selection? Were you inspired to read the rest of any of the books excerpted in that unit? If so, what made you want to read more?

Responding Based on what you have read of Walter Dean Myers's work, write a review for one of the selections. Your target audience is next year's eighth-grade class, and your purpose is to give them some guidance as they study Walter Dean Myers. In your review, consider such elements as the power of the story, your interest in the characters, and Myers's writing style. Give specific reasons and use examples from his work to support your opinion. Be sure to revise your draft and make a final copy.

Evaluation Criteria

The writer responds directly to the prompt and

* develops and supports the main ideas, using examples and quotations from the selection

* uses transition words such as *for instance, moreover,* and *additionally* to connect and organize ideas

* uses a personal writer's voice that connects with the reader

* uses synonyms and pronouns to avoid repeating words

* varies sentence structure and writes fluent sentences

* edits and proofreads for accurate copy

The *Daybook* assessments are designed to help you evaluate students' progress toward understanding what they read. The assessments include a Pretest, four Reading Strategy Assessments, and a Posttest, as described below. Each assessment includes one or two passages that were created for the assessment and are based on the types of selections found in the *Daybook*.

PRETEST

The Pretest has one long and two short, paired texts. This test is designed to be administered at the beginning of the school year. Because each of the sixteen questions covers a particular reading strategy, the test can help you determine students' beginning levels and indicate what you might need to emphasize in your teaching. The test also provides a baseline for measuring students' progress through the *Daybook*.

READING STRATEGY ASSESSMENTS

These assessments can help you monitor students' progress and inform your teaching plans for using the *Daybook*. Each assessment requires students to apply a particular reading strategy to a text. Units not listed below are assessed only through the more appropriate method of the writing prompts (see page 230). The following list shows the strategy focus of each assessment and suggests when to administer the assessment.

Assessment	To be administered after . . .
1. Interacting with the Text	Unit 2 or Unit 9
2. Making Connections	Unit 3 or Unit 10
3. Exploring Multiple Perspectives	Unit 4 or Unit 11
4. Focusing on Language and Craft	Unit 5 or Unit 12

Note: If you administer the assessment after completing the first unit and students do not score well, you may want to administer the assessment again after the second unit of instruction for the same strategy.

POSTTEST

The Posttest contains the same types of selections and the same number of questions as the Pretest and measures the same strategies. It should be administered at the completion of the *Daybook* to help determine how much progress students have made.

DIRECTIONS FOR ADMINISTERING ASSESSMENTS

To administer, distribute copies of the test pages to each student. Have students write their name at the top of each page. Then have students read the selections and answer the questions. For multiple-choice questions, students should choose the best answer to each question and circle the letter of the answer. For written-response questions, students should write their answers in complete sentences on the writing lines provided on the test page.

DIRECTIONS FOR SCORING ASSESSMENTS

All multiple-choice items are worth 1 point each; written-response questions are worth 2 points each. (A partially correct written response may be awarded 1 point.) Use a copy of the Scoring Chart on page 244 to record students' scores.

Pretest & Posttest—Add the total number of points earned and write the result under "Points" on the Scoring Chart for each test. To find the "Percent," multiply the total points × 5. (For example, 15 points × 5 = 75%).

Reading Strategy Assessments—Add the total number of points earned and write the result under "Points" on the Scoring Chart for each assessment. To find the "Percent," multiply the total points × 10. (For example, 7 points × 10 = 70%).

Students should score at least 70% correct on each test. For students who score 70% or lower, you may want to analyze the test responses more closely and focus instruction on particular strategies.

Multiple Choice   (1 point each)

Item	Answer	Reading Strategy
1	C	Making Connections: Stepping into the Story
2	D	Making Connections: Deciding What's Important
3	B	Focusing on Language and Craft: More Style Choices
4	C	Focusing on Language and Craft: Style and Structure in Prose
5	D	Making Connections: Images and Symbols Suggest Themes
6	A	Making Connections: Events Reveal Themes

Written Responses   (2 points each)

7 **Answers vary.** Acceptable responses will suggest a plausible explanation and will be an inference drawn from information presented in the passage. (Making Connections: Inferring Meaning through the Story)

8 **Answers vary.** Acceptable responses will quote an example of Joey's use of formal language and explain that he uses it to appear mature, serious, official, rule-abiding, or something similar. (Focusing on Language and Craft: Style and Structure in Prose)

Multiple Choice   (1 point each)

Item	Answer	Reading Strategy
9	D	Examining Multiple Perspectives: Choosing a Perspective
10	C	Examining Multiple Perspectives: In Their Own Words
11	A	Examining Multiple Perspectives: Examining the Details
12	D	Interacting with the Text: Visualizing
13	B	Interacting with the Text: Questioning
14	A	Interacting with the Text: Making Inferences

Written Responses   (2 points each)

15 **Answers vary.** Acceptable responses will identify two facts that appear in both passages. Examples: the earthquake lasted 15 seconds, light poles swayed, part of I-880 collapsed. (Examining Multiple Perspectives: Examining the Details)

16 **Answers vary.** Answers will vary. An acceptable response will identify "The 1989 Earthquake" as a passage to be read for information and "Something Terrible" as a passage to be read more for entertainment. It should also explain that reading more than one passage about an event provides different perspectives and different information about the event. (Interacting with the Text: Setting a Purpose)

READING STRATEGY ASSESSMENTS ANSWER KEY

ASSESSMENT 1   Interacting with the Text

Answers: 1–B   2–C   3–A   4–A   5–C   6–D   (1 point each)

Written responses   (2 points each)

7 **Answers vary.**   Acceptable responses will mention at least two physical features of the snakehead mentioned in the passage. Examples: long, tube-like body; long fins on back; small, snake-like head; many sharp teeth.

8 **Answers vary.**   Acceptable responses will depict the story of a man dumping fish from an aquarium (or bucket) into the pond.

ASSESSMENT 2   Making Connections

Answers: 1–C   2–B   3–A   4–D   5–A   6–C   (1 point each)

Written responses   (2 points each)

7 **Answers vary.**   Acceptable responses will describe two things that surprised Theresa. Examples: She found out there was a big demand for girls' clothes, and she found that there are children living at the shelter.

8 **Answers vary.**   Acceptable responses will tell what Theresa realizes when she sees the girl in her sweater (for example, that the girl is homeless or lives at the shelter) and will give evidence to support the realization.

ASSESSMENT 3   Exploring Multiple Perspectives

Answers: 1–A   2–D   3–B   4–C   5–C   6–A   (1 point each)

Written responses   (2 points each)

7 **Answers vary.**   Acceptable responses will cite at least two facts presented in Passage 1. Examples: Japanese bombers attacked Pearl Harbor on December 7, 1941, and American factories started making war goods.

8 **Answers vary.**   Acceptable responses will suggest that the passages present different views (for example, Passage 1 presents a more negative view than Passage 2) and present details from each passage to support this conclusion.

ASSESSMENT 4   Focusing on Language and Craft

Answers: 1–A   2–D   3–B   4–C   5–D   6–B   (1 point each)

Written responses   (2 points each)

7 **Answers vary.**   Acceptable responses will note the cardinals' apparent happiness and the parents' apparently unhappy marriage.

8 **Answers vary.**   Acceptable responses will identify a sentence or phrase that uses highly formal language and restate the sentence or phrase in more informal language. Example: "My mother lost the opportunity to groom herself to her satisfaction" could be restated as "My mother didn't get a chance to fix herself up as she wanted to."

Multiple Choice   (1 point each)

Item	Answer	Reading Strategy
1	C	Making Connections: Stepping into the Story
2	C	Making Connections: Deciding What's Important
3	B	Focusing on Language and Craft: More Style Choices
4	D	Focusing on Language and Craft: Style and Structure in Prose
5	D	Making Connections: Images and Symbols Suggest Themes
6	A	Making Connections: Events Reveal Themes

Written Responses   (2 points each)

7 **Answers vary.** Acceptable responses will describe how Cory was feeling and use information from the passage to support this inference. (Making Connections: Inferring Meaning through the Story)

8 **Answers vary.** Acceptable responses will indicate that the dialogue is mostly informal language and describe an effect of informal dialogue. Examples: enhancing the realism of the story, establishing a mood. or suggesting close relationships among the characters. (Focusing on Language and Craft: Style and Structure in Prose)

Multiple Choice   (1 point each)

Item	Answer	Reading Strategy
9	B	Examining Multiple Perspectives: Tone
10	D	Interacting with the Text: Visualizing
11	C	Examining Multiple Perspectives: Choosing a Perspective
12	B	Examining Multiple Perspectives: Structuring an Argument
13	A	Interacting with the Text: Setting a Purpose
14	D	Interacting with the Text: Questioning

Written Responses   (2 points each)

15 **Answers vary.** Acceptable responses will mention two details from the passage to support the author's statement that her daughter's school schedule prevents her from getting adequate sleep. Examples: many schools begin at 7:30 A.M., but research says teens should sleep till 8 A.M.; the teen in the story is supposed to go to bed at 10:30 P.M., but research says teens typically can't fall asleep prior to 11:00 P.M. (Examining Multiple Perspectives: Examining the Details)

16 **Answers vary.** Answers will vary. An acceptable response will discuss the different times shown on the clock in each panel and the change of the window view from nighttime in the first panel to daytime in the second panel. (Interacting with the Text: Making Inferences)

Student Name	Pretest			Assess 1		Assess 2		Assess 3		Assess 4		Posttest	
	Date	Points	%		%		%		%		%		%

DIRECTIONS: Read this passage about what happens when a boy worries about people who break the rules. Then answer questions 1–8.

Silver's Rule

When his doorbell buzzed, Mr. Armando peered through the peephole and saw the curly top of Joey's head. Smiling to himself, Mr. Armando wondered which tenant Joey had caught violating a rule. As superintendent of the Cliffside Apartments, Mr. Armando thought he did a fine job of managing the complex. But 13-year-old Joey from Apartment 301 seemed to think otherwise. Since moving in last year, Joey had made it his business to notify Mr. Armando whenever he thought a tenant was misbehaving.

Mr. Armando opened his door, and Joey strode in swiftly, brandishing a dog-eared copy of the standard Cliffside Apartments rental agreement. In an official-sounding tone, Joey announced, "I am here to report a violation of Item 13, which states that tenants shall be prohibited from keeping dogs or cats in their apartments."

Looking at Joey's earnest expression, Mr. Armando had to force himself to stifle a chuckle. Though he realized now where the conversation was headed, he decided to play along just because he got such a kick out of Joey. So, nodding gravely, Mr. Armando replied, "Tell me, Joey, is a Cliffside tenant violating Item 13 of the rental agreement?"

"Yes, indeed!" exclaimed Joey. "It's my neighbor across the hall—you know, Ms. Oletta in 304—and she's got a *cat!* I hear it mewing by the door sometimes when Ms. Oletta is at work."

"You don't say . . . ," Mr. Armando responded thoughtfully. Then he added, "Come to think of it, I vaguely recall giving Ms. Oletta special permission to keep a cat."

"But that's against the rules!" insisted Joey, his voice screeching like a siren. "Why are you letting Ms. Oletta *break the rules?"*

"You know, Joey, I don't remember anymore," fibbed Mr. Armando, "but I do remember she had a good reason." Guiding Joey toward the door, Mr. Armando suggested, "Run along and ask Ms. Oletta yourself. She'll tell you how she talked me into bending the 'no pets' rule for her."

A short while later, Ms. Oletta ushered Joey into her apartment, and in a pleasant voice said, "I'm so happy to see you, my dear. To what do I owe the honor of your presence?"

Ms. Oletta's warm welcome took Joey aback for a moment. After clearing his throat, he held up his copy of the rental agreement and declared, "It has come to my attention that, in violation of Item 13, you are keeping a cat in your apartment. Mr. Armando says you've got a good reason, and I'd like to know what it is."

A look of surprise mixed with amusement crossed Ms. Oletta's face. Gesturing for Joey to sit on the couch, she walked out of the living room and returned with a tabby cat in her arms. Explaining that the cat was afraid of strangers, Ms.Oletta sat in a far corner of the room and let the cat settle into her lap. But as soon as Joey leaned forward to get a better look, the skittish feline leaped from Ms. Oletta's lap and raced out of the room.

Name _____ Date _____

“Silver has actually come a long way since I found her about a month ago in the parking lot, on top of the dumpster,” began Ms. Oletta. “It took a whole week of coaxing—and about ten cans of gourmet cat food—before I could get her to come near me. Then the car ride to the animal shelter terrified her, poor thing. She hissed and growled the whole way there.”

“Hold on, I must have missed something,” Joey broke in. “If you brought the cat to the animal shelter, why is she here in your apartment?”

“Well, the fellow at the animal shelter practically guaranteed me that no one would adopt such a nervous cat. More than likely, she'd be put away, and I couldn't bear to think of that. It made me sorry I'd caught her and brought her in.”

“So you decided to adopt her yourself?” asked Joey.

“No, I never considered that an option because of the ‘no pets’ rule here. The man at the shelter explained that placing Silver in a temporary home—a foster home, he called it—might give her the chance to settle down a bit and become a friendlier, more trusting cat—an adoptable cat, in other words. So, with Mr. Armando's permission, I brought her home.”

“So when Silver is ready, she'll go back to the shelter and you'll give her up?” asked Joey.

Ms. Oletta smiled reassuringly and said, “Yes, Joey, don't worry. Before long, Silver will be gone from Cliffside.”

Joey was quiet for a moment. Then he said, “You know, Ms. Oletta, I'm glad you rescued Silver, but I'm still kind of surprised that Mr. Armando would bend the rules for you.”

Nodding, Ms. Oletta replied, “I was surprised, too, until Mr. Armando told me something about his childhood that I think he'd like you to know, too.”

“What did Mr. Armando tell you?” asked Joey.

“When Mr. Armando was two years old,” Ms. Oletta began, “he was placed in a foster home. Apparently he was a pretty sickly kid, and his mother, who was going through some tough times of her own, was too overwhelmed to care for him anymore. Mr. Armando doesn't have any memories of his foster parents, but he says he's grateful that they were willing to care for him and nurse him back to health until—just a year later—he was ready to be adopted.”

As Ms. Oletta spoke, Silver crept cautiously back into the living room and jumped into her lap. After chatting with Ms. Oletta a few minutes more, Joey politely excused himself and went home. Closing the door behind Joey, Ms. Oletta noticed his copy of the rental agreement on the couch where he'd left it.

QUESTIONS 1–6: Circle the letter of the best answer to each question.

1. At the beginning of the story, the author creates the impression that Mr. Armando —

A is gruff and grumpy.
B likes to avoid hard work.
C is patient and easy going.
D gets too involved in other people's business.

Name ______

DAYBOOK (8) © GREAT SOURCE. COPYING IS PERMITTED; SEE PAGE ii.

Name

2. **As the story unfolds, which of these facts seems most important?**

   A Joey is 13 years old.

   B Ms. Oletta lives in Apartment 304.

   C Joey has lived at Cliffside Apartments for a year.

   D Mr. Armando is bending a rule for Ms. Oletta.

3. **Which sentence from the story contains a simile?**

   A Mr. Armando opened his door, and Joey strode in swiftly, brandishing a dog-eared copy of the standard Cliffside Apartments rental agreement.

   B "But that's against the rules!" insisted Joey, his voice screeching like a siren.

   C Looking at Joey's earnest expression, Mr. Armando had to force himself to stifle a chuckle.

   D Guiding Joey toward the door, Mr. Armando suggested, "Run along and ask Ms. Oletta yourself."

4. **Which sentence from the story is an example of informal language?**

   A Since moving in last year, Joey had made it his business to notify Mr. Armando whenever he thought a tenant was misbehaving.

   B Mr. Armando opened his door, and Joey strode in swiftly, brandishing a dog-eared copy of the standard Cliffside Apartments rental agreement.

   C Though he realized now where the conversation was headed, he decided to play along just because he got such a kick out of Joey.

   D A short while later, Ms. Oletta ushered Joey into her apartment, and in a pleasant voice said, "I'm so happy to see you, my dear."

5. **The rental agreement that Joey carries with him in this story symbolizes which of these?**

   A sacrifice and loss

   B beauty and perfection

   C sympathy and understanding

   D expectations and obedience

6. **At the end of the story, Joey leaves the rental agreement behind in Ms. Oletta's apartment. What does this action suggest?**

   A Joey recognizes that special circumstances can justify changing a rule.

   B Joey has become forgetful and disorganized.

   C Joey wants to remind Ms. Oletta of the importance of rules.

   D Joey realizes that adults are always in charge.

✳ *QUESTIONS 7 and 8:* **Write your answers on the lines.**

7. **Why does Mr. Armando tell Joey that he can't remember the reason he let Ms. Oletta break a rule?**

_____

_____

_____

_____

8. Give an example of dialogue spoken by Joey that uses formal language. Then explain what Joey's use of formal language suggests about him.

_____

_____

_____

_____

DIRECTIONS: Read these two passages about an event that took place in San Francisco. Then answer questions 9–16.

PASSAGE 1

The 1989 Earthquake

On the afternoon of October 17, 1989, baseball fans were streaming into Candlestick Park in San Francisco for the third game of the World Series. The 1989 World Series was already destined to be memorable since it matched up two California teams, the Oakland Athletics and the San Francisco Giants. With only the San Francisco Bay separating the teams' home stadiums, the fans' rivalrous enthusiasm was intense.

But at 5:04 P.M., before the game had even started, something unforgettable happened. At that moment, the stands began shaking and the light poles started swaying—movements that continued for 15 seconds. The fans, who were mostly central Californians, realized they had just experienced an earthquake. Relieved that the shaking was over and no one was hurt, they cheered loudly. Some even chanted, "Play ball! Play ball!" But that wasn't going to happen. Like the rest of the city, the stadium had no power. Using bullhorns, police announced that the game had been called off and told the disappointed fans to leave Candlestick Park.

As they headed for the exits, the fans began to sense that the earthquake had caused serious damage outside the stadium's walls. To the north they could see smoke rising in the sky. They heard the wailing sirens of rescue vehicles. Some fans switched on portable radios to listen to emergency news bulletins. With growing dread, the fans made their way home to see what awaited them.

As it turned out, the earthquake, centered 70 miles south of the stadium near Santa Cruz, was the area's worst since the San Francisco earthquake of 1906 virtually flattened the city. This time, earthquake-resistant construction helped to limit damage to buildings. Still, the cities of Oakland, Alameda, Santa Cruz, and Monterey sustained heavy property damage. San Francisco's hardest-hit area was the Marina District, where several old buildings collapsed and burned.

But the most dramatic—and deadliest—damage caused by the earthquake affected roadways and bridges. When the top portion of a two-tier stretch of Interstate 880 collapsed on the road below it, 42 people were killed in their cars. Another motorist was killed when a section of the Bay Bridge between Oakland and San Francisco gave way. All around the region, major transportation routes were closed for repairs. Others were simply demolished

In all, the earthquake caused 63 deaths, 3,757 injuries, and $6 billion in property damage. Bay area residents knew that recovering from the disaster would be a long and difficult process. Yet just ten days after the earthquake struck, baseball fans returned to Candlestick Park for the third World Series game, and millions more tuned in to watch on television. For the Bay area and the rest of the country, it was time once again to play ball. ❖

Something Terrible

When I saw Dad waiting for me outside the school entrance, I thought something terrible must have happened. Instead he handed me an envelope and said, "My boss just got called out of town unexpectedly. He can't use these, so he gave them to me. It's our lucky day, son!"

Reaching into the envelope, I pulled out two tickets: third-row box seats to that night's World Series game. I let out a hoot and started doing a crazed happy dance right there on the sidewalk, and Dad laughed.

We decided to head straight for the city to avoid the afternoon rush hour, and then grab something to eat at Candlestick Park. Unfortunately, the drive from Oakland to San Francisco across the Bay Bridge took a little longer than we'd expected; the rush hour seemed to have already started. "I guess everyone's heading home to watch the game on television," Dad suggested.

I laughed and added, "Everyone who doesn't have tickets, that is."

We got to our seats in Candlestick as the Oakland Athletics were wrapping up their batting practice. With just enough time to get some hot dogs and drinks, Dad and I headed for the concession area. At that moment I heard a rumbling sound—low at first, but then louder—and I automatically started searching the sky for a jet. Then the steps under my feet started shifting, and I wheeled around to see the light poles jiggling and swaying. My father bellowed, "Earthquake!" as he grabbed my arm and yanked me back down the steps, out from under the upper deck. Holding the back of an aisle seat to steady myself, I squeezed my eyes shut and counted to 15 before the shaking stopped. After a brief, stunned silence, the crowd erupted in rowdy cheers. I heard myself hooting again, just like when Dad handed me the tickets. Instead of laughing, though, Dad leaned toward me and gravely murmured, "We're leaving now, as fast as we can go without running."

"What, and miss a World Series game? Are you kidding?" I demanded, but Dad was moving up the aisle, and I knew better than to hang back. While some die-hard fans chanted for the game to start, the exits began to fill with others who had made the same calculation as Dad: the quake may have already damaged Candlestick, and a strong aftershock might cause it to collapse.

As the crowd moved along, fans with radios tuned in to news bulletins about the earthquake damage and then shouted urgent summaries to the rest of us. We heard about crumbling buildings, fires, overloaded telephone lines, and power blackouts. We heard that part of Interstate 880 had collapsed and that the Bay Bridge was damaged and closed. We heard that bridges, overpasses, and exit ramps all over the Bay area might be unstable and that the major roads throughout the Bay area were a disastrous tangle of detours, closings, and gridlock. As Dad and I hurried out of Candlestick Park toward our car, we had no idea how or when we would ever get back to Oakland. ❖

✳ QUESTIONS 9–14: Circle the letter of the best answer to each question.

9. "The 1989 Earthquake" is best described as —
   A a fictional account.
   B an opinion piece.
   C an eyewitness perspective.
   D a factual account.

10. The information in "Something Terrible" is based mostly on —
   A newspaper accounts of the event.
   B scientific research and data.
   C one person's recollections.
   D the author's conversations with others.

11. Compared with the author of "Something Terrible," the author of "The Earthquake" is more interested in —
   A using numbers to give information.
   B telling events in sequence.
   C describing thoughts and emotions.
   D using vivid, colorful language.

12. Which detail from "The 1989 Earthquake" best helps you visualize the moment the earthquake struck?
   A ". . . baseball fans were streaming into Candlestick Park . . ."
   B ". . . the fans' rivalrous enthusiasm was intense."
   C ". . . before the game even started, something unforgettable happened."
   D ". . . the stands began shaking and the light poles started swaying."

13. The words and the picture in this visual text suggest which of these emotions?

    A disappointment and annoyance

    B shock and worry

    C relief and acceptance

    D anger and scorn

14. Which of these questions is answered by "Something Terrible"?

    A When did the author realize how serious the earthquake was?

    B How did the author and his father get back home to Oakland after the earthquake?

    C Did the author return ten days after the earthquake to see the third game of the World Series?

    D Which California team won the World Series of 1989?

✳ *QUESTIONS 15 and 16:* Write your answers on the lines.

15. Write two facts about the earthquake that are explained in both passages.

_____

_____

_____

16. Think about why you would read these two passages. How does reading more than one passage about a single event help you understand the event better?

_____

_____

_____

_____

Name _____

INTERACTING WITH THE TEXT

DIRECTIONS: Read this passage about an unusual creature. Then answer questions 1–8.

Fearsome Fish

In May of 2002, two friends were fishing at a pond in Crofton, Maryland. When one of the men reeled in an unfamiliar fish, he decided to throw it back into the water. But first he took a few photographs, which he passed along to biologists at the state fisheries department.

Initially the biologists were stumped by the photos, which showed a fish unlike any they had ever seen. Its body was tube-shaped, with long fins that ran along its back and its underside. Although the fish had a small, snake-like head, its mouth was large and filled with sharp teeth. With a bit of research, the biologists identified the fish as a northern snakehead. Since snakeheads are native to China, the presence of one in the Crofton pond was a mystery. It was also a potentially serious problem. Why? Snakeheads are aggressive predators, and in a non-native ecosystem, they likely had no natural enemies to keep their numbers under control. Moreover, snakeheads can live out of water for up to three days and can use their fins to wriggle slowly across land. So the biologists worried that a thriving population of snakeheads could wipe out the native fish species in the pond and then move on to invade nearby ponds, streams, and rivers.

On the other hand, if the snakehead in the photos was the only one in the pond, the problem was minor. Without a mate, the snakehead could not reproduce. Someone could probably fish the snakehead out of the pond to keep it from eating native species. Even if no one ever caught the snakehead again, it would eventually die.

With fingers crossed, officials set out to evaluate their snakehead problem. They soon realized the problem was big—and getting bigger. In June, a 26-inch snakehead was caught in the Crofton pond. In July, officials announced that they had found the person who introduced snakefish to the pond—an unnamed man who'd bought two young snakeheads in New York to keep as pets. When the fish outgrew their aquarium, he released them in the pond. Soon after this announcement, 99 young snakefish were netted in the pond.

Officials moved quickly to get rid of the snakeheads by poisoning the water. Within days, 1,200 dead snakeheads were removed from the pond, along with 1,100 pounds of other fish. Then, after the poison had dissolved and the water was safe again, the Crofton pond was restocked with native fishes.

With the demise of the snakefish in Crofton, Maryland wildlife officials assumed they had seen the last of the fearsome fish. However, in April of 2004, a snakehead was fished from Pine Lake in Wheaton, Maryland. Around the same time, nine snakeheads turned up in the Potomac River, which forms the boundary between Maryland and Virginia. Further investigations brought both good news and bad news: Pine Lake

DAYBOOK (8) © GREAT SOURCE. COPYING IS PERMITTED; SEE PAGE ii.

Name _____

Date _____

was drained and no more snakeheads were found. Yet in 2005, nearly 100 snakeheads turned up in a creek that feeds into the Potomac. Testing showed that these fish were probably spawned by snakeheads released directly into the Potomac and were not related to the ones found in Crofton or Wheaton. Consequently, officials have concluded that the snakehead population appears to be well established and growing in the Potomac, a major river that cannot be poisoned or drained. ❖

✳ *QUESTIONS 1–6:* Circle the letter of the best answer to each question.

1. **The information in the first paragraph helps you set which of the following purposes for reading this article?**

   A learning some tips for photographing fish
   B finding out more about a mysterious fish
   C learning some tips for fishing in ponds
   D finding out more about Maryland

2. **Which detail from the article helps you picture the snakehead in your mind?**

   A A man caught an unfamiliar fish.
   B The biologists had never seen a fish like the one in the photos.
   C The fish's small head had a large mouth filled with large teeth.
   D Snakeheads are native to China.

3. **Which information from the visual text is narration?**

   A The biologists made an alarming discovery . . .
   B This fish appears to be a snakehead!
   C We need to find out if there are more snakeheads in Maryland.
   D Yes, before they wipe out the native species!

Name

4. **Which of these questions is answered in the article?**

   A How did snakeheads get into the pond in Crofton?
   B How was Pine Lake drained?
   C Which kinds of fish do snakeheads eat?
   D How long do snakeheads usually live?

5. **Which detail best supports the idea that snakeheads are "fearsome fish"?**

   A The man who fished the snakehead from the Crofton pond threw it back in the water.
   B The photos of the snakehead stumped biologists.
   C Snakeheads could wipe out native fish in one pond and then invade other ponds and streams.
   D Pine Lake was drained, but no other snakeheads were found.

6. **The discovery of nearly 100 snakeheads in a creek that feeds into the Potomac River suggests that —**

   A officials are doing an effective job of finding and eliminating snakeheads.
   B snakeheads prefer rivers and creeks to lakes or ponds.
   C snakeheads probably have some natural enemies in the Potomac River.
   D the Potomac River may have a growing snakehead population.

✳ *QUESTIONS 7 and 8:* **Draw your answers in the boxes.**

7. **Based on the information in the article, how would you draw the body of a snakehead?**

8. **Based on this text, draw a picture of the course of action that caused the problem in the Crofton pond.**

MAKING CONNECTIONS

DIRECTIONS: Read this passage about a teenager's experience with homelessness. Then answer questions 1–8.

The Sweater

Theresa sighed regretfully at the clothes piled high on her bed. She'd just finished emptying her drawers and closet of everything that didn't fit her anymore. She was in the midst of a dramatic growth spurt, and, for the first time in her life, Theresa had outgrown her clothes faster than she'd grown tired of them. Among the things that were too small was a sweater Grandma Bea had knitted from turquoise and pink yarns chosen specifically to set off Theresa's bronze complexion and black hair.

An hour later, Papa and Theresa put two bags of her old clothes in the car and drove downtown. They pulled up in front of a large brick building, took the bags from the car, and carried them inside. "Clothing donations go down the hall and to the left," directed a friendly man seated at a desk in the lobby. Papa and Theresa passed rooms for food, furniture, and toy donations before they located the clothing room. It was brimming with boxes and bags of clothing, which several workers were sorting and organizing.

"We've got two bags of clothes for girls," Papa began.

"Fantastic, we've got a big demand for those!" replied one of the workers.

As they walked back down the hallway, Theresa murmured quizzically to her father, "Why is there a big demand for girls clothes? I thought homeless people were mostly adults." Stepping outside again, Theresa heard shouts and laughter coming from behind the building. Looking back, she saw more than a dozen children playing four-square and basketball on a paved lot.

"*All* those kids are living *here?*" Theresa asked in a bewildered tone.

"Yes," Papa replied, "until their parents can get back on their feet."

As they drove home, Papa and Theresa talked about homelessness. "There are a lot of negative stereotypes about homeless people being lazy or irresponsible," Papa explained, "but the fact is that homelessness can happen to almost anyone. You might get seriously ill or be laid off from a job and in no time you don't have enough money to keep a roof over your head. If you've got a family depending on you, it's even worse."

"Could those things happen to us, Papa? Could we end up living in a homeless shelter?" Theresa asked anxiously.

Papa eased the car into the driveway, turned the engine off, and looked Theresa straight in the eye. "Could I lose my job or get sick? Yes, those things are always possible. Would we have to live in a homeless shelter if one of those things happened to me? No, probably not, because we're fortunate enough to have a tremendous support system—grandparents, aunts and uncles, and friends—who would do everything they could to help us over a rough patch."

A few weeks later, Theresa was surprised to catch a glimpse of a turquoise-and-pink sweater in the hallway at school. Theresa didn't know the girl who was wearing the sweater, but she was struck by how well its colors complemented the girl's bronze skin and black hair. Suddenly Theresa felt an odd jumble of emotions—relief, sympathy, and hopefulness—wash over her. Watching the girl disappear into a river of students, Theresa found herself wondering what else they might have in common. ❖

✳ QUESTIONS 1–6: Circle the letter of the best answer to each question.

1. About what does Theresa feel regretful at the beginning of the story?

- **A** being taller than she wants to be
- **B** missing her grandmother
- **C** outgrowing some favorite clothes
- **D** having to stay home to do chores

2. Where did Papa take Theresa in the car?

- **A** to a school
- **B** to a homeless shelter
- **C** to a hotel
- **D** to a department store

3. As Theresa learns more about homelessness, what seems most important to her?

- **A** She was able to help others by donating clothes.
- **B** She would never wear her favorite sweater again.
- **C** Many homeless people are viewed as lazy or irresponsible.
- **D** The children living at the homeless shelter got plenty of exercise.

4. The author of this story creates the impression that Theresa and her father are —

- **A** upset by the behavior of people working at the shelter.
- **B** disgusted by homeless people who don't have jobs.
- **C** confident that they will never need help from anyone.
- **D** concerned about homeless people and trying to help.

5. At the end of this story, the sweater symbolizes —

- **A** something Theresa and the homeless girl have in common.
- **B** a final end to homelessness.
- **C** Theresa's love for her grandmother.
- **D** Theresa's selfish disregard for other people.

6. Which statement expresses a theme of this story?

- **A** Homelessness is becoming less common.
- **B** Most people will be homeless at some time.
- **C** Homelessness could happen to anyone.
- **D** Most homeless people do not really need any help.

✳ *QUESTIONS 7 and 8:* Write your answers on the lines.

7. Think of what Theresa saw and heard when she and Papa dropped off the bags of clothing. What two things surprised and bothered Theresa the most?

_____

_____

_____

_____

_____

_____

8. What does Theresa realize when she sees the girl in the turquoise-and-pink sweater? Explain how you know.

_____

_____

_____

_____

_____

_____

EXPLORING MULTIPLE PERSPECTIVES

DIRECTIONS: Read these two passages about some changes that came about as a result of World War II. Then answer questions 1–8.

PASSAGE 1

Help Wanted

On December 7, 1941, Japanese bombers attacked Pearl Harbor, a United States naval base in Hawaii. In response, the United States entered World War II against the Axis powers: Japan, Italy, and Germany. President Franklin Roosevelt called on Americans to join the war effort with "righteous might." With no time to waste, American men enlisted and headed for the battlefronts of Europe and Asia.

As American men flooded into the armed services, factories in the United States switched from making domestic goods to war goods—and at a feverish pace, too. As a result, the country suddenly faced a serious shortage of factory workers. To pick up the slack, the government launched a campaign to bring women into the workforce.

Before World War II, most of the American women who worked held traditional jobs as teachers, nurses, secretaries, and store clerks. There was also a myth accepted by men and women alike that women were not suited for factory work. To counter the myth and attract women to factory jobs, the government made a poster of a determined-looking woman, clad in overalls and flexing her arm muscles. This striking image appeared beneath a slogan that proclaimed, "We Can Do It!" Other posters, ads, and radio spots played to women's sense of patriotism. Both types of appeals worked well. During the war years, more than three million American women took jobs in defense industries. The best jobs paid forty dollars a week, which was a very good wage at the time.

When the war ended in 1945, American men came home. Many women wanted to keep their factory jobs, but employers had promised to give them back to returning soldiers. As a result, just as sharply as they'd risen, the numbers of women factory workers fell. Most women who wished to work had to settle once again for lower-paying jobs. It would be another twenty years before the women's rights movement helped reopen the doors of America's factories to women workers. ❖

PASSAGE 2

A Working Woman

The war years were a time of transformation for my parents' marriage. To be sure, Father and Mother weren't seeking any kind of change; rather, it was brought on by circumstances beyond their control. Afterward, there was no going back: their marriage had achieved a new balance, and their relationship would never be the same.

The seeds of the transformation were planted on December 7, 1941, when the Japanese bombed Pearl Harbor. As we listened to the radio bulletin, my parents sized up the situation. The attack meant the United States would enter World War II, they concluded. Then Father noted regretfully that his lame leg, the result of a bout with polio, would keep him out of the action. Mother quickly assured him he would find a way to contribute to the war effort.

The way became clear within a couple of months, as the government launched its campaign to recruit women into the workforce. All around us posters, newspaper ads, newsreels, and radio announcements urged women to do their patriotic duty by taking factory jobs. One day, as my mother drove me home from school, a voice from the radio claimed, "Ladies, if you can drive a car, you can run a machine." Turning to look at me, Mother smiled and winked.

Father hated the idea of Mother donning overalls to work in a factory. He called it "unfeminine" and insisted that her place was in the home, but he really never stood a chance of keeping Mother there. By appealing both to his pride and his patriotism, she held the upper hand. Some of Father's good friends, as well as his brother, had enlisted. "No one expects you to fight, of course," Mother countered smoothly, "but letting me go to work is a sacrifice you can make."

Before long, Mother took a job as a machinist at an aircraft factory. She worked the day shift, so as not to disrupt our routines too much. Still, some inconvenient adjustments had to be made: Father began riding a bus to and from his office so that Mother could drive to the factory, and I spent two hours after school each day at a child-care center.

For a while, Mother's absence from the house also meant simple and sometimes slapdash dinners, untidy rooms, and a shortage of clean laundry. Father grumbled mightily that the place was coming apart at the seams, until he noticed how nicely Mother's paychecks were padding the savings account. The day our leaky roof was replaced, the grumbling stopped for good. Father also started pitching in with household chores and yipping at me to do more, too.

Mother gave up her factory job when the war ended, but she had another career in her sights. With some of her savings, she put herself through night school, earning a degree as a librarian and eventually taking a position at a library just a few blocks from Father's office. Once a week for the next twenty years, Father and Mother had lunch together at a nearby restaurant—and they split the check each time. ❖

✳ QUESTIONS 1–6: Circle the letter of the best answer to each question.

1. **Passage 1 is best described as —**

   A a factual report.

   B a comparison of several perspectives.

   C an opinion essay.

   D a personal account.

2. **The information in Passage 2 is based mostly on —**

   A data collected by historians.

   B the author's interviews with others.

   C newspaper accounts.

   D the author's memories.

3. Both Passage 1 and Passage 2 provide information about which of these?

    A what adjustments families made when women went to work

    B how the government recruited women into the workforce

    C why some men did not enlist in the armed services

    D how most men felt about women who worked in factories

4. The author's main purpose in Passage 1 was to —

    A show how the government used advertising to influence women.

    B encourage women to show their patriotism by working in factories.

    C explain the effects of World War II on women's employment.

    D compare past and present manufacturing jobs.

5. The author's main purpose in Passage 2 was to —

    A compare today's women to women during World War II.

    B encourage women to try more than one career.

    C describe how a marriage changed when a housewife took a job.

    D praise American women for contributing to war efforts.

6. What impression does Passage 2 give you of the narrator's mother?

    A She truly enjoyed having a career.

    B She worked in a factory only because it seemed patriotic.

    C She was bossy and short-tempered.

    D She was interested in earning a lot of money.

✳ QUESTIONS 7 and 8: Write your answers on the lines.

7. Write two facts you learned from reading Passage 1.

8. Do you think Passage 1 and Passage 2 present similar or different views about how the end of World War II affected women factory workers? Use details from the passages to support your opinion.

FOCUSING ON LANGUAGE AND CRAFT

DIRECTIONS: **Read these two short pieces. Then answer questions 1–8.**

Neighbors

I've named them Mr. and Mrs. Cardinal,
and think of them as the next-door neighbors.
They live, after all, next to our kitchen door
in a downy nest hidden in the lilacs.

He decks himself out in scarlet, flashy as a movie star.
She cloaks herself in browns that say, "Ignore me."
Yet he doesn't. They are mated for life.
Happily, devotedly, they raise their broods.

From my seat at the kitchen window
I hear the rumble of my parents' quarrel.
The sounds rise sharply, then fade. It's over,
But there will be another.

A different sound rises from the lilacs.
Mrs. Cardinal sings notes as sweet and golden as honey.
As the notes fade, a response swiftly follows—
a flash of scarlet crosses the sky and settles in the nest. ❖

— Janet Callahan

Graduation Day

Purchased for the winter holiday pageant, my dress pants hadn't left my closet since then. Now, on the morning of my middle-school graduation, they cleared the tops of my shoes by a good inch and a half. With her hair uncombed and her make-up only half applied, my mother took one look at me and groaned. "You're not a child, you're a *weed!*" she exclaimed. Handing me my bathrobe, she added, "Put this on while I let down the cuffs. Hurry now!"

With this last-minute tailoring task, my mother lost the opportunity to groom herself to her satisfaction. Hence, in the photo of us on the front steps that my father snapped that morning, my mother's curls are haphazardly arranged and the dark circles under her eyes are unconcealed. More vivid and apparent, however, are her upturned chin, broad smile, and shining eyes. My mother was savoring one of her proudest moments, and it showed. ❖

✳ **QUESTIONS 1–6:** Circle the letter of the best answer to each question.

1. In "Neighbors" the speaker compares the male cardinal to —

    A a movie star.   **C** a brown cloak.

    B a lilac bush.   **D** a quarrel.

2. Which line from "Neighbors" uses a simile?

    A I've named them Mr. and Mrs. Cardinal,

    B Happily, devotedly, they raise their broods.

    C I hear the rumble of my parents' quarrel.

    D Mrs. Cardinal sings notes as sweet and golden as honey.

3. What attitude does the speaker in "Neighbors" express toward the cardinals?

    A pity and concern   **C** amusement and boredom

    B appreciation and admiration   **D** annoyance and resentment

4. Which words best describe the atmosphere created by the author in "Graduation Day"?

    A nervousness and uncertainty   **C** excitement and happiness

    B resentment and irritation   **D** disappointment and acceptance

5. Which sentence from "Graduation Day" includes a metaphor?

    A My dress pants hadn't left my closet since then.

    B They cleared the tops of my shoes by a good inch and a half.

    C My mother took one look at me and groaned.

    D "You're not a child, you're a *weed!*" she exclaimed.

6. The sensory language in "Graduation Day" mostly describes what the narrator —

    A touched or felt.   **C** tasted or smelled.

    B saw with the eyes.   **D** heard or listened to.

✳ **QUESTIONS 7 and 8:** Write your answers on the lines.

7. Explain how the cardinals and the speaker's parents are opposites in "Neighbors."

_____

_____

_____

_____

8. Give an example of a sentence from "Graduation Day" that is written in formal language. Then rewrite the sentence in more informal language.

_____

_____

_____

_____

DIRECTIONS: **Read this passage about a family that experiences change. Then answer questions 1–8.**

Empty

One last box sealed with packing tape was left in the bedroom. Cory struggled mightily to lift it from the floor, but he hardly budged it. Watching from the doorway, Malcolm chuckled, "Hey, I know you're desperate to get rid of me, kid, but it's not worth busting a gut over." With that, Malcolm lifted the box, hoisted it onto one shoulder, and carried it effortlessly out to the car. Then he embraced his mother, kissed her cheek, and slid into the front passenger seat.

At the last minute, Cory decided to go along with Dad, who was driving Malcolm to the state university. "It's a three-hour ride each way," warned Dad as Cory climbed into the backseat. "That's a lot of sitting time on one of the last days of your summer vacation."

"That's why I'm coming along," replied Cory, "to keep you company on the way back."

"Better you than your mother, I guess," laughed Dad affectionately as Mom, standing in the driveway, clutched a crumpled tissue. Malcolm smiled and waved at Mom as Dad started the engine. Cory, feeling a sudden pang of empathy and understanding for her, had to look away.

A few hours later, as they said goodbye to Malcolm on the steps of his dormitory, Cory marveled that Dad didn't seem the least bit wistful. "This is an exciting time for Malcolm," Dad explained to Cory as they pulled onto the interstate on the way back, "so I'm happy for him, and proud of him, too." As Dad talked and talked about Malcolm's promising future, he was like a helium balloon drifting ever higher in the sky. Dad was not usually that much of a talker. As he kept going on, Cory wondered if Dad wasn't trying to cover up his own emotions by talking nonstop.

Much to his surprise, Cory realized that he was feeling a sense of loss himself, though he wasn't sure why. He and Malcolm had completely different personalities and interests, and as a result they frequently clashed. All summer long the brothers had taunted each other with the same back-and-forth: first Cory would declare how glad he'd be when Malcolm finally cleared out of their room, and then Malcolm would counter that any roommate he had at college would be an improvement over Cory. Perhaps, Cory reasoned, he'd feel happier about having the room to himself once he had a chance to settle into it.

When they returned home that evening, Mom's mood had improved noticeably. "Nothing like moving furniture around to cure the blues," she joked as everyone sat down for dinner. Glancing from the kitchen to the family room, Cory wondered aloud what had been moved.

"Not in here, in your room!" Mom exclaimed. "I put Malcolm's desk and dresser into the garage—for now, anyway—he may want them for an apartment once he graduates. Then I emptied his closet, and—" Seeing Cory's bewildered expression, Mom stopped and asked, "What's wrong?"

"How could you clear all of Malcolm's stuff out of our room?" Cory demanded incredulously. "I mean, he's gone to college, not to Mars. He's still gonna be home for Thanksgiving and winter break and summer vacation for the next four years, and he's still gonna need a room!"

"We thought you couldn't wait to have your own room, Cory," Dad responded, "and of course, Malcolm's going to be back, but his stays will be relatively short. The guest room is small, but it'll be more than adequate."

Then Mom added, "Malcolm had his own room for three years before you were born, so it's your turn. Enjoy it, dear."

For the rest of the meal, Dad filled Mom in on the details of dropping off Malcolm at the university, regaling her with a hilarious description of Malcolm's new room-mate, who'd already plastered the room with posters of Malcolm's least favorite band. Cory tried unsuccessfully to laugh along with his parents before finally excus-ing himself from the table.

Two hours later, Cory was reading a magazine, stretched out on the top bunk bed with Malcolm's empty bed beneath him, when Mom looked in on him. Surprised and exasperated, Mom declared, "Cory, after years of listening to you complain about sleeping on the top bunk, I could just about pull my hair out to find you there now!" The bunk bed arrangement had always been a point of contention between Cory and Malcolm. Tall and lanky, both boys had difficulty squeezing themselves into the top bunk without bumping the ceiling, but as the younger, slightly shorter brother, Cory was the logical choice for the higher berth.

Tossing the magazine aside, Cory stretched his arms out slowly and pretended to yawn wearily. He actually wasn't the least bit tired, but the yawn bought him some time to think of something to say. Apparently Malcolm's absence wasn't upset-ting Mom that much, so Cory wasn't about to admit how he was feeling, especially since his reaction was the last thing anyone would have predicted. So Cory said, "You know, Mom, I actually tried getting into the bottom bunk, but it reeks of that nasty cologne Malcolm likes to wear." Shuddering for dramatic effect, Cory added, "After just five minutes down there, I had a horrible headache."

Smiling sympathetically, Mom stepped into the room and yanked the bedclothes off the lower bunk. "We'll leave the mattress like that for a while, just until it airs out," she explained. "You'll need to give it a little time, but eventually, you'll be able to have the lower bunk, just like you've always wanted."

Mom left the room, and Cory listened as her footsteps faded down the hallway. Thinking about what she'd said, he felt reassured. Like the scent of bad cologne, he

DAYBOOK (8) © GREAT SOURCE. COPYING IS PERMITTED; SEE PAGE ii.

realized, the empty feeling he had inside would eventually go away. It was probably just a matter of time and a little fresh air. ❖

✳ *QUESTIONS 1–6:* Circle the letter of the best answer to each question.

1. At the beginning of the story, the author creates the impression that Malcolm —

   A is concerned about his mother.
   B demands a lot from other people.
   C is excited about going off to college.
   D does not have much self-confidence.

2. As the story unfolds, which of these facts seems most important?

   A The state university is three hours away.
   B Cory's summer vacation is almost over.
   C Cory is not enthusiastic about Malcolm's departure.
   D Malcolm's roommate plastered their room with posters.

3. Which sentence from the story contains a *simile*?

   A Mom, standing in the driveway, clutched a crumpled tissue.
   B As Dad talked and talked about Malcolm's promising future, he was like a helium balloon drifting ever higher in the sky.
   C Much to his surprise, Cory realized that he was feeling a sense of loss himself, though he wasn't sure why.
   D Tossing the magazine aside, Cory stretched his arms out slowly and pretended to yawn wearily.

4. Which sentence from the story is the best example of informal language?

   A With that, Malcolm lifted the box, hoisted it onto one shoulder, and carried it effortlessly out to the car.
   B He and Malcolm had completely different personalities and interests, and as a result they frequently clashed.
   C The bunk bed arrangement had always been a point of contention between Cory and Malcolm.
   D He's still gonna be home for Thanksgiving and winter break and summer vacation for the next four years, and he's still gonna need a room!

5. For Cory, the dresser and desk that Mom has moved to the garage suggest that Malcolm —

   A is stronger than Cory.
   B doesn't get along with Cory.
   C is going to miss Cory.
   D is moving out of Cory's life.

6. The events of this story illustrate which of these themes?

   A Growing up means learning to accept change and loss.
   B It's better never to count on anyone but yourself.
   C People who truly love you will never hurt you.
   D Parents can learn a lot from their children.

✳ *QUESTIONS 7 and 8:* Write your answers on the lines.

7. **What emotion was Cory feeling as Dad started the car engine? Explain how you know.**

_____

_____

_____

_____

_____

8. **Does dialogue spoken by the characters in this story use mostly simple or mostly complex vocabulary? Describe what effect this kind of vocabulary creates.**

_____

_____

_____

_____

_____

DIRECTIONS: Read these two passages about teenagers' sleep habits. Then answer questions 9–16.

PASSAGE 1

Let's Help Our Teens Get More Sleep!

Get in bed, turn off the light, and get to sleep IMMEDIATELY, or you'll be a zombie in school tomorrow! I deliver some variation of this rant to my 14-year-old daughter every school night. My goal, of course, is to make sure she gets enough sleep to stay healthy and function well in school. But every single day, I fail to achieve this goal. Why? Like most teens, my daughter has a school schedule that keeps her from getting the sleep she needs. Although middle schools and high schools in most communities have starting times of 7:30 A.M. or so, research shows that teens should still be sleeping at this hour. Parents have the responsibility to do something about this unhealthy situation. Since we can't change teens' sleep requirements, we should demand that schools change their schedules.

But what exactly are teens' sleep requirements? According to leading sleep researchers, teens need nine hours of sleep a night. However, the research also shows that *when* teens need to sleep is just as important as *how long.* Typically, teens can't fall asleep before 11 P.M.—a fact that parents quickly discover when

DAYBOOK (8) © GREAT SOURCE. COPYING IS PERMITTED; SEE PAGE ii.

they try to enforce earlier bed times. Plain and simple, the research boils down to this: a good night's sleep for a typical teen is from 11 P.M. to 8 A.M.

Obviously, school starting times of 7:30 A.M., which necessitate early wake-up times, are robbing our teenage children of much-needed sleep. As a result, they drag listlessly through their classes, have trouble concentrating on what's being taught, and often fall fast asleep on their desks. We shouldn't be surprised when, as a consequence of being constantly overtired, our children do poorly in school, get sick often, become irritable and withdrawn, and sleep the weekends away. Instead, we should be concerned and determined to right what's wrong. Let's get together as parents to persuade school administrators to adjust school schedules so that our teens can get a decent night's sleep. ❖

No Easy Solutions for Tired Teens

As the superintendent of schools, I'm well aware of middle- and high-school students' sleep problems. I've read the latest research, and I've met with many parents concerned about their sleep-deprived children. Most important, I'm raising two teenagers of my own who can barely get out of bed on school mornings, yet seem to get a second wind just when they need to be turning in for the night. So no one needs to persuade me that the school system should make some schedule changes to help teens get more sleep. But adjusting teens' schools schedules to accommodate their sleep needs is more difficult than most parents realize, for several reasons.

Name

Why can't we just push back the school start time for middle- and high-school students to, say, 8:30 or 9:00 A.M.? The biggest obstacle is bus transportation. Currently, our buses operate on an early shift for middle and high schools and a later shift for elementary schools, both in the mornings and in the afternoons. We don't have nearly enough buses to transport all of our students at the same time. And with our tight budget, purchasing more buses is definitely not an option.

All right then, why don't we just swap the start times of elementary schools with middle and high schools? I hear this proposal a lot from the parents of middle- and high-school students. Yet parents of younger students strongly oppose it. Why? For working parents, an earlier elementary school start time (and dismissal time) may mean paying for more hours in after-school care programs. Many parents cannot afford this added expense. Such a switch would also be a hardship for families that count on middle- or high-school children to care for younger siblings until the parents get home from work.

Additionally, a major change in school start times would affect students' after-school activities. Unless everyone follows the same schedule, our student athletes can't participate in after-school events with teams from other school systems. A later start time would also cut into the hours students can spend working after-school jobs and still be home for dinner.

Is it just too difficult to adjust school start times so that teens can sleep better? No, I don't believe that. However, parents cannot realistically expect a quick and painless fix for this problem. Many issues, such as our budget, working parents' needs and after-school activities, must be considered as we try to solve this problem. With open minds and patience, we can find the best solution for everyone. ❖

❋ *QUESTIONS 9–14:* Circle the letter of the best answer to each question.

9. The tone of passage 1 is best described as—
   A humorous and playful.
   B serious and persuasive.
   C polite and respectful.
   D angry and bitter.

10. Which information from Passage 1 helps create a vivid image of the problem the author is describing?
   A Middle schools and high schools begin around 7:30 A.M.
   B Teens need nine hours of sleep a night.
   C When teens sleep is as important as how long.
   D Students often fall asleep on their desks.

11. Which of these best describes Passage 2?
   A an emotional appeal backed up with research
   B a personal account of an experience
   C a factual discussion of a complicated issue
   D an argument against scientific evidence

12. **Which sentence from Passage 2 expresses the author's thesis?**
    - A I've read the latest research, and I've met with parents concerned about their sleep-deprived children.
    - B But adjusting teens' school schedules to accommodate their sleep needs is more difficult than most parents realize, for several reasons.
    - C We don't have nearly enough buses to transport all of our students at the same time.
    - D Unless everyone follows the same schedule, our student athletes cannot participate in after-school events with teams from other school systems.

13. **The titles "Let's Help Our Teens Get More Sleep" and "No Easy Solutions for Tired Teens" provide the reader with clues that the passages—**
    - A present different views on the same topic.
    - B are intended mostly to amuse the reader.
    - C present information objectively.
    - D are fictional stories about the same characters.

14. **Which of these questions does Passage 2 answer?**
    - A Are elementary school children getting enough sleep?
    - B How much would it cost to purchase more buses?
    - C When do after-school sports activities start?
    - D Why is it hard for school schedules to meet the sleep needs of teens?

✳ *QUESTIONS 15 and 16:* **Write your answers on the lines.**

15. **In Passage 1, the author states, "Like most teens, my daughter has a school schedule that keeps her from getting the sleep she needs." Write two details from the passage that provide supporting evidence for this statement.**

_____

_____

_____

_____

16. **In the visual text, how does the artist show the passage of time from the first panel to the second? Describe two ways.**

_____

_____

_____

_____

_____

_____

REPRODUCIBLE GRAPHIC ORGANIZERS

Graphic organizers are great for helping students organize their thinking, whether they are analyzing something they've read; planning their own writing; or exploring relationships among words, phrases, and ideas.

CHARACTER MAP, Page 275

Using a Character Map allows readers to notice, record, and organize details from various perspectives. It can also be used for planning the writing of a story or a character sketch.

PLOT DIAGRAM, Page 276

Keeping track of the events of the plot helps readers comprehend and remember the action of the story. While many stories have the five-part structure presented in unit 3, some stories may have fewer or more parts. This diagram can also be used for planning the writing of a story.

THEME ORGANIZER, Page 277

This graphic offers students a step-by-step way to organize their thinking about the important messages and ideas in a story. Because *theme* can be a fairly abstract concept, students benefit from collecting concrete details as they try to understand and articulate a theme.

WORD SPLASH, Page 278

Use this graphic to preview the vocabulary in something students are about to read. First give students the list of key vocabulary that they may not know but will need to understand in order to get the key concepts in the story. Then provide them with definitions or have them find their own definitions to write next to the words. Ask them to suggest the subject of the article and tell why they think so, accounting for all of the words and phrases. Once you have discussed the possibilities, read the selection independently or as a group. Discuss students' guesses and how close they are to the actual text. Make sure students understand that the point of the activity is to get them thinking about the words; it is not about guessing correctly. Surprises should be welcome. They will inspire interesting discussions about word meanings and language.

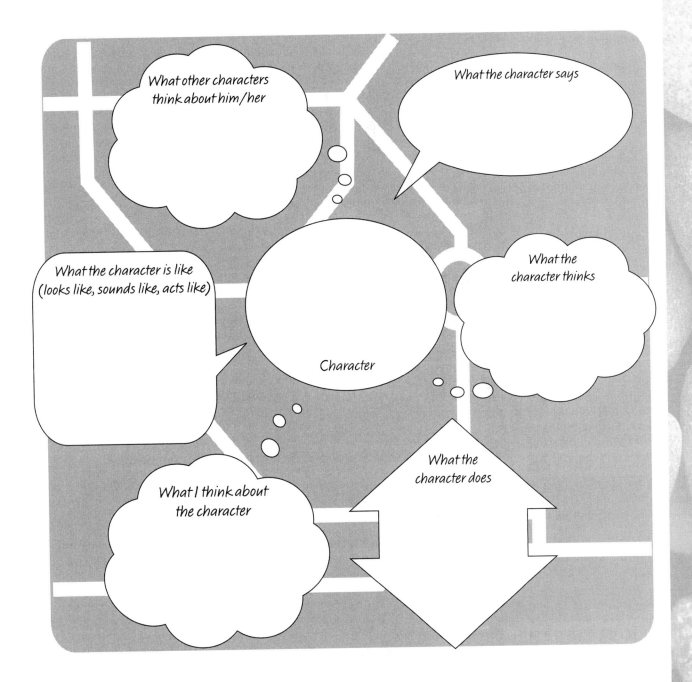

What other characters think about him/her

What the character says

What the character is like (looks like, sounds like, acts like)

What the character thinks

Character

What I think about the character

What the character does

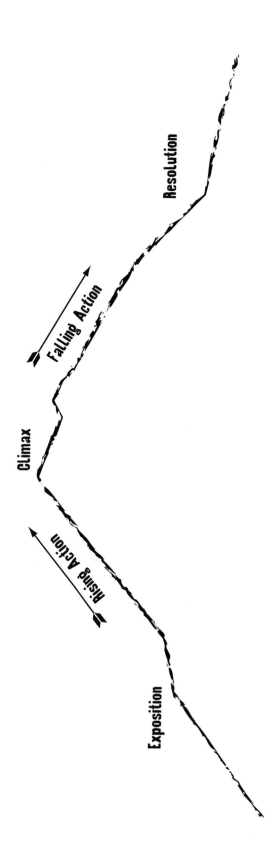

1. Important Quotes   What I Think About This

2. What Characters Do and Say

Meaning to the Story

3. Big Ideas

4. Lessons Learned

SELECTION VOCABULARY

Write the selection vocabulary on the lines below. Write a definition for each word. Read the words and their definitions and then guess what the selection will be about. Remember, all the words will be used in the selection. Compare your guess with your classmates and talk about the reasons for each person's guess. Then read the selection to see if anyone's guess was close to the topic.

Word

Definition

What the selection will be about _____